PERCY'S RELIQUES.

RELIQUES OF

Ancient English Poetry,

CONSISTING OF

OLD HEROIC BALLADS, SONGS, AND OTHER

PIECES OF OUR EARLIER POETS,

TOGETHER WITH SOME FEW

OF LATER DATE,

BY THOMAS PERCY, D.D.

BISHOP OF DROMORE,

EDITED, WITH A GENERAL INTRODUCTION, ADDITIONAL

PREFACES, NOTES, GLOSSARY, ETC., BY

HENRY B. WHEATLEY, F.S.A.

IN THREE VOLUMES.

VOL. III.

NEW YORK

DOVER PUBLICATIONS, INC.

This Dover edition, first published in 1966, is an unabridged and unaltered republication of the work originally published by Swan Sonneschein, Lebas, & Lowrey in 1886.

The publisher is grateful to the Columbia University Libraries for making a copy of this work available for purpose of reproduction.

Library of Congress Catalog Card Number: 66-20326

Manufactured in the United States of America
Dover Publications, Inc.
180 Varick Street
New York, N. Y. 10014

CONTENTS OF VOLUME THE THIRD.

BOOK THE FIRST.

(*Poems on King Arthur, &c.*)

Page

BOOK THE THIRD.

CONTENTS.

RELIQUES OF ANCIENT POETRY, ETC

SERIES THE THIRD.

BOOK I.

"An ordinary song or ballad, that is the delight of the common people, cannot fail to please all such readers, as are not unqualified for the entertainment by their affectation or their ignorance; and the reason is plain, because the same paintings of nature which recommend it to the most ordinary reader, will appear beautiful to the most refined."—ADDISON, in *Spectator*, No. 70.

POEMS ON KING ARTHUR, ETC.

HE third volume being chiefly devoted to romantic subjects, may not be improperly introduced with a few slight strictures on the old metrical romances: a subject the more worthy attention, as it seems not to have been known to such as have written on the nature and origin of books of chivalry, that the first compositions of this kind were in verse, and usually sung to the harp.*

I.

THE BOY AND THE MANTLE

AS printed verbatim from the old MS. described in the Preface.† The Editor believes it more ancient than it will appear to be at first sight; the transcriber of that manuscript having reduced the orthography and style in many instances to the standard of his own times.

The incidents of the *Mantle and the Knife* have not, that I can recollect, been borrowed from any other writer. The former of these evidently suggested to Spenser his conceit of *Florimel's Girdle*, b. iv. c. 5, st. 3.

[* See Appendix.

† Percy folio MS. ed. Hales and Furnivall, vol. ii. pp. 301-311.]

> " That girdle gave the virtue of chaste love
> And wivehood true to all that did it beare ;
> But whosoever contrarie doth prove,
> Might not the same about her middle weare,
> But it would loose or else asunder teare."

So it happened to the false Florimel, st. 16, when

> " Being brought, about her middle small
> They thought to gird, as best it her became,
> But by no means they could it thereto frame,
> For ever as they fastned it, it loos'd
> And fell away, as feeling secret blame, &c.
> That all men wondred at the uncouth sight
> And each one thought as to their fancies came.
> But she herself did think it done for spight,
> And touched was with secret wrath and shame
> Therewith, as thing deviz'd her to defame :
> Then many other ladies likewise tride
> About their tender loynes to knit the same,
> But it would not on none of them abide,
> But when they thought it fast, eftsoones it was untide.
> Thereat all knights gan laugh and ladies lowre,
> Till that at last the gentle Amoret
> Likewise assayed to prove that girdle's powre.
> And having it about her middle set
> Did find it fit withouten breach or let,
> Whereat the rest gan greatly to envie.
> But Florimel exceedingly did fret
> And snatching from her hand," &c.

As for the trial of the *Horne*, it is not peculiar to our poet : it occurs in the old romance, intitled *Morte Arthur*, which was translated out of French in the time of K. Edw. IV., and first printed anno 1484. From that romance Ariosto is thought to have borrowed his tale of the *Enchanted Cup*, c. 42, &c. See Mr. Warton's *Observations on the Faerie Queen*, &c.

The story of the *Horn* in *Morte Arthur* varies a good deal from this of our poet, as the reader will judge from the following extract :—" By the way they met with a knight that was sent from Morgan la Faye to king Arthur, and this knight had a fair horne all garnished with gold, and the horne had such a virtue, that there might no ladye or gentlewoman drinke of that horne, but if she were true to her husband : and if shee were false she should spill all the drinke, and if shee were true unto her lorde, shee might drink peaceably : and because of queene Guenever and in despite of Sir Launcelot du Lake, this horne was sent unto king Arthur."

This horn is intercepted and brought unto another king named Marke, who is not a whit more fortunate than the British hero, for he makes " his qeene drinke thereof and an hundred ladies moe, and there were but foure ladies of all those that drank cleane," of which number the said queen proves not to be one (book ii. chap. 22, ed. 1632).

In other respects the two stories are so different, that we have just reason to suppose this ballad was written before that romance was translated into English.

As for queen Guenever, she is here represented no otherwise than in the old histories and romances. Holinshed observes, that "she was evil reported of, as noted of incontinence and breach of faith to hir husband" (vol. i. p. 93).

Such readers, as have no relish for pure antiquity, will find a more modern copy of this ballad at the end of the volume.

[For Percy's further notes on this ballad see the modernized version (book iii. No. 18). Professor Child prints the ballad in his *English and Scottish Ballads* (vol. i. p. 1) with a full notice of the various forms of the story by way of introduction. He writes :—" No incident is more common in romantic fiction than the employment of some magical contrivance as a test of conjugal fidelity, or of constancy in love. In some romances of the Round Table, and tales founded upon them, this experiment is performed by means either of an enchanted horn, of such properties that no dishonoured husband or unfaithful wife can drink from it without spilling, or of a mantle which will fit none but chaste women. The earliest known instances of the use of these ordeals are afforded by the *Lai du Corn*, by Robert Bikez, a French minstrel of the twelfth or thirteenth century, and the *Fabliau du Mantel Mautaillé*, which, in the opinion of a competent critic, dates from the second half of the thirteenth century, and is only the older lay worked up into a new shape (Wolf, *Ueber die Lais*, 327, sq., 342, sq.). We are not to suppose, however, that either of these pieces presents us with the primitive form of this humorous invention. Robert Bikez tells us that he learned his story from an abbot, and that ' noble ecclesiast' stood but one further back in a line of tradition which curiosity will never follow to its source."

Here follows a list of "the most remarkable cases of the use of these and similar talismans in imaginative literature." To these may be added the garland described in the curious old story of the *Wright's Wife*, which has been printed since the publication of Mr. Child's work.

> " Haue here thys garlond of roses ryche,
> In alle thys lond ys none yt lyche ;
> For ytt wylle euer be newe.

Wete þou wele withowtyn fable,
Alle the whyle thy wyfe ys stable
   The chaplett wolle hold hewe ;
And yf thy wyfe vse putry,
Or tolle eny man to lye her by,
   Than wolle yt change hewe ;
And by the garlond þou may see,
Fekylle or fals yf þat sche be,
   Or ellys yf sche be trewe."

The Wright's Chaste Wife (E. E. Text Soc. 1865, l. 55-66).]

N the third day of may,
    To Carleile did come
    A kind curteous child,
    That cold[1] much of wisdome.

A kirtle and a mantle   5
This child had uppon,
With ' brouches' and ringes
Full richelye bedone.[2]

He had a sute of silke
About his middle drawne ;   10
Without he cold of curtesye
He thought itt much shame.

God speed thee, king Arthur,
Sitting at thy meate :
And the goodly queene Guénever,   15
I cannott her forgett.

I tell you, lords, in this hall ;
I hett[3] you all to ' heede' ;
Except you be the more surer
Is you for to dread.   20

Ver. 7. branches, MS.   V. 18. heate, MS.

[[1] knew.   [2] ornamented.   [3] bid.]

He plucked out of his ' poterner,'[1]
And longer wold not dwell,
He pulled forth a pretty mantle,
Betweene two nut-shells.

Have thou here, king Arthur;   25
Have thou heere of mee :
Give itt to thy comely queene
Shapen as itt is alreadye.

Itt shall never become that wiffe,
That hath once done amisse.   30
Then every knight in the kings court
Began to care for ' his.'

Forth came dame Guénever;
To the mantle shee her 'hied';
The ladye shee was newfangle,   35
But yett shee was affrayd.

When shee had taken the mantle;
She stoode as shee had beene madd :
It was from the top to the toe
As sheeres had itt shread.   40

One while was itt 'gule';[2]
Another while was itt greene;
Another while was itt wadded :[3]
Ill itt did her beseeme.

Another while was it blacke   45
And bore the worst hue :
By my troth, quoth king Arthur,
I thinke thou be not true.

Ver. 21. potewer, MS.   V. 32. his wiffe, MS.   V. 34. biled, MS.
V. 41. gaule, MS.

[[1] probably a pouch or bag, but there is no authority for the
word.   [2] red.   [3] light blue or woad coloured.]

Shee threw downe the mantle,
That bright was of blee ;[1]   50
Fast with a rudd[2] redd,
To her chamber can[3] shee flee.

She curst the weaver, and the walker,[4]
That clothe that had wrought ;
And bade a vengeance on his crowne,   55
That hither hath itt brought.

I had rather be in a wood,
Under a greene tree ;
Then in king Arthurs court
Shamed for to bee.   60

Kay called forth his ladye,
And bade her come neere ;
Saies, Madam, and thou be guiltye,
I pray thee hold thee there.

Forth came his ladye   65
Shortlye and anon ;
Boldlye to the mantle
Then is shee gone.

When she had tane the mantle,
And cast it her about ;   70
Then was shee bare
' Before all the rout.'

Then every knight,
That was in the kings court,
Talked, laughed, and showted   75
Full oft att that sport.

[Ver. 72. all above the buttockes, MS.]   V. 75. lauged, **MS.**

colour.   [2] ruddy.   [3] began.   [4] fuller.]

Shee threw downe the mantle,
That bright was of blee;
Fast, with a red rudd,
To her chamber can[1] shee flee.   80

Forth came an old knight
Pattering ore a creede,
And he proferred to this litle boy
Twenty markes to his meede;

And all the time of the Christmasse   85
Willinglye to ffeede;
For why this mantle might
Doe his wiffe some need.

When she had tane the mantle,
Of cloth that was made,   90
Shee had no more left on her,
But a tassell and a threed:
Then every knight in the kings court
Bade evill might shee speed.

Shee threw downe the mantle,   95
That bright was of blee;
And fast, with a redd rudd,
To her chamber can[1] shee flee.

Craddocke called forth his ladye,
And bade her come in;   100
Saith, Winne this mantle, ladye,
With a litle dinne.

Winne this mantle, ladye,
And it shal be thine,
If thou never did amisse   105
Since thou wast mine.

[[1] began.]

Forth came Craddockes ladye
Shortlye and anon ;
But boldlye to the mantle
Then is shee gone.   110

When shee had tane the mantle,
And cast itt her about,
Upp att her great toe
It began to crinkle and crowt :[1]
Shee said, bowe downe, mantle,   115
And shame me not for nought.

Once I did amisse,
I tell you certainlye,
When I kist Craddockes mouth
Under a greene tree ;   120
When I kist Craddockes mouth
Before he marryed mee.

When shee had her shreeven,
And her sines shee had tolde ;
The mantle stoode about her   125
Right as shee wold :

Seemelye of coulour
Glittering like gold :
Then every knight in Arthurs court
Did her behold.   130

Then spake dame Guénever
To Arthur our king ;
She hath tane yonder mantle
Not with right, but with wronge.

See you not yonder woman,   135
That maketh her self soe 'cleane'?
I have seene tane out of her bedd
Of men fiveteene ;

Ver. 134. wright, MS.   V. 136. cleare, MS.
[[1] draw close together, another form of *crowd*.]

Priests, clarkes, and wedded men
From her bedeene:[1] 140
Yett shee taketh the mantle,
And maketh her self cleane.

Then spake the litle boy,
That kept the mantle in hold ;
Sayes, king, chasten thy wiffe, 145
Of her words shee is to bold :

Shee is a bitch and a witch,
And a whore bold :
King, in thine owne hall
Thou art a cuckold. 150

The litle boy stoode
Looking out a dore ;
[And there as he was lookinge
He was ware of a wyld bore.]

He was ware of a wyld bore, 155
Wold have werryed a man :
He pulld forth a wood kniffe,
Fast thither that he ran :
He brought in the bores head,
And quitted him like a man. 160

He brought in the bores head,
And was wonderous bold :
He said there was never a cuckolds kniffe
Carve itt that cold.

Some rubbed their knives 165
Uppon a whetstone :
Some threw them under the table,
And said they had none.

Ver. 140. by deene, MS. [V. 151. a little boy, MS. V. 152.
looking over. V. 155-6. these two lines belong to the former
stanza.]

[1 forthwith.]

King Arthur, and the child
Stood looking upon them;
All their knives edges
Turned backe againe.   170

Craddocke had a litle knive
Of iron and of steele;
He britled[1] the bores head   175
Wonderous weele;
That every knight in the kings court
Had a morssell.

The litle boy had a horne,
Of red gold that ronge: 180
He said, there was noe cuckolde
Shall drinke of my horne;
But he shold it sheede[2]
Either behind or beforne.

Some shedd on their shoulder,   185
And some on their knee;
He that cold not hitt his mouthe,
Put it in his eye:
And he that was a cuckold
Every man might him see.   190

Craddocke wan the horne,
And the bores head:
His ladie wan the mantle
Unto her meede.
Everye such a lovely ladye   195
God send her well to speede.

Ver. 170. them upon, MS.   V. 175. *or* birtled, MS.

[1 carved.   2 shed.]

II.

THE MARRIAGE OF SIR GAWAINE

IS chiefly taken from the fragment of an old ballad in the Editor's MS., which he has reason to believe more ancient than the time of *Chaucer*, and what furnished that bard with his *Wife of Bath's Tale*. The original was so extremely mutilated, half of every leaf being torn away, that without large supplements, &c. it was deemed improper for this collection: these it has therefore received, such as they are. They are not here particularly pointed out, because the *Fragment* itself will now be found printed at the end of this volume.

[Sir Frederic Madden supposed this ballad to be founded upon the *Weddynge of Syr Gawen and Dame Ragnell*, which he printed from the Rawlinson MS. c. 86, fol. 128 b, in his *Syr Gawaine*.

Mr. Hales writes as follows respecting the various forms in which the story appears in literature. "The wonderful 'metamorphosis' on which this story turns is narrated in Gower's *Confessio Amantis*, as the story of Florent and the King of Sicily's Daughter, taken by him, as Tyrwhitt conjectures, from the *Gesta Romanorum*, or some such collection. It appears again, as the reader will remember, in Chaucer's *Wyf of Bathes Tale*. 'Worked over,' says Prof. Child, 'by some ballad-monger of the sixteenth century, and of course reduced to ditch-water, this tale has found its way into the *Crown Garland of Golden Roses*, part i. p. 68 (*Percy Society*, vol. vi.), 'Of a Knight and a Faire Virgin.' On a similar transformation depends the story of 'King Henrie' in Scott's *Minstrelsy*, edited from Mrs. Brown's MS., with corrections from a recited fragment, and modernized as 'Courteous King Jamie' in Lewis's *Tales of Wonder*. 'The prime original,' says Scott, 'is to be found in an Icelandic Saga.'"*

Mr. Child prints (*English and Scottish Ballads*, vol. viii. p. 139) two versions of a Scotch ballad entitled *Kempy Kaye*, which he supposes to be an extravagant parody of *The Marriage of Sir Gawaine*.]

[* Percy folio MS. ed. Hales and Furnivall, vol. i. p. 104.]

PART THE FIRST.

ING Arthur lives in merry Carleile,
 And seemely is to see;
And there with him queene Guenever,
 That bride soe bright of blee.[1]

And there with him queene Guenever, 5
 That bride so bright in bowre:
And all his barons about him stoode,
 That were both stiffe and stowre.[2]

The king a royale Christmasse kept,
 With mirth and princelye cheare; 10
To him repaired many a knighte,
 That came both farre and neare.

And when they were to dinner sette,
 And cups went freely round;
Before them came a faire damsèlle, 15
 And knelt upon the ground.

A boone, a boone, O kinge Arthùre,
 I beg a boone of thee;
Avenge me of a carlish knighte,
 Who hath shent[3] my love and mee. 20

At Tearne-Wadling* his castle stands,
 Near to that lake so fair,
And proudlye rise the battlements,
 And streamers deck the air.

---

* *Tearne-Wadling* is the name of a small lake [in Inglewood Forest] near Hesketh in Cumberland, on the road from Penrith to Carlisle. There is a tradition, that an old castle once stood near the lake, the remains of which were not long since visible. *Tarn*, in the dialect of that country, signifies a small lake, and is still in use. ["Tarn-Wadling . . . has been for the last ten years a wide meadow grazed by hundreds of sheep."—J. S. Glennie, in *Macmillan's Mag.* Dec. 1867, p. 167, col. 2.]

[[1] complexion. [2] strong. [3] abused.]

Noe gentle knighte, nor ladye gay,   25
   May pass that castle-walle :
But from that foule discurteous knighte,
   Mishappe will them befalle.

Hee's twyce the size of common men,
   Wi' thewes, and sinewes stronge,   30
And on his backe he bears a clubbe,
   That is both thicke and longe.

This grimme baròne 'twas our harde happe,
   But yester morne to see ;
When to his bowre he bare my love,   35
   And sore misused mee.

And when I told him, king Arthùre
   As lyttle shold him spare ;
Goe tell, sayd hee, that cuckold kinge,
   To meete mee if he dare.   40

Upp then sterted king Arthùre,
   And sware by hille and dale,
He ne'er wolde quitt that grimme baròne,
   Till he had made him quail.

Goe fetch my sword Excalibar :   45
   Goe saddle mee my steede ;
Nowe, by my faye, that grimme baròne
   Shall rue this ruthfulle deede.

And when he came to Tearne Wadlinge
   Benethe the castle walle :   50
" Come forth ; come forth ; thou proude baròne,
   Or yielde thyself my thralle."

On magicke grounde that castle stoode,
   And fenc'd with many a spelle :
Noe valiant knighte could tread thereon,   55
   But straite his courage felle.

Forth then rush'd that carlish[1] knight,
  King Arthur felte the charme:
His sturdy sinewes lost their strengthe,
  Downe sunke his feeble arme.   60

Nowe yield thee, yield thee, kinge Arthùre,
  Now yield thee, unto mee:
Or fighte with mee, or lose thy lande,
  Noe better termes maye bee,

Unlesse thou sweare upon the rood,   65
  And promise on thy faye,
Here to returne to Tearne-Wadling,
  Upon the new-yeare's daye;

And bringe me worde what thing it is
  All women moste desyre;   70
This is thy ransome, Arthur, he sayes,
  Ile have noe other hyre.

King Arthur then helde up his hande,
  And sware upon his faye,[2]
Then tooke his leave of the grimme barone   7
  And faste hee rode awaye.

And he rode east, and he rode west,
  And did of all inquyre,
What thing it is all women crave,
  And what they most desyre.   80

Some told him riches, pompe, or state;
  Some rayment fine and brighte;
Some told him mirthe; some flatterye;
  And some a jollye knighte.

[1 churlish.   2 faith.]

In letters all king Arthur wrote,   85
    And seal'd them with his ringe:
But still his minde was helde in doubte,
    Each tolde a different thinge.

As ruthfulle he rode over a more,
    He saw a ladye sette   90
Betweene an oke, and a greene holléye,
    All clad in red* scarlette.

Her nose was crookt and turnd outwàrde,
    Her chin stoode all awrye;
And where as sholde have been her mouthe, 95
    Lo! there was set her eye:

Her haires, like serpents, clung aboute
    Her cheekes of deadlye hewe:
A worse-form'd ladye than she was,
    No man mote ever viewe.   100

To hail the king in seemelye sorte
    This ladye was fulle faine;
But king Arthùre all sore amaz'd,
    No aunswere made againe.

What wight art thou, the ladye sayd,   105
    That wilt not speake to mee;
Sir, I may chance to ease thy paine,
    Though I be foule to see.

If thou wilt ease my paine, he sayd,
    And helpe me in my neede;   110
Ask what thou wilt, thou grimme ladyè,
    And it shall bee thy meede.

---

* This was a common phrase in our old writers; so Chaucer, in his prologue to the *Cant. Tales,* says of the wife of Bath:—

    " Her hosen were of fyne scarlet red."

O sweare mee this upon the roode,
 And promise on thy faye;
And here the secrette I will telle,   115
 That shall thy ransome paye.

King Arthur promis'd on his faye,
 And sware upon the roode;
The secrette then the ladye told,
 As lightlye well shee cou'de.   120

Now this shall be my paye, sir king,
 And this my guerdon bee,
That some yong fair and courtlye knight,
 Thou bringe to marrye mee.

Fast then pricked king Arthùre   125
 Ore hille, and dale, and downe:
And soone he founde the barone's bowre:
 And soone the grimme baroùne.

He bare his clubbe upon his backe,
 Hee stoode bothe stiffe and stronge; 130
And, when he had the letters reade,
 Awaye the lettres flunge.

Nowe yielde thee, Arthur, and thy lands,
 All forfeit unto mee;
For this is not thy paye, sir king,   135
 Nor may thy ransome bee.

Yet hold thy hand, thou proud baròne,
 I praye thee hold thy hand;
And give mee leave to speake once more
 In reskewe of my land.   140

This morne, as I came over a more,
 I saw a ladye sette
Betwene an oke, and a greene hollèye,
 All clad in red scarlètte.

Shee sayes, all women will have their wille, 145
    This is their chief desyre;
Now yield, as thou art a barone true,
    That I have payd mine hyre.

An earlye vengeaunce light on her!
    The carlish baron swore: 150
Shee was my sister tolde thee this,
    And shee's a mishapen whore.

But here I will make mine avowe,
    To do her as ill a turne:
For an ever I may that foule theefe gette, 155
    In a fyre I will her burne.

PART THE SECONDE.

OMEWARDE pricked king Arthùre,
    And a wearye man was hee;
And soone he mette queene Guenever,
    That bride so bright of blee.

What newes! what newes! thou noble king, 5
    Howe, Arthur, hast thou sped?
Where hast thou hung the carlish knighte?
    And where bestow'd his head?

The carlish knight is safe for mee,
    And free fro mortal harme: 10
On magicke grounde his castle stands,
    And fenc'd with many a charme.

To bowe to him I was fulle faine,
    And yielde mee to his hand:
And but for a lothly ladye, there 15
    I sholde have lost my land.

And nowe this fills my hearte with woe,
    And sorrowe of my life;
I swore a yonge and courtlye knight,
    Sholde marry her to his wife.   20

Then bespake him sir Gawàine,
    That was ever a gentle knighte:
That lothly ladye I will wed;
    Therefore be merrye and lighte.

Nowe naye, nowe naye, good sir Gawàine;   25
    My sister's sonne yee bee;
This lothlye ladye's all too grimme,
    And all too foule for yee.

Her nose is crookt and turn'd outwàrde;
    Her chin stands all awrye;   30
A worse form'd ladye than shee is
    Was never seen with eye.

What though her chin stand all awrye,
    And shee be foule to see:
I'll marry her, unkle, for thy sake,   35
    And I'll thy ransome bee.

Nowe thankes, nowe thankes, good sir Gawàine;
    And a blessing thee betyde!
To-morrow wee'll have knights and squires,
    And wee'll goe fetch thy bride.   40

And wee'll have hawkes and wee'll have houndes,
    To cover our intent;
And wee'll away to the greene forèst,
    As wee a hunting went.

Sir Lancelot, sir Stephen * bolde,   45
    They rode with them that daye;
And foremoste of the companye
    There rode the stewarde Kaye:

[* Sir F. Madden remarks that Sir Stephen does not appear in the Round Table Romances.]

Soe did sir Banier * and sir Bore,†
   And eke sir Garratte ‡ keene ;   50
Sir Tristram too, that gentle knight,
   To the forest freshe and greene.

And when they came to the greene forrèst,
   Beneathe a faire holley tree
There sate that ladye in red scarlètte   55
   That unseemelye was to see.

Sir Kay beheld that lady's face,
   And looked upon her sweere ;[1]
Whoever kisses that ladye, he sayes,
   Of his kisse he stands in feare.   60

Sir Kay beheld that ladye againe,
   And looked upon her snout ;
Whoever kisses that ladye, he sayes,
   Of his kisse he stands in doubt.

Peace, brother Kay, sayde sir Gawàine,   65
   And amend thee of thy life :
For there is a knight amongst us all,
   Must marry her to his wife.

What marry this foule queane, quoth Kay,
   I' the devil's name anone ;   70
Gett mee a wife wherever I maye,
   In sooth shee shall be none.

Then some tooke up their hawkes in haste,
   And some took up their houndes ;
And sayd they wolde not marry her,   75
   For cities, nor for townes.

[* Perhaps intended for Bedver, the King's Constable, Tennyson's
Bedivere, but more probably Ban of Benoyk, the brother of Bors.
  † Bors de Gauves, or Gaunes.
  ‡ Gareth, or Gaheret, Sir Gawain's younger brother.
       [1] neck.]

Then bespake him king Arthùre,
   And sware there by this daye;
For a little foule sighte and mislikìnge,
   Yee shall not say her naye.   80

Peace, lordings, peace; sir Gawaine sayd;
   Nor make debate and strife;
This lothlye ladye I will take,
   And marry her to my wife.

Nowe thankes, nowe thankes, good sir Gawaine, 85
   And a blessinge be thy meede!
For as I am thine owne ladyè,
   Thou never shalt rue this deede.

Then up they took that lothly dame,
   And home anone they bringe: 90
And there sir Gawaine he her wed,
   And married her with a ringe.

And when they were in wed-bed laid,
   And all were done awaye:
"Come turne to mee, mine owne wed-lord   95
   Come turne to mee I praye."

Sir Gawaine scant could lift his head,
   For sorrowe and for care;
When, lo! instead of that lothelye dame,
   Hee sawe a young ladye faire.   100

Sweet blushes stayn'd her rud-red cheeke,
   Her eyen were blacke as sloe:
The ripening cherrye swellde her lippe,
   And all her necke was snowe.

Sir Gawaine kiss'd that lady faire,   105
   Lying upon the sheete:
And swore, as he was a true knighte,
   The spice was never soe sweete.

Sir Gawaine kiss'd that lady brighte,
   Lying there by his side: 110
" The fairest flower is not soe faire :
   Thou never can'st bee my bride."

I am thy bride, mine owne deare lorde,
   The same whiche thou didst knowe,
That was soe lothlye, and was wont   115
   Upon the wild more to goe.

Nowe, gentle Gawaine, chuse, quoth shee,
   And make thy choice with care;
Whether by night, or else by daye,
   Shall I be foule or faire ?   120

" To have thee foule still in the night,
   When I with thee should playe !
I had rather farre, my lady deare,
   To have thee foule by daye."

What when gaye ladyes goe with their lordes 125
   To drinke the ale and wine;
Alas ! then I must hide myself,
   I must not goe with mine ?

" My faire ladyè, sir Gawaine sayd,
   I yield me to thy skille;   130
Because thou art mine owne ladyè
   Thou shalt have all thy wille."

Nowe blessed be thou, sweete Gawàine,
   And the daye that I thee see ;
For as thou seest mee at this time,   135
   Soe shall I ever bee.

My father was an aged knighte,
   And yet it chanced soe,
He tooke to wife a false ladyè,
   Whiche broughte me to this woe.   140

Shee witch'd mee, being a faire yonge maide,
  In the greene forèst to dwelle;
And there to abide in lothlye shape,
  Most like a fiend of helle.

Midst mores and mosses; woods, and wilds;   145
  To lead a lonesome life:
Till some yong faire and courtlye knighte
  Wolde marrye me to his wife:

Nor fully to gaine mine owne trewe shape,
  Such was her devilish skille;   150
Until he wolde yielde to be rul'd by mee,
  And let mee have all my wille.

She witchd my brother to a carlish boore,
  And made him stiffe and stronge;
And built him a bowre on magicke grounde,   155
  To live by rapine and wronge.

But now the spelle is broken throughe,
  And wronge is turnde to righte;
Henceforth I shall bee a faire ladyè,
  And hee be a gentle knighte.   160

*_**

III.

KING RYENCE'S CHALLENGE.

THIS song is more modern than many of those which follow it, but is placed here for the sake of the subject. It was sung before queene Elizabeth at the grand entertainment at Kenelworth-castle in 1575, and was probably composed for that occasion. In a letter describing those festivities, it is thus mentioned: "A Minstral came forth with a sollem song, warranted for story out of K. Arthur's acts, whereof I gat a copy, and is this:

"So it fell out on a Pentecost, &c."

After the song the narrative proceeds : " At this the Minstrell made a pause and a curtezy for Primus Passus. More of the song is thear, but I gatt it not."

The story in Morte Arthur, whence it is taken, runs as follows : " Came a messenger hastely from king Ryence of North-Wales,— saying, that king Ryence had discomfited and overcomen eleaven kings, and everiche of them did him homage, and that was this : they gave him their beards cleane flayne off.—wherefore the messenger came for king Arthur's beard, for king Ryence had purfeled a mantell with kings beards, and there lacked for one a place of the mantell, wherefore he sent for his beard, or else he would enter into his lands, and brenn and slay, and never leave till he have thy head and thy beard. Well, said king Arthur, thou hast said thy message, which is the most villainous and lewdest message that ever man heard sent to a king. Also thou mayest see my beard is full young yet for to make a purfell of, but tell thou the king that —or it be long he shall do to me homage on both his knees, or else he shall leese his head." [B. i. c. 24. See also the same Romance, b. i. c. 92.]

The thought seems to be originally taken from Jeff. Monmouth's *Hist.* b. x. c. 3. which is alluded to by Drayton in his *Poly-Olb. Song.* 4 and by Spenser in *Faer. Qu.* 6. 1. 13. 15. See the Observations on Spenser, vol. ii. p. 223.

The following text is composed of the best readings selected from three different copies. The first in Enderbie's *Cambria Triumphans*, p. 197. The second in the Letter abovementioned. And the third inserted in MS. in a copy of *Morte Arthur*, 1632, in the Bodleian Library.

Stow tells us, that king Arthur kept his round table at "diverse places, but especially at Carlion, Winchester, and Camalet in Somersetshire." This *Camalet*, sometimes a famous towne or castle, is situate on a very high tor or hill," &c. (See an exact description in Stowe's *Annals*, ed. 1631, p. 55.)

AS it fell out on a Pentecost day,
 King Arthur at Camelot kept his court
  royall,
 With his faire queene dame Guenever the
   gay ;
And many bold barons sitting in hall ;
With ladies attired in purple and pall ;   5

And heraults in hewkes,[1] hooting on high,
Cryed, *Largesse, Largesse, Chevaliers tres-hardie.**

A doughty dwarfe to the uppermost deas[2]
　Right pertlye gan pricke, kneeling on knee;
With steven[3] fulle stoute amids all the preas,[4]　　　10
　Sayd, Nowe sir king Arthur, God save thee, and see!
　Sir Ryence of North-gales[5] greeteth well thee,
And bids thee thy beard anon to him send,
Or else from thy jaws he will it off rend.

For his robe of state is a rich scarlet mantle,　　　15
　With eleven kings beards bordered † about,
And there is room lefte yet in a kantle,[6]
　For thine to stande, to make the twelfth out:
　This must be done, be thou never so stout;
This must be done, I tell thee no fable,　　　20
Maugre[7] the teethe of all thy round table.

When this mortal message from his mouthe past,
　Great was the noyse bothe in hall and in bower:
The king fum'd; the queene screecht; ladies were
　　aghast;
　Princes puffd; barons blustred; lords began lower;
　Knights stormed; squires startled, like steeds in
　　a stower;　　　26
Pages and yeomen yell'd out in the hall,
Then in came sir Kay, the 'king's' seneschal.

---

　* *Largesse, Largesse.* The heralds resounded these words as oft
as they received of the bounty of the knights. See *Memoires de la
Chevalerie*, tom. i. p. 99.—The expression is still used in the form
of installing knights of the garter.
　† *i.e.* set round the border, as furs are now round the gowns of
Magistrates.

　　[[1] party-coloured coats.　　　[2] dais or upper table.
　　[3] voice.　　　　[4] press.　　　　[5] North Wales.
　　[6] corner.　　　　[7] in spite of.]

Silence, my soveraignes, quoth this courteous knight,
   And in that stound the stowre[1] began still :   30
' Then' the dwarfe's dinner full deerely was dight ;[2]
   Of wine and wassel he had his wille :
And, when he had eaten and drunken his fill,
An hundred pieces of fine coyned gold
Were given this dwarf for his message bold.   35

But say to sir Ryence, thou dwarf, quoth the king,
   That for his bold message I do him defye;
And shortlye with basins and pans will him ring
   Out of North-gales; where he and I
With swords, and not razors, quickly shall trye, 40
Whether he, or king Arthur will prove the best
   barbor :
And therewith he shook his good sword Excalàbor.
     *   *   *   *   *   *

†⌊† Strada, in his *Prolusions*, has ridiculed the story of the Giant's Mantle, made of the Beards of Kings.

IV.

KING ARTHUR'S DEATH.

A Fragment.

HE subject of this ballad is evidently taken from the old romance *Morte Arthur*, but with some variations, especially in the concluding stanzas; in which the author seems rather to follow the traditions of the old Welsh Bards, who believed that King Arthur was not dead, "but conveied awaie by the Fairies into some pleasant place, where he should remaine for a time, and then returne againe and reign in as great

---

[[1] that moment the tumult.   [2] decked.]

authority as ever." Holinshed, b. 5, c. 14, or as it is expressed in
an old Chronicle printed at Antwerp 1493, by Ger. de Leew,
" The Bretons supposen, that he [K. Arthur]—shall come yet and
conquere all Bretaigne, for certes this is the prophicye of Merlyn :
He sayd, that his deth shall be doubteous; and sayd soth, for men
thereof yet have doubte, and shullen for ever more,—for men wyt
not whether that he lyveth or is dede." See more ancient testi-
monies in Selden's *Notes on Polyolbion, Song III.*

This fragment being very incorrect and imperfect in the original
MS. hath received some conjectural emendations, and even a sup-
plement of three or four stanzas composed from the romance of
Morte Arthur.

[The two ballads here entitled *King Arthur's Death* and *The
Legend of King Arthur* are united in the Folio MS. (ed. Hales and
Furnivall, vol. i. p. 497), but they are evidently two distinct songs.
The first ballad forms part ii. of the MS. copy, which has fourteen
verses at the end not printed here. The last four verses are
printed at the end of the next ballad. Percy has taken great
liberties with his original, and has not left a single line unaltered,
as will be seen by comparing it with the original printed at the
end. Additional lines are also interpolated which are now enclosed within brackets, and it will be seen that these unnecessary
amplifications do not improve the effect of the poem. It will also
be seen that in vv. 41-44 the father and son of the original are
changed into uncle and nephew.

This last scene in the life of King Arthur is the most beautiful
and touching portion of his history, and the romancers and minstrels were never tired of telling it in every form.

According to one tradition Arthur still sleeps under St. Michael's
Mount ("the guarded Mount" of Milton's *Lycidas*), and according
to another beneath Richmond Castle, Yorkshire.

Mr. Willmott, in his edition of the *Reliques*, writes, " according
to popular superstition in Sicily, Arthur is preserved alive by his
sister la Fata Morgana, whose fairy palace is occasionally seen
from Reggio in the opposite sea of Messina."]

*   *   *   *   *

N Trinitye Mondaye in the morne,
  This sore battayle was doom'd to bee;
Where manye a knighte cry'd, Well-awaye!
  Alacke, it was the more pittie.

Ere the first crowinge of the cocke,   5
   When as the kinge in his bed laye,
He thoughte sir Gawaine to him came,*
   And there to him these wordes did saye.

Nowe, as you are mine unkle deare,
   And as you prize your life, this daye   10
O meet not with your foe in fighte ;
   Putt off the battayle, if yee maye.

For sir Launcelot is now in Fraunce,
   And with him many an hardye knighte :
Who will within this moneth be backe,   15
   And will assiste yee in the fighte.

The kinge then call'd his nobles all,
   Before the breakinge of the daye ;
And tolde them howe sir Gawaine came,
   And there to him these wordes did saye.   20

His nobles all this counsayle gave,
   That earlye in the morning, hee
Shold send awaye an herauld at armes,
   To aske a parley faire and free.

Then twelve good knightes king Arthure chose,   25
   The best of all that with him were :
To parley with the foe in field,
   And make with him agreement faire.

The king he charged all his hoste,
   In readinesse there for to bee :   30
But noe man sholde noe weapon sturre,
   Unlesse a sword drawne they shold see

---

* Sir Gawaine had been killed at Arthur's landing on his return
from abroad.   See the next ballad, ver. 73.

And Mordred on the other parte,
   Twelve of his knights did likewise bringe;
The beste of all his companye,   35
   To hold the parley with the kinge.

Sir Mordred alsoe charged his hoste,
   In readinesse there for to bee;
But noe man sholde noe weapon sturre,
   But if a sworde drawne they shold see.   40

For he durste not his unkle truste,
   Nor he his nephewe, sothe to tell:
Alacke! it was a woefulle case,
   As ere in Christentye befelle.

But when they were together mette,   45
   And both to faire accordance broughte;
And a month's league betweene them sette,
   Before the battayle sholde be foughte;

An addere crept forth of a bushe,
   Stunge one o' th' king's knightes on the knee: 50
Alacke! it was a woefulle chance,
   As ever was in Christentie.

When the knighte found him wounded sore,
   And sawe the wild-worme[1] hanginge there;
His sworde he from his scabberde drewe;   55
   A piteous case as ye shall heare.

For when the two hostes sawe the sworde,
   They joyned battayle instantlye;
Till of soe manye noble knightes,
   On one side there were left but three.   60

[Ver. 41, 42, the folio MS. reads father . . . sonne.
[1] serpent.]

For all were slain that durst abide,
   And but some fewe that fled awaye:
Ay mee! it was a bloodye fielde,
   As ere was foughte on summer's daye.

Upon king Arthur's own partyè,   65
   Onlye himselfe escaped there,
And Lukyn duke of Gloster free,
   And the king's butler Bedevere.

And when the king beheld his knightes,
   All dead and scattered on the molde;   70
⌊The teares fast trickled downe his face;
   That manlye face in fight so bolde.

Nowe reste yee all, brave knights, he said,
   Soe true and faithful to your trust:
And must yee then, ye valiant hearts,   75
   Be lefte to moulder into dust!

Most loyal have yee been to mee,
   Most true and faithful unto deathe:
And, oh! to rayse yee up againe,
   How freelye could I yield my breathe!⌋   80

But see the traitor's yet alive,
   Lo where hee stalkes among the deade!
Nowe bitterlye he shall abye:[1]
   And vengeance fall upon his head.

O staye, my liege, then sayd the duke;   85
   O staye for love and charitìe;
⌈Remember what the vision spake,
   Nor meete your foe, if it may bee.

[1 pay for or expiate.]

O, staye mee not, thou worthye wight,
   This debt my loyal knights I owe: 90
Betide me life, betide me death,
   I will avenge them of their foe.]

Then straite he grasp'd his trustye speare,
   And on his horse then mounted hee:
As his butler holpe him to his horse,   95
   His bowels gushed to his knee.

Alas! then sayd the noble king,
   That I should live this sight to see!
To see this good knight here be slaine,
   All for his love in helping mee!   100

He put his speare into his reste,
   And to sir Mordred loud gan crye;
[Nowe sette thyself upon thy guarde,
   For, traitor, nowe thy death is nye.

Sir Mordred lifted up his sworde,   105
   And fierce to meet the king ran hee:]
The king his speare he through him thrust;
   A fathom thorow his bodìe.

When Mordered felt the stroke of death,
   And found that he was wounded soe;   110
He thruste himselfe upon the speare,
   And strucke the king a deadlye blowe.

Then grimmlye dyed sir Mordered,
   Presentlye upon that tree:
And bloody streames ranne from the kinge   115
   Ere to the duke returned hee.

Sir Lukyn then he thus bespake,
   Sir knighte, thou hast beene faithfulle tryde,
Nowe take my sword Excalibar,*
   That hangs so freelye by my syde: 120

---

* More commonly called, *Caliburn.* In the folio MS. *Escall-
berd.* [Percy notes in the MS. that "Caliburn was presented A.D.

O take my sword Excalibar,
   And there into the river throwe :
For here, henceforth, benethe this tree,
   All use of weapons I foregoe.

[And fare thee well, thou trustye sword,   125
   A better neer had valiant knighte,
With thee full ofte, and manye a daye,
   Have I withstood my foe in fighte.

With this good fauchion in my hande,
   Oft have I reapd the bloody feelde :   1 0
But nowe the fatalle houre is come,
   That never more I may thee weelde.]

The duke to the river side he went,
   And there his owne sword in threwe he :
But he kept back Excalibar,   135
   He kept it back in privitie.

[For all of coleyne[1] was the blade ;
   And all the hilte of precious stone :
And ever alacke! then sayd the knighte,
   Must such a sword awaye be throwne ?]   140

Then backe he came unto the kinge,
   Who sayd, Sir Lukyn, what did yee see ?
Nothing, my liege, save that the winde
   Blewe oer the waters faire and free.

O goe againe, then said the kinge,   145
   O good sir Lukyn, goe againe :
Into the rivere throwe my sword,
   Nor keepe me lingering here in paine.

1191 to Tancred, King of Sicily, by our King Richard I.   See
Rapin, vol. i."
       [1] Cologne steel.]

The duke then to the river went,
   And the kings scabberd in threwe hee ;   150
But hee kept backe Excalibar,
   And hid it undernethe a tree.

Then backe he came to tell the kinge,
   Who sayde, Sir Lukyn sawe ye oughte ?
Nothinge, my liege, save that the winde   155
   Nowe with the angrye waters fought.

O Lukyn, Lukyn, said the kinge,
   [Twice haste thou dealt deceytfullye :
Alacke, whom may wee ever truste,
   When suche a knighte soe false can bee ?   160

Saye, wouldst thou have thy master dead ;
   All for a sword, that wins thine eye :
Nowe goe againe, and throwe it in,
   Or here the one of us shall dye.]

The duke, all shent with this rebuke,   165
   No aunswere made unto the kinge :
But to the rivere tooke the sworde,
   And threwe it far as he coulde flinge.

A hande and an arme did meete the sworde,
   And flourishd three times in the air ;   170
[Then sunke benethe the renninge streme,
   And of the duke was seene noe mair.

All sore astonied stood the duke ;
   He stood as still, as still mote bee :]
Then hastend backe to telle the kinge ;   175
   But he was gone from under the tree.

But to what place he cold not tell,
   For never after hee did him spye :

Ver. 178, see MS.

But hee sawe a barge goe from the land,
    And hee heard ladyes howle and crye*.   180

And whether the kinge were there, or not,
    Hee never knewe, nor ever colde:
[For from that sad and direfulle daye,
    Hee never more was seene on molde.]

                           ***

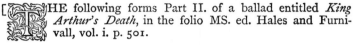

[T]HE following forms Part II. of a ballad entitled *King Arthur's Death*, in the folio MS. ed. Hales and Furnivall, vol. i. p. 501.

> but vpon a Monday after Trinity Sonday
> this battaile foughten cold bee,
> where many a Knight cryed well-away!
> alacke, the more pittye!

> but vpon Sunday in the euening then,   5
> when the King in his bedd did Lye,
> he thought Sir Gawaine to him came,
> & thus to him did say:

> "Now as you are my vnckle deere,
> I pray you be ruled by mee,   10
> doe not fight as to-morrow day,
> but put the battelle of if you may;

> "for Sir Lancelott is now in france,
> & many Knights with him full hardye,
> & with-in this Month here hee wilbe,   15
> great aide wilbe to thee."

---

* Not unlike that passage in Virgil.

    "Summoque ulularunt vertice nymphæ."

Ladies was the word our old English writers used for *Nymphs:* As in the following lines of an old song in the Editor's folio MS.

    "When scorching Phœbus he did mount,
    Then Lady Venus went to hunt:
      To whom Diana did resort,
    With all the Ladyes of hills, and valleys
    Of springs, and floodes, &c.

hee wakened forth of his dreames ;
to his Nobles that told hee,
how he thought Sir Gawaine to him came,
& these words sayd Certainly.   20

& then thé gaue the King councell all,
vpon Munday Earlye
that hee shold send one of his heralds of armes
to parle with his sonne, if itt might bee.

& 12 knights King Arthur chose,   25
the best in his companye,
that they shold goe to meete his sonne,
to agree if itt cold bee.

& the King charged all his host
in readynesse for to bee,   30
that Noe man shold noe weapons stur
with-out a sword drawne amongst his Knights thé see.

& Mordred vpon the other part,
12 of his Knights chose hee
that they shold goe to meete his father   35
betweene those 2 hosts fayre & free.

& Mordred charged his ost
in like mannor most certainely,
that noe man shold noe weapons sturr
with-out a sword drawne amongst them thé see ;   40

for he durst not his father trust,
nor the father the sonne certainley.
Alacke ! this was a woefull case
as euer was in christentye !

but when they were mett together there,   45
& agreed of all things as itt shold bee,
& a monthes League then there was
before the battele foughten shold bee,

an Adder came forth of Bush,
stunge one of king Arthirs Knights below his knee ;   50
alacke ! this was a woefull chance
as euer was in christentye !

the Knight he found him wounded there,
& see the wild worme there to bee ;
his sword out of his scabberd he drew ;   55
alas ! itt was the more pittye !

& when these 2 osts saw they sword drawen,
thé Ioyned battell certainlye,
Till of a 100 : 1000 : men
of one side was left but 3.   60

but all were slaine that durst abyde,
but some awaye that did flee.
King Arthur vpon his owne partye
himselfe aliue cold be,

& Lukin the Duke of Gloster,   65
& Bedever his Butler certainlye
the King looked about him there
& saw his Knights all slaine to bee;

"Alas!" then sayd noble King Arthur
"that ever this sight I see!   70
to see all my good Knights lye slaine,
& the traitor yett aliue to bee !

loe where he leanes vpon his sword hillts
amongst his dead men certainlye !
I will goe slay him att this time;   75
neuer att better advantage I shall him see."

"Nay! stay here, my Leege!" then said the Duke,
for loue and charitye !
for wee haue the battell woone,
for yett aliue we are but 3 : "   80

the king wold not be perswaded then,
but his horsse then mounted hee;
his Butler [that] helped him to horsse,
his bowells gushed to his knee.

"Alas!" then said noble king Arthur,   85
"that this sight I euer see,
to see this good knight for to be slaine
for loue for to helpe mee !"

he put his speare into his rest,
& att his sonne he ryd feirclye,   90
& through him there his speare he thrust
a fatham thorrow his body.

the sonne he felld him wounded there,
& knew his death then to bee ;
he thrust himselfe vpon his speare,   95
& gaue his father a wound certainlye.

but there dyed Sir Mordred
presently vpon that tree.
but or ere the King returned againe,
his butler was dead certainlye.   100

then bespake him Noble King Arthur,
these were the words sayd hee,
sayes " take my sword Escalberd
from my side fayre & free,
& throw itt into this riuer heere ;   105
for all the vse of weapons Ile deliuer vppe,
heere vnderneath this tree."

the Duke to the riuer side he went,
& his sword in threw hee ;
& then he kept Escalberd,   110
I tell you certainlye ;

& then he came to tell the King,
the king said, " Lukin what did thou see ? "
noe thing, my leege," the[n] sayd the duke,
" I tell you certainlye."   115

" O goe againe," said the king
for loue & charitye,
& throw my sword into that riuer,
that neuer I doe itt see."

the Duke to the riuer side he went,   120
& the kings scaberd in threw hee ;
& still he kept Escalberd
for vertue sake faire & free.

he came againe to tell the King ;
the King sayd, " Lukin what did thou see ? "   125
" nothing my leege," then sayd the Duke,
" I tell you certainlye."

" O goe againe Lukin," said the King,
or the one of vs shall dye."
then the Duke to the riuer sid went,   130
& then Kings sword then threw hee :

A hand & an arme did meete that sword,
& flourished 3 times certainlye
he came againe to tell the King,
but the king was gone from vnder the tree   135

but to what place, he cold not tell,
for neuer after hee did him see,
but he see a barge from the land goe,
& hearde Ladyes houle & cry certainlye ;

but whether the king was there or noe   140
he knew not certainlye.
the Duke walked by that Riuers side
till a chappell there found hee,

& a preist by the aulter side there stood.
the Duke kneeled downe there on his knee   145
& prayed the preists, " for Christs sake
the rights of the church bestow on mee ! "

for many dangerous wounds he had vpon him
& liklye he was to dye.
& there the Duke liued in prayer   150
till the time that hee did dye.

King Arthur liued King 22 yeere
in honor and great fame,
& thus by death suddenlye   155
was depriued from the same.

ffins.]

V.

THE LEGEND OF KING ARTHUR.

WE have here a short summary of K. Arthur's History
as given by Jeff. of Monmouth and the old chronicles,
with the addition of a few circumstances from the romance Morte Arthur.—The ancient chronicle of Ger.
de Leew (quoted above in p. 28), seems to have been chiefly
followed : upon the authority of which we have restored some of
the names which were corrupted in the MS. and have transposed
one stanza, which appeared to be misplaced, (*viz.* that beginning
at ver. 49, which in the MS. followed ver. 36.)
Printed from the Editor's ancient folio Manuscript.

[This ballad as previously stated is the first part of the poem in
the MS. and precedes the one here printed before it.   Percy made
comparatively few alterations in this part and all of them are now
noted at the foot of the page.]

F Brutus' blood, in Brittaine borne,
King Arthur I am to name;
Through Christendome, and Heathynesse,[1]
Well knowne is my worthy fame.

In Jesus Christ I doe beleeve;   5
I am a christyan bore:[2]
The Father, Sone, and Holy Gost
One God, I doe adore.

In the four hundred ninetieth yeere,
Over Brittaine I did rayne,   10
After my savior Christ his byrth:
What time I did maintaine

The fellowshipp of the table round,
Soe famous in those dayes;
Whereatt a hundred noble knights,   15
And thirty sat alwayes:

Who for their deeds and martiall feates,
As bookes done yett record,
Amongst all other nations
Wer feared throwgh the world.   20

And in the castle off Tyntagill[3]
King Uther mee begate
Of Agyana a bewtyous ladye,
And come of "hie" estate.

Ver. 1. Bruite his, MS. [V. 6. borne, MS.] V. 9. He began
his reign A.D. 515, according to the Chronicles. [V. 16. sit, MS.
V. 19. all nations, MS.] V. 23. She is named Igerna in the old
Chronicles. V. 24. his, MS.

[1 heathendom.   2 born.
3 pronounced "Tintadgell;" the remains of the castle still exist
on the north coast of Cornwall.]

And when I was fifteen yeere old,   25
    Then was I crowned kinge :
All Brittaine that was att an upròre,
    I did to quiett bringe.

And drove the Saxons from the realme,
    Who had opprest this land ;   30
All Scotland then throughe manly feats
    I conquered with my hand.

Ireland, Denmarke, Norway,
    These countryes wan I all ;
Iseland, Gotheland, and Swethland ;   35
    And made their kings my thrall.

I conquered all Gallya,
    That now is called France ;
And slew the hardye Froll in feild
    My honor to advance.   40

And the ugly gyant Dynabus
    Soe terrible to vewe,
That in Saint Barnards mount did lye,
    By force of armes I slew :

And Lucyus the emperour of Rome   45
    I brought to deadly wracke ;
And a thousand more of noble knightes
    For feare did turne their backe :

Five kinges of " paynims "[1] I did kill
    Amidst that bloody strife ;   50
Besides the Grecian emperour
    Who alsoe lost his liffe.

[Ver. 31-2. And then I conquered througe manly feats,
    All Scottlande with my hands, MS.]
V. 39. Froland feild, MS. Froll, according to the Chronicles, was
a Roman knight governor of Gaul. V. 41. Danibus, MS. V. 49.
of Pavye, MS. [V. 49-52. this stanza occurs after v. 36 in the MS.]

[1 Pagans.]

Whose carcasse I did send to Rome
　Cladd poorlye on a beere;
And afterward I past Mount-Joye　　　　55
　The next approaching yeere.

Then I came to Rome, where I was mett
　Right as a conquerour,
And by all the cardinalls solempnelye
　I was crowned an emperour.　　　　60

One winter there I made abode:
　Then word to mee was brought
How Mordred had oppressd the crowne:
　What treason he had wrought

Att home in Brittaine with my queene;　　　65
　Therfore I came with speede
To Brittaine backe, with all my power,
　To quitt that traiterous deede:

And soone at Sandwiche I arrivde,
　Where Mordred me withstoode:　　　70
But yett at last I landed there,
　With effusion of much blood.

For there my nephew sir Gawaine dyed,
　Being wounded in that sore,
The whiche sir Lancelot in fight　　　75
　Had given him before.

Thence chased I Mordered away,
　Who fledd to London right,
From London to Winchester, and
　To Cornewalle tooke his flyght.　　　80

[Ver. 69. and when at Sandwich I did land. V. 74. on that.
V. 75. that Sir Lancelott. V. 80. he tooke. MS.]

And still I him pursued with speed
    Till at the last we mett:
Whereby an appointed day of fight
    Was there agreed and sett.

Where we did fight, of mortal life   85
    Eche other to deprive,
Till of a hundred thousand men
    Scarce one was left a live.

There all the noble chivalrye
    Of Brittaine tooke their end.   90
O see how fickle is their state
    That doe on feates depend!

There all the traiterous men were slaine
    Not one escapte away;
And there dyed all my vallyant knightes.   95
    Alas! that woefull day!

Two and twenty yeere I ware the crowne
    In honor and great fame;
And thus by death was suddenlye
    Deprived of the same.   100

[Ver. 83. Wherby appointed. V. 84. was agreed. V. 85-6.

    Where wee did fight soe mortallye
    Of live eche other to deprive.

V. 92. upon.]   V. 92. perhaps fates.   [V. 96 is the end of the first part in the MS., the stanza

    King Arthur lived King 22 yeere
      in honor and great fame
    and thus by death suddenlye
      was deprived from the same

ends the second part, which is printed by Percy as *King Arthur's death,* see previous ballad.]

VI.

A DYTTIE TO HEY DOWNE.

Copied from an old MS. in the Cotton Library [British Museum]
(Vesp. A. xxv. fol. 170), intitled, "Divers things of Hen. viij's
time."

HO sekes to tame the blustering winde,
    Or causse the floods bend to his wyll,
  Or els against dame nature's kinde
    To "change" things frame by cunning
      skyll :
That man I thinke bestoweth paine,   5
Thoughe that his laboure be in vaine.

Who strives to breake the sturdye steele,
  Or goeth about to staye the sunne ;
Who thinks to causse an oke to reele,
  Which never can by force be done :   10
That man likewise bestoweth paine,
Thoughe that his laboure be in vaine.

Who thinks to stryve against the streame,
  And for to sayle without a maste ;
Unlesse he thinks perhapps to faine,   15
  His travell ys forelorne and waste ;
And so in cure of all his paine,
His travell ys his cheffest gaine.

So he lykewise, that goes about
  To please eche eye and every eare,   20
Had nede to have withouten doubt
  A golden gyft with hym to beare ;
For evyll report shall be his gaine,
Though he bestowe both toyle and paine.

---

* Ver. 4. causse, MS.

God grant eche man one to amend ;   25
  God send us all a happy place ;
And let us pray unto the end,
  That we may have our princes grace :
Amen, Amen ! so shall we gaine
A dewe reward for all our paine.   30

VII.

GLASGERION.

AN ingenious Friend thinks that the following old Ditty (which is printed from the Editor's folio MS.) may possibly have given birth to the Tragedy of the *Orphan*, in which Polidore intercepts Monimia's intended favours to Castalio.

See what is said concerning the hero of this song, (who is celebrated by *Chaucer* under the name of *Glaskyrion*) in the Essay affixed to vol. i. note H. pt. iv. (2).

[The hero of this ballad is the same as " gret Glascurion," placed by Chaucer in the *House of Fame* by the side of Orpheus, and also associated with Orpheus by Gawain Douglas in the *Palice of Honour*. Percy's note in the Folio MS. is " It was not necessary to correct this much for the press ;" (ed. Hales and Furnivall, vol. i. p. 246). It will be seen, however, by the collations at the foot of the page that several corrections were made, not always for the better. Thus ver. 96, " who did his ladye grieve," is certainly weaker than the original,—

    " And asked noe man noe leave."

Jamieson (*Popular Ballads*, 1806, vol. i. p. 91) prints an inferior version under the name of *Glenkindie*. Mr. Hale points out, however, that " the Scotch version is more perfect in one point—in the test question put to the page before the assignation is disclosed to him :—

    ' O mith I tell you, Gib my man,
    Gin I a man had slain ? '

Some such question perhaps would give more force to vv. 85-88 of our version." He also very justly observes, " perhaps there is no ballad that represents more keenly the great gulf fixed between churl and noble—a profounder horror at the crossing over it."]

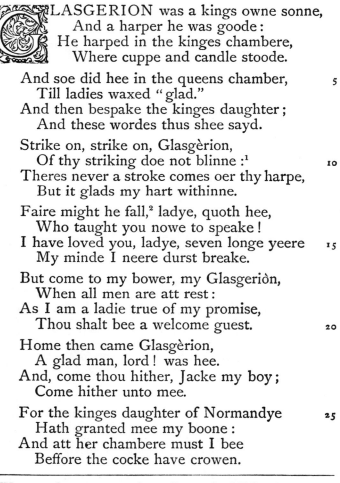LASGERION was a kings owne sonne,
  And a harper he was goode:
He harped in the kinges chambere,
  Where cuppe and candle stoode.

And soe did hee in the queens chamber,   5
  Till ladies waxed "glad."
And then bespake the kinges daughter;
  And these wordes thus shee sayd.

Strike on, strike on, Glasgèrion,
  Of thy striking doe not blinne:[1]   10
Theres never a stroke comes oer thy harpe,
  But it glads my hart withinne.

Faire might he fall,[2] ladye, quoth hee,
  Who taught you nowe to speake!
I have loved you, ladye, seven longe yeere   15
  My minde I neere durst breake.

But come to my bower, my Glasgeriòn,
  When all men are att rest:
As I am a ladie true of my promise,
  Thou shalt bee a welcome guest.   20

Home then came Glasgèrion,
  A glad man, lord! was hee.
And, come thou hither, Jacke my boy;
  Come hither unto mee.

For the kinges daughter of Normandye   25
  Hath granted mee my boone:
And att her chambere must I bee
  Beffore the cocke have crowen.

[Ver. 4. where cappe and candle yoode, MS.]   V. 6. wood,
MS.   [V. 8. sayd shee, MS.   V. 9. saide, strike.   V. 11. over
this.   V. 13. you fall.   V. 15. 7 yeere.   V. 16. my hart I durst
neere breake.   V. 21. but whom then.   V. 24. her love is granted
mee.]

[1 cease.   2 well may be thine.]

O master, master, then quoth hee,
  Lay your head downe on this stone:
For I will waken you, master deere,
  Afore it be time to gone.

But up then rose that lither[1] ladd,
  And hose and shoone did on:
A coller he cast upon his necke,
  Hee seemed a gentleman.

And when he came to the ladies chamber,
  He thrild upon a pinn.*
The lady was true of her promise,
  Rose up and lett him in.

He did not take the lady gaye
  To boulster nor to bed:
"Nor thoughe hee had his wicked wille,
  "A single word he sed."

[Ver. 29. but come you hither Master, quoth he. V. 34. and did on hose and shoone. V. 42. nor noe bed. V. 43-4.

but downe upon her chamber flore
full soone he hath her layd.]

* This is elsewhere expressed "*twirled the pin*," or "*tirled at the pin*" (see b. ii. s. vi. v. 3.) and seems to refer to the turning round the button on the outside of a door, by which the latch rises, still used in cottages.

[The explanation given by Percy in this note is an unfounded guess. The Risp or tirling pin was very generally used in the north to do the duty afterwards performed by the knocker. There are several of these curious contrivances in the Antiquarian Museum at Edinburgh, and they are described by D. Wilson in his *Memorials of Edinburgh in the Olden Time*, as follows,—"These antique precursors of the knocker and bell are still frequently to be met with in the steep turnpikes of the Old Town, notwithstanding the cupidity of the Antiquarian collectors. The ring is drawn up and down the notched iron rod and makes a very audible noise within." (1848, vol. i. p. 97).]

[[1] wicked.]

He did not kisse that ladyes mouthe,   45
    Nor when he came, nor youd :[1]
And sore mistrusted that ladye gay,
    He was of some churls bloud.

But home then came that lither ladd,
    And did off his hose and shoone;   50
And cast the coller from off his necke :
    He was but a churlès sonne.

Awake, awake, my deere master,
    [The cock hath well-nigh crowen.
Awake, awake, my master deere,]   55
    I hold it time to be gone.

For I have saddled your horsse, mastèr,
    Well bridled I have your steede :
And I have served you a good breakfast :
    For thereof ye have need.   60

Up then rose, good Glasgeriòn,
    And did on hose and shoone;
And cast a coller about his necke :
    For he was a kinge his sonne.

And when he came to the ladyes chamber,   65
    He thrild upon the pinne :
The ladye was more than true of promise,
    And rose and let him in.

Saies, whether have you left with me
    Your bracelett or your glove ?   70
Or are you returned backe againe
    To know more of my love ?

[Ver. 45. that lady gay.   Ver. 46. when he came nor when he
youd.   V. 51. that coller from about.   V. 53. awaken quoth hee
my master deere.   V. 54-5. not in MS.   V. 59. have not I served a.
V. 60. when times comes I have need.   V. 61. but up.   V. 64. he
was a kinges sonne.   V. 65. that ladies.   V. 66. upon a.   V. 68.
rose up and.   V. 71. you are. MS]
[1 went.]

Glasgèrion swore a full great othe
  By oake, and ashe, and thorne ;
Lady, I was never in your chambèr,   7 ;
  Sith the time that I was borne.

O then it was your lither foot-page,
  He hath beguiled mee.
Then shee pulled forth a little pen-kniffe,
  That hanged by her knee :   80

Sayes, there shall never noe churlès blood
  Within my bodye spring :
[No churlès blood shall ever defile
  The daughter of a kinge.]

Home then went Glasgèrion,   85
  And woe, good lord, was hee.
Sayes, come thou hither, Jacke my boy,
  Come hither unto mee.

If I had killed a man to night,
  Jacke, I would tell it thee :   90
But if I have not killed a man to night
  Jacke, thou hast killed three.

And he puld out his bright browne sword,
  And dryed it on his sleeve,
And he smote off that lither ladds head,   95
  Who did his ladye grieve.

He sett the swords poynt till his brest,
  The pummil untill a stone :
Throw the falsenesse of that lither ladd,
  These three lives werne all gone.   100

Ver. 77. litle, MS. [V. 78. falsly hath. V. 79. and then. V. 82. spring within my body. V. 83-4. not in MS. V. 85. but home then. V. 86. a woe man good was hee. V. 87. come hither thou. V. 88. come thou. V. 89. ffor if. V. 96. and asked noe man noe leave. V. 98. till a. MS.]

VIII.

OLD ROBIN OF PORTINGALE.

FROM an ancient copy in the Editor's folio MS. which was judged to require considerable corrections.

In the former edition the hero of this piece had been called Sir Robin, but that title not being in the MS. is now omitted.

Giles, steward to a rich old merchant trading to *Portugal*, is qualified with the title of *Sir*, not as being a knight, but rather, I conceive, as having received an inferior order of priesthood.

[Percy's note in the MS. is as follows, "When I first set to examine this I had not yet learnt to hold this old MS. in much regard." Every line is altered, so that it has been necessary to add a copy of the original, although the interest of the ballad itself is not very great. Percy's most notable correction is the introduction of 20 good knights to help Robin against his wife's twenty-four traitors.]

LET never again soe old a man
　　Marrye soe yonge a wife,
　As did old Robin of Portingale ;
　　Who may rue all the dayes of his life.

For the mayors daughter of Lin, god wott,　5
　　He chose her to his wife,
And thought with her to have lived in love,
　　By they fell to hate and strife.

They scarce were in their wed-bed laid,
　　And scarce was hee asleepe,　　　　　10
But upp shee rose, and forth shee goes,
　　To the steward, and gan to weepe.

Sleepe you, wake you, faire sir **Gyles**?
  Or be you not within?
Sleepe you, wake you, faire sir **Gyles**,   1 5
  Arise and let me inn.

O, I am waking, sweete, he said,
  Sweete ladye, what is your will?
I have unbethought me of a wile
  How my wed-lord weell spill.[1]   20

Twenty-four good knights, shee sayes,
  That dwell about this towne,
Even twenty-four of my next cozèns,
  Will helpe to dinge[2] him downe.

All that beheard his litle footepage,   25
  As he watered his masters steed;
And for his masters sad perille
  His verry heart did bleed.

He mourned still, and wept full sore;
  I sweare by the holy roode   30
The teares he for his master wept
  Were blent water and bloude.

And that beheard his deare mastèr
  As he stood at his garden pale:
Sayes, Ever alacke, my litle foot-page,   35
  What causes thee to wail?

Hath any one done to thee wronge
  Any of thy fellowes here?
Or is any of thy good friends dead,
  That thou shedst manye a teare?   40

Ver. 19. *unbethought*, (properly *onbethought*) this word is still
used in the Midland counties in the same sense as *bethought*.
V. 32. blend, MS.

  [[1] spoil or kill.   [2] knock.]

Or, if it be my head bookes-man,[1]
  Aggrieved he shal bee :
For no man here within my howse,
  Shall doe wrong unto thee.

O, it is not your head bookes-man,   45
  Nor none of his degree :
But, on to-morrow ere it be noone
  All deemed[2] to die are yee.

And of that bethank your head stewàrd,
  And thank your gay ladie.   50
If this be true, my litle foot-page,
  The heyre of my land thoust bee.

If it be not true, my dear mastèr,
  No good death let me die.
If it be not true, thou litle foot-page,   55
  A dead corse shalt thou lie.

O call now downe my faire ladye,
  O call her downe to mee :
And tell my ladye gay how sicke,
  And like to die I bee.   60

Downe then came his ladye faire,
  All clad in purple and pall :
The rings that were on her fingèrs,
  Cast light thorrow the hall.

What is your will, my owne wed-lord ?   65
  What is your will with mee ?
O see, my ladye deere, how sicke,
  And like to die I bee.

Ver. 47. or to-morrow, MS.   V. 56. bee, MS.

[[1] clerk.   [2] doomed.]

And thou be sicke, my own wed-lord,
   Soe sore it grieveth me: 70
But my five maydens and myselfe
   Will " watch thy " bedde for thee:

And at the waking of your first sleepe,
   We will a hott drinke make:
And at the waking of your " next " sleepe,   75
   Your sorrowes we will slake.

He put a silk cote on his backe,
   And mail of manye a fold:
And hee putt a steele cap on his head,
   Was gilt with good red gold.   80

He layd a bright browne sword by his side,
   And another att his feete:
" And twentye good knights he placed at hand,
   To watch him in his sleepe."

And about the middle time of the night,   85
   Came twentye-four traitours inn:
Sir Giles he was the foremost man,
   The leader of that ginn.[1]

Old Robin with his bright browne sword,
   Sir Gyles head soon did winn: 90
And scant of all those twenty-four,
   Went out one quick[2] agenn.

None save only a litle foot page,
   Crept forth at a window of stone:
And he had two armes when he came in,   95
   And he went back with one.

Ver. 72. make the, MS.   V. 75. first, **MS.**

[[1] snare.   [2] alive.]

Upp then came that ladie gaye
  With torches burning bright:
She thought to have brought sir Gyles a drinke,
  Butt she found her owne wedd knight.   100

The first thinge that she stumbled on
  It was sir Gyles his foote:
Sayes, Ever alacke, and woe is mee!
  Here lyes my sweete hart-roote.

The next thinge that she stumbled on   105
  It was sir Gyles his heade;
Sayes, Ever, alacke, and woe is me!
  Heere lyes my true love deade.

Hee cutt the pappes beside her brest,
  And did her body spille;   110
He cutt the eares beside her heade,
  And bade her love her fille.

He called then up his litle foot-page,
  And made him there his heyre;
And sayd henceforth my worldlye goodes   115
  And countrye I forsweare.

He shope[1] the crosse on his right shoulder,
  Of the white " clothe " and the redde,*
And went him into the holy land,
  Wheras Christ was quicke and dead.   120

Ver. 118. fleshe, MS.

* Every person who went on a *Croisade* to the Holy Land,
usually wore a cross on his upper garment, on the right shoulder,
as a badge of his profession. Different nations were distinguished
by crosses of different colours: The English wore white; the
French red; &c. This circumstance seems to be confounded in
the ballad. (V. Spelman, *Gloss.*)

[1 shaped.]

THE following is the original ballad from the Folio MS. ed. Hales and Furnivall, vol. i. p. 235.

God! let neuer soe old a man
marry so yonge a wiffe
as did old Robin of portingale!
he may rue all the dayes of his liffe.   4

ffor the Maiors daughter of Lin, god wott,
he chose her to his wife,
& thought to haue liued in quiettnesse
with her all the dayes of his liffe.   8

they had not in their wed bed laid,
scarcly were both on sleepe,
but vpp shee rose, & forth shee goes
to Sir Gyles, & fast can weepe,   12

Saies, "sleepe you, wake you, faire Sir Gyles,
or be not you within?"

"but I am waking, sweete," he said,
"Lady, what is your will?"   16
"I haue vnbethought me of a will,
how my wed Lord we shall spill.

"24 knights, she sayes,
that dwells about this towne,   20
eene 24 of my Next Cozens,
will helpe to dinge him downe."

with that beheard his litle foote page
as he was watering his Masters steed,   24
Soe s   *   *   *   *
his verry heart did bleed;

he mourned, sist, and wept full sore;
I sweare by the holy roode,   28
the teares he for his Master wept
were blend water & bloude.

with that beheard his deare Master
as in his garden sate,   32
says, "euer alacke my litle page!
what causes thee to weepe?

"hath any one done to thee wronge,
any of thy fellowes here,   36
or is any of thy good friends dead
which makes thee shed such teares?

" or if it be my head bookes man,
grieued againe he shalbe,   4⁽⁾
nor noe man within my howse
shall doe wrong vnto thee."

" but it is not your head bookes man,
nor none of his degree,   44
but or to morrow, ere it be Noone,
you are deemed to die ;

" & of that thanke your head Steward,
& after your gay Ladie."   48
" If it be true, my little foote page,
Ile make thee heyre of all my land."

" if it be not true, my deare Master,
god let me neuer dye."   52
" if it be not true, thou little foot page,
a dead corse shalt thou be."

he called downe his head kookes man,
cooke in kitchen super to dresse :   56
" all & anon, my deare Master,
anon at your request."

" & call you downe my faire Lady,
this night to supp with mee."   60

& downe then came that fayre Lady,
was cladd all in purple & palle,
the rings that were vpon her fingers
cast light thorrow the hall.   64

" What is your will, my owne wed Lord,
what is your will with mee ? "
" I am sicke, fayre Lady,
sore sicke, & like to dye."   68

" but & you be sicke, my owne wed Lord,
soe sore it greiueth mee,
but my 5 maydens & my selfe
will goe & make your bedd,   72

" & at the wakening of your first sleepe,
you shall haue a hott drinke Made,
& at the wakening of your first sleepe
your sorrowes will haue a slake."   76

he put a silke cote on his backe,
was 13 inches folde,
& put a steele cap vpon his head,
was gilded with good red gold ;   80

& he layd a bright browne sword by his side,
& another att his ffeete,
& full well knew old Robin then
whether he shold wake or sleepe.   84

& about the Middle time of the Night
came 24 good knights in,
Syr Gyles he was the formost man,
soe well he knew that ginne.   88

Old Robin with a bright browne sword
Sir Gyles head he did winne,
soe did he all those 24,
neuer a one went quicke out [agen ;]   92

none but one litle foot page
crept forth at a window of stone,
& he had 2 armes when he came in
And [when he went out he had none].   96

Vpp then came that Ladie bright
with torches burning light ;
shee thought to haue brought Sir Gyles a drinke,
but shee found her owne wedd Knight,   100

& the first thinge that this Ladye stumbled vpon,
was of Sir Gyles his ffoote,
sayes, " euer alacke, and woe is me,
heere lyes my sweete hart roote !"   104

& the 2^d thing that this Ladie stumbled on,
was of Sir Gyles his head,
sayes, " euer alacke, and woe is me,
heere lyes my true loue deade !"   108

hee cutt the papps beside he[r] brest,
& bad her wish her will,
& he cutt the eares beside her heade,
& bade her wish on still.   112

" Mickle is the mans blood I haue spent
to doe thee & me some good,"
sayes, " euer alacke, my fayre Lady,
I thinke that I was woode ? "   116

he calld then vp his litle foote page,
& made him heyre of all his land,
& he shope the crosse in his right sholder
of the white flesh & the redd.   120
& he sent him into the holy land
wheras Christ was quicke & dead."

ffins.]

IX.

CHILD WATERS.

HILD is frequently used by our old writers, as a Title. It is repeatedly given to Prince Arthur in the Fairie Queen: and the son of a king is in the same poem called "Child Tristram." (B. 5. c. 11. st. 8. 13.—B. 6. c. 2. st. 36.—*Ibid.* c. 8. st. 15.) In an old ballad quoted in Shakespeare's *K. Lear*, the hero of Ariosto is called *Child Roland.* Mr. Theobald supposes this use of the word was received along with their romances from the Spaniards, with whom *Infante* signifies a "Prince." A more eminent critic tells us, that "in the old times of chivalry, the noble youth, who were candidates for knighthood, during the time of their probation were called *Infans, Varlets, Damoysels, Bacheliers.* The most noble of the youth were particularly called *Infans.*" (Vid. Warb. Shakesp.) A late commentator on Spenser observes, that the Saxon word cniht, knight, signifies also a "child." (See Upton's gloss to the F. Q.)

The Editor's folio MS. whence the following piece is taken (with some corrections), affords several other ballads, wherein the word *Child* occurs as a title: but in none of these it signifies "Prince." See the song intitled *Gil Morrice*, in this volume.

It ought to be observed, that the Word *Child* or *Chield* is still used in North Britain to denominate a Man, commonly with some contemptuous character affixed to him, but sometimes to denote Man in general.

[This ballad gives us a curious insight into ancient manners, and shows what were our forefathers' notions of the perfection of female character. They would have agreed with the propounder of the question—What is woman's mission? answer, sub-mission. Like patient Grissel, Ellen bears worse sufferings than the Nut-Brown Maid has to hear of, and in spite of the worst usage she

never swerves from her devotion.   This English version was the
first published, but the story is the same as *Lai le Frêne*, preserved
in English in the Auchinleck MS. and in Norman in the *Lais* of
Marie, which were written about the year 1250.

Jamieson (*Popular Ballads and Songs*, 1806, vol. i. p. 113) published his Scottish version under the more appropriate name of
Burd Ellen, who is the real heroine rather than the ruffian Waters
is the hero.   Adopting the idea of Mrs. Hampden Pye, who wrote
a ballad on the same subject, he changes the character of the
catastrophe by adding three concluding stanzas to wind up the
story in an unhappy manner.   Another version of the ballad, which
ends happily, is given in Kinloch's *Ancient Scottish Ballads* under
the title of Lady Margaret.   A German version of this ballad was
made by the poet Bürger.]

HILDE WATERS in his stable stoode
    And stroakt his milke white steede
To him a fayre yonge ladye came
    As ever ware womans weede.

Sayes, Christ you save, good Childe Waters ;   5
    Sayes, Christ you save, and see :
My girdle of gold that was too longe,
    Is now too short for mee.

And all is with one chyld of yours,
    I feele sturre att my side ;   10
My gowne of greene it is too straighte ;
    Before, it was too wide.

If the child be mine, faire Ellen, he sayd,
    Be mine as you tell mee ;
Then take you Cheshire and Lancashire both,   15
    Take them your owne to bee.

[Ver. 3. to him came, MS.   V. 4. as ere did weare, MS.   V. 7.
which was. MS.   V. 15. then not in MS.]

If the childe be mine, faire Ellen, he sayd,
   Be mine, as you doe sweare :
Then take you Cheshire and Lancashire both,
   And make that child your heyre.   20

Shee saies, I had rather have one kisse,
   Child Waters, of thy mouth ;
Than I wolde have Cheshire and Lancashire both,
   That lye by north and south.

And I had rather have one twinkling,   25
   Childe Waters, of thine ee :
Then I wolde have Cheshire and Lancashire both
   To take them mine owne to bee.

To morrow, Ellen, I must forth ryde
   Farr into the north countrie ;   30
The fairest lady that I can find,
   Ellen, must goe with mee.

[Thoughe I am not that lady fayre,
   Yet let me go with thee.]
And ever I pray you, Child Watèrs,   35
   Your foot-page let me bee.

If you will my foot-page be, Ellèn,
   As you doe tell to mee ;
Then you must cut your gowne of greene,
   An inch above your knee :   40

Soe must you doe your yellowe lockes,
   An inch above your ee :
You must tell no man what is my name ;
   My foot-page then you shall bee.

[V. 24. that lyes. V. 25. have a. V. 26. of your eye. V. 30. soe ffarr. V. 38. tell itt mee. V. 42. another inch above your eye. MS.]

Shee, all the long day Child Waters rode,   45
   Ran barefoote by his side;
Yett was he never so courteous a knighte,
   To say, Ellen, will you ryde?

Shee, all the long day Child Waters rode,
   Ran barefoote thorow the broome;   50
Yett hee was never soe curteous a knighte,
   To say, put on your shoone.

Ride softlye, shee sayd, O Childe Waters,
   Why doe you ryde soe fast?
The childe, which is no mans but thine,   55
   My bodye itt will brast.

Hee sayth, seest thou yonder water, Ellen,
   That flows from banke to brimme.—
I trust to God, O Child Waters,
   You never will see* mee swimme.   60

But when shee came to the waters side,
   Shee sayled to the chinne:
Except the Lord of heaven be my speed,
   Now must I learne to swimme.

The salt waters bare up her clothes;   65
   Our Ladye bare upp her chinne:
Childe Waters was a woe man, good Lord,
   To see faire Ellen swimme.

And when shee over the water was,
   Shee then came to his knee: 70
He said, Come hither, thou faire Ellèn,
   Loe yonder what I see.

[Ver. 45. all this long. *Shee* not in MS. V. 46. shee ran.
V. 49. but all this day. V. 50. shee ran. V. 52. as to say. V. 53.
O not in MS. V. 55. but yours. V. 56. burst. V. 57. he sayes,
sees. V. 59. Child Waters, shee said. V. 65. Ellen's clothes.
V. 67. and Child Waters. V. 71. *thou* not in MS.]

* *i.e.* permit, suffer, &c.

Seest thou not yonder hall, Ellèn?
  Of redd gold shines the yate:
Of twenty foure faire ladyes there,   75
  The fairest is my mate.

Seest thou not yonder hall, Ellèn?
  Of redd gold shines the towre:
There are twenty four faire ladyes there,
  The fairest is my paramoure.   80

I see the hall now, Child Waters,
  Of redd gold shines the yate:
God give you good now of yourselfe,
  And of your worthye mate.

I see the hall now, Child Waters,   85
  Of redd golde shines the towre:
God give you good now of yourselfe,
  And of your paramoure.

There twenty four fayre ladyes were
  A playing att the ball: 90
And Ellen the fairest ladye there,
  Must bring his steed to the stall.

There twenty four fayre ladyes were
  A playinge at the chesse;
And Ellen the fayrest ladye there,   95
  Must bring his horse to gresse.

And then bespake Childe Waters sister,
  These were the wordes said shee:
You have the prettyest foot-page, brother,
  That ever I saw with mine ee.   100

[Ver. 74. shine the yates. MS. V. 75. theres 24 ffayre ladyes.
V. 76. the ffairest is my worldlye make. V. 78. Shineth. V. 79. there
is 24 ffaire ladyes. V. 81, 85. I doe see. V. 82, 86. that of redd
gold shineth the yates. V. 83, 87. God give good then. V. 84.
worldlye make. V. 89. there were 24 ladyes. V. 90. were playing. V. 91. Ellen was the fairest ladye. V. 93. there were.
V. 94. was playing. V. 95. shee was the ffairest ladye. V. 96.
grasse. V. 98. and these. V. 100. eye. MS.]

But that his bellye it is soe bigg,
  His girdle goes wonderous hie :
And let him, I pray you, Childe Watèrs,
  Goe into the chamber with mee.

[It is not fit for a little foot-page,   105
  That has run throughe mosse and myre,
To go into the chamber with any ladye,
  That weares soe riche attyre.]

It is more meete for a litle foot-page,
  That has run throughe mosse and myre,   110
To take his supper upon his knee,
  And sitt downe by the kitchen fyer.

But when they had supped every one,
  To bedd they tooke theyr waye :
He sayd, come hither, my little foot-page,   115
  And hearken what I saye.

Goe thee downe into yonder towne,
  And low into the street;
The fayrest ladye that thou can finde,
  Hyer her in mine armes to sleepe,   120
And take her up in thine armes twaine,
  For filinge * of her feete.

Ellen is gone into the towne,
  And low into the streete :
The fairest ladye that shee cold find,   125
  Shee hyred in his armes to sleepe;

[Ver. 103. and ever I pray. MS. V. 104. let him goe. After
v. 112 the two lines

      then goe into the chamber with any ladye
      that weares soe . . . . attyre

occur in the MS. V. 114. they waye. V. 116. hearken what I
doe say. V. 117. and goe thy. V. 121. armes 2. MS.]

  * *i.e.* defiling. See Warton's *Observ.* vol. ii. p. 158.

And tooke her up in her armes twayne,
  For filing of her feete.

I praye you nowe, good Childe Watèrs,
  Let mee lye at your bedds feete :   130
For there is noe place about this house,
  Where I may 'saye a slepe*.

[He gave her leave, and faire Ellèn
  Down at his beds feet laye :]
This done the nighte drove on apace,   135
  And when it was neare the daye,

Hee sayd, Rise up, my litle foot-page,
  Give my steede corne and haye ;
And soe doe thou the good black oats,
  To carry mee better awaye.   140

Up then rose the faire Ellèn
  And gave his steede corne and hay :
And soe shee did the good blacke oates,
  To carry him the better away.

Shee leaned her backe to the manger side,   145
  And grievouslye did groane :
[Shee leaned her back to the manger side,
  And there shee made her moane.]

And that beheard his mother deere,
  Shee heard her there monand.   150
Shee sayd, Rise up, thou Child Watèrs,
  I think thee a cursed man.

[V. 127. and tooke her in her armes 2.   V. 130. that I may
creape in att.   V. 135-6.

          this and itt drove now afterward
          till itt was neere the day.

V. 138. and give.   V. 140. that he may carry me the better
away.   V. 141. and up then rose the.   V. 143. did on.   V. 144.
that he might carry him.   V. 145. she layned.   V. 150. and
heard her make her moane.   V. 152. I think thou art a. MS.]

          * Ver. 132. *i.e.* essay, attempt.

For in thy stable is a ghost,
   That grievouslye doth grone:
Or else some woman laboures of childe,   155
   She is soe woe-begone.

Up then rose Childe Waters soon,
   And did on his shirte of silke;
And then he put on his other clothes,
   On his body as white as milke.   160

And when he came to the stable dore,
   Full still there hee did stand,
That hee mighte heare his fayre Ellèn,
   Howe shee made her monànd*.

She sayd, Lullabye, mine owne deere child,   165
   Lullabye, dere child, dere:
I wold thy father were a king,
   Thy mother layd on a biere.

Peace now, hee said, good faire Ellèn.
   Be of good cheere, I praye;   170
And the bridal and the churching both
   Shall bee upon one day.

[Ver. 153. for yonder is a ghost in thy stable. V. 157. but up then rose Childe Waters. V. 159. *and* not in MS. V. 162. full still that. V. 163. heare now faire. V. 165. my owne. V. 170. and be of good cheere I thee pray. V. 172. they shall, MS.]

* *sic* in MS., *i.e.* moaning, bemoaning, &c.

X.

PHILLIDA AND CORYDON.

HIS Sonnet is given from a small quarto MS. in the Editor's possession, written in the time of Q. Elizabeth. Another Copy of it containing some variations, is reprinted in the *Muses' Library*, p. 295, from an ancient miscellany, intitled *England's Helicon*, 1600, 4to. The author was *Nicholas Breton*, a writer of some fame in the reign of Elizabeth; who also published an interlude intitled *An old man's lesson and a young man's love*, 4to., and many other little pieces in prose and verse, the titles of which may be seen in Winstanley, Ames' *Typog.* and Osborne's *Harl. Catalog.* &c.—He is mentioned with great respect by *Meres*, in his 2d pt. of *Wit's Common-wealth*, 1598, f. 283, and is alluded to in Beaumont and Fletcher's *Scornful Lady*, act ii., and again in *Wit without Money*, act iii.—See Whalley's *Ben Jonson*, vol. iii. p. 103.

The present Edition is improved by a copy in *England's Helicon*, edit. 1614, 8vo.

This little Pastoral is one of the Songs in "The Honourable Entertainment gieven to the Queenes Majestie in Progresse at Elvetham in Hampshire, by the R. H. the Earle of Hertford, 1591, 4to." (Printed by Wolfe. No name of author.) See in that pamphlet,

"The thirde daies Entertainment.

"On Wednesday morning about 9 o'clock, as her Majestie opened a casement of her gallerie window, ther were 3 excellent musitians, who being disguised in auncient country attire, did greet her with a pleasant song of *Corydon and Phillida*, made in 3 parts of purpose. The song, as well for the worth of the dittie as the aptnesse of the note thereto applied, it pleased her Highnesse after it had been once sung to command it againe, and highly to grace it with her cheerefull acceptance and commendation.

THE PLOWMAN'S SONG.

In the merrie month of May, &c."

The splendour and magnificence of Elizabeth's reign is nowhere more strongly painted than in these little diaries of some of her summer excursions to the houses of her nobility; nor could a more acceptable present be given to the world, than a republication of a select number of such details as this of the entertainment at *Elvetham*, that at *Killingworth*, &c., &c., which so strongly mark the spirit of the times, and present us with scenes so very remote from modern manners.

Since the above was written, the public hath been gratified with a most compleat work on the foregoing subject, intitled, *The Progresses and Public Processions of Queen Elizabeth, &c. By John Nichols, F.A.S., Edinb. and Perth,* 1788, 2 vols. 4to.

[The author of this elegant little poem was a most voluminous author, and "is supposed to be the same Capt. Nicholas Breton, who was of Norton in Northamptonshire, and dying there June 22, 1624, has a monument in that church." * Dr. Rimbault (*Musical Illustrations of Percy's Reliques*) writes as follows of the music :— " We have here two settings of this beautiful pastoral, the first as it was sung by the 'three excellent musitians' before Queen Elizabeth in 1591; the second as it was reset in the following century. The first is extracted from *Madrigals to* 3, 4, *and* 5 *parts, apt for viols and voices*, newly composed by Michael Este, 1604; the second from *Cheerfull Ayres or Ballads, set for three voyces*, by Dr. John Wilson, Oxford, 1660. The latter became extremely popular, and is included in D'Urfey's *Pills to Purge Melancholy*, 1719, and several other musical miscellanies of subsequent date."]

N the merrie moneth of Maye,
In a morne by break of daye,
With a troope of damselles playing
Forthe " I yode" forsooth a maying :

When anon by a wood side, 5
Where as Maye was in his pride,
I espied all alone
Phillida and Corydon.

Much adoe there was, god wot ;
He wold love, and she wold not. 10
She sayde, never man was trewe ;
He sayes, none was false to you.

Ver. 4. the wode, MS.

[* England's *Helicon* (Brydges' *British Bibliographer*, vol. iii.)]

He sayde, hee had lovde her longe :
She sayes, love should have no wronge.
Corydon wold kisse her then :   15
She sayes, maydes must kisse no men,

Tyll they doe for good and all.
When she made the shepperde call
All the heavens to wytnes truthe,
Never loved a truer youthe.   20

Then with manie a prettie othe,
Yea and nay, and, faith and trothe ;
Suche as seelie shepperdes use
When they will not love abuse ;

Love, that had bene long deluded,   25
Was with kisses sweete concluded ;
And Phillida with garlands gaye
Was made the lady of the Maye.

XI.

LITTLE MUSGRAVE AND LADY BARNARD.

THIS ballad is ancient, and has been popular; we find it quoted in many old plays. See Beaum. and Fletcher's *Knight of the Burning Pestle*, 4to. 1613, act v. sc. iii. *The Varietie, a comedy*, 12mo. 1649, act iv. &c. In Sir William Davenant's play, *The Witts*, a. iii. a gallant thus boasts of himself :

" Limber and sound ! besides I sing Musgrave,
And for Chevy-chace no lark comes near me."

In the Pepys *Collection*, vol. iii. p. 314, is an imitation of this old song, in 33 stanzas, by a more modern pen, with many alterations, but evidently for the worse.

This is given from an old printed copy in the British Museum, with corrections; some of which are from a fragment in the Editor's folio MS.   It is also printed in Dryden's *Collection of Miscellaneous Poems*.

[The copy of this ballad in the Folio MS. (ed. Hales and Furnivall, vol. i. p. 119) is a mutilated fragment consisting of only ten complete stanzas and three half ones.   The oldest entire copy is to be found in *Wit Restor'd*, 1658, where it is called *the* old *ballad of little Musgrave*, which is given by Professor Child (*English and Scottish Ballads*, vol. ii. p. 15) in preference to Percy's.   This version, not very exactly transcribed, is printed in Dryden's *Miscellany Poems* (1716, vol. iii. 312), and Ritson (*Ancient Songs and Ballads*, vol. ii. p. 116) copied it from thence.   Ritson writes of one of Percy's statements above : " Dr. Percy indeed, by some mistake, gives it as from an old printed copy in the British Museum ; observing that ' In the Pepys collection is an imitation of this old song in a different measure, by a more modern pen, with many alterations, but evidently for the worse.'   It is very true, and not less so that the only copies in the museum (for there are two) are more recent impressions of this identical *imitation*."

It is the 14th stanza slightly altered which is quoted in the *Knight of the Burning Pestle.*

> " And some they whistled, and some they sung,
>   Hey down down !
> And some did loudly say
> Ever as Lord Barnet's horn blew,
>   Away Musgrave, away."

There are several Scottish versions, in which the reciters have altered the locality.   Jamieson has printed one which he calls *Lord Barnaby* (*Popular Ballads and Songs*, i. 170).   He states that he had heard it repeated both in Morayshire and in the southern counties.

Motherwell gives the air in his *Minstrelsy* which he noted down from oral communication, and this verse—

> " It fell upon a Martinmas time
>   When the nobles were a drinking wine,
> That little Mushiegrove to the kirk he did go
>   For to see the ladies come in."

Mr. J. H. Dixon includes a version entitled *Lord Burnett and Little Munsgrove* in his Scottish Traditional Versions of Ancient Ballads (Percy Society, vol. xvii.)

Home adopted the name of Lady Barnard in his *Douglas* before he took that of Lady Randolph, see No. 18, Gil Morrice.

There is another ballad called *The Bonny Birdy*, with a similar story. Jamieson (i. 162) prints it and alters the title to *Lord Randal.*]

S it fell out on a highe holye daye,
　　As many bee in the yeare,
　　When yong men and maides together do
　　　goe
　　Their masses and mattins to heare,

Little Musgràve came to the church door,　　5
　　The priest was at the mass ;
But he had more mind of the fine womèn,
　　Then he had of our Ladyes grace.

And some of them were clad in greene,
　　And others were clad in pall ;　　　　1c
And then came in my lord Barnardes wife,
　　The fairest among them all.

Shee cast an eye on little Musgràve
　　As bright as the summer sunne :
O then bethought him little Musgràve,　　15
　　This ladyes heart I have wonne.

Quoth she, I have loved thee, little Musgràve,
　　Fulle long and manye a daye.
So have I loved you, ladye faire,
　　Yet word I never durst saye.　　　　20

I have a bower at Bucklesford-Bury,*
　　Full daintilye bedight,
If thoult wend thither, my little Musgràve,
　　Thoust lig in mine armes all night.

---

* Bucklefield-berry, fol. MS.

Quoth hee, I thanke yee, ladye faire,   25
   This kindness yee shew to mee;
And whether it be to my weale or woe,
   This night will I lig with thee.

All this beheard a litle foot-page,
   By his ladyes coach as he ranne :   30
Quoth he, thoughe I am my ladyes page,
   Yet Ime my lord Barnardes manne.

My lord Barnàrd shall knowe of this,
   Although I lose a limbe.
And ever whereas the bridges were broke,   35
   He layd him downe to swimme.

Asleep or awake, thou lord Barnàrd,
   As thou art a man of life,
Lo! this same night at Bucklesford-Bury
   Litle Musgrave's in bed with thy wife.   40

If it be trew, thou litle foote-page,
   This tale thou hast told to mee,
Then all my lands in Bucklesford-Bury
   I freelye will give to thee.

But and it be a lye, thou litle foot-page,   45
   This tale thou hast told to mee,
On the highest tree in Bucklesford-Bury
   All hanged shalt thou bee.

Rise up, rise up, my merry men all,
   And saddle me my good steede;   50
This night must I to Bucklesford-bury;
   God wott, I had never more neede.

Then some they whistled, and some they sang,
   And some did loudlye saye,
Whenever lord Barnardes horne it blewe,   55
   Awaye, Musgràve, away.

Methinkes I heare the throstle cocke,
  Methinkes I heare the jay,
Methinkes I heare lord Barnards horne ;
  I would I were awaye.   60

Lye still, lye still, thou little Musgràve,
  And huggle me from the cold ;
For it is but some shephardes boye
  A whistling his sheepe to the fold.

Is not thy hawke upon the pearche,   65
  Thy horse eating corne and haye ?
And thou a gay lady within thine armes :
  And wouldst thou be awaye ?

By this lord Barnard was come to the dore,
  And lighted upon a stone :   70
And he pulled out three silver keyes,
  And opened the dores eche one.

He lifted up the coverlett,
  He lifted up the sheete ;
How now, how now, thou little Musgràve,   75
  Dost find my gaye ladye sweete ?

I find her sweete, quoth little Musgràve,
  The more is my griefe and paine ;
Ide gladlye give three hundred poundes
  That I were on yonder plaine.   80

Arise, arise, thou little Musgràve,
  And put thy cloathes nowe on,
It shall never be said in my countree,
  That I killed a naked man.

Ver. 64. Is whistling sheepe ore the mold, fol. MS.

I have two swordes in one scabbàrde,85
Full deare they cost my purse;
And thou shalt have the best of them,
And I will have the worse.

The first stroke that little Musgrave strucke,
He hurt lord Barnard sore;90
The next stroke that lord Barnard strucke,
Little Musgrave never strucke more.

With that bespake the ladye faire,
In bed whereas she laye,
Althoughe thou art dead, my little Musgràve,95
Yet for thee I will praye:

And wishe well to thy soule will I,
So long as I have life;
So will I not do for thee, Barnàrd,
Thoughe I am thy wedded wife.100

He cut her pappes from off her brest;
Great pitye it was to see
The drops of this fair ladyes bloode
Run trickling downe her knee.

Wo worth, wo worth ye, my merrye men all,105
You never were borne for my goode:
Why did you not offer to stay my hande,
When you sawe me wax so woode?¹

For I have slaine the fairest sir knighte,
That ever rode on a steede;110
So have I done the fairest lady,
That ever ware womans weede.*

[* See the last stanza of *Childe Maurice* from Folio MS., book i.
No. 18, which is almost identical with this.

¹ wildly angry.]

A grave, a grave, Lord Barnard cryde,
   To putt these lovers in ;
But lay my ladye o' the upper hande,   115
   For she comes o' the better kin.

✝╪✝ That the more modern copy is to be dated about the middle
of the last century, will be readily conceived from the tenor of the
concluding stanza, viz.

" This sad Mischief by Lust was wrought ;
   Then let us call for Grace,
That we may shun the wicked vice,
   And fly from Sin a-pace."

XII.

THE EW-BUGHTS, MARION.

A Scottish Song.

HIS sonnet appears to be ancient : that and its simplicity of sentiment have recommended it to a place
here.

[This is marked in Ramsay's *Tea Table Miscellany* as
an old song with additions.   It is not known who wrote the song
or who composed the air belonging to it.   They are both old.]

ILL ye gae to the ew-bughts,[1] Marion,
      And wear in[2] the sheip wi' mee ?
The sun shines sweit, my Marion,
      But nae half sae sweit as thee.
O Marion's a bonnie lass ;   5
      And the blyth blinks[3] in her ee :
And fain wad I marrie Marion,
      Gin Marion wad marrie mee.

[[1] the pens in which the ewes are milked.   [2] gather in.
               [3] joy sparkles.]

Theire's gowd in your garters, Marion;
   And siller on your white hauss-bane*:   10
Fou faine wad I kisse my Marion
   At eene quhan I cum hame.
Theire's braw lads in Earnslaw, Marion,
   Quha gape and glowr wi' their ee
At kirk, quhan they see my Marion;   15
   Bot nane of them lues[1] like mee.

Ive nine milk-ews, my Marion,
   A cow and a brawney quay;[2]
Ise gie tham au to my Marion,
   Just on her bridal day.   20
And yees get a grein sey[3] apron,
   And waistcote o' London broun;
And wow bot ye will be vaporing
   Quhaneir ye gang to the toun.

Ime yong and stout, my Marion,   25
   None dance lik mee on the greine;
And gin ye forsak me, Marion,
   Ise een gae draw up wi' Jeane.
Sae put on your pearlins,[4] Marion,
   And kirtle oth' cramasie;[5]   30
And sune as my chin has nae haire on,
   I sall cum west, and see yee.

---

* *Hauss bane*, *i. e.* The neck-bone. Marion had probably a silver locket on, tied close to her neck with a ribband, an usual ornament in Scotland; where a sore throat is called "*a sair hause*," properly *halse*.

[1 loves.   2 young heifer.   3 woollen cloth.
4 a kind of lace made of thread or silk.   5 crimson.]

XIII.

THE KNIGHT, AND SHEPHERD'S DAUGHTER.

HIS ballad (given from an old black-letter copy, with some corrections) was popular in the time of Q. Elizabeth, being usually printed with her picture before it, as Hearne informs us in his preface to *Gul. Neubrig. Hist. Oxon.* 1719, 8vo. vol. i. p. lxx. It is quoted in Fletcher's comedy of the *Pilgrim*, act iv. sc. 2.

[It is also quoted in *The Knight of the Burning Pestle:*

"He set her on a milk white steed." (l. 85.)

There are several Scottish versions given by Buchan, Kinloch, and Motherwell. The latter claims greater antiquity for his over Percy's. It appears, however, to be a southern ballad adapted by the Scotch and improved in its humour. The heroine practices various artifices to maintain the character of a "beggar's brat" when riding back with *Earl Richard.*]

HERE was a shepherd's daughter
　　Came tripping on the waye;
And there by chance a knighte shee mett,
　　Which caused her to staye.

Good morrowe to you, beauteous maide,　　5
　　These words pronounced hee:
O I shall dye this daye, he sayd,
　　If Ive not my wille of thee.

The Lord forbid, the maide replyde,
　　That you shold waxe so wode!　　10
"But for all that shee could do or saye,
　　He wold not be withstood."

Sith you have had your wille of mee,
   And put me to open shame,
Now, if you are a courteous knighte,   15
   Tell me what is your name?

Some do call mee Jacke, sweet heart,
   And some do call mee Jille;[1]
But when I come to the kings faire courte
   They call me Wilfulle Wille.   20

He sett his foot into the stirrup,
   And awaye then he did ride;
She tuckt her girdle about her middle,
   And ranne close by his side.

But when she came to the brode watèr,   25
   She sett her brest and swamme;
And when she was got out againe,
   She tooke to her heels and ranne.

He never was the courteous knighte,
   To saye, faire maide, will ye ride?   30
" And she was ever too loving a maide"
   To saye, sir knighte abide.

When she came to the kings faire courte,
   She knocked at the ring;
So readye was the king himself   35
   To let this faire maide in.

Now Christ you save, my gracious liege,
   Now Christ you save and see,
You have a knighte within your courte
   This daye hath robbed mee.   40

---

[1] Jill is sometimes used as a woman's name and at other times
as a man's.]

What hath he robbed thee of, sweet heart?
    Of purple or of pall?
Or hath he took thy gaye gold ring
    From off thy finger small?

He hath not robbed mee, my leige,   45
    Of purple nor of pall:
But he hath gotten my maiden head,
    Which grieves mee worst of all.

Now if he be a batchelor,
    His bodye Ile give to thee;   50
But if he be a married man,
    High hanged he shall bee.

He called downe his merrye men all,
    By one, by two, by three;
Sir William used to bee the first,   55
    But nowe the last came hee.

He brought her downe full fortye pounde,
    Tyed up withinne a glove:
Faire maid, Ile give the same to thee;
    Go, seeke thee another love.   60

O Ile have none of your gold, she sayde,
    Nor Ile have none of your fee;
But your faire bodye I must have,
    The king hath granted mee.

Sir William ranne and fetchd her then   65
    Five hundred pound in golde,
Saying, faire maide, take this to thee,
    Thy fault will never be tolde.

Ver. 50. *His bodye Ile give to thee.*] This was agreeable to the feudal customs: The Lord had a right to give a wife to his vassals. See Shakespeare's *All's well that ends well.*

Tis not the gold that shall mee tempt,
   These words then answered shee,   70
But your own bodye I must have,
   The king hath granted mee.

Would I had dranke the water cleare,
   When I did drinke the wine,
Rather than any shepherds brat   75
   Shold bee a ladye of mine!

Would I had drank the puddle foule,
   When I did drink the ale,
Rather than ever a shepherds brat
   Shold tell me such a tale!   80

A shepherds brat even as I was,
   You mote have let me bee,
I never had come othe kings faire courte,
   To crave any love of thee.

He sett her on a milk-white steede,   85
   And himself upon a graye;
He hung a bugle about his necke,
   And soe they rode awaye.

But when they came unto the place,
   Where marriage-rites were done,   90
She proved herself a dukes daughtèr,
   And he but a squires sonne.

Now marrye me, or not, sir knight,
   Your pleasure shall be free:
If you make me ladye of one good towne,   95
   Ile make you lord of three.

Ah! cursed bee the gold, he sayd,
   If thou hadst not been trewe,
I shold have forsaken my sweet love,
   And have changed her for a newe.   100

And now their hearts being linked fast,
   They joyned hand in hande :
Thus he had both purse, and person too,
   And all at his commande.

*

XIV.

THE SHEPHERD'S ADDRESS TO HIS MUSE.

T HIS poem, originally printed from the small MS. volume, mentioned above in No. X., has been improved by a more perfect copy in *England's Helicon*, where the author is discovered to be *N. Breton*.

OOD Muse, rocke me aslepe
   With some sweete harmony :
This wearie eyes is not to kepe
   Thy wary company.

Sweete Love, begon a while,   5
   Thou seest my heavines :
Beautie is borne but to beguyle
   My harte of happines.

See howe my little flocke,
   That lovde to feede on highe,   10
Doe headlonge tumble downe the rocke,
   And in the valley dye.

The bushes and the trees,
   That were so freshe and greene,
Doe all their deintie colors leese,   15
   And not a leafe is seene.

The blacke birde and the thrushe,
  That made the woodes to ringe,
With all the rest, are now at hushe,
  And not a note they singe.   20

Swete Philomele, the birde
  That hath the heavenly throte,
Doth nowe, alas! not once afforde
  Recordinge of a note.

The flowers have had a frost,   25
  The herbs have loste their savoure;
And Phillida the faire hath lost
  " For me her wonted " favour.

Thus all these careful sights,
  So kill me in conceit;   30
That now to hope upon delights,
  It is but meere deceite.

And therefore, my sweete Muse,
  That knowest what helpe is best,
Doe nowe thy heavenlie conninge use   35
  To sett my harte at rest :

And in a dreame bewraie
  What fate shal be my frende ;
Whether my life shall still decaye,
  Or when my sorrowes ende.   40

XV.

LORD THOMAS AND FAIR ELLINOR

 S given (with corrections) from an ancient copy in black letter, in the Pepys collection, intitled, *A tragical ballad on the unfortunate love of lord Thomas and fair Ellinor, together with the downfall of the browne girl.*—In the same collection may be seen an attempt to modernize this old song, and reduce it to a different measure: A proof of its popularity.

The reader will find a Scottish song on a similar subject to this, towards the end of this volume, intitled, *Lord Thomas and Lady Annet.*

[This is one of the ballads still kept in print in Seven Dials, and Ritson describes it as having "every appearance of being originally a minstrel song."

There is a series of ballads on the same subject—

1. *Lord Thomas and Fair Annet*, (see book iii. No. 4.)
2. *Fair Margaret and Sweet William*, (see book ii. No. 4.)
3. *Sweet Willie and Fair Annie*, (Jamieson's *Popular Ballads*, i. 22.)

The last named ballad is a combination of the first two, the first part being similar to *Lord Thomas*, and the second part to *Fair Margaret.*]

 ORD Thomas he was a bold forrestèr,
    And a chaser of the kings deere;
Faire Ellinor was a fine womàn,
    And lord Thomas he loved her deare.

Come riddle my riddle, dear mother, he sayd,   5
    And riddle us both as one;
Whether I shall marrye with faire Ellinòr,
    And let the browne girl alone?

The browne girl she has got houses and lands,
   Faire Ellinor she has got none,   10
And therefore I charge thee on my blessìng,
   To bring me the browne girl home.

And as it befelle on a high holidaye,
   As many there are beside,
Lord Thomas he went to faire Ellinòr,   15
   That should have been his bride.

And when he came to faire Ellinors bower,
   He knocked there at the ring,
And who was so readye as faire Ellinòr,
   To lett lord Thomas withinn.   20

What newes, what newes, lord Thomas, she sayd?
   What newes dost thou bring to mee?
I am come to bid thee to my weddìng,
   And that is bad newes for thee.

O God forbid, lord Thomas, she sayd,   25
   That such a thing should be done;
I thought to have been the bride my selfe,
   And thou to have been the bridegrome.

Come riddle my riddle, dear mother, she sayd,
   And riddle it all in one;   30
Whether I shall goe to lord Thomas his wedding,
   Or whether shall tarry at home?

There are manye that are your friendes, daughtèr,
   And manye a one your foe,
Therefore I charge you on my blessing,   35
   To lord Thomas his wedding don't goe.

Ver. 29. It should probably be, *Read me, read, &c.*, *i.e.* Advise
me, advise.

There are manye that are my friendes, mothèr ;
  But were every one my foe,
Betide me life, betide me death,
  To lord Thomas his wedding I'ld goe.   40

She cloathed herself in gallant attire,
  And her merrye men all in greene ;
And as they rid through every towne,
  They took her to be some queene.

But when she came to lord Thomas his gate,   45
  She knocked there at the ring ;
And who was so readye as lord Thomàs,
  To lett faire Ellinor in.

Is this your bride, fair Ellinor sayd ?
  Methinks she looks wonderous browne ;   50
Thou mightest have had as faire a womàn,
  As ever trod on the grounde.

Despise her not, fair Ellin, he sayd,
  Despise her not unto mee ;
For better I love thy little fingèr,   55
  Than all her whole bodèe.

This browne bride had a little penknife,
  That was both long and sharpe,
And betwixt the short ribs and the long,
  She prickd faire Ellinor's harte.   60

O Christ thee save, lord Thomas, hee sayd,
  Methinks thou lookst wonderous wan ;
Thou usedst to look with as fresh a colòur,
  As ever the sun shone on.

Oh, art thou blind, lord Thomas ? she sayd,   65
  Or canst thou not very well see ?
Oh ! dost thou not see my owne hearts bloode
  Run trickling down my knee.

Lord Thomas he had a sword by his side;
  As he walked about the halle,   70
He cut off his brides head from her shoulders,
  And threw it against the walle.

He set the hilte against the grounde,
  And the point against his harte.
There never three lovers together did meete,   75
  That sooner againe did parte.

XVI.

CUPID AND CAMPASPE.

HIS elegant little sonnet is found in the third act of an old play intitled *Alexander and Campaspe*, written by John Lilye, a celebrated writer in the time of queen Elizabeth. That play was first printed in 1591; but this copy is given from a later edition.

[These pretty epigrammatic verses occur in act iii. sc. 5. of Lilly's play as a song by Apelles. The first edition of *Campaspe* was printed in 1584, and that of 1591, mentioned above, is the second edition. This song, however, was omitted in all the editions printed before that of E. Blount (*Si. Court Comedies*, 1632.)]

UPID and my Campaspe playd
  At cardes for kisses; Cupid payd:
  He stakes his quiver, bow and arrows,
  His mothers doves, and teame of sparrows;
Loses them too; then down he throws   5
The coral of his lippe, the rose
Growing on's cheek (but none knows how)
With these, the crystal of his browe,
And then the dimple of his chinne;
All these did my Campaspe winne.   10

At last he set her both his eyes,
She won, and Cupid blind did rise.
 O Love! has she done this to thee?
What shall, alas! become of mee?

XVII.

THE LADY TURNED SERVING-MAN

S given from a written copy, containing some improvements (perhaps modern ones), upon the popular ballad,
intitled, *The famous flower of Serving-men:* or the *Lady
turned Serving-man.*

[It is printed in the *Collection of Old Ballads* (i. 216) without
the *improvements*. After verse 56 the first person is changed to
the third in the original, but Percy altered this and made the first
person run on throughout. Kinloch (*Ancient Scottish Ballads*,
p. 95) gives a very mutilated and varied version of this ballad in
the Scottish dress under the title of *Sweet Willie*, which was taken
down from the recitation of an old woman in Lanark. There is a
similar story in Swedish and Danish.]

OU beauteous ladyes, great and small,
 I write unto you one and all,
 Whereby that you may understand
 What I have suffered in the land.

I was by birth a lady faire,   5
An ancient barons only heire,
And when my good old father dyed,
Then I became a young knightes bride.

And there my love built me a bower,
Bedeck'd with many a fragrant flower;   10
A braver bower you ne'er did see
Then my true-love did build for mee.

And there I livde a ladye gay,
Till fortune wrought our loves decay;
For there came foes so fierce a band,   15
That soon they over-run the land.

They came upon us in the night,
And brent my bower, and slew my knight;
And trembling hid in mans array,
I scant with life escap'd away.   20

In the midst of this extremitìe,
My servants all did from me flee:
Thus was I left myself alone,
With heart more cold than any stone.

Yet though my heart was full of care,   25
Heaven would not suffer me to dispaire,
Wherefore in haste I chang'd my name
From faire Elise, to sweet Williame:

And therewithall I cut my haire,
Resolv'd my man's attire to weare;   30
And in my beaver, hose and band,
I travell'd far through many a land.

At length all wearied with my toil,
I sate me downe to rest awhile;
My heart it was so fill'd with woe,   35
That downe my cheeke the teares did flow.

It chanc'd the king of that same place
With all his lords a hunting was,
And seeing me weepe, upon the same
Askt who I was, and whence I came.   40

Then to his grace I did replye,
I am a poore and friendlesse boye,
Though nobly borne, nowe forc'd to bee
A serving-man of lowe degree.

Stand up, faire youth, the king reply'd,　　45
For thee a service I'll provyde :
But tell me first what thou canst do ;
Thou shalt be fitted thereunto.

Wilt thou be usher of my hall,
To wait upon my nobles all ?　　50
Or wilt be taster of my wine,
To 'tend on me when I shall dine ?

Or wilt thou be my chamberlaine,
About my person to remaine ?
Or wilt thou be one of my guard,　　55
And I will give thee great reward ?

Chuse, gentle youth, said he, thy place.
Then I reply'd, If it please your grace
To shew such favour unto mee,
Your chamberlaine I faine would bee.　　60

The king then smiling gave consent,
And straitwaye to his court I went;
Where I behavde so faithfullie,
That hee great favour showd to mee.

Now marke what fortune did provide;　　65
The king he would a hunting ride
With all his lords and noble traine,
Sweet William must at home remaine.

Thus being left alone behind,
My former state came in my mind :　　70
I wept to see my mans array ;
No longer now a ladye gay.

And meeting with a ladyes vest,
Within the same myself I drest ;
With silken robes, and jewels rare,　　75
I deckt me, as a ladye faire :

And taking up a lute straitwaye,
Upon the same I strove to play;
And sweetly to the same did sing,
As made both hall and chamber ring.   80

" My father was as brave a lord,
As ever Europe might afford;
My mother was a lady bright;
My husband was a valiant knight:

" And I myself a ladye gay,   85
Bedeckt with gorgeous rich array;
The happiest lady in the land,
Had not more pleasure at command.

" I had my musicke every day
Harmonious lessons for to play;   90
I had my virgins fair and free,
Continually to wait on mee.

" But now, alas! my husband's dead,
And all my friends are from me fled,
My former days are past and gone,   95
And I am now a serving-man."

And fetching many a tender sigh,
As thinking no one then was nigh,
In pensive mood I laid me lowe,
My heart was full, the tears did flowe.   100

The king, who had a huntinge gone,
Grewe weary of his sport anone,
And leaving all his gallant traine,
Turn'd on the sudden home againe:

And when he reach'd his statelye tower,   105
Hearing one sing within his bower,
He stopt to listen, and to see
Who sung there so melodiouslie.

Thus heard he everye word I sed,
And saw the pearlye teares I shed,   110
And found to his amazement there,
Sweete William was a ladye faire.

Then stepping in, Faire ladye, rise,
And dry, said he, those lovelye eyes,
For I have heard thy mournful tale,   115
The which shall turne to thy availe.

A crimson dye my face orespred,
I blusht for shame, and hung my head,
To find my sex and story knowne,
When as I thought I was alone.   120

But to be briefe, his royall grace
Grewe so enamour'd of my face,
The richest gifts he proffered mee,
His mistress if that I would bee.

Ah! no, my liege, I firmlye sayd,   125
I'll rather in my grave be layd,
And though your grace hath won my heart,
I ne'er will act soe base a part.

Faire ladye, pardon me, sayd hee,
Thy virtue shall rewarded bee,   130
And since it is soe fairly tryde
Thou shalt become my royal bride.

Then strait to end his amorous strife,
He tooke sweet William to his wife.
The like before was never seene,   135
A serving-man became a queene.

***

XVIII.

GIL MORRICE.

A Scottish Ballad.

HE following piece hath run thro' two editions in Scotland: the second was printed at Glasgow in 1755, 8vo. Prefixed to them both is an advertisement, setting forth that the preservation of this poem was owing "to a lady, who favoured the printers with a copy, as it was carefully collected from the mouths of old women and nurses;" and "any reader that can render it more correct or complete," is desired to oblige the public with such improvements. In consequence of this advertisement sixteen additional verses have been produced and handed about in manuscript, which are here inserted in their proper places: (these are from ver. 109, to ver. 121, and from ver. 124, to ver. 129, but are perhaps, after all, only an ingenious interpolation.)

As this poem lays claim to a pretty high antiquity, we have assigned it a place among our early pieces: though, after all, there is reason to believe it has received very considerable modern improvements: for in the Editor's ancient MS. collection is a very old imperfect copy of the same ballad: wherein though the leading features of the story are the same, yet the colouring here is so much improved and heightened, and so many additional strokes are thrown in, that it is evident the whole has undergone a revisal.

This little pathetic tale suggested the plot of the tragedy of *Douglas.*

Since it was first printed, the Editor has been assured that the foregoing ballad is still current in many parts of Scotland, where the hero is universally known by the name of *Child Maurice*, pronounced by the common people *Cheild* or *Cheeld;* which occasioned the mistake.

It may be proper to mention that other copies read ver. 110, thus:

"Shot frae the golden sun."

And ver. 116, as follows:

"His een like azure sheene."

N.B. The Editor's MS. instead of "lord Barnard," has "John Stewart;" and instead of "Gil Morrice," *Child Maurice,* which last is probably the original title. See above, p. 58.

[*Gil Maurice* is one of the most popular of the old ballads and it is also one of the most corrupt.   The present copy is so tinkered that it is not surprising Burns regarded the ballad as a modern composition and classed it with *Hardyknute*, a position afterwards taken up by Robert Chambers in his pamphlet *The Romantic Scottish Ballads, their epoch and authorship.*   The fact however that the story is preserved in the Folio MS. and also in several other forms obtained from tradition prove it to be an authentic ballad.   Jamieson thinks it has all the appearance of being a true narrative of some incident that had really taken place.   Motherwell devotes several pages of his *Minstrelsy* (pp. 257-286) to an account of the various versions.   He says that tradition points out the "green wood" of the ballad in the ancient forest of Dundaff in Stirlingshire.

The request for additions mentioned above by Percy was a tempting bait eagerly caught at, and the edition of 1755 was a made up text with additional verses.   Besides vv. 109-120, 125-128, which are known to be interpolations, Professor Child (*English and Scottish Ballads*, vol. ii. p. 38) also degrades to the foot of the page the verses from 177 to the end, on the authority of Jamieson, who says, that " having been attentive to all the proceedings in most of the trials at the bar of ballad criticism I may venture to hazard an opinion that the genuine text ends with " ver. 176."   Ritson and Motherwell are of the same opinion.   Sir Walter Scott notes on the interpolated verses, " In the beautiful and simple ballad of *Gil Morris* some affected person has stuck in one or two factitious verses which, like vulgar persons in a drawing room, betray themselves by their over-finery."

The fine copy in the Folio MS. (ed. Hales and Furnivall, vol. ii. p. 500), which Jamieson thought debased and totally unworthy of the subject, which Chambers calls " a poor, bald imperfect composition," and Mr. Hales more accurately designates as " a noble specimen of our ballad poetry in all its strength," was first printed by Jamieson (*Popular Ballads and Songs*, 1806, vol. i. p. 8), and is now added to the present version.   The last stanza of the Folio MS. copy is identical with the last stanza but one of *Little Musgrave and Lady Barnard*, with which it seems to have some connection both in subject and name.

Prof. Aytoun points out that vv. 51-58 of Percy's copy, which are now placed within brackets, are taken from *Lady Maisry*, a ballad obtained from recitation and printed by Jamieson (vol. i. p. 73).

      " O whan he came to broken briggs
        He bent his bow and swam,
      And whan he came to the green grass growin'
        He slack'd his shoon and ran.

> And whan he came to Lord William's yeats
> He badena to chap or ca',
> But set his bent bow to his breast
> And lightly lap the wa'."

It is however only fair to Percy to say that he printed *Gil Morice* before *Lady Maisry* was published.

Gray wrote to a friend, " I have got the old Scotch ballad on which *Douglas* was founded; it is divine, and as long as from hence [Cambridge] to Aston."

Jamieson says, on the authority of Sir Walter Scott, that after the appearance of Home's *Douglas* six additional stanzas, beginning—

> " She heard him speak, but fell despair
> Sat rooted in her heart
> She heard him, and she heard nae mair
> Though sair she rued the smart,"

were written to complete the ballad, and in accordance with the final catastrophe of the tragedy Lord Barnard rushes into the thickest of the fight—

> " and meets the death he sought."

When the play was produced in Edinburgh in 1756 the heroine was named Lady Barnard, and the alteration to Lady Randolph was made on its appearance in England in the following year.

Jamieson gives three stanzas of a traditional version of the ballad, the whole of which neither he nor Motherwell could recover, although Mr. Sharpe told the latter that they were incorporated in an Annandale version which contained a novel feature in the story.

Motherwell prints a version called *Chield Morice*, which he took down from the recitation of an old woman of 70 in 1827, and which she had learned in infancy from her grandmother. She told Motherwell " that at a later period of her life she also committed to memory *Gill Morice*, which began with young lasses like her to be a greater favourite, and more fashionable than the set which her grandmother and other old folks used to sing under the title of *Chield Morice.*" He also prints *Child Moryce*, taken down from the singing of widow M'Cormick of Paisley in 1825, and adds his opinion that Morice and Maurice are evident corruptions of Norice—a foster child. The story of Langhorne's *Owen of Carron* is also taken from this ballad.]

IL MORRICE was an erlès son,
  His name it waxed wide;
It was nae for his great richès,
  Nor yet his mickle pride;
Bot it was for a lady gay,   5
  That livd on Carron side.

Quhair sall I get a bonny boy,
  That will win hose and shoen;
That will gae to lord Barnards ha',
  And bid his lady cum?   10
And ye maun rin my errand, Willie;
  And ye may rin wi' pride;
Quhen other boys gae on their foot,
  On horse-back ye sall ride.

O no! Oh no! my master dear!   15
  I dare nae for my life;
I'll no gae to the bauld baròns,
  For to triest furth his wife.
My bird Willie, my boy Willie;
  My dear Willie, he sayd: 20
How can ye strive against the stream?
  For I sall be obeyd.

Bot, O my master dear! he cryd,
  In grene wod ye're your lain;[1]
Gi owre sic thochts, I walde ye rede,[2]   25
  For fear ye should be tain.
Haste, haste, I say, gae to the ha',
  Bid hir cum here wi speid:
If ye refuse my heigh command,
  Ill gar your body bleid.   30

Ver. 11. something seems wanting here.

[1 alone by yourself.   2 advise.]

Gae bid hir take this gay mantèl,
   'Tis a' gowd bot the hem ;
Bid hir cum to the gude grene wode,
   And bring nane bot hir lain :
And there it is, a silken sarke,   35
   Her ain hand sewd the sleive ;
And bid hir cum to Gill Morice,
   Speir nae bauld barons leave.

Yes, I will gae your black errand,
   Though it be to your cost ;   40
Sen ye by me will nae be warn'd,
   In it ye sall find frost.
The baron he is a man of might,
   He neir could bide to taunt,
As ye will see before its nicht,   45
   How sma' ye hae to vaunt.

And sen I maun your errand rin
   Sae sair against my will,
I'se mak a vow and keip it trow,
   It sall be done for ill.   50
[And quhen he came to broken brigue,
   He bent his bow and swam ;
And quhen he came to grass growing,
   Set down his feet and ran.

And quhen he came to Barnards ha',   55
   Would neither chap[1] nor ca' :
Bot set his bent bow to his breist,
   And lichtly lap the wa'.]
He wauld nae tell the man his errand,
   Though he stude at the gait ;   60
Bot straiht into the ha' he cam,
   Quhair they were set at meit.

Ver. 32, and 68, perhaps, *'bout the hem.* V. 58. Could this be the wall of the castle ?

[1 knock.]

Hail! hail! my gentle sire and dame!
  My message winna waite;
Dame, ye maun to the gude grene wod   65
  Before that it be late.
Ye're bidden tak this gay mantèl,
  Tis a' gowd bot the hem:
You maun gae to the gude grene wode,
  Ev'n by your sel alane.   70

And there it is, a silken sarke,
  Your ain hand sewd the sleive;
Ye maun gae speik to Gill Morìce;
  Speir nae bauld barons leave.
The lady stamped wi' hir foot,   75
  And winked wi' hir ee;
Bot a' that she coud say or do,
  Forbidden he wad nae bee.

Its surely to my bow'r-womàn;
  It neir could be to me.   80
I brocht it to lord Barnards lady;
  I trow that ye be she.
Then up and spack the wylie nurse,
  (The bairn upon hir knee)
If it be cum frae Gill Morìce,   85
  It's deir welcum to mee.

Ye leid, ye leid, ye filthy nurse,
  Sae loud I heird ye lee;
I brocht it to lord Barnards lady;
  I trow ye be nae shee.   90
Then up and spack the bauld baròn,
  An angry man was hee;

Ver. 88. Perhaps, *loud say I heire.*

He's tain the table wi' his foot,
　　Sae has he wi' his knee;
Till siller cup and 'mazer'* dish　　95
　　In flinders he gard flee.[1]

Gae bring a robe of your clidìng,[2]
　　That hings upon the pin;
And I'll gae to the gude grene wode,
　　And speik wi' your lemmàn.　　100
O bide at hame, now lord Barnàrd,
　　I warde ye bide at hame;
Neir wyte[3] a man for violence,
　　That neir wate[4] ye wi' nane.

Gil Morice sate in gude grene wode,　　105
　　He whistled and he sang':
O what mean a' the folk comìng,
　　My mother tarries lang.
[His hair was like the threeds of gold,
　　Drawne frae Minervas loome:　　110
His lipps like roses drapping dew,
　　His breath was a' perfume.

His brow was like the mountain snae
　　Gilt by the morning beam:
His cheeks like living roses glow:　　115
　　His een like azure stream.
The boy was clad in robes of grene,
　　Sweete as the infant spring:
And like the mavis on the bush,
　　He gart the vallies ring.]　　120

The baron came to the grene wode,
　　Wi' mickle dule and care,
And there he first spied Gill Morìce
　　Kameing his yellow hair:

---

* *i.e.* a drinking cup of maple: other edit. read *ezar*.
[1 in splinters he made fly.　2 clothing.　3 blame.
4 blamed.]

[That sweetly wavd around his face,   125
   That face beyond compare:
He sang sae sweet it might dispel,
   A' rage but fell despair.]

Nae wonder, nae wonder, Gill Morìce,
   My lady loed thee weel,   130
The fairest part of my bodie
   Is blacker than thy heel.
Yet neir the less now, Gill Morìce,
   For a' thy great beautiè,
Ye's rew the day ye eir was born;   135
   That head sall gae wi' me.

Now he has drawn his trusty brand,
   And slaited on the strae;[1]
And thro' Gill Morice' fair body
   He's gar cauld iron gae.   140
And he has tain Gill Morice' head
   And set it on a speir;
The meanest man in a' his train
   Has gotten that head to bear.

And he has tain Gill Morice up,   145
   Laid him across his steid,
And brocht him to his painted bowr
   And laid him on a bed.
The lady sat on castil wa',
   Beheld baith dale and doun;   150
And there she saw Gill Morice' head
   Cum trailing to the toun.

Ver. 128. So Milton,—

   "Vernal delight and joy: able to drive
   All sadness but despair."—   B. iv. v. 155.

   [1 and wiped it on the grass.]

Far better I loe that bluidy head,
  Both and that yellow hair,
Than lord Barnard, and a' his lands,   155
  As they lig here and thair.
And she has tain her Gill Morice,
  And kissd baith mouth and chin :
I was once as fow of Gill Morice,
  As the hip is o' the stean.¹   160

I got ye in my father's house,
  Wi' mickle sin and shame ;
I brocht thee up in gude grene wode,
  Under the heavy rain.
Oft have I by thy cradle sitten,   165
  And fondly seen thee sleip ;
But now I gae about thy grave,
  The saut tears for to weip.

And syne she kissd his bluidy cheik,
  And syne his bluidy chin :   170
O better I loe my Gill Morice
  Than a' my kith and kin !
Away, away, ye ill womàn,
  And an il deith mait ye dee :
Gin I had kend he'd bin your son,   175
  He'd neir bin slain for mee.

[Obraid me not, my lord Barnard !
  Obraid me not for shame !
Wi' that saim speir O pierce my heart !
  And put me out o' pain.   180
Since nothing bot Gill Morice head
  Thy jelous rage could quell,
Let that saim hand now tak hir life,
  That neir to thee did ill.

[¹ as the berry is of the stone.]

To me nae after days nor nichts   185
  Will eir be saft or kind;
I'll fill the air with heavy sighs,
  And greet till I am blind.
Enouch of blood by me's bin spilt,
  Seek not your death frae mee;   190
I rather lourd it had been my sel
  Than eather him or thee.

With waefo wae I hear your plaint;
  Sair, sair I rew the deid,
That eir this cursed hand of mine   195
  Had gard his body bleid.
Dry up your tears, my winsome dame,
  Ye neir can heal the wound;
Ye see his head upon the speir,
  His heart's blude on the ground.   200

I curse the hand that did the deid,
  The heart that thocht the ill;
The feet that bore me wi' silk speid,
  The comely youth to kill.
I'll ay lament for Gill Morice,   205
  As gin he were mine ain;
I'll neir forget the dreiry day
  On which the youth was slain.]

HE following is copied from the Folio MS. (ed. H. & F.
vol. 2. pp. 502-506.)

Childe Maurice hunted ithe siluen wood,
  he hunted itt round about,
& noebodye that he ffound therin,
  nor none there was with-out.   4

& he tooke his siluer combe in his hand,
  to kembe his yellow lockes;
he sayes, " come hither, thou litle ffoot page,
  that runneth lowlye by my knee;   8
ffor thou shalt goe to Iohn stewards wiffe
  & pray her speake with mee.

" & as itt ffalls out many times,
    as knotts beene knitt on a kell,   12
or Marchant men gone to Leeue London
    either to buy ware or sell,

" I, and greete thou doe that Ladye well,
    euer soe well ffroe mee,—   16
And as itt ffalles out many times
    as any hart can thinke,

" as schoole masters are in any schoole house
    writting with pen and Iinke,—   20
ffor if I might, as well as shee may,
    this night I wold with her speake.

" & heere I send her a mantle of greene,
    as greene as any grasse,   24
& bidd her come to the siluer wood
    to hunt with Child Maurice;

" & there I send her a ring of gold,
    a ring of precyous stone,   28
& bidd her come to the siluer wood;
    let ffor no kind of man."

one while this litle boy he yode,
    another while he ran;   32
vntill he came to Iohn Stewards hall,
    I-wis he neuer blan.

& of nurture the child had good;
    hee ran vp hall & bower ffree,   36
& when he came to this Lady ffaire,
    sayes, " god you saue and see !

" I am come ffrom Ch[i]ld Maurice,
    a message vnto thee;   40
& Child Maurice, he greetes you well,
    & euer soe well ffrom mee.

" & as itt ffalls out oftentimes,
    as knotts beene knitt on a kell,   44
or Marchant men gone to leeue London,
    either ffor to buy ware or sell,

" & as oftentimes he greetes you well
    as any hart can thinke,   48
or schoole masters in any schoole
    wryting with pen and inke;

" & heere he sends a Mantle of greene,
 as greene as any grasse,   52
& he bidds you come to the siluer wood,
 to hunt with Child Maurice.

" & heere he sends you a ring of gold,
 a ring of the precyous stone,   56
he prayes you to come to the siluer wood,
 let ffor no kind of man."

"now peace, now peace, thou litle ffootpage,
 ffor Christes sake, I pray thee! 60
ffor if my lord heare one of these words,
 thou must be hanged hye!"

Iohn steward stood vnder the Castle wall,
 & he wrote the words euerye one, 64
& he called vnto his horskeeper,
 "make readye you my steede!"
I, and soe hee did to his Chamberlaine,
 "make readye then my weede!" 68

& he cast a lease[1] vpon his backe,
 & he rode to the siluer wood;
& there he sought all about,
 about the siluer wood,   72

& there he ffound him Child Maurice
 sitting vpon a blocke,
with a siluer combe in his hand
 kembing his yellow locke.   76

he sayes, "how now, how now, Child Maurice?
 alacke! how may this bee?"
but then stood vp him Child Maurice,
 & sayd these words trulye: 80

" I doe not know your Ladye," he said,
 " if that I doe her see."
" ffor thou hast sent her loue tokens,
 more now then 2 or 3;   84

" ffor thou hast sent her a mantle of greene,
 as greene as any grasse,
& bade her come to the siluer woode
 to hunt with Child Maurice; 88

---

[1] leash, thong, cord?—F.

" & thou [hast] sent her a ring of gold,
  a ring of precyous stone,
& bade her come to the siluer wood,
  let ffor noe kind of man.   92

" and by my ffaith, now, Child Maurice,
  the tone of vs shall dye ! "
" Now be my troth," sayd Child Maurice,
  " & that shall not be I."   96

but hee pulled forth a bright browne sword
  & dryed itt on the grasse,
& soe ffast he smote att Iohn Steward,
  I-wisse he neuer rest.   100

then hee pulled fforth his bright browne sword,
  & dryed itt on his sleeue ;
& the ffirst good stroke Iohn stewart stroke,
  Child Maurice head he did cleeue ;   104

& he pricked itt on his swords poynt,
  went singing there beside,
& he rode till he came to that Ladye ffaire
  wheras this ladye Lyed ;   108

and sayes " dost thou know Child Maurice head
  if that thou dost itt see ?
& lapp itt soft, & kisse itt offt,
  ffor thou louedst him better then mee." 112

but when shee looked on Child Maurice head
  shee neuer spake words but 3,
" I neuer beare no Child but one,
  & you haue slaine him trulye."   116

sayes, " wicked by my merry men all,
  I gaue Meate, drinke, & Clothe !
but cold they not haue holden me
  when I was in all that wrath ?   120

" ffor I haue slaine one of the curteouse[s]t **Knights**
  that euer bestrode a steed !
soe haue I done one [of] the fairest Ladyes
  that euer ware womans weede ! "   124
                ffins]

THE END OF THE FIRST BOOK.

RELIQUES OF ANCIENT POETRY, ETC.

SERIES THE THIRD.

BOOK II.

I.

THE LEGEND OF SIR GUY

CONTAINS a short summary of the exploits of this famous champion, as recorded in the old story books; and is commonly intitled, "A pleasant song of the valiant deeds of chivalry atchieved by that noble knight sir Guy of Warwick, who, for the love of fair Phelis, became a hermit, and dyed in a cave of craggy rocke, a mile distant from Warwick."

The history of Sir Guy, tho' now very properly resigned to children, was once admired by all readers of wit and taste: for taste and wit had once their childhood. Although of English growth, it was early a favourite with other nations: it appeared in French in 1525; and is alluded to in the old Spanish romance *Tirante el Blanco*, which, it is believed, was written not long after the year 1430. See advertisement to the French translation, 2 vols. 12mo.

The original whence all these stories are extracted is a very ancient romance in old English verse, which is quoted by Chaucer as a celebrated piece even in his time (viz. :—

> " Men speken of romances of price,
> Of Horne childe and Ippotis,
>   Of Bevis, and sir Guy," &c.—*R. of Thop.*)

and was usually sung to the harp at Christmas dinners and brideales, as we learn from Puttenham's *Art of Poetry*, 4to. 1589.

This ancient romance is not wholly lost. An imperfect copy in black letter, " Imprynted at London —— for Wylliam Copland," in 34 sheets 4to. without date, is still preserved among Mr. Garrick's collection of old plays. As a specimen of the poetry of this antique rhymer, take his description of the dragon mentioned in v. 105 of the following ballad :—

" —— A messenger came to the king.
Syr king, he sayd, lysten me now,
For bad tydinges I bring you,
In Northumberlande there is no man,
But that they be slayne everychone :
For there dare no man route,
By twenty myle rounde aboute,
For doubt of a fowle dragon,
That sleath men and beastes downe.
He is blacke as any cole,
Rugged as a rough fole ;
His bodye from the navill upwarde
No man may it pierce it is so harde ;
His neck is great as any summere ;
He renneth as swifte as any distrere ;
Pawes he hath as a lyon :
All that he toucheth he sleath dead downe.
Great winges he hath to flight,
That is no man that bare him might.
There may no man fight him agayne,
But that he sleath him certayne :
For a fowler beast then is he,
Ywis of none never heard ye."

Sir William Dugdale is of opinion that the story of Guy is not wholly apocryphal, tho' he acknowledges the monks have sounded out his praises too hyperbolically. In particular, he gives the duel fought with the Danish champion as a real historical truth, and fixes the date of it in the year 926, Ætat. Guy, 67. See his *Warwickshire*.

The following is written upon the same plan as ballad v. book i., but which is the original and which the copy cannot be decided. This song is ancient, as may be inferred from the idiom preserved in the margin, v. 94, 102 : and was once popular, as appears from Fletcher's *Knight of the Burning Pestle*, act 2, sc. ult.

It is here published from an ancient MS. copy in the editor's old folio volume, collated with two printed ones, one of which is in black letter in the Pepys collection.

[Guy was one of the most popular of the heroes of romance, and the Folio MS. contains three pieces upon his history, viz., the two printed here and *Guy and Colbrand*.

The original of the present ballad in the Folio MS., entitled *Guy and Phillis* (ed. Hales and Furnivall, vol. ii. p. 201), is a mere fragment beginning with verse 89. Percy tore out certain leaves to send to the printer, and in consequence the whole of

King Estmere and the beginning of this ballad are lost. Alterations have been made in nearly every verse by the help of the printed copies. *Guy and Phillis* was entered on the Stationers' books, 5th January, 1591-2.

We are told by Dugdale that an English traveller, about the year 1410, was hospitably received at Jerusalem by the Soldan's lieutenant, who, hearing that Lord Beauchamp "was descended from the famous Guy of Warwick, whose story they had in books of their own language, invited him to his palace; and royally feasting him, presented him with three precious stones of great value, besides divers cloaths of silk and gold given to his servants." Dugdale's authority for this story was John Rous, a priest of the chapel at Guy's Cliff, near Warwick, who compiled a biography of the hero, in which all the incidents of the romance are narrated as sober fact. The constant praises of the hero bored some people, and Corbet, in his *Iter Boreale*, expressed the hope that he should hear no more of him—

> " May all the ballads be call'd in and dye
> Which sing the warrs of Colebrand and Sir Guy."

Much valuable information on this subject will be found in Mr. Hale's interesting introduction to the Guy poems in the Folio MS.]

AS ever knight for ladyes sake
  Soe tost in love, as I sir Guy
  For Phelis fayre, that lady bright
  As ever man beheld with eye?

She gave me leave myself to try,
 The valiant knight with sheeld and speare,
Ere that her love shee wold grant me;
 Which made mee venture far and neare.

Then proved I a baron bold,
 In deeds of armes the doughtyest knight
That in those dayes in England was,
 With sworde and speare in feild to fight.

Ver. 9. The proud Sir Guy, *PC.*

An English man I was by birthe :
   In faith of Christ a christyan true :
The wicked lawes of infidells   15
   I sought by prowesse to subdue.

' Nine' hundred twenty yeere and odde
   After our Saviour Christ his birth,
When ,king Athèlstone wore the crowne,
   I lived heere upon the earth.   20

Sometime I was of Warwicke erle,
   And, as I sayd, of very truth
A ladyes love did me constraine
   To seeke strange ventures in my youth.

To win me fame by feates of armes   25
   In strange and sundry heathen lands ;
Where I atchieved for her sake
   Right dangerous conquests with my hands.

For first I sayled to Normandye,
   And there I stoutlye wan in fight   30
The emperours daughter of Almaine,
   From manye a vallyant worthye knight.

Then passed I the seas to Greece
   To helpe the emperour in his right ;
Against the mightye souldans hoaste   35
   Of puissant Persians for to fight.

Where I did slay of Sarazens,
   And heathen pagans, manye a man ;
And slew the souldans cozen deere,
   Who had to name doughtye Coldràn.   40

Eskeldered a famous knight
   To death likewise I did pursue :
And Elmayne king of Tyre alsoe,
   Most terrible in fight to viewe.

Ver. 17. Two hundred, MS. and P.

I went into the souldans hoast,   45
   Being thither on embassage sent,
And brought his head awaye with mee;
   I having slaine him in his tent.

There was a dragon in that land
   Most fiercelye mett me by the waye   50
As hee a lyon did pursue,
   Which I myself did alsoe slay.

Then soon I past the seas from Greece,
   And came to Pavye land aright:
Where I the duke of Pavye killed,   55
   His hainous treason to requite.

To England then I came with speede,
   To wedd faire Phelis lady bright:
For love of whome I travelled farr
   To try my manhood and my might.   60

But when I had espoused her,
   I stayd with her but fortye dayes,
Ere that I left this ladye faire,
   And went from her beyond the seas.

All cladd in gray, in pilgrim sort,   65
   My voyage from her I did take
Unto the blessed Holy-land,
   For Jesus Christ my Saviours sake.

Where I erle Jonas did redeeme,
   And all his sonnes which were fifteene, 70
Who with the cruell Sarazens
   In prison for long time had beene.

I slew the gyant Amarant
   In battel fiercelye hand to hand:
And doughty Barknard killed I,   75
   A treacherous knight of Pavye land.

Then I to England came againe,
  And here with Colbronde fell I fought :
An ugly gyant, which the Danes
  Had for their champion hither brought.   80

I overcame him in the feild,
  And slewe him soone right valliantlye ;
Wherebye this land I did redeeme
  From Danish tribute utterlye.

And afterwards I offered upp   85
  The use of weapons solemnlye
At Winchester, whereas I fought,
  In sight of manye farr and nye.

' But first,' neare Winsor, I did slaye
  A bore of passing might and strength ;   90
Whose like in England never was
  For hugenesse both in bredth, and length.

Some of his bones in Warwicke yett,
  Within the castle there doe lye :
One of his sheeld-bones to this day   95
  Hangs in the citye of Coventrye.

On Dunsmore heath I alsoe slewe
  A monstrous wyld and cruell beast,
Calld the Dun-cow of Dunsmore heath ;
  Which manye people had opprest.   100

Some of her bones in Warwicke yett
  Still for a monument doe lye ;
And there exposed to lookers viewe
  As wonderous strange, they may espye.

A dragon in Northumberland,   105
  I alsoe did in fight destroye,
Which did bothe man and beast oppresse,
  And all the countrye sore annoye.

Ver. 94, 102, doth lye, MS.

At length to Warwicke I did come,
　Like pilgrim poore and was not knowne;　110
And there I lived a hermitts life
　A mile and more out of the towne.

Where with my hands I hewed a house
　Out of a craggy rocke of stone;
And lived like a palmer poore　　　　115
　Within that cave myself alone:

And daylye came to begg my bread
　Of Phelis att my castle gate;
Not knowne unto my loved wiffe
　Who dailye mourned for her mate.　　120

Till att the last I fell sore sicke,
　Yea sicke soe sore that I must dye;
I sent to her a ring of golde,
　By which shee knew me presentlye.

Then shee repairing to the cave　　　125
　Before that I gave up the ghost;
Herself closd up my dying eyes:
　My Phelis faire, whom I lovd most.

Thus dreadful death did me arrest,
　To bring my corpes unto the grave;　130
And like a palmer dyed I,
　Wherby I sought my soule to save.

My body that endured this toyle,
　Though now it be consumed to mold;
My statue faire engraven in stone,　　135
　In Warwicke still you may behold.

II.

GUY AND AMARANT.

THE Editor found this Poem in his ancient folio manu-script among the old ballads; he was desirous therefore that it should still accompany them; and as it is not altogether devoid of merit, its insertion here will be pardoned.

Although this piece seems not imperfect, there is reason to believe that it is only part of a much larger poem, which contained the whole history of sir Guy: for upon comparing it with the common story book 12mo. we find the latter to be nothing more than this poem reduced to prose: which is only effected by now and then altering the rhyme, and throwing out some few of the poetical ornaments. The disguise is so slight, that it is an easy matter to pick complete stanzas in any page of that book.

The author of this poem has shown some invention. Though he took the subject from the old romance quoted before, he has adorned it afresh, and made the story intirely his own.

This poem has been discovered to be a fragment of, " The famous historie of Guy earl of Warwicke, by *Samuel Rowlands*, London, printed by J. Bell, 1649, 4to." in xii cantos, beginning thus:

" When dreadful Mars in armour every day."

Whether the edition in 1649, was the first, is not known, but the author *Sam. Rowlands* was one of the minor poets who lived in the reigns of Q. Elizabeth and James I. and perhaps later. His other poems are chiefly of the religious kind, which makes it probable that the hist. of Guy was one of his earliest performances.— There are extant of his (1.) " *The betraying of Christ, Judas in dispaire, the seven words of our Saviour on the crosse, with other poems on the passion, &c.* 1598, 4to. (Ames Typ. p. 428.)—(2.) *A Theatre of delightful Recreation.* Lond. printed for A. Johnson, 1605," 4to. (Penes editor.) This is a book of poems on subjects chiefly taken from the old Testament. (3.) " *Memory of Christ's miracles, in verse.* Lond. 1618, 4to." (4.) " *Heaven's glory, earth's vanity, and hell's horror.* Lond. 1638, 8vo." (These two in Bod. Cat.)

In the present edition the following poem has been much improved from the printed copy.

[This poem is a very poor thing and looks very like a joke in
some parts. In the Folio MS. Percy has written " By the elegance
of language and easy flow of the versification this poem should be
more modern than the rest."

Mr. Furnivall adds to this expression of opinion the following
note, " the first bombastic rhodomontade affair in the book. Certainly modern and certainly bad" (Folio MS. ed. Hales and Furnivall, vol. ii. p. 136.) Collations from the MS. are added at the
foot of the page.]

UY journeyes towards that sanctifyed
  ground,
 Whereas the Jewes fayre citye some-
  time stood,
Wherin our Saviour's sacred head was crowned,
 And where for sinfull man he shed his blood :
To see the sepulcher was his intent,   5
The tombe that Joseph unto Jesus lent.

With tedious miles he tyred his wearye feet,
 And passed desart places full of danger,
At last with a most woefull wight* did meet,
 A man that unto sorrow was noe stranger :   10
For he had fifteen sonnes, made captives all
To slavish bondage, in extremest thrall.

A gyant called Amarant detaind them,
 Whom noe man durst encounter for his strength :
Who in a castle, which he held, had chaind them : 15
 Guy questions, where ? and understands at length
The place not farr.—Lend me thy sword, quoth hee,
Ile lend my manhood all thy sonnes to free.

With that he goes, and lays upon the dore,
 Like one that sayes, I must, and will come in :   20

[Ver. 1. journeyed ore the. V. 20. he sayes that must. MS.]

  * Erle Jonas, mentioned in the foregoing ballad.

The gyant never was soe rowz'd before;
 For noe such knocking at his gate had bin:
Soe takes his keyes, and clubb, and cometh out
Staring with ireful countenance about.

Sirra, quoth hee, what busines hast thou heere? 25
 Art come to feast the crowes about my walls?
Didst never heare, noe ransome can him cleere,
 That in the compasse of my furye falls:
For making me to take a porters paines,
With this same clubb I will dash out thy braines. 30

Gyant, quoth Guy, y'are quarrelsome I see,
 Choller and you seem very neere of kin:
Most dangerous at the clubb belike you bee;
 I have bin better armed, though nowe goe thin;
But shew thy utmost hate, enlarge thy spight, 35
Keene is my weapon, and shall doe me right.

Soe draws his sword, salutes him with the same
 About the head, the shoulders, and the side:
Whilst his erected clubb doth death proclaime,
 Standinge with huge Colossus' spacious stride, 40
Putting such vigour to his knotty beame,
That like a furnace he did smoke extreame.

But on the ground he spent his strokes in vaine,
 For Guy was nimble to avoyde them still,
And ever ere he heav'd his clubb againe, 45
 Did brush his plated coat against his will:
Att such advantage Guy wold never fayle,
To bang him soundlye in his coate of mayle.

[Ver. 21. the gyant, he was neere soe. V. 25. sais hee. V. 26. my crowes about the walls. V. 27. cold him. V. 31. saies Guy your quarrelsome. V. 32. are something neere. V. 33. *most* not in MS., a club. V. 36. heere is the wepon that must doe. V. 37. Soe takes. V. 38. sides. V. 45. and ere he cold recovers clubb againe. V. 46. did beate. V. 48. to beate.]

Att last through thirst the gyant feeble grewe,
   And sayd to Guy, As thou'rt of humane race,   50
Shew itt in this, give natures wants their dewe,
   Let me but goe, and drinke in yonder place :
Thou canst not yeeld to " me" a smaller thing,
Than to graunt life, thats given by the spring.

I graunt thee leave, quoth Guye, goe drink thy last, 55
   Go pledge the dragon, and the salvage bore * :
Succeed the tragedyes that they have past,
   But never thinke to taste cold water more :
Drinke deepe to Death and unto him carouse :
Bid him receive thee in his earthen house.   60

Soe to the spring he goes, and slakes his thirst ;
   Takeing the water in extremely like
Some wracked shipp that on a rocke is burst,
   Whose forced hulke against the stones does stryke ;
Scooping it in soe fast with both his hands,   65
That Guy admiring to behold it stands.

Come on, quoth Guy, let us to worke againe,
   Thou stayest about thy liquor overlong ;
The fish, which in the river doe remaine,
   Will want thereby ; thy drinking doth them wrong :
But I will see their satisfaction made,   71
With gyants blood they must, and shall be payd.

Villaine, quoth Amarant, Ile crush thee streight ;
   Thy life shall pay thy daring toungs offence :
This clubb, which is about some hundred weight, 75
   Is deathes commission to dispatch thee hence :

[Ver. 49. att last through strength, Amarant feeble grew. V. 51.
natnre wants her. V. 54. then to grant. V. 55. I give. V. 56.
to pledge, beare. V. 58. to drinke cold. V. 59. and after that
carrouse. V. 63. on some rocke. V. 64. bulke doe stryke. V. 66.
behold him. V. 67. lets to one. V. 76. has deathes.]

    * Which Guy had slain before

Dresse thee for ravens dyett I must needes ;
And breake thy bones, as they were made of reedes.

Incensed much by these bold pagan bostes,
　　Which worthye Guy cold ill endure to heare,　　80
He hewes upon those bigg supporting postes,
　　Which like two pillars did his body beare :
Amarant for those wounds in choller growes
And desperatelye att Guy his clubb he throwes :

Which did directly on his body light,　　　　　85
　　Soe violent, and weighty there-withall,
That downe to ground on sudden came the knight ;
　　And, ere he cold recover from the fall,
The gyant gott his clubb againe in fist,
And aimd a stroke that wonderfullye mist.　　90

Traytor, quoth Guy, thy falshood Ile repay,
　　This coward act to intercept my bloode.
Sayes Amarant, Ile murther any way,
　　With enemyes all vantages are good :
O could I poyson in thy nostrills blowe,　　　95
Besure of it I wold dispatch thee soe.

Its well, said Guy, thy honest thoughts appeare,
　　Within that beastlye bulke where devills dwell ;
Which are thy tenants while thou livest heare,
　　But will be landlords when thou comest in hell :　100
Vile miscreant, prepare thee for their den,
Inhumane monster, hatefull unto men.

But breathe thy selfe a time, while I goe drinke,
　　For flameing Phœbus with his fyerye eye
Torments me soe with burning heat, I thinke　　105
　　My thirst wold serve to drinke an ocean drye :

[Ver. 79. att this bold pagans bostes. V. 86. soe heavy and soe
weaghtye. V. 88. his fall. V. 89. in his fist. V. 90. and stroke a
blow. V. 96. I wold destroy. V. 102. hurtfull.]

Forbear a litle, as I delt with thee.
Quoth Amarant, 'Thou hast noe foole of mee.

Noe, sillye wretch, my father taught more witt,
   How I shold use such enemyes as thou;   110
By all my gods I doe rejoice at itt,
   To understand that thirst constraines thee now;
For all the treasure, that the world containes,
One drop of water shall not coole thy vaines.

Releeve my foe! why, 'twere a madmans part: 115
   Refresh an adversarye to my wrong!
If thou imagine this, a child thou art:
   Noe, fellow, I have known the world too long
To be soe simple: now I know thy want,
A minutes space of breathing I'll not grant.   120

And with these words heaving aloft his clubb
   Into the ayre, he swings the same about:
Then shakes his lockes, and doth his temples rubb,
   And, like the Cyclops, in his pride doth strout:[1]
Sirra, sayes hee, I have you at a lift,   125
Now you are come unto your latest shift.

Perish forever: with this stroke I send thee
   A medicine, that will doe thy thirst much good;
Take noe more care for drinke before I end thee,
   And then wee'll have carouses of thy blood: 130
Here's at thee with a butchers downright blow,
To please my furye with thine overthrow.

Infernall, false, obdurate feend, said Guy,
   That seemst a lumpe of crueltye from hell;
Ungratefull monster, since thou dost deny   135
   The thing to mee wherin I used thee well:

[Ver. 120. space to thee I will not.   V. 128. *that* not in MS.
V. 133. Guy said.   V. 134. seemes.   V. 135. ingratefull monster
since thou hast denyd.]

[1 strut.]

With more revenge, than ere my sword did make,
On thy accursed head revenge Ile take.

Thy gyants longitude shall shorter shrinke,
    Except thy sun-scorcht skin be weapon proof : 140
Farewell my thirst; I doe disdaine to drinke,
    Streames keepe your waters to your owne behoof;
Or let wild beasts be welcome thereunto ;
With those pearle drops I will not have to do.

Here, tyrant, take a taste of my good-will,   145
    For thus I doe begin my bloodye bout :
You cannot chuse but like the greeting ill ;
    It is not that same clubb will beare you out ;
And take this payment on thy shaggye crowne.—
A blowe that brought him with a vengeance downe. 150

Then Guy sett foot upon the monsters brest,
    And from his shoulders did his head divide ;
Which with a yawninge mouth did gape, unblest ;
    Noe dragons jawes were ever seene soe wide
To open and to shut, till life was spent.   155
Then Guy tooke keyes and to the castle went.

Where manye woefull captives he did find,
    Which had beene tyred with extremityes ;
Whom he in freindly manner did unbind,
    And reasoned with them of their miseryes :   160
Eche told a tale with teares, and sighes, and cryes,
All weeping to him with complaining eyes.

There tender ladyes in darke dungeons lay,
    That were surprised in the desart wood,
And had noe other dyett everye day,   165
    But flesh of humane creatures for their food :
Some with their lovers bodyes had beene fed,
And in their wombes their husbands buryed.

[Ver. 140. doe weapon prove. V. 142. behoves. V. 145. Hold,
tyrant. V. 160. miserye. V. 163. dungeon. V. 166. then flesh.]

Now he bethinkes him of his being there, 169
To enlarge the wronged brethren from their woes ;
And, as he searcheth, doth great clamours heare,
By which sad sound's direction on he goes,
Untill he findes a darksome obscure gate,
Arm'd strongly ouer all with iron plate.

That he unlockes, and enters, where appeares, 175
The strangest object that he ever saw ;
Men that with famishment of many yeares,
Were like deathes picture, which the painters draw ;
Divers of them were hanged by eche thombe ;
Others head-downward : by the middle some. 180

With diligence he takes them from the walle,
With lybertye their thraldome to acquaint :
Then the perplexed knight their father calls,
And sayes, Receive thy sonnes though poore and
faint :
I promisd you their lives, accept of that ; 185
But did not warrant you they shold be fat.

The castle I doe give thee, heere's the keyes,
Where tyranye for many yeeres did dwell :
Procure the gentle tender ladyes ease,
For pittyes sake, use wronged women well : 190
Men easilye revenge the wrongs men do :
But poore weake women have not strength thereto.

The good old man, even overjoyed with this,
Fell on the ground, and wold have kist Guys feete :
Father, quoth he, refraine soe base a kiss, 195
For age to honor youth I hold unmeete :
Ambitious pryde hath hurt mee all it can,
I goe to mortifie a sinfull man.

[Ver. 178. Will were. V. 181. walls. V. 183. the father. V. 186.
promise you. V. 190. pittye sake. V. 191. men may easilye
revenge the deeds men doe. V. 192. no strength. MS.]

III.

THE AULD GOOD-MAN.

A Scottish Song.

 HAVE not been able to meet with a more ancient copy of this humourous old song, than that printed in the *Tea-Table miscellany, &c.* which seems to have admitted some corruptions.

[This song is printed in Ramsay's *Tea-Table Miscellany* as old, and it is also given in the *Orpheus Caledonius*, 1725. "Auld goodman" means a first husband.]

 ATE in an evening forth I went
    A little before the sun gade down,
And there I chanc't, by accident,
    To light on a battle new begun :
A man and his wife wer fawn[1] in a strife,   5
    I canna weel tell ye how it began ;
But aye she wail'd her wretched life,
    Cryeng, Evir alake, mine auld goodman !

He.

Thy auld goodman, that thou tells of,
    The country kens where he was born,   10
Was but a silly poor vagabond,
    And ilka ane leugh him to scorn :
For he did spend and make an end
    Of gear ' his fathers nevir' wan ;
He gart the poor stand frae the door ;   15
    Sae tell nae mair of thy auld goodman.

[1 fallen.]

SHE.

My heart, alake! is liken to break,
    Whan I think on my winsome John,
His blinkan ee, and gait sae free,
    Was naithing like thee, thou dosend[1] drone; 20
Wi' his rosie face, and flaxen hair,
    And skin as white as ony swan,
He was large and tall, and comely withall;
    Thou'lt nevir be like mine auld goodman.

HE.

Why dost thou plein?[2] I thee maintein;   25
    For meal and mawt thou disna want:
But thy wild bees I canna please,
    Now whan our gear gins to grow scant:
Of houshold stuff thou hast enough;
    Thou wants for neither pot nor pan;   30
Of sicklike ware he left thee bare;
    Sae tell nae mair of thy auld goodman.

SHE.

Yes I may tell, and fret my sell,
    To think on those blyth days I had,
Whan I and he, together ley   35
    In armes into a well-made bed :
But now I sigh and may be sad,
    Thy courage is cauld, thy colour wan,
Thou falds thy feet and fa's asleep;
    Thou'lt nevir be like mine auld goodman.   40

Then coming was the night sae dark,
    And gane was a' the light of day?
The carle was fear'd to miss his mark,
    And therefore wad nae longer stay :

[1 dozing or stupid.   2 complain.]

Then up he gat, and ran his way,   45
   I trowe, the wife the day she wan;
And aye the owreword[1] of the fray
   Was, Evir alake! mine auld goodman.

IV.

FAIR MARGARET AND SWEET
WILLIAM.

HIS seems to be the old song quoted in Fletcher's *Knight of the burning pestle*, acts 2d and 3d; altho' the six lines there preserved are somewhat different from those in the ballad, as it stands at present. The reader will not wonder at this, when he is informed that this is only given from a modern printed copy picked up on a stall. It's full title is *Fair Margaret's Misfortunes; or Sweet William's frightful dreams on his wedding night, with the sudden death and burial of those noble lovers.*—
The lines preserved in the play are this distich,

    "You are no love for me, Margaret,
      I am no love for you."

And the following stanza,

    "When it was grown to dark midnight,
      And all were fast asleep,
    In came Margarets grimly ghost
      And stood at Williams feet."

These lines have acquired an importance by giving birth to one of the most beautiful ballads in our own or any language. See the song intitled *Margaret's Ghost*, at the end of this volume.
Since the first edition some improvements have been inserted, which were communicated by a lady of the first distinction, as she had heard this song repeated in her infancy.

[The ballads on the two lovers Margaret and William are numerous, culminating as they do in Mallet's *William and Mar-*

[1 last word or burden.]

garet. See *Sweet William's Ghost* (No. 6 in this book) and Mallet's ballad (No. 16 of book iii). The present ballad is also in the Douce Collection and in that of the late Mr. George Daniel. Jamieson prints (*Popular Ballads and Songs*, 1806, vol. i. p. 22) a ballad entitled *Sweet Willie and Fair Annie*, which may be divided into two parts, the first resembling *Lord Thomas and Fair Elinor*, and the second, *Fair Annie's Ghost*, is still more like the following ballad.

Mr. Chappell remarks, "Another point deserving notice in the old ballad is that one part of it has furnished the principal subject of the modern burlesque ballad *Lord Lovel*, and another that of T. Hood's song, *Mary's Ghost.*"]

S it fell out on a long summer's day
　　　Two lovers they sat on a hill;
　　They sat together that long summer's day,
　　　And could not talk their fill.

I see no harm by you, Margarèt,　　　　　　5
　　And you see none by mee;
Before to-morrow at eight o' the clock
　　A rich wedding you shall see.

Fair Margaret sat in her bower-window,
　　Combing her yellow hair;　　　　　　10
There she spyed sweet William and his bride,
　　As they were a riding near.

Then down she layd her ivory combe,
　　And braided her hair in twain:
She went alive out of her bower,　　　　　15
　　But ne'er came alive in't again.

When day was gone, and night was come,
　　And all men fast asleep,
Then came the spirit of fair Marg'ret,
　　And stood at Williams feet.　　　　　　20

Are you awake, sweet William ? shee said ;
  Or, sweet William, are you asleep ?
God give you joy of your gay bride-bed,
  And me of my winding-sheet.

When day was come, and night was gone,   25
  And all men wak'd from sleep,
Sweet William to his lady sayd,
  My dear, I have cause to weep.

I dreamt a dream, my dear ladyè,
  Such dreames are never good :   30
I dreamt my bower was full of red ' wine,'
  And my bride-bed full of blood.

Such dreams, such dreams, my honoured Sir,
  They never do prove good ;
To dream thy bower was full of red ' wine,'   35
  And thy bride-bed full of blood.

He called up his merry men all,
  By one, by two, and by three ;
Saying, I'll away to fair Marg'ret's bower,
  By the leave of my ladiè.   40

And when he came to fair Marg'ret's bower,
  He knocked at the ring ;
And who so ready as her seven brethrèn
  To let sweet William in.

Then he turned up the covering-sheet,   45
  Pray let me see the dead ;
Methinks she looks all pale and wan,
  She hath lost her cherry red.

I'll do more for thee, Margarèt,
  Than any of thy kin ;   50
For I will kiss thy pale wan lips,
  Though a smile I cannot win.

Ver. 31, 35. Swine, *PCC.*

With that bespake the seven brethrèn,
   Making most piteous mone :
You may go kiss your jolly brown bride,   55
   And let our sister alone.

If I do kiss my jolly brown bride,
   I do but what is right ;
I neer made a vow to yonder poor corpse
   By day, nor yet by night.   60

Deal on, deal on, my merry men all,
   Deal on your cake and your wine * :
For whatever is dealt at her funeral to-day,
   Shall be dealt to-morrow at mine.

Fair Margaret dyed to-day, to-day,   65
   Sweet William dyed the morrow :
Fair Margaret dyed for pure true love,
   Sweet William dyed for sorrow.

Margaret was buryed in the lower chancèl,
   And William in the higher :   70
Out of her brest there sprang a rose,
   And out of his a briar.

They grew till they grew unto the church-top,
   And then they could grow no higher ;
And there they tyed in a true lovers knot,   75
   Which made all the people admire.

Then came the clerk of the parìsh,
   As you the truth shall hear,
And by misfortune cut them down,
   Or they had now been there.   80

---

* Alluding to the dole anciently given at funerals.

V.

BARBARA ALLEN'S CRUELTY.

IVEN, with some corrections, from an old black letter copy, intitled, *Barbara Allen's cruelty, or the young man's tragedy.*

[It is not clear why Percy separated this English version of *Barbara Allen* from the Scottish version entitled *Sir John Grehme and Barbara Allan* (No. 7).

Goldsmith in his third Essay says, " the music of the finest singer is dissonance to what I felt when our dairy maid sung me into tears with *Johnny Armstrong's Last Good Night*, or the *Cruelty of Barbara Allen*.

It has been suggested that for " Scarlet towne " in the first verse should be read Carlisle town, but as some printed copies have Reading town we may suppose that a pun is intended.]

N Scarlet towne, where I was borne,
    There was a faire maid dwellin,
    Made every youth crye, Wel-awaye!
    Her name was Barbara Allen.

All in the merrye month of may,   5
    When greene buds they were swellin,
Yong Jemmye Grove on his death-bed lay,
    For love of Barbara Allen.

He sent his man unto her then,
    To the town, where shee was dwellin;   10
You must come to my master deare,
    Giff your name be Barbara Allen.

For death is printed on his face,
    And ore his hart is stealin :
Then haste away to comfort him,   15
    O lovelye Barbara Allen.

Though death be printed on his face,
   And ore his harte is stealin,
Yet little better shall he bee,
   For bonny Barbara Allen.   20

So slowly, slowly, she came up,
   And slowly she came nye him;
And all she sayd, when there she came,
   Young man, I think y'are dying.

He turnd his face unto her strait,   25
   With deadlye sorrow sighing;
O lovely maid, come pity mee,
   Ime on my deth-bed lying.

If on your death-bed you doe lye,
   What needs the tale you are tellin: 30
I cannot keep you from your death;
   Farewell, sayd Barbara Allen.

He turnd his face unto the wall,
   As deadlye pangs he fell in:
Adieu! adieu! adieu to you all,   35
   Adieu to Barbara Allen.

As she was walking ore the fields,
   She heard the bell a knellin;
And every stroke did seem to saye,
   Unworthy Barbara Allen.   40

She turnd her bodye round about,
   And spied the corps a coming:
Laye down, laye down the corps, she sayd,
   That I may look upon him.

With scornful eye she looked downe,   45
   Her cheeke with laughter swellin;
Whilst all her friends cryd out amaine,
   Unworthye Barbara Allen.

When he was dead, and laid in grave,
  Her harte was struck with sorrowe,   50
O mother, mother, make my bed,
  For I shall dye to-morrowe.

Hard harted creature him to slight,
  Who loved me so dearlye :
O that I had beene more kind to him,   55
  When he was alive and neare me !

She, on her death-bed as she laye,
  Beg'd to be buried by him ;
And sore repented of the daye,
  That she did ere denye him.   60

Farewell, she sayd, ye virgins all,
  And shun the fault I fell in :
Henceforth take warning by the fall
  Of cruel Barbara Allen.

*_*_*

VI.

SWEET WILLIAM'S GHOST.

A SCOTTISH BALLAD.

FROM Allan Ramsay's *Tea-Table Miscellany.* The concluding stanza of this piece seems modern.

[In the previous ballad (No. 4) and in Mallet's *William and Margaret* it is Margaret who appears to William, but
in the present one and in some other versions William is made
to die first. In *Clerk Saunders* (*Minstrelsy of the Scottish Border*) Scott has joined two distinct stories, and the second part, in
which the spirit of Clerk Saunders appears to May Margaret,
closely resembles the present ballad. Besides these there are
two other versions Kinloch's, entitled *Sweet William and May*

Margaret, and Motherwell's *William and Marjorie*. Dr. Rimbault points out that the chief incidents in Bürger's *Leonora* resemble those in this ballad.

The last two stanzas are probably Ramsay's own.]

HERE came a ghost to Margaret's door,
    With many a grievous grone,
And ay he tirled at the pin ;*
    But answer made she none.

Is this my father Philip ?   5
    Or is't my brother John ?
Or is't my true love Willie,
    From Scotland new come home?

'Tis not thy father Philip ;
    Nor yet thy brother John :   10
But tis thy true love Willie
    From Scotland new come home,

O sweet Margret ! O dear Margret !
    I pray thee speak to mee :
Give me my faith and troth, Margret,   15
    As I gave it to thee.

Thy faith and troth thou'se nevir get,
    ' Of me shalt nevir win,'
Till that thou come within my bower,
    And kiss my cheek and chin.   20

If I should come within thy bower,
    I am no earthly man :
And should I kiss thy rosy lipp,
    Thy days will not be lang.

[* See note, *ante*, p. 47.]

O sweet Margret, O dear Margret, 25
 I pray thee speak to mee:
Give me my faith and troth, Margret,
 As I gave it to thee.

Thy faith and troth thou'se nevir get,
 'Of me shalt nevir win,' 30
Till thou take me to yon kirk yard,
 And wed me with a ring.

My bones are buried in a kirk yard
 Afar beyond the sea,
And it is but my sprite, Margret, 35
 That's speaking now to thee.

She stretched out her lilly-white hand,
 As for to do her best:
Hae there your faith and troth, Willie,
 God send your soul good rest. 40

Now she has kilted her robes of green,
 A piece below her knee:
And a' the live-lang winter night
 The dead corps followed shee.

Is there any room at your head, Willie? 45
 Or any room at your feet?
Or any room at your side, Willie,
 Wherein that I may creep?

There's nae room at my head, Margret,
 There's nae room at my feet, 50
There's no room at my side, Margret,
 My coffin is made so meet.

Then up and crew the red red cock,
 And up then crew the gray:
Tis time, tis time, my dear Margret, 55
 That 'I' were gane away.

[No more the ghost to Margret said,
   But, with a grievous grone,
Evanish'd in a cloud of mist,
   And left her all alone.   60

O stay, my only true love, stay,
   The constant Margret cried:
Wan grew her cheeks, she clos'd her een,
   Stretch'd her saft limbs, and died.]

VII.

SIR JOHN GREHME AND BARBARA ALLAN.

A Scottish Ballad.

RINTED, with a few conjectural emendations, from a written copy.

[Pepys, in Jan. 1665-1666, heard Mrs. Knipp, the actress, sing "her little Scotch song of *Barbery Allen*" at Lord Brouncker's, and he was "in perfect pleasure to hear her sing" it. It was first printed in Ramsay's *Tea-Table Miscellany* (ii. 171).

"I remember," says Mr. C. Kirkpatrick Sharpe, "that the peasantry of Annandale sang many more verses of this ballad than have appeared in print, but they were of no merit, containing numerous magnificent offers from the lover to his mistress, and amongst others some ships in sight, which may strengthen the belief that this song was composed near the shores of the Solway." —*Addit. Illustrations to Stenhouse.*]

T was in and about the Martinmas time,
   When the greene leaves wer a fallan;
That Sir John Grehme o' the west
     countrye,
   Fell in luve wi' Barbara Allan.

He sent his man down throw the towne,   5
   To the plaice wher she was dwellan :
O haste and cum to my maister deare,
   Gin ye bin Barbara Allan.

O hooly, hooly raise she up,
   To the plaice wher he was lyan;   10
And whan she drew the curtain by,
   Young man, I think ye're dyan.*

O its I'm sick, and very very sick,
   And its a' for Barbara Allan.
O the better for me ye'se never be,   15
   Though your harts blude wer spillan.

Remember ye nat in the tavern, sir,
   Whan ye the cups wer fillan;
How ye made the healths gae round and round,
   And slighted Barbara Allan?   20

He turn'd his face unto the wa'
   And death was with him dealan;
Adiew! adiew! my dear friends a',
   Be kind to Barbara Allan.

Then hooly, hooly raise she up,   25
   And hooly, hooly left him;
And sighan said, she could not stay,
   Since death of life had reft him.

She had not gane a mile but twa,
   Whan she heard the deid-bell knellan;   30
And everye jow the deid-bell geid,
   Cried, Wae to Barbara Allan!

---

* An ingenious friend thinks the rhymes *Dyand* and *Lyand*
ought to be transposed; as the taunt *Young man, I think ye're
yand*, would be very characteristical.

O mither, mither, mak my bed,
  O make it saft and narrow :
Since my love died for me to-day,   35
  Ise die for him to morrowe.

**

VIII.

THE BAILIFF'S DAUGHTER OF
ISLINGTON.

ROM an ancient black-letter copy in the Pepys *Collection,* with some improvements communicated by a lady as she had heard the same recited in her youth. The full title is, *True love requited: Or, the Bailiff's daughter of Islington.*
Islington in Norfolk is probably the place here meant.

[Copies of this charming old ballad are found in all the large collections, and two tunes are associated with it.

Percy's suggestion that Islington in Norfolk is referred to is not a probable one, and there seems to be no reason for depriving the better known Islington of the south of the honour of having given birth to the bailiff's daughter. Islington at the time when this ballad was written was a country village quite unconnected with London, and a person who represented "a squier minstrel of Middlesex" made a speech before Queen Elizabeth at Kenilworth in 1575, in which he declared "how the worshipful village of Islington [was] well knooen too bee one of the most auncient and best tounz in England, next to London."

HERE was a youthe, and a well-beloved
    youthe,
  And he was a squires son :
He loved the bayliffes daughter deare,
  That lived in Islington.

Yet she was coye and would not believe   5
   That he did love her soe,
Noe nor at any time would she
   Any countenance to him showe.

But when his friendes did understand
   His fond and foolish minde,   10
They sent him up to faire London
   An apprentice for to binde.

And when he had been seven long yeares,
   And never his love could see :
Many a teare have I shed for her sake,   15
   When she little thought of mee.

Then all the maids of Islington
   Went forth to sport and playe,
All but the bayliffes daughter deare ;
   She secretly stole awaye.   20

She pulled off her gowne of greene,
   And put on ragged attire,
And to faire London she would go
   Her true love to enquire.

And as she went along the high road,   25
   The weather being hot and drye,
She sat her downe upon a green bank,
   And her true love came riding bye.

She started up, with a colour soe redd,
   Catching hold of his bridle-reine ;   30
One penny, one penny, kind sir, she sayd,
   Will ease me of much paine.

Before I give you one penny, sweet-heart,
   Praye tell me where you were borne.
At Islington, kind sir, sayd shee,   35
   Where I have had many a scorne.

I prythee, sweet-heart, then tell to mee,
   O tell me, whether you knowe
The bayliffes daughter of Islington,
   She is dead, sir, long agoe.   40

If she be dead, then take my horse,
   My saddle and bridle also;
For I will into some farr countrye,
   Where noe man shall me knowe.

O staye, O staye, thou goodlye youthe,   45
   She standeth by thy side;
She is here alive, she is not dead,
   And readye to be thy bride.

O farewell griefe, and welcome joye,
   Ten thousand times therefore;   50
For nowe I have founde mine owne true love,
   Whom I thought I should never see more.

IX.

THE WILLOW TREE.

A PASTORAL DIALOGUE.

FROM the small black-letter collection, intitled, *The Golden Garland of princely delights;* collated with two other copies, and corrected by conjecture.

[Dr. Rimbault gives the melody of this pretty little pastoral on the favourite subject of wearing the willow from a MS. dated 1639 in the Advocate's Library, Edinburgh. It is also to be found in the celebrated Skene MS. in the same library, and again in all the editions of Forbes's *Cantus.*]

WILLY.

OW now, shepherde, what meanes that?
Why that willowe in thy hat?
Why thy scarffes of red and yellowe
Turn'd to branches of greene willowe?

CUDDY.

They are chang'd, and so am I;   5
Sorrowes live, but pleasures die:
Phillis hath forsaken mee,
Which makes me weare the willowe-tree.

WILLY.

Phillis! shee that lov'd thee long?
Is shee the lass hath done thee wrong?   10
Shee that lov'd thee long and best,
Is her love turn'd to a jest?

CUDDY.

Shee that long true love profest,
She hath robb'd my heart of rest:
For she a new love loves, not mee;   15
Which makes me wear the willowe-tree.

WILLY.

Come then, shepherde, let us joine,
Since thy happ is like to mine:
For the maid I thought most true,
Mee hath also bid adieu.   20

CUDDY.

Thy hard happ doth mine appease,
Companye doth sorrowe ease:
Yet, Phillis, still I pine for thee,
And still must weare the willowe-tree.

WILLY.

Shepherde, be advis'd by mee, 25
Cast off grief and willowe-tree :
For thy grief brings her content,
She is pleas'd if thou lament.

CUDDY.

Herdsman, I'll be rul'd by thee,
There lyes grief and willowe-tree : 30
Henceforth I will do as they,
And love a new love every day.

_

X.

THE LADY'S FALL

S given (with corrections) from the Editor's ancient folio MS.* collated with two printed copies in black-letter; one in the British Museum, the other in the Pepys Collection. Its old title is, *A lamentable ballad of the Lady's fall.* To the tune of, *In Pescod time, &c.*—The ballad here referred to is preserved in the *Muses Library*, 8vo. p. 281. It is an allegory or vision, intitled, *The Shepherd's Slumber*, and opens with some pretty rural images, viz.

" In pescod time when hound to horn
    Gives eare till buck be kil'd,
And little lads with pipes of corne
    Sate keeping beasts a-field."

" I went to gather strawberries
    By woods and groves full fair, &c."

[Mr. Hales thinks it possible that this ballad was written by the same author as *The Children in the Wood*—" the same facility of

---

[* Ed. Hales and Furnivall, vol. ii. p. 246.]

language and of rhyme, the same power of pathos, the same extreme simplicity characterise both ballads."

Mr. Chappell says that *Chevy Chace* was sometimes sung to the tune of *In Pescod time*, as were the *Bride's burial* (No. 12), and *Lady Isabella's Tragedy* (No. 14). The various readings from the original MS. are noted at the foot of the page.]

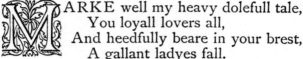

ARKE well my heavy dolefull tale,
 You loyall lovers all,
 And heedfully beare in your brest,
  A gallant ladyes fall.
Long was she wooed, ere shee was wonne, 5
 To lead a wedded life,
But folly wrought her overthrowe
 Before she was a wife.

Too soone, alas! shee gave consent
 And yeelded to his will, 10
Though he protested to be true,
 And faithfull to her still.
Shee felt her body altered quite,
 Her bright hue waxed pale,
Her lovelye cheeks chang'd color white, 15
 Her strength began to fayle.

Soe that with many a sorrowful sigh,
 This beauteous ladye milde,
With greeved hart, perceived herselfe
 To have conceived with childe. 20
Shee kept it from her parents sight
 As close as close might bee,
And soe put on her silken gowne
 None might her swelling see.

[Ver. 15. her faire red cheekes changed color quite. V. 17. and soe with. V. 20. to be conceived. V. 24. none shold. MS.]

Unto her lover secretly   25
   Her greefe shee did bewray,
And walking with him hand in hand,
   These words to him did say;
Behold, quoth shee, a maids distresse
   By love brought to thy bowe;   3c
Behold I goe with childe by thee,
   Tho none thereof doth knowe.

The litle babe springs in my wombe
   To heare its fathers voyce,
Lett it not be a bastard called,   35
   Sith I made thee my choyce:
[Come, come, my love, perform thy vowe
   And wed me out of hand;
O leave me not in this extreme
   Of griefe, alas! to stand.]   40

Think on thy former promises,
   Thy oathes and vowes eche one;
Remember with what bitter teares
   To mee thou madest thy moane.
Convay me to some secrett place,   45
   And marry me with speede;
Or with thy rapyer end my life,
   Ere further shame proceede.

Alacke! my beauteous love, quoth hee,
   My joye, and only dear;   50
Which way can I convay thee hence,
   When dangers are so near?

[Ver. 29. a ladyes distress. V. 30. your bowe. V. 31. See how
I goe with chyld with thee. V. 33. my litle. V. 35. O lett.
V. 37-40. not in MS. V. 42. thy wordes. V. 48. lest further.
V. 49. my derest. V. 50. my greatest joy on earthe. V. 51.
shold I convay you. V. 52. to scape a sudden death.]

Thy friends are all of hye degree,
  And I of meane estate;
Full hard it is to gett thee forthe   55
  Out of thy fathers gate.

Dread not thy life to save my fame,
  For if thou taken bee,
My selfe will step betweene the swords,
  And take the harme on mee: 60
Soe shall I scape dishonor quite;
  And if I should be slaine
What could they say, but that true love
  Had wrought a ladyes bane.

But feare not any further harme;   65
  My selfe will soe devise,
That I will ryde away with thee
  Unknowen of mortall eyes:
Disguised like some pretty page
  Ile meete thee in the darke,   70
And all alone Ile come to thee
  Hard by my fathers parke.

And there, quoth hee, Ile meete my deare
  If God soe lend me life,
On this day month without all fayle   75
  I will make thee my wife.
Then with a sweet and loving kisse,
  They parted presentlye,
And att their partinge brinish teares
  Stoode in eche others eye,   80

[Ver. 53. your friends. V. 55. gett you. V. 56. your ffathers.
V. 57. your liffe . . . your fame. V. 58. you. V. 59. sword.
V. 60. to take . . . of thee. V. 61. soe may you. V. 62. if soe
you. V. 64. ladyes paine. V. 67. I will safely ryd with thee.
V. 76. Ile make the then. V. 77. and with.]

Att length the wished day was come,
    On which this beauteous mayd,
With longing eyes, and strange attire,
    For her true lover stayd.
When any person shee espyed   85
    Come ryding ore the plaine,
She hop'd it was her owne true love :
    But all her hopes were vaine.

Then did shee weepe and sore bewayle
    Her most unhappy fate;   90
Then did shee speake these woefull words,
    As succourless she sate;
O false, forsworne, and faithlesse man,
    Disloyall in thy love,
Hast thou forgott thy promise past,   95
    And wilt thou perjured prove ?

And hast thou now forsaken mee
    In this my great distresse,
To end my dayes in open shame,
    Which thou mightst well redresse ?   100
Woe worth the time I eer believ'd
    That flattering tongue of thine :
Wold God that I had never seene
    The teares of thy false eyne.

And thus with many a sorrowful sigh,   105
    Homewards shee went againe;
Noe rest came in her waterye eyes,
    Shee felt such privye paine.

[Ver. 81. wherin this lovely maid. V. 85. if any person shee
had spyed. V. 86. came. V. 87. shee thought. V. 92. when
succourles. V. 93. *and* not in MS. V. 99. in heavinesse. V. 100.
which well thou might. V. 101. I did beleeve. V. 105. soe that
with many a grievous groane. V. 106. amaine. V. 108. shee
found.]

In travail strong shee fell that night,
  With many a bitter throwe ;   110
What woefull paines shee then did feel,
  Doth eche good woman knowe.

Shee called up her waiting mayd,
  That lay at her bedds feete,
Who musing at her mistress woe,   115
  Began full fast to weepe.
Weepe not, said shee, but shutt the dores,
  And windowes round about,
Let none bewray my wretched state,
  But keepe all persons out.   120

O mistress, call your mother deare ;
  Of women you have neede,
And of some skilfull midwifes helpe,
  That better may you speed.
Call not my mother for thy life,   125
  Nor fetch no woman here ;
The midwives helpe comes all too late,
  My death I doe not feare.

With that the babe sprang from her wombe
  No creature being nye,   130
And with one sighe, which brake her hart,
  This gentle dame did dye.
The lovely litle infant younge,
  [The mother being dead,]
Resigned its new received breath,   135
  To him that had it made.

[Ver. 110. thraw. V. 111. shee felt that night. V. 113. mayd.
V. 114. who lay. V. 115. and musing at her great woe. V. 117.
shee sayth. V. 118. all about. V. 123. and to some. V. 124.
the better. V. 130. being by. V. 132. gallant dame. V. 133.
litle lovely. V. 134. the pretty smiling babe.]

Next morning came her own true love,
  Affrighted at the newes,
And he for sorrow slew himselfe,
  Whom eche one did accuse.   140
The mother with her new borne babe,
  Were laide both in one grave :
Their parents overworne with woe,
  No joy thenceforth cold have.

Take heed, you dayntye damsells all,   145
  Of flattering words beware,
And to the honour of your name
  Have an especial care.
[Too true, alas ! this story is,
  As many one can tell :   150
By others harmes learne to be wise,
  And you shall do full well.]

XI.

WALY WALY, LOVE BE BONNY.

A Scottish Song.

 HIS is a very ancient song, but we could only give it from a modern copy. Some editions instead of the four last lines in the second stanza have these, which have too much merit to be wholly suppressed :

"Whan cockle shells turn siller bells,
  And muscles grow on every tree,
When frost and snaw sall warm us aw',
  Than sall my love prove true to me."
             See the *Orpheus Caledonius, &c.*

[Ver. 138. with this newes.   V. 144. no joy that they.   V. 148. have you a specyall care.   V. 149-152. not in MS.]

Arthur's-seat mentioned in ver. 17, is a hill near Edinborough; near the bottom of which is St. Anthony's well.

[There has been considerable difference of opinion among ballad collectors relative to this beautiful song. Some suppose it to be a portion of the ballad entitled *Lord Jamie Douglas*, which relates to James Douglas, second Marquis of Douglas, who married Lady Barbara Erskine, eldest daughter of John, ninth Earl of Mar, on the seventh of September, 1670, and afterwards repudiated her on account of a false accusation of adultery made against her by Lowrie, laird of Blackwood. Prof. Aytoun, however, believes that certain verses of *Waly Waly* have wrongly been mixed up with *Lord Jamie Douglas*. There is very little doubt that the song was in existence long before 1670, and it also appears to be the lamentation of a forsaken girl rather than of a wife. Mr. Stenhouse and others considered it to belong to the age of Queen Mary and to refer to some affair at Court. Aytoun writes, " there is also evidence that it was composed before 1566, for there is extant a MS. of that year in which some of the lines are transcribed," but Mr. Maidment gives the following opinion—" that the ballad is of ancient date is undoubted, but we are not quite prepared to admit that it goes back as far as 1566, the date of the manuscript transcribed by Thomas Wode from an ancient church music book compiled by Dean John Angus, Andrew Blackhall, and others, in which it said the first [second] stanza is thus parodied :—

> Hey trollie lollie, love is jollie,
>   A quhile, quhil itt is new
> Quhen it is old, it grows full cold,
>   Wae worth the love untrue.

Never having had access to the MS., we may be permitted to remark that the phraseology of the burlesque is not exactly that of the reign of Queen Mary" (*Scottish Ballads and Songs*, 1868, vol. ii. p. 49.)

Allan Ramsay was the first to publish the song, and he marked it as ancient.

> " When cockle shells turn silver bells,
>   When wine drieps red frae ilka tree,
> When frost and snaw will warm us a'
>   Then I'll cum down and dine wi' thee,"

is the fourth stanza of *Jamie Douglas*, printed by John Finlay, in his *Scottish Historical and Romantic Ballads* (vol. ii.)]

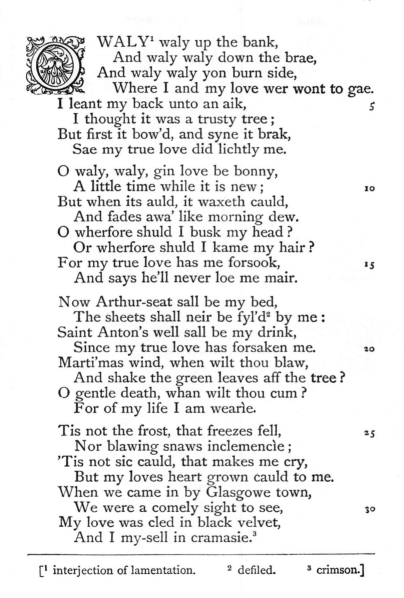

WALY[1] waly up the bank,
  And waly waly down the brae,
And waly waly yon burn side,
  Where I and my love wer wont to gae.
I leant my back unto an aik,   5
  I thought it was a trusty tree;
But first it bow'd, and syne it brak,
  Sae my true love did lichtly me.

O waly, waly, gin love be bonny,
  A little time while it is new;   10
But when its auld, it waxeth cauld,
  And fades awa' like morning dew.
O wherfore shuld I busk my head?
  Or wherfore shuld I kame my hair?
For my true love has me forsook,   15
  And says he'll never loe me mair.

Now Arthur-seat sall be my bed,
  The sheets shall neir be fyl'd[2] by me:
Saint Anton's well sall be my drink,
  Since my true love has forsaken me. 20
Marti'mas wind, when wilt thou blaw,
  And shake the green leaves aff the tree?
O gentle death, whan wilt thou cum?
  For of my life I am wearìe.

Tis not the frost, that freezes fell, 25
  Nor blawing snaws inclemencìe;
'Tis not sic cauld, that makes me cry,
  But my loves heart grown cauld to me.
When we came in by Glasgowe town,
  We were a comely sight to see,   30
My love was cled in black velvet,
  And I my-sell in cramasie.[3]

[[1] interjection of lamentation.   [2] defiled.   [3] crimson.]

But had I wist, before I kisst,
   That love had been sae ill to win;
I had lockt my heart in a case of gowd,   35
   And pinnd it with a siller pin.
And, oh! if my young babe were born,
   And set upon the nurses knee,
And I my sell were dead and gane!
   For a maid again Ise never be.   40

XII.

THE BRIDE'S BURIAL.

 ROM two ancient copies in black-letter: one in the Pepys Collection; the other in the British Museum.

To the tune of *The Lady's Fall.*

 OME mourne, come mourne with mee,
   You loyall lovers all;
Lament my loss in weeds of woe,
   Whom griping grief doth thrall.

Like to the drooping vine,   5
   Cut by the gardener's knife,
Even so my heart, with sorrow slaine,
   Doth bleed for my sweet wife.

By death, that grislye ghost,
   My turtle dove is slaine,   10
And I am left, unhappy man,
   To spend my dayes in paine.

Her beauty late so bright,
   Like roses in their prime,
Is wasted like the mountain snowe,   15
   Before warme Phebus' shine.

Her faire red colour'd cheeks
  Now pale and wan; her eyes,
That late did shine like crystal stars;
  Alas, their light it dies :   20

Her prettye lilly hands,
  With fingers long and small,
In colour like the earthly claye,
  Yea, cold and stiff withall.

When as the morning star   25
  Her golden gates had spred,
And that the glittering sun arose
  Forth from fair Thetis' bed ;

Then did my love awake,
  Most like a lilly-flower,   30
And as the lovely queene of heaven,
  So shone shee in her bower.

Attired was shee then,
  Like Flora in her pride,
Like one of bright Diana's nymphs,   35
  So look'd my loving bride.

And as fair Helen's face,
  Did Grecian dames besmirche,
So did my dear exceed in sight,
  All virgins in the church.   40

When we had knitt the knott
  Of holy wedlock-band,
Like alabaster joyn'd to jett,
  So stood we hand in hand ;

Then lo ! a chilling cold   45
  Strucke every vital part,
And griping grief, like pangs of death,
  Seiz'd on my true love's heart.

Down in a swoon she fell,
  As cold as any stone;   50
Like Venus picture lacking life,
  So was my love brought home.

At length her rosye red,
  Throughout her comely face,
As Phœbus beames with watry cloudes   55
  Was cover'd for a space.

When with a grievous groane,
  And voice both hoarse and drye,
Farewell, quoth she, my loving friend,
  For I this daye must dye;   60

The messenger of God,
  With golden trumpe I see,
With manye other angels more,
  Which sound and call for mee.

Instead of musicke sweet,   65
  Go toll my passing-bell;
And with sweet flowers strow my grave,
  That in my chamber smell.

Strip off my bride's arraye,
  My cork shoes from my feet;   70
And, gentle mother, be not coye
  To bring my winding-sheet.

My wedding dinner drest,
  Bestowe upon the poor,
And on the hungry, needy, maimde,   75
  Now craving at the door.

Instead of virgins yong,
  My bride-bed for to see,
Go cause some cunning carpenter,
  To make a chest for mee.   80

My bride laces of silk
  Bestowd, for maidens meet,
May fitly serve, when I am dead,
  To tye my hands and feet.

And thou, my lover true,   85
  My husband and my friend,
Let me intreat thee here to staye,
  Until my life doth end.

Now leave to talk of love,
  And humblye on your knee,   90
Direct your prayers unto God :
  But mourn no more for mee.

In love as we have livde,
  In love let us depart;
And I, in token of my love,   95
  Do kiss thee with my heart.

O staunch those bootless teares,
  Thy weeping tis in vaine ;
I am not lost, for wee in heaven
  Shall one daye meet againe.   100

With that shee turn'd aside,
  As one dispos'd to sleep,
And like a lamb departed life ;
  Whose friends did sorely weep.

Her true love seeing this,   105
  Did fetch a grievous groane,
As tho' his heart would burst in twaine,
  And thus he made his moane.

O darke and dismal daye,
  A daye of grief and care,   110
That hath bereft the sun so bright,
  Whose beams refresht the air.

Now woe unto the world,
　　And all that therein dwell,
O that I were with thee in heaven,　　　　115
　　For here I live in hell.

And now this lover lives
　　A discontented life,
Whose bride was brought unto the grave
　　A maiden and a wife.　　　　120

A garland fresh and faire
　　Of lillies there was made,
In sign of her virginitye,
　　And on her coffin laid.*

Six maidens, all in white,　　　　125
　　Did beare her to the ground :
The bells did ring in solemn sort,
　　And made a dolefull sound.

In earth they laid her then,
　　For hungry wormes a preye ;　　　　130
So shall the fairest face alive
　　At length be brought to claye.

[* " It was an ancient and pleasing custom to place a garland
made of white flowers and white riband upon the coffin of a
maiden ; it was afterwards hung up over her customary seat in
church. Sometimes a pair of white gloves, or paper cut to the
shape of gloves, was hung beneath the garland. Chaplets of the
kind still hang in some of the Derbyshire churches, and at Hather-
sage in that county the custom is still retained."—(*Transactions of
the Essex Archæological Society*, vol. i. 1858, p. 118.) See *Corydon's
Doleful Knell*, vol. ii. book ii. No. 27, p. 275.   Ophelia is "allowed
her virgin crants" (or garland)—*Hamlet*, act v. sc. 1.   See also an
interesting article on *Funeral Garlands* by Llewellyn Jewitt in the
Reliquary, vol. i. (1860), p. 5.]

XIII.

DULCINA.

GIVEN from two ancient copies, one in black-print, in the Pepys Collection: the other in the Editor's folio MS. Each of these contained a stanza not found in the other. What seemed the best readings were selected from both.

This song is quoted as very popular in Walton's *Compleat Angler*, chap. ii. It is more ancient than the ballad of *Robin Good-Fellow* printed below, which yet is supposed to have been written by Ben. Jonson.

[The Milk-woman in Walton's *Angler* says, " What song was it, I pray you? Was it *Come shepherds deck your heads*, or *As at noon Dulcina rested* ? "

In the Registers of the Stationers' Company, under date of May 22, 1615, there is an entry transferring the right of publication from one printer to another of *A Ballett of Dulcina to the tune of Forgoe me nowe, come to me sone*. Mr. Chappell also tells us that *Dulcina* was one of the tunes to the " Psalms and Songs of Sion," turned into the language and set to the tunes of a strange land," 1642.

The editors of the Folio MS., more scrupulous than the bishop, have not printed this song in its proper place, but have turned it into the Supplement of *Loose and Humourous Songs* (p. 32). The third stanza of the MS. beginning

" Words whose hopes might have enjoyned "

is not printed in the present copy. The third stanza here is the fourth of the MS., and the fourth stanza is not in the MS. at all.

Cayley and Ellis attribute this song to Raleigh, but without sufficient authority.]

S at noone Dulcina rested
　　　In her sweete and shady bower ;
　　Came a shepherd, and requested
　　　In her lapp to sleepe an hour.
　　　　But from her looke　　　　5
　　　　A wounde he tooke

Soe deepe, that for a further boone
  The nymph he prayes.
  Wherto shee sayes,
Forgoe me now, come to me soone.   10

But in vayne shee did conjure him
  To depart her presence soe ;
Having a thousand tongues to allure him,
  And but one to bid him goe :
    Where lipps invite,   15
    And eyes delight,
  And cheekes, as fresh as rose in june,
    Persuade delay ;
    What boots, she say,
Forgoe me now, come to me soone ?   20

He demands what time for pleasure
  Can there be more fit than now :
She sayes, night gives love that leysure,
  Which the day can not allow.
    He sayes, the sight   25
    ‘ Improves delight.
  ‘ Which she denies : Nights mirkie noone
    In Venus’ playes
    Makes bold, shee sayes ;
Forgoe me now, come to mee soone.   30

But what promise or profession
  From his hands could purchase scope ?
Who would sell the sweet possession
  Of suche beautye for a hope ?
    Or for the sight   35
    Of lingering night
  Foregoe the present joyes of noone ?
    Though ne’er soe faire
    Her speeches were,
Forgoe me now, come to me soone.   40

How, at last, agreed these lovers ?
  Shee was fayre, and he was young :
The tongue may tell what th'eye discovers ;
  Joyes unseene are never sung.
      Did shee consent,   45
      Or he relent ;
Accepts he night, or grants shee noone ;
      Left he her a mayd,
      Or not ; she sayd
Forgoe me now, come to me soone.   50

XIV.

THE LADY ISABELLA'S TRAGEDY.

HIS ballad is given from an old black-letter copy in the Pepys Collection, collated with another in the British Museum, H. 263, folio. It is there intitled, "*The Lady Isabella's Tragedy, or the Step-Mother's Cruelty:* being a relation of a lamentable and cruel murther, committed on the body of the lady Isabella, the only daughter of a noble duke, &c. To the tune of, *The Lady's Fall.*" To some copies are annexed eight more modern stanzas, intitled, *The Dutchess's and Cook's Lamentation.*

HERE was a lord of worthy fame,
    And a hunting he would ride,
    Attended by a noble traine
      Of gentrye by his side.

And while he did in chase remaine,   5
  To see both sport and playe ;
His ladye went, as she did feigne,
  Unto the church to praye.

This lord he had a daughter deare,
　　Whose beauty shone so bright,　　　　10
She was belov'd, both far and neare,
　　Of many a lord and knight.

Fair Isabella was she call'd,
　　A creature faire was shee;
She was her father's only joye;　　　　15
　　As you shall after see.

Therefore her cruel step-mothèr
　　Did envye her so much;
That daye by daye she sought her life,
　　Her malice it was such.　　　　20

She bargain'd with the master-cook,
　　To take her life awaye:
And taking of her daughters book,
　　She thus to her did saye.

Go home, sweet daughter, I thee praye,　25
　　Go hasten presentlie;
And tell unto the master-cook
　　These wordes that I tell thee.

And bid him dresse to dinner streight
　　That faire and milk-white doe,　　　30
That in the parke doth shine so bright,
　　There's none so faire to showe.

This ladye fearing of no harme,
　　Obey'd her mothers will;
And presentlye she hasted home,　　　35
　　Her pleasure to fulfill.

She streight into the kitchen went,
　　Her message for to tell;
And there she spied the master-cook,
　　Who did with malice swell.　　　　40

Nowe, master-cook, it must be soe,
    Do that which I thee tell :
You needes must dresse the milk-white doe,
    Which you do knowe full well.

Then streight his cruell bloodye hands,   45
    He on the ladye layd ;
Who quivering and shaking stands,
    While thus to her he sayd :

Thou art the doe, that I must dresse ;
    See here, behold my knife ;   50
For it is pointed presently
    To rid thee of thy life.

O then, cried out the scullion-boye,
    As loud as loud might bee ;
O save her life, good master-cook,   55
    And make your pyes of mee !

For pityes sake do not destroye
    My ladye with your knife ;
You know shee is her father's joye,
    For Christes sake save her life.   60

I will not save her life, he sayd,
    Nor make my pyes of thee ;
Yet if thou dost this deed bewraye,
    Thy butcher I will bee.

Now when this lord he did come home   65
    For to sit downe and eat ;
He called for his daughter deare,
    To come and carve his meat.

Now sit you downe, his ladye sayd,
    O sit you downe to meat :   70
Into some nunnery she is gone ;
    Your daughter deare forget.

Then solemnlye he made a vowe,
  Before the companìe :
That he would neither eat nor drinke,   75
  Until he did her see.

O then bespake the scullion-boye,
  With a loud voice so hye :
If now you will your daughter see,
  My lord, cut up that pye :   80

Wherein her fleshe is minced small,
  And parched with the fire ;
All caused by her step-mothèr,
  Who did her death desire.

And cursed bee the master-cook,   85
  O cursed may he bee !
I proffered him my own hearts blood,
  From death to set her free.

Then all in blacke this lord did mourne ;
  And for his daughters sake,   90
He judged her cruell step-mothèr
  To be burnt at a stake.

Likewise he judg'd the master-cook
  In boiling lead to stand ;
And made the simple scullion-boye   95
  The heire of all his land.

XV.

A HUE AND CRY AFTER CUPID.

HIS song is a kind of translation of a pretty poem of Tasso's, called *Amore fuggitivo,* generally printed with his *Aminta,* and originally imitated from the first Idyllium of Moschus.

It is extracted from Ben Jonson's Masque at the marriage of lord viscount Hadington, on Shrove-Tuesday, 1608. One stanza full of dry mythology is here omitted, as it had been dropped in a copy of this song printed in a small volume called *Le Prince d'Amour.* Lond. 1660, 8vo.

[The stanza of the first Grace which Percy left out is as follows:—

" At his sight the sun hath turn'd,
Neptune in the waters burn'd;
Hell hath felt a greater heat;
Jove himself forsook his seat:
From the centre to the sky
Are his trophies reared high."]

[1 *Grace.*]

EAUTIES have yee seen a toy,
Called Love, a little boy,
Almost naked, wanton, blinde;
Cruel now; and then as kinde?
If he be amongst yee, say;   5
He is Venus' run away.

[2 *Grace.*] Shee, that will but now discover
Where the winged wag doth hover,
Shall to-night receive a kisse,
How and where herselfe would wish: 10
But who brings him to his mother
Shall have that kisse, and another.

[3 *Grace.*] Markes he hath about him plentie;
You may know him among twentie:
All his body is a fire,   15
And his breath a flame entire:
Which, being shot, like lightning, in,
Wounds the heart, but not the skin.

               *   *   *   *   *

[2 *Grace.*] Wings he hath, which though yee clip,
He will leape from lip to lip,   20
Over liver, lights, and heart;
Yet not stay in any part.
And, if chance his arrow misses,
He will shoot himselfe in kisses.

[3 *Grace.*] He doth beare a golden bow,   25
And a quiver hanging low,
Full of arrowes, which outbrave
Dian's shafts; where, if he have
Any head more sharpe than other,
With that first he strikes his mother.   30

[1 *Grace.*] Still the fairest are his fuell,
When his daies are to be cruell;
Lovers hearts are all his food,
And his baths their warmest bloud:
Nought but wounds his hand doth season,   35
And he hates none like to Reason.

[2 *Grace.*] Trust him not: his words, though sweet,
Seldome with his heart doe meet:
All his practice is deceit;
Everie gift is but a bait;   40
Not a kisse but poyson beares;
And most treason's in his teares.

[3 *Grace.*] Idle minutes are his raigne;
Then the straggler makes his gaine,

By presenting maids with toyes   45
And would have yee thinke hem joyes ;
'Tis the ambition of the elfe
To have all childish as himselfe.

[1 *Grace.*] If by these yee please to know him,
Beauties, be not nice, but show him.   50
[2 *Grace.*] Though ye had a will to hide him,
Now, we hope, yee'le not abide him
[3 *Grace.*] Since yee heare this falser's play,
And that he is Venus' run-away.

XVI.

THE KING OF FRANCE'S DAUGHTER.

HE story of this ballad seems to be taken from an incident in the domestic history of Charles the Bald, king
of France. His daughter Judith was betrothed to
Ethelwulph king of England : but before the marriage
was consummated, Ethelwulph died, and she returned to France :
whence she was carried off by Baldwyn, Forester of Flanders ;
who, after many crosses and difficulties, at length obtained the
king's consent to their marriage, and was made Earl of Flanders.
This happened about A.D. 863.—See Rapin, Henault, and the
French historians.

The following copy is given from the Editor's ancient folio MS.
collated with another in black-letter in the Pepys Collection, intitled, *An excellent Ballad of a prince of England's courtship to the
king of France's daughter, &c.* To the tune of *Crimson Velvet.*

Many breaches having been made in this old song by the hand
of time, principally (as might be expected) in the quick returns
of the rhime ; an attempt is here made to repair them.

[This ballad was written by Thomas Deloney, who included it
in his *Garland of Goodwill* (Percy Society, vol. xxx. p. 52). It is,
as Percy points out, founded on history, but Deloney paid little
attention to facts. All the first part of the poem, which tells of the
miserable end of the English prince of suitable age to the young

French princess, is fiction.   Judith was Ethelwulf's wife for about
two years, and on the death of her husband she married his son
Ethelbert.   The only historical fact that is followed in the ballad
is the marriage of Judith with Baldwin, Great Forester of France,
from which union descended Matilda, the wife of William the Conqueror.

The copy in the Folio MS. (ed. Hales and Furnivall, vol. iii.
p. 441) is entitled " In the Dayes of Olde."   Percy altered it con-
siderably, sometimes following the printed copy and sometimes the
MS.

Mr. Hales suggests that the name of the tune is derived from
the dress of the princess, described in vv. 185-6,—

> " Their mothers riche array
> Was of crimson velvet,"

and Mr. Chappell agrees with him.]

N the dayes of old,
  When faire France did flourish,
 Storyes plaine have told,
  Lovers felt annoye.
The queene a daughter bare,   5
 Whom beautye's queene did nourish :
She was lovelye faire
 She was her father's joye.
A prince of England came,
Whose deeds did merit fame,   10
 But he was exil'd, and outcast :
Love his soul did fire,
Shee granted his desire,
 Their hearts in one were linked fast.
Which when her father proved,   15
Sorelye he was moved,
 And tormented in his minde.
He sought for to prevent them ;
And, to discontent them,
 Fortune cross'd these lovers kinde. 20

When these princes twaine
  Were thus barr'd of pleasure,
Through the kinges disdaine,
  Which their joyes withstoode:
The lady soone prepar'd   25
  Her jewells and her treasure;
Having no regard
  For state and royall bloode;
In homelye poore array
She went from court away,   30
  To meet her joye and hearts delight;
Who in a forest great
Had taken up his seat,
  To wayt her coming in the night.
But, lo! what sudden danger   35
To this princely stranger
  Chanced, as he sate alone!
By outlawes he was robbed,
And with ponyards stabbed,
  Uttering many a dying grone.   40

The princesse, arm'd by love,
  And by chaste desire,
All the night did rove
  Without dread at all:
Still unknowne she past   45
  In her strange attire;
Coming at the last
  Within echoes call,—
You faire woods, quoth shee,
Honoured may you bee,   50
  Harbouring my heart's delight;
Which encompass here
My joye and only deare,
  My trustye friend, and comelye knight.
Sweete, I come unto thee,   55
Sweete, I come to woo thee;

That thou mayst not angry bee
For my long delaying;
For thy curteous staying
   Soone amendes Ile make to thee.   60

Passing thus alone
   Through the silent forest,
Many a grievous grone
   Sounded in her eares:
She heard one complayne   65
   And lament the sorest,
Seeming all in payne,
   Shedding deadly teares.
Farewell, my deare, quoth hee,
Whom I must never see;   70
   For why my life is att an end,
Through villaines crueltye:
For thy sweet sake I dye,
   To show I am a faithfull friend.
Here I lye a bleeding,   75
While my thoughts are feeding
   On the rarest beautye found.
O hard happ, that may be!
Little knows my ladye
   My heartes blood lyes on the ground.   80

With that a grone he sends
   Which did burst in sunder
All the tender bands
   Of his gentle heart.
She, who knewe his voice,   85
   At his wordes did wonder;
All her former joyes
   Did to griefe convert.
Strait she ran to see,
Who this man shold bee,   90
   That soe like her love did seeme:

Her lovely lord she found
Lye slaine upon the ground,
　　Smear'd with gore a ghastlye streame.
Which his lady spying,　　　　　　　95
Shrieking, fainting, crying,
　　Her sorrows could not uttered bee :
Fate, she cryed, too cruell :
For thee—my dearest jewell,
　　Would God ! that I had dyed for thee.　　100

His pale lippes, alas !
　　Twentye times she kissed,
And his face did wash
　　With her trickling teares :
Every gaping wound　　　　　　　105
　　Tenderlye she pressed,
And did wipe it round
　　With her golden haires.
Speake, faire love, quoth shee,
Speake, fair prince, to mee,　　　　　110
　　One sweete word of comfort give :
Lift up thy deare eyes,
Listen to my cryes,
　　Thinke in what sad griefe I live.
All in vain she sued,　　　　　　　115
All in vain she wooed,
　　The prince's life was fled and gone.
There stood she still mourning,
Till the suns retourning,
　　And bright day was coming on.　　　120

In this great distresse
　　Weeping, wayling ever,
Oft shee cryed, alas !
　　What will become of mee ?
To my fathers court　　　　　　　125
　　I returne will never :

But in lowlye sort
  I will a servant bee.
While thus she made her mone,
Weeping all alone,   130
  In this deepe and deadlye feare :
A for'ster all in greene,
Most comelye to be seene,
  Ranging the woods did find her there.
Moved with her sorrowe,   135
Maid, quoth hee, good morrowe,
  What hard happ has brought thee here ?
Harder happ did never
Two kinde hearts dissever :
  Here lyes slaine my brother deare.   140

Where may I remaine,
  Gentle for'ster, shew me,
'Till I can obtaine
  A service in my neede ?
Paines I will not spare :   145
  This kinde favour doe me,
It will ease my care ;
  Heaven shall be thy meede.
The for'ster all amazed,
On her beautye gazed,   150
  Till his heart was set on fire.
If, faire maid, quoth hee,
You will goe with mee,
  You shall have your hearts desire.
He brought her to his mother,   155
And above all other
  He sett forth this maidens praise.
Long was his heart inflamed,
At length her love he gained,
  And fortune crown'd his future dayes. 160

Thus unknowne he wedde
  With a kings faire daughter ;

Children seven they had,
   Ere she told her birth.
Which when once he knew,   165
   Humblye he besought her,
He to the world might shew
   Her rank and princelye worth.
He cloath'd his children then,
(Not like other men)   170
   In partye-colours strange to see;
The right side cloth of gold,
The left side to behold,
   Of woollen cloth still framed hee*.
Men thereat did wonder;   175
Golden fame did thunder
   This strange deede in every place:
The king of France came thither,
It being pleasant weather,
   In those woods the hart to chase.   180

The children then they bring,
   So their mother will'd it,
Where the royall king
   Must of force come bye:
Their mothers riche array,   185
   Was of crimson velvet:
Their fathers all of gray,
   Seemelye to the eye.

---

* This will remind the reader of the livery and device of Charles Brandon, a private gentleman, who married the Queen Dowager of France, sister of Henry VIII. At a tournament which he held at his wedding, the trappings of his horse were half Cloth of gold, and half Frieze, with the following Motto :—

      "Cloth of Gold, do not despise,
      Tho' thou art matcht with Cloth of Frize;
      Cloth of Frize, be not too bold,
      Tho' thou art matcht with Cloth of Gold."

See Sir W. Temple's *Misc.* vol. iii. p. 356.

Then this famous king,
Noting every thing,   190
   Askt how he durst be so bold
To let his wife soe weare,
And decke his children there
   In costly robes of pearl and gold.
The forrester replying,   195
And the cause descrying*,
   To the king these words did say,
Well may they, by their mother,
Weare rich clothes with other,
   Being by birth a princesse gay.   200

The king aroused thus,
   More heedfullye beheld them,
Till a crimson blush
   His remembrance crost.
The more I fix my mind   205
   On thy wife and children,
The more methinks I find
   The daughter which I lost.
Falling on her knee,
I am that child, quoth shee;   210
   Pardon mee, my soveraine liege.
The king perceiving this,
His daughter deare did kiss,
   While joyfull teares did stopp his speeche.
With his traine he tourned,   215
And with them sojourned.
   Strait he dubb'd her husband knight;
Then made him erle of Flanders,
And chiefe of his commanders:
   Thus were their sorrowes put to flight. 220

                                                   **

---

* *i.e.* describing.

XVII.

THE SWEET NEGLECT.

HIS little madrigal (extracted from Ben. Jonson's *Silent Woman*, act i. sc. 1, first acted in 1609) is in imitation of a Latin Poem printed at the end of the Variorum Edit. of Petronius, beginning, *Semper munditias, semper Basilissa, decoras,* &c.   See Whalley's *Ben Jonson,* vol. ii. p. 420.

TILL to be neat, still to be drest,
   As you were going to a feast:
   Still to be pou'dred, still perfum'd:
   Lady, it is to be presum'd,
Though art's hid causes are not found,   5
All is not sweet, all is not sound.

Give me a looke, give me a face,
That makes simplicitie a grace;
Robes loosely flowing, haire as free:
Such sweet neglect more taketh me,   10
Than all th' adulteries of art,
That strike mine eyes, but not my heart.

XVIII.

THE CHILDREN IN THE WOOD.

HE subject of this very popular ballad (which has been set in so favourable a light by the *Spectator*, No. 85.) seems to be taken from an old play, intitled, *Two lamentable Tragedies; The one of the murder of Maister Beech, a chandler in Thames streete, &c. The other of a young child murthered in a wood by two ruffins, with the consent of his unkle.* By Rob. Yarrington, 1601, 4to. Our ballad-maker has strictly followed the play in the description of the father and mother's dying charge: in the uncle's promise to take care of their issue: his hiring two ruffians to destroy his ward, under pretence of sending him to school : their chusing a wood to perpetrate the murder in : one of the ruffians relenting, and a battle ensuing, &c. In other respects he has departed from the play. In the latter the scene is laid in Padua: there is but one child: which is murdered by a sudden stab of the unrelenting ruffian: he is slain himself by his less bloody companion ; but ere he dies gives the other a mortal wound : the latter living just long enough to impeach the uncle; who, in consequence of this im peachment, is arraigned and executed by the hand of justice, &c. Whoever compares the play with the ballad, will have no doubt but the former is the original: the language is far more obsolete, and such a vein of simplicity runs through the whole performance, that, had the ballad been written first, there is no doubt but every circumstance of it would have been received into the drama: whereas this was probably built on some Italian novel.

Printed from two ancient copies, one of them in black-letter in the Pepys Collection. Its title at large is, *The Children in the Wood; or, The Norfolk Gentleman's Last Will and Testament : To the tune of Rogero, &c.*

[Ritson thought he had refuted Percy's statement that the play was older than the ballad by pointing out that the latter was entered in the Stationers' books in 1595, but I find in Baker's *Biographia Dramatica* an assertion that Yarrington's play was not printed "till many years after it was written." The following is the form of the entry at Stationers' Hall, "15 Oct. 1595. Thomas Millington entred for his copie under th[e h]andes of bothe the Wardens a ballad intituled *The Norfolk Gent, his Will and Testa-ment and howe he commytted the keepinge of his children to his owne brother whoe delte most wickedly with them and howe God plagued him for it.*" Sharon Turner and Miss Halsted favoured the rather untenable opinion that the wicked uncle was intended to represent Richard III., and therefore that the date of the ballad was much earlier than that usually claimed for it. Turner writes in his *His-tory of England*, "I have sometimes fancied that the popular ballad may have been written at this time on Richard and his nephews before it was quite safe to stigmatize him more openly."

Wailing, or Wayland Wood, a large cover near Walton in Nor-folk is the place which tradition assigns to the tragedy, but the people of Wood Dalling also claim the honour for their village.

Addison speaks of the ballad as " one of the darling songs of the common people, [which] has been the delight of most English-

men in some part of their age," and points out that the circumstance

> . . . . robin-red-breast piously
> Did cover them with leaves,

has a parallel in Horace, who tells us that when he was a child,
fallen asleep in a desert wood, the turtle doves took pity on him
and covered him with leaves.

The popular belief that the robin covers dead bodies with leaves
(probably founded on the habits of the bird) is of considerable
antiquity. The passage in Cymbeline (act iv. sc. 2) naturally
occurs as the chief illustration :—

> . . . . "the ruddock would,
> With charitable bill . . . . .
> . . . . . bring thee all this,
> Yea and furr'd moss besides, when flowers are none,
> To winter-ground thy corse."

In Webster's *White Devil*, act v., we read :—

> "Call for the robin red breast and the wren
> Since o'er shady groves they hover
> And with leaves and flowers do cover
> The friendless bodies of unburied men."

The critics suppose Webster to have imitated Shakespere here,
but there is no ground for any such supposition. The industry of
Reed, Steevens, and Douce has supplied us with several passages
from old literature in which this characteristic of the robin is referred to.

In "*Cornucopiæ, or, divers Secrets;* wherein is contained the rare
secrets of man, beasts, fowles, fishes, trees, plants, stones, and
such like, most pleasant and profitable, and not before committed
to bee printed in English. Newlie drawen out of divers Latine
Authors into English by Thomas Johnson," 4to. London, 1596,
occurs the following passage :—"The robin red-breast if he find a
man or woman dead will cover all his face with mosse, and some
thinke that if the body should remaine unburied that hee woulde
cover the whole body also."

This little secret of Johnson is copied by Thomas Lupton into
his *A Thousand Notable Things of sundrie sorts newly corrected*,
1601, where it appears as No. 37 of book i.

Michael Drayton has the following lines in his poem, *The Owl:*

> "Cov'ring with moss the dead's unclosed eye
> The little red-breast teacheth charitie."

In Dekker's *Villanies discovered by lanthorn and candlelight*, 1616, we read, "They that cheere up a prisoner but with their sight are Robin red-breasts, that bring strawes in their bils to cover a dead man in extremitie." This is sufficient evidence that the belief was wide-spread.]

NOW ponder well, you parents deare,
  These wordes, which I shall write;
A doleful story you shall heare,
  In time brought forth to light.
A gentleman of good account   5
  In Norfolke dwelt of late,
Who did in honour far surmount
  Most men of his estate.

Sore sicke he was, and like to dye,
  No helpe his life could save;   10
His wife by him as sicke did lye,
  And both possest one grave.
No love between these two was lost,
  Each was to other kinde,
In love they liv'd, in love they dyed,   15
  And left two babes behinde :

The one a fine and pretty boy,
  Not passing three yeares olde;
The other a girl more young than he,
  And fram'd in beautyes molde.   20
The father left his little son,
  As plainlye doth appeare,
When he to perfect age should come,
  Three hundred poundes a yeare.

And to his little daughter Jane   25
  Five hundred poundes in gold,
To be paid down on marriage-day,
  Which might not be controll'd :

But if the children chance to dye,
 Ere they to age should come,   30
Their uncle should possesse their wealth ;
 For so the wille did run.

Now, brother, said the dying man,
 Look to my children deare ;
Be good unto my boy and girl,   35
 No friendes else have they here :
To God and you I recommend
 My children deare this daye ;
But little while be sure we have
 Within this world to staye.   40

You must be father and mother both,
 And uncle all in one ;
God knowes what will become of them,
 When I am dead and gone.
With that bespake their mother deare, 45
 O brother kinde, quoth shee,
You are the man must bring our babes
 To wealth or miserie :

And if you keep them carefully,
 Then God will you reward ;   50
But if you otherwise should deal,
 God will your deedes regard.
With lippes as cold as any stone,
 They kist their children small :
God bless you both, my children deare ; 55
 With that the teares did fall.

These speeches then their brother spake
 To this sicke couple there,
The keeping of your little ones
 Sweet sister, do not feare ;   60
God never prosper me nor mine,
 Nor aught else that I have,
If I do wrong your children deare,
 When you are layd in grave.

The parents being dead and gone,   65
   The children home he takes,
And bringes them straite unto his house,
   Where much of them he makes.
He had not kept these pretty babes
   A twelvemonth and a daye,   70
But, for their wealth, he did devise
   To make them both awaye.

He bargain'd with two ruffians strong,
   Which were of furious mood,
That they should take these children young,   75
   And slaye them in a wood.
He told his wife an artful tale,
   He would the children send
To be brought up in faire Londòn,
   With one that was his friend.   80

Away then went those pretty babes,
   Rejoycing at that tide,
Rejoycing with a merry minde,
   They should on cock-horse ride.
They prate and prattle pleasantly,   85
   As they rode on the waye,
To those that should their butchers be,
   And work their lives decaye :

So that the pretty speeche they had,
   Made Murder's heart relent ;   90
And they that undertooke the deed,
   Full sore did now repent.
Yet one of them more hard of heart,
   Did vowe to do his charge,
Because the wretch, that hired him,   95
   Had paid him very large.

The other won't agree thereto,
   So here they fall to strife ;
With one another they did fight,
   About the childrens life :   100

And he that was of mildest mood,
  Did slaye the other there,
Within an unfrequented wood;
  The babes did quake for feare!

He took the children by the hand,   105
  Teares standing in their eye,
And bad them straitwaye follow him,
  And look they did not crye:
And two long miles he ledd them on,
  While they for food complaine: 110
Staye here, quoth he, I'll bring you bread,
  When I come back againe.

These pretty babes, with hand in hand,
  Went wandering up and downe;
But never more could see the man   115
  Approaching from the town:
Their prettye lippes with black-berries,
  Were all besmear'd and dyed,
And when they sawe the darksome night,
  They sat them downe and cryed.   120

Thus wandered these poor innocents,
  Till deathe did end their grief,
In one anothers armes they dyed,
  As wanting due relief:
No burial 'this' pretty 'pair'   125
  Of any man receives,
Till Robin-red-breast piously
  Did cover them with leaves.

And now the heavy wrathe of God
  Upon their uncle fell;   130
Yea, fearfull fiends did haunt his house,
  His conscience felt an hell:

Ver. 125. these . . . babes. *P.P.*

His barnes were fir'd, his goodes consum'd,
  His landes were barren made,
His cattle dyed within the field,   135
  And nothing with him stayd.

And in a voyage to Portugal*
  Two of his sonnes did dye;
And to conclude, himselfe was brought
  To want and miserye: 140
He pawn'd and mortgaged all his land
  Ere seven yeares came about.
And now at length this wicked act
  Did by this meanes come out:

The fellowe, that did take in hand   145
  These children for to kill,
Was for a robbery judg'd to dye,
  Such was God's blessed will:
Who did confess the very truth,
  As here hath been display'd: 150
Their uncle having dyed in gaol,
  Where he for debt was layd.

You that executors be made,
  And overseers eke
Of children that be fatherless,   155
  And infants mild and meek;
Take you example by this thing,
  And yield to each his right,
Lest God with such like miserye
  Your wicked minds requite.   160

[* Ritson has the following note (*Ancient Songs*, 1829, vol. ii. p. 155): "*the* voyage, A.D. 1588. See the Catalogue of the Harl. MSS. No. 167 (15). Dr. Percy, not knowing that the text alludes to a particular event, has altered it to *a* voyage."]

XIX.

A LOVER OF LATE.

RINTED, with a few slight corrections, from the Editor's folio MS.

[This song is printed, Hales and Furnivall's edition
of the MS. vol. iii. p. 389.]

 LOVER of late was I,
    For Cupid would have it soe,
The boy that hath never an eye,
    As every man doth know :
I sighed and sobbed, and cryed, alas!   5
For her that laught, and called me ass.

Then knew not I what to doe,
    When I saw itt was in vaine
A lady soe coy to wooe,
    Who gave me the asse soe plaine :   10
Yet would I her asse freelye bee,
Soe shee would helpe, and beare with mee.

An' I were as faire as shee,
    Or shee were as kind as I,
What payre cold have made, as wee,   15
    Soe prettye a sympathye :
I was as kind as she was faire,
But for all this wee cold not paire.

[Ver. 8. when I see itt was vaine. V. 10. and gave.] V. 13.
faine, MS. [V. 14. and shee, MS.]

Paire with her that will for mee,
    With her I will never paire;   20
That cunningly can be coy,
    For being a little faire.
The asse Ile leave to her disdaine;
And now I am myselfe againe.

XX.

THE KING AND MILLER OF

MANSFIELD.

T has been a favourite subject with our English ballad-makers to represent our kings conversing, either by accident or design, with the meanest of their subjects. Of the former kind, besides this song of the King and the Miller; we have K. Henry and the Soldier; K. James I. and the Tinker; K. William III. and the Forrester &c. Of the latter sort, are K. Alfred and the Shepherd; K. Edward IV. and the Tanner;* K. Henry VIII. and the Cobler, &c.—A few of the best of these are admitted into this collection. Both the author of the following ballad, and others who have written on the same plan, seem to have copied a very ancient poem, intitled *John the Reeve*, which is built on an adventure of the same kind, that happened between K. Edward Longshanks, and one of his Reeves or Bailiffs. This is a piece of great antiquity, being written before the time of Edward IV. and for its genuine humour, diverting incidents, and faithful picture of rustic manners, is infinitely superior to all that have been since written in imitation of it. The Editor has a copy in his ancient folio MS. but its length rendered it improper for this volume, it consisting of more than 900 lines. It contains also some corruptions, and the Editor chuses to defer its publication in hopes that some time or other he shall be able to remove them.

The following is printed, with corrections, from the editor's folio MS. collated with an old black-letter copy in the Pepys Col-

[* See vol. ii. book i. No. 15.]

lection, intitled *A pleasant ballad of K. Henry II. and the Miller of Mansfield, &c.*

[This ballad of *Henry II. and the Miller of Mansfield* cannot be traced farther back than the end of Elizabeth's reign or the beginning of James's. One of the three copies in the Roxburghe Collection is dated by Mr. Chappell between 1621 and 1655, and the copy in the Folio MS. (ed. Hales and Furnivall, vol. ii. p. 147) was written about the same period. (See Roxburghe *Ballads*, ed. Chappell, vol. i. p. 538.)

As there are earlier copies than the one in the Folio MS. it has not been thought necessary to add Collations.

John the Reeve, referred to above, is one of the earliest and most interesting of this large class of tales. It was printed for the first time in Hales and Furnivall's edition of the MS. (vol. ii. p. 550) with a valuable introduction.

This spirited poem was probably written originally in the middle of the fifteenth century. "It professes to describe an incident that took place in the days of King Edward. It adds :

> Of that name were Kings *three*
> But Edward with the long shanks was he,
> A lord of great renown.

The poem then was written after the death of Edward III.; that is, after 1377, and before the accession of Edward IV., that is before 1461."]

Part the First.

ENRY, our royall king, would ride a hunting
To the greene forest so pleasant and faire ;
To see the harts skipping, and dainty does
    tripping :
Unto merry Sherwood his nobles repair :
Hawke and hound were unbound, all things prepar'd 5
For the game, in the same, with good regard.

All a long summers day rode the king pleasantlye,
  With all his princes and nobles eche one ;

Chasing the hart and hind, and the bucke gallantlye,
   Till the dark evening forc'd all to turne home.   10
Then at last, riding fast, he had lost quite
All his lords in the wood, late in the night.

Wandering thus wearilye, all alone, up and downe,
   With a rude miller he mett at the last:
Asking the ready way unto faire Nottingham;   15
   Sir, quoth the miller, I meane not to jest,
Yet I thinke, what I thinke, sooth for to say,
You doe not lightlye ride out of your way.

Why, what dost thou think of me, quoth our king
      merrily,
   Passing thy judgment upon me so briefe?   20
Good faith, sayd the miller, I meane not to flatter thee;
   I guess thee to be but some gentleman thiefe;
Stand thee backe, in the darke; light not adowne,
Lest that I presentlye cracke thy knaves crowne.

Thou dost abuse me much, quoth the king, saying
      thus;   25
   I am a gentleman; lodging I lacke.
Thou hast not, quoth th' miller, one groat in thy
      purse;
   All thy inheritance hanges on thy backe.
*I have gold to discharge all that I call;
If it be forty pence, I will pay all.   30

If thou beest a true man, then quoth the miller,
   I sweare by my toll-dish, I'll lodge thee all night.
Here's my hand, quoth the king, that was I ever.
   Nay, soft, quoth the miller, thou may'st be a sprite.
Better I'll know thee, ere hands we will shake;   35
With none but honest men hands will I take.

---

* The king says this.

Thus they went all along unto the miller's house ;
   Where they were seething of puddings and souse :[1]
The miller first enter'd in, after him went the king ;
   Never came hee in soe smoakye a house.   40
Now, quoth hee, let me see here what you are.
Quoth our king, looke your fill, and doe not spare.

I like well thy countenance, thou hast an honest face
   With my son Richard this night thou shalt lye.
Quoth his wife, by my troth, it is a handsome youth, 45
   Yet it's best, husband, to deal warilye.
Art thou no run away, prythee, youth, tell ?
Shew me thy passport, and all shal be well.

Then our king presentlye, making lowe courtesye,
   With his hatt in his hand, thus he did say ;   50
I have no passport, nor never was servitor,
   But a poor courtyer, rode out of my way :
And for your kindness here offered to mee,
I will requite you in everye degree.

Then to the miller his wife whisper'd secretlye,   55
   Saying, It seemeth, this youth's of good kin,
Both by his apparel, and eke by his manners ;
   To turne him out, certainlye, were a great sin.
Yea, quoth hee, you may see, he hath some grace
When he doth speake to his betters in place.   60

Well, quo' the millers wife, young man, ye're wel-
   come here ;
   And, though I say it, well lodged shall be :
Fresh straw will I have, laid on thy bed so brave,
   And good brown hempen sheets likewise, quoth
      shee.
Aye, quoth the good man ; and when that is done, 65
Thou shalt lye with no worse, than our own sonne.

[1 The head, feet, and ears of swine boiled and pickled for
eating.—*Halliwell's Dictionary.*]

Nay, first, quoth Richard, good-fellowe, tell me true,
    Host thou noe creepers within thy gay hose?
Or art thou not troubled with the scabbado?
    I pray, quoth the king, what creatures are those? 70
Art thou not lowsy, nor scabby? quoth he:
    If thou beest, surely thou lyest not with mee.

This caus'd the king, suddenlye, to laugh most
      heartilye,
    Till the teares trickled fast downe from his eyes.
Then to their supper were they set orderlye,   75
    With hot bag-puddings, and good apple-pyes;
Nappy ale, good and stale, in a browne bowle,
Which did about the board merrilye trowle.

Here, quoth the miller, good fellowe, I drinke to thee,
    And to all 'cuckholds, wherever they bee.'   80
I pledge thee, quotth our king, and thanke thee
      heartilye
    For my good welcome in everye degree:
And here, in like manner, I drinke to thy sonne.
Do then, quoth Richard, and quicke let it come.

Wife, quoth the miller, fetch me forth lightfoote,   85
    And of his sweetnesse a little we'll taste.
A fair ven'son pastye brought she out presentlye.
    Eate, quoth the miller, but, sir, make no waste.
Here's dainty lightfoote! In faith, sayd the king,
I never before eat so daintye a thing.   90

I wis, quoth Richard, no daintye at all it is,
    For we doe eate of it everye day.
In what place, sayd our king, may be bought like to
      this?
    We never pay pennye for itt, by my fay:
From merry Sherwood we fetch it home here;   95
Now and then we make bold with our kings deer.

Ver. 80. courtnalls, that courteous be. *MS. and P.*

Then I thinke, sayd our king, that it is venison.
　Eche foole, quoth Richard, full well may know that:
Never are wee without two or three in the roof,
　Very well fleshed, and excellent fat:　　　100
But, prythee, say nothing wherever thou goe;
We would not, for two pence, the king should it knowe.

Doubt not, then sayd the king, my promist secresye;
　The king shall never know more on't for mee.
A cupp of lambs-wool[1] they dranke unto him then,　105
　And to their bedds they past presentlie.
The nobles, next morning, went all up and down,
For to seeke out the king in everye towne.

At last, at the miller's 'cott,' soone they espy'd him
　　out,
　As he was mounting upon his faire steede;　　110
To whom they came presently, falling down on their
　　knee;
　Which made the millers heart wofully bleede;
Shaking and quaking, before him he stood,
Thinking he should have been hang'd, by the rood.

The king perceiving him fearfully trembling,　　115
　Drew forth his sword, but nothing he sed:
The miller downe did fall, crying before them all,
　Doubting the king would have cut off his head.
But he his kind courtesye for to requite,
Gave him great living, and dubb'd him a knight.　120

[1 A favourite liquor among the common people, composed of ale and roasted apples, the pulp of the apple worked up with the ale till the mixture formed a smooth beverage. *Nares' Glossary.*]

PART THE SECONDE.

WHEN as our royall king came home from
    Nottingham,
    And with his nobles at Westminster lay ;
    Recounting the sports and pastimes they
      had taken,
In this late progress along on the way ;
Of them all, great and small, he did protest,   5
The miller of Mansfield's sport liked him best.

And now, my lords, quoth the king, I am determined
    Against St. Georges next sumptuous feast,
That this old miller, our new confirm'd knight,
    With his son Richard, shall here be my guest : 10
For, in this merryment, 'tis my desire
To talke with the jolly knight, and the young squire.

When as the noble lords saw the kinges pleasantness,
    They were right joyfull and glad in their hearts :
A pursuivant there was sent straighte on the busi-
      ness,   15
    The which had often-times been in those parts.
When he came to the place, where they did dwell,
His message orderlye then 'gan he tell.

God save your worshippe, then said the messenger,
    And grant your ladye her own hearts desire ; 20
And to your sonne Richard good fortune and happi-
      ness ;
    That sweet, gentle, and gallant young squire.
Our king greets you well, and thus he doth say,
You must come to the court on St. George's day ;

Therfore, in any case, faile not to be in place. 25
    I wis, quoth the miller, this is an odd jest :

What should we doe there ? faith, I am halfe afraid.
  I doubt, quoth Richard, to be hang'd at the least.
Nay, quoth the messenger, you doe mistake ;
Our king he provides a great feast for your sake.   30

Then sayd the miller, By my troth, messenger,
  Thou hast contented my worshippe full well.
Hold here are three farthings, to quite thy gentlenesse,
  For these happy tydings, which thou dost tell.
Let me see, hear thou mee ; tell to our king,   35
We'll wayt on his mastershipp in everye thing.

The pursuivant smiled at their simplicitye,
  And, making many leggs, tooke their reward ;
And his leave taking with great humilitye
  To the kings court againe he repair'd ;   40
Shewing unto his grace, merry and free,
The knightes most liberall gift and bountie.

When he was gone away, thus gan the miller say,
  Here come expences and charges indeed ;
Now must we needs be brave, tho' we spend all we
    have ;   45
  For of new garments we have great need :
Of horses and serving-men we must have store,
With bridles and saddles, and twentye things more.

Tushe, sir John, quoth his wife, why should you frett,
  or frowne ?
You shall ne'er be att no charges for mee ;   50
For I will turne and trim up my old russet gowne,
  With everye thing else as fine as may bee ;
And on our mill-horses swift we will ride,
With pillowes and pannells, as we shall provide.

In this most statelye sort, rode they unto the court, 55
  Their jolly sonne Richard rode foremost of all ;

Who set up, for good hap, a cocks feather in his cap,
    And so they jetted[1] downe to the kings hall;
The merry old miller with hands on his side;
His wife, like maid Marian, did mince at that tide. 60

The king and his nobles that heard of their coming,
    Meeting this gallant knight with his brave traine;
Welcome, sir knight, quoth he, with your gay lady:
    Good sir John Cockle, once welcome againe:
And soe is the squire of courage soe free.   65
Quoth Dicke, A bots on you! do you know mee?

Quoth our king gentlye, how should I forget thee?
    That wast my owne bed-fellowe, well it I wot.
Yea, sir, quoth Richard, and by the same token,
    Thou with thy farting didst make the bed hot. 70
Thou whore-son unhappy knave, then quoth the
        knight,
Speake cleanly to our king, or else go sh***.

The king and his courtiers laugh at this heartily,
    While the king taketh them both by the hand;
With the court-dames, and maids, like to the queen
        of spades   75
    The millers wife did soe orderlye stand.
A milk-maids courtesye at every word;
And downe all the folkes were set to the board.

There the king royally, in princelye majestye,
    Sate at his dinner with joy and delight;   80
When they had eaten well, then he to jesting fell,
    And in a bowle of wine dranke to the knight:

Ver. 57. *for good hap: i. e.* for good luck; they were going on
an hazardous expedition.
    Ver. 60. Maid Marian in the Morris dance, was represented by
a man in woman's cloaths, who was to take short steps in order to
sustain the female character.

[1 strutted.]

Here's to you both, in wine, ale and beer;
Thanking you heartilye for my good cheer.

Quoth sir John Cockle, I'll pledge you a pottle,   85
   Were it the best ale in Nottinghamshire:
But then said our king, now I think of a thing;
   Some of your lightfoote I would we had here.
Ho! ho! quoth Richard, full well I may say it,
'Tis knavery to eate it, and then to betray it.   90

Why art thou angry? quoth our king merrilye;
   In faith, I take it now very unkind:
I thought thou wouldst pledge me in ale and wine
      heartily.
   Quoth Dicke, You are like to stay till I have din'd:
You feed us with twatling dishes soe small;   95
Zounds, a blacke-pudding is better than all.

Aye, marry, quoth our king, that were a daintye thing,
   Could a man get but one here for to eate.
With that Dicke straite arose, and pluckt one from
      his hose,
   Which with heat of his breech gan to sweate.   100
The king made a proffer to snatch it away:—
'Tis meat for your master: good sir, you must stay.

Thus in great merriment was the time wholly spent;
   And then the ladyes prepared to dance.
Old Sir John Cockle, and Richard, incontinent[1]   105
   Unto their places the king did advance.
Here with the ladyes such sport they did make,
The nobles with laughing did make their sides ake.

Many thankes for their paines did the king give them,
   Asking young Richard then, if he would wed; 110
Among these ladyes free, tell me which liketh thee?
   Quoth he, Jugg Grumball, Sir, with the red head:

[¹ forthwith.]

She's my love, she's my life, her will I wed ;
She hath sworn I shall have her maidenhead.

Then sir John Cockle the king called unto him,   115
    And of merry Sherwood made him o'er seer ;
And gave him out of hand three hundred pound
        yearlye :
    Take heed now you steale no more of my deer :
And once a quarter let's here have your view ;
And now, sir John Cockle, I bid you adieu.   120

XXI.

THE SHEPHERD'S RESOLUTION.

THIS beautiful old song was written by a poet, whose
name would have been utterly forgotten, if it had not
been preserved by *Swift*, as a term of contempt.
Dryden and *Wither* are coupled by him like the
Bavius and *Mœvius* of Virgil. *Dryden*, however, has had justice done him by posterity : and as for *Wither*, though of subor-
dinate merit, that he was not altogether devoid of genius, will be
judged from the following stanzas. The truth is, *Wither* was a
very voluminous party-writer : and as his political and satyrical
strokes rendered him extremely popular in his life-time ; so afterwards, when these were no longer relished, they totally consigned
his writings to oblivion.

George Wither was born June 11, 1588, and in his younger
years distinguished himself by some pastoral pieces, that were not
inelegant ; but growing afterwards involved in the political and
religious disputes in the times of James I. and Charles I. he
employed his poetical vein in severe pasquils on the court and
clergy, and was occasionally a sufferer for the freedom of his pen.
In the civil war that ensued, he exerted himself in the service of
the Parliament, and became a considerable sharer in the spoils.
He was even one of those provincial tyrants, whom Oliver dis-
tributed over the kingdom, under the name of Major Generals ;
and had the fleecing of the county of Surrey : but surviving the
Restoration, he outlived both his power and his affluence ; and

giving vent to his chagrin in libels on the court, was long a prisoner in Newgate and the Tower. He died at length on the 2d of May, 1667.

During the whole course of his life, *Wither* was a continual publisher; having generally for opponent, *Taylor* the Water-poet. The long list of his productions may be seen in Wood's *Athenæ. Oxon.* vol. ii. His most popular satire is intitled, *Abuses whipt and stript*, 1613. His most poetical pieces were eclogues, intitled, *The Shepherd's Hunting*, 1615, 8vo. and others printed at the end of Browne's *Shepherd's Pipe*, 1614, 8vo. The following sonnet is extracted from a long pastoral piece of his, intitled, *The Mistresse of Philarete*, 1622, 8vo. which is said in the preface to be one of the Author's first poems; and may therefore be dated as early as any of the foregoing.

[This favourite song appeared in 1619, appended to Wither's *Fidelia*, and again in his *Juvenilia* in 1633 in *Fair Virtue the mistress of Philarete*. It was reprinted again and again, and occurs in the Folio MS. (ed. Hales and Furnivall, vol. ii. p. 50).

Mr. Chappell refers to a copy in the Pepys Collection entitled, *A New Song of a young man's opinion of the difference between good and bad women*, the first line of which is, "Shall I *wrestling* in despaire?" This reading seems to have been pretty popular, as Mr. Chappell gives two instances of the tune being called "*Shall I wrastle in despair?*" Mr. Chappell prints a song in the same metre and with a similar burden, which has been attributed on insufficient evidence to Sir Walter Raleigh. The first stanza is as follows:—

> " Shall I like a hermit dwell
> On a rock or in a cell?
> Calling home the smallest part
> That is missing of my heart,
> To bestow it where I may
> Meet a rival every day?
> If she undervalues me
> What care I how fair she be."

Popular Music of the Olden Time, vol. i. p. 315.]

SHALL I, wasting in dispaire,
　　Dye because a woman's faire?
　　Or make pale my cheeks with care,
　　'Cause another's rosie are?
Be shee fairer then the day,　　　　　5
Or the flowery meads in may;
　　If she be not so to me,
　　What care I how faire shee be?

Shall my foolish heart be pin'd,
'Cause I see a woman kind?　　　　　10
Or a well-disposed nature
Joyned with a lovely feature?
Be she meeker, kinder, than
The turtle-dove or pelican:
　　If shee be not so to me,　　　　　15
　　What care I how kind shee be?

Shall a woman's virtues move
Me to perish for her love?
Or, her well-deservings knowne,
Make me quite forget mine owne?　　　20
Be shee with that goodnesse blest,
Which may merit name of Best;
　　If she be not such to me,
　　What care I how good she be?

Cause her fortune seems too high,　　25
Shall I play the foole and dye?
Those that beare a noble minde,
Where they want of riches find,

[Ver. 7. if shee thinke not well of mee, MS.　V. 23. soe to me,
MS.　V. 25-32. this stanza is not in the MS.]

Think what with them they would doe,
That without them dare to woe;   30
   And, unlesse that minde I see,
   What care I how great she be?

Great or good, or kind or faire,
I will ne'er the more dispaire:
If she love me, this beleeve;   35
I will die ere she shall grieve.
If she slight me when I wooe,
I can scorn and let her goe:
   If shee be not fit for me,
   What care I for whom she be?   40

XXII.

QUEEN DIDO.

UCH is the title given in the editor's folio MS.* to this excellent old ballad, which, in the common printed copies, is inscribed, *Eneas, wandering Prince of Troy.* It is here given from that MS. collated with two different printed copies, both in black-letter, in the Pepys Collection.

The reader will smile to observe with what natural and affecting simplicity, our ancient ballad-maker has engrafted a Gothic conclusion on the classic story of Virgil, from whom, however, it is probable he had it not. Nor can it be denied, but he has dealt out his poetical justice with a more impartial hand, than that celebrated poet.

[This once popular ballad was entered on the Registers of the Stationers Company in 1564-5 as "a ballett intituled *The Wanderynge Prince.*" Its great popularity is evidenced by the frequent references in literature and the large number of ballads sung to the tune of *Queen Dido* or *Troy towne.* In *The Penniless Parliament of Threadbare Poets,* 1608, ale-knights are said to " sing *Queen Dido*

[* Ed. Hales and Furnivall, vol. iii. p. 502.]

over a cup and tell strange news over an ale-pot," and the same song is referred to in Fletcher's *Captain* (act iii. sc. 3) and his *Bonduca*, act i. sc. 2.

The only tune that Mr. Chappell could find for the ballad was one by Dr. John Wilson (the Jack Wilson of Shakspere's stage according to Dr. Rimbault), which is printed in his *Cheerful Ayres or Ballads*, Oxford, 1660.]

HEN Troy towne had, for ten yeeres "past,"
    Withstood the Greekes in manfull wise,
Then did their foes encrease soe fast,
    That to resist none could suffice :
Wast lye those walls, that were soe good,   5
And corne now growes where Troy towne stoode.

Æneas, wandering prince of Troy,
    When he for land long time had sought,
At length arriving with great joy,
    To mighty Carthage walls was brought;   10
Where Dido queene, with sumptuous feast,
Did entertaine that wandering guest.

And, as in hall at meate, they sate,
    The queene, desirous newes to heare,
" Says, of thy Troys unhappy fate "   15
    Declare to me thou Trojan deare :
The heavy hap and chance soe bad,
That thou, poore wandering prince, hast had,

And then anon this comelye knight,
    With words demure, as he cold well,   20
Of his unhappy ten yeares "fight,"
    Soe true a tale began to tell,
With words soe sweete, and sighes so deepe,
That oft he made them all to weepe.

Ver. 1. 21. war. MS. and *PP.*

And then a thousand sighes he fet,[1]   25
    And every sigh brought teares amaine;
That where he sate the place was wett,
    As though he had seene those warrs againe;
Soe that the queene, with ruth therfore,
Said, worthy prince, enough, no more.   30

And then the darksome night drew on,
    And twinkling starres the skye bespred;
When he his dolefull tale had done,
    And every one was layd in bedd:
Where they full sweetly tooke their rest,   35
Save only Dido's boyling brest.

This silly woman never slept,
    But in her chamber, all alone,
As one unhappye, alwayes wept,
    And to the walls shee made her mone;   40
That she shold still desire in vaine
The thing, she never must obtaine.

And thus in grieffe she spent the night,
    Till twinkling starres the skye were fled,
And Phœbus, with his glistering light,   45
    Through misty cloudes appeared red;
Then tidings came to her anon,
That all the Trojan shipps were gone.

And then the queene with bloody knife
    Did arme her hart as hard as stone,   50
Yet, something loth to loose her life,
    In woefull wise she made her mone;
And, rowling on her carefull bed,
With sighes and sobbs, these words shee sayd:

O wretched Dido queene! quoth shee,   55
    I see thy end approacheth neare;

---

[1] fetched.

For hee is fled away from thee,
   Whom thou didst love and hold so deare :
What is he gone, and passed by ?
O hart, prepare thyselfe to dye.   60

Though reason says, thou shouldst forbeare,
   And stay thy hand from bloudy stroke ;
Yet fancy bids thee not to fear,
   Which fetter'd thee in Cupids yoke.
Come death, quoth shee, resolve my smart !—   65
And with those words shee peerced her hart.

When death had pierced the tender hart
   Of Dido, Carthaginian queene ;
Whose bloudy knife did end the smart,
   Which shee sustain'd in mournfull teene[1] ;   70
Æneas being shipt and gone,
Whose flattery caused all her mone ;

Her funerall most costly made,
   And all things finisht mournfullye ;
Her body fine in mold was laid,   75
   Where itt consumed speedilye :
Her sisters teares her tombe bestrewde ;
Her subjects griefe their kindnesse shewed.

Then was Æneas in an ile
   In Grecya, where he stayd long space,   80
Wheras her sister in short while
   Writt to him to his vile disgrace ;
In speeches bitter to his mind
Shee told him plaine he was unkind.

False-harted wretch, quoth shee, thou art ;   85
   And traiterouslye thou hast betraid
Unto thy lure a gentle hart,
   Which unto thee much welcome made ;

[¹ trouble.]

My sister deare, and Carthage' joy,
Whose folly bred her deere annoy.   90

   Yett on her death-bed when shee lay,
     Shee prayd for thy prosperitye,
   Beseeching god, that every day
     Might breed thy great felicitye :
Thus by thy meanes I lost a friend ;   95
Heavens send thee such untimely end.

   When he these lines, full fraught with gall,
     Perused had, and wayed them right,
   His lofty courage then did fall ;
     And straight appeared in his sight   100
Queene Dido's ghost, both grim and pale ;
Which made this valliant souldier quaile.

   Æneas, quoth this ghastly ghost,
     My whole delight when I did live,
   Thee of all men I loved most ;   105
     My fancy and my will did give ;
For entertainment I thee gave,
Unthankefully thou didst me grave.

   Therfore prepare thy flitting soule
     To wander with me in the aire ;   110
   Where deadlye griefe shall make it howle,
     Because of me thou tookst no care :
Delay not time, thy glasse is run,
Thy date is past, thy life is done.

   O stay a while, thou lovely sprite,   115
     Be not soe hasty to convay
   My soule into eternall night,
     Where itt shall ne're behold bright day.
O doe not frowne ; thy angry looke,
Hath " all my soule with horror shooke."   120

Ver. 120. MS. *Hath* made my breath my life forsooke.

But, woe is me! all is in vaine,
　　And bootless is my dismall crye;
Time will not be recalled againe,
　　Nor thou surcease before I dye.
O lett me live, and make amends　　　125
To some of thy most deerest friends.

But seeing thou obdurate art,
　　And wilt no pittye on me show,
Because from thee I did depart,
　　And left unpaid what I did owe :　　130
I must content myselfe to take
What lott to me thou wilt partake.

And thus, as one being in a trance,
　　A multitude of uglye feinds
About this woffull prince did dance;　　135
　　He had no helpe of any friends :
His body then they tooke away,
And no man knew his dying day.

XXIII.

THE WITCHES' SONG

FROM Ben Jonson's *Masque of Queens* presented at Whitehall, Feb. 2, 1609.

The editor thought it incumbent on him to insert some old pieces on the popular superstition concerning witches, hobgoblins, fairies, and ghosts. The last of these make their appearance in most of the tragical ballads; and in the following songs will be found some description of the former.

It is true, this song of the Witches, falling from the learned pen of Ben Jonson, is rather an extract from the various incantations of classical antiquity, than a display of the opinions of our own vulgar. But let it be observed, that a parcel of learned wiseacres had just before busied themselves on this subject, in compliment to K. James I. whose weakness on this head is well known : and these had so ransacked all writers, ancient and modern, and so blended and kneaded together the several superstitions of different times and nations, that those of genuine English growth could no longer be traced out and distinguished.

By good luck the whimsical belief of fairies and goblins could furnish no pretences for torturing our fellow-creatures, and therefore we have this handed down to us pure and unsophisticated.

1 WITCH.*

HAVE been all day looking after
A raven feeding upon a quarter ;
And, soone as she turn'd her beak to the
        south,
I snatch'd this morsell out of her mouth.

2 WITCH.

I have beene gathering wolves haires,   5
The madd dogges foames, and adders eares ;
The spurging of a deadmans eyes :
And all since the evening starre did rise.

3 WITCH.

I last night lay all alone
O' the ground, to heare the mandrake grone ; 10
And pluckt him up, though he grew full low :
And, as I had done, the cocke did crow.

4 WITCH.

And I ha' beene chusing out this scull
From charnell houses that were full ;

[* These witches are called Hags by Jonson.]

From private grots, and publike pits ;   15
And frighted a sexton out of his wits.

5 WITCH.

Under a cradle I did crepe
By day ; and, when the childe was a-sleepe
At night, I suck'd the breath ; and rose,
And pluck'd the nodding nurse by the nose.   20

6 WITCH.

I had a dagger : what did I with that ?
Killed an infant to have his fat.
A piper it got at a church-ale,[1]
I bade him again blow wind i' the taile.

7 WITCH.

A murderer, yonder, was hung in chaines ;   25
The sunne and the wind had shrunke his veines :
I bit off a sinew ; I clipp'd his haire ;
I brought off his ragges, that danc'd i' the ayre.

8 WITCH.

The scrich-owles egges and the feathers blacke,
The bloud of the frogge, and the bone in his backe 30
I have been getting ; and made of his skin
A purset, to keep sir Cranion[2] in.

9 WITCH.

And I ha' beene plucking (plants among)
Hemlock, henbane, adders-tongue,
Night-shade, moone-wort, libbards-bane[3] ;   35
And twise by the dogges was like to be tane.

[[1] a wake or feast in commemoration of the dedication of a church.   [2] skull.   [3] the herb wolfbane.]

10 WITCH.

I from the jawes of a gardiner's bitch
Did snatch these bones, and then leap'd the ditch:
Yet went I back to the house againe,
Kill'd the blacke cat, and here is the braine. 40

11 WITCH.

I went to the toad, breedes under the wall,
I charmed him out, and he came at my call;
I scratch'd out the eyes of the owle before;
I tore the batts wing: what would you have more?

DAME.*

Yes: I have brought, to helpe your vows, 45
Horned poppie, cypresse boughes,
The fig-tree wild, that growes on tombes,
And juice, that from the larch-tree comes,
    The basiliskes bloud, and the viper's skin:
And now our orgies let's begin. 50

XXIV.

ROBIN GOOD-FELLOW,

LIAS *Pucke,* alias *Hobgoblin,* in the creed of ancient
superstition, was a kind of merry sprite, whose character
and atchievements are recorded in this ballad, and in
those well-known lines of Milton's *L'Allegro,* which the
antiquarian Peck supposes to be owing to it:

" Tells how the drudging *Goblin* swet
To earn his creame-bowle duly set;
When in one night ere glimpse of morne,
His shadowy flail hath thresh'd the corn

---

* [Jonson meant the Dame to represent Ate or the goddess of
Mischief.]

That ten day-labourers could not end;
Then lies him down the lubber fiend,
And stretch'd out all the chimneys length,
Basks at the fire his hairy strength,
And crop-full out of doors he flings,
Ere the first cock his matins rings."

The reader will observe that our simple ancestors had reduced all these whimsies to a kind of system, as regular, and perhaps more consistent, that many parts of classic mythology : a proof of the extensive influence and vast antiquity of these superstitions. Mankind, and especially the common people, could not every where have been so unanimously agreed concerning these arbitrary notions, if they had not prevailed among them for many ages. Indeed, a learned friend in Wales assures the Editor, that the existence of Fairies and Goblins is alluded to by the most ancient British Bards, who mention them under various names, one of the most common of which signifies, *The spirits of the mountains.* See also Preface to Song XXV.

This song, which Peck attributes to Ben Jonson, (tho' it is not found among his works) is chiefly printed from an ancient black-letter copy in the British Museum. It seems to have been originally intended for some Masque.

It is intitled, in the old black-letter copies, *The mad merry Prankes of Robin Goodfellow.* To the tune of *Dulcina,* &c. (See No. XIII. above.)

To one, if not more of the old copies, are prefixed two wooden cuts, said to be taken from Bulwer's *Artificial Changeling, &c.,* which, as they seem to correspond with the notions then entertained of the whimsical appearances of this fantastic spirit, and perhaps were copied in the dresses in which he was formerly exhibited on the stage, are, to gratify the curious, engraven below.

[The copy in the Roxburghe *Collection* (ed. Chappell, vol. ii. pl. i. p. 80) is printed by H[enry] G[osson], who was a contemporary of Ben Jonson. Some little books in prose on *Robin Goodfellow*, written in the seventeenth century, were printed for the Percy Society by Mr. J. P. Collier.]

ROM Oberon, in fairye land,
　　The king of ghosts and shadowes there,
Mad Robin I, at his command,
　　Am sent to viewe the night-sports here.
　　What revell rout　　　　　　　5
　　Is kept about,
In every corner where I go,
　　I will o'ersee,
　　And merry bee,
And make good sport, with ho, ho, ho!　　10

More swift than lightening can I flye
　　About this aery welkin soone,
And, in a minutes space, descrye
　　Each thing that's done belowe the moone,
　　There's not a hag　　　　　　　15
　　Or ghost shall wag,
Or cry, ware Goblins! where I go;
　　But Robin I
　　Their feates will spy,
And send them home, with ho, ho, ho!　　20

Whene'er such wanderers I meete,
　　As from their night-sports they trudge home;
With counterfeiting voice I greete
　　And call them on, with me to roame
　　Thro' woods, thro' lakes,　　　　25
　　Thro' bogs, thro' brakes;
Or else, unseene, with them I go,
　　All in the nicke
　　To play some tricke
And frolicke it, with ho, ho, ho!　　30

Sometimes I meete them like a man;
　　Sometimes, an ox, sometimes, a hound;
And to a horse I turn me can;
　　To trip and trot about them round.

But if, to ride,   35
My backe they stride,
More swift than wind away I go,
Ore hedge and lands,
Thro' pools and ponds
I whirry, laughing, ho, ho, ho!   40

When lads and lasses merry be,
With possets and with juncates fine;
Unseene of all the company,
I eat their cakes and sip their wine;
And, to make sport,   45
I fart and snort;
And out the candles I do blow:
The maids I kiss;
They shrieke—Who's this?
I answer nought, but ho, ho, ho!   50

Yet now and then, the maids to please,
At midnight I card up their wooll;
And while they sleepe, and take their ease,
With wheel to threads their flax I pull.
I grind at mill   55
Their malt up still;
I dress their hemp, I spin their tow.
If any 'wake,
And would me take,
I wend me, laughing, ho, ho, ho!   60

When house or harth doth sluttish lye,
I pinch the maidens blacke and blue;
The bed-clothes from the bedd pull I,
And lay them naked all to view.
'Twixt sleepe and wake,   65
I do them take,

[Ver. 61. this begins the second part in the Roxburghe copy.]

And on the key-cold floor them throw.
　　If out they cry,
　　Then forth I fly,
And loudly laugh out, ho, ho, ho!　　　70

When any need to borrowe ought,
　　We lend them what they do require;
And for the use demand we nought;
　　Our owne is all we do desire.
　　　　If to repay,　　　　　　　　75
　　　　They do delay,
　　Abroad amongst them then I go,
　　　　And night by night,
　　　　I them affright
　　With pinchings, dreames, and ho, ho, ho!　80

When lazie queans have nought to do,
　　But study how to cog and lye;
To make debate and mischief too,
　　'Twixt one another secretlye:
　　　　I marke their gloze,　　　　85
　　　　And it disclose,
　　To them whom they have wronged so;
　　　　When I have done,
　　　　I get me gone,
　　And leave them scolding, ho, ho, ho!　90

When men do traps and engins set
　　In loop-holes, where the vermine creepe,
Who from their foldes and houses, get
　　Their duckes and geese, and lambes and sheepe:
　　　　I spy the gin,　　　　　　95
　　　　And enter in,
　　And seeme a vermine taken so;
　　　　But when they there
　　　　Approach me neare,
　　I leap out laughing, ho, ho, ho!　　100

By wells and rills,[1] in meadowes greene,
    We nightly dance our hey-day guise;[2]
And to our fairye king, and queene,
    We chant our moon-light minstrelsies.
        When larks 'gin sing,   105
        Away we fling;
    And babes new borne steal as we go,
        And else in bed,
        We leave instead,
    And wend us laughing, ho, ho, ho!   110

From hag-bred Merlin's time have I
    Thus nightly revell'd to and fro:
And for my pranks men call me by
    The name of Robin Good-fellow.
        Fiends, ghosts, and sprites,   115
        Who haunt the nightes,
    The hags and goblins do me know;
        And beldames old
        My feates have told;
    So *Vale, Vale;* ho, ho, ho!   120

XXV.

THE FAIRY QUEEN.

E have here a short display of the popular belief concerning *Fairies.* It will afford entertainment to a con-
templative mind to trace these whimsical opinions up
to their origin. Whoever considers, how early, how
extensively, and how uniformly, they have prevailed in these

---

[1] gills=rivulets, *Roxb. copy.*
[2] a misprint for heydegies=rustic dances. The word occurs in
Lily's *Endymion,* 1591, and in Wm. Bulleyn's *Dialogue,* 1564,
where the minstrel daunces "Trenchmore" and "Heie de gie."—
Chappell.]

nations, will not readily assent to the hypothesis of those, who fetch them from the east so late as the time of the Croisades. Whereas it is well known that our Saxon ancestors, long before they left their German forests, believed the existence of a kind ot diminutive demons, or middle species between men and spirits, whom they called *Duergar* or *Dwarfs*, and to whom they attributed many wonderful performances, far exceeding human art. Vid. Hervarer Saga Olaj Verelj. 1675. Hickes' Thesaur., &c.

This Song is given (with some corrections by another copy) from a book intitled, *The Mysteries of Love and Eloquence, &c* Lond. 1658, 8vo.

[Dr. Rimbault points out that this song occurs in a rare tract published more than twenty years before the book mentioned above. It is entitled, *A description of the King and Queen of the Fayries, their habit, fare, abode, pomp and state, being very delightfut to the sense and full of mirth.* London, 1635. The song was to be sung to the tune of the *Spanish Gypsie*, which began—

> " O follow, follow me
> For we be gypsies three."

Martin Parker wrote a sort of parody called *The three merry Cobblers*, commencing—

> " Come follow, follow me
> To the alehouse we'll march all three ;
> Leave awl, last, thread and leather,
> And let's go all together."

Mr. Chappell prints the first, eighth, fourteenth and last stanzas (*Popular Music*, vol. i. p. 272.)]

OME, follow, follow me,
   You, fairy elves that be :
   Which circle on the greene,
   Come follow Mab your queene.
Hand in hand let's dance around,   5
For this place is fairye ground.

When mortals are at rest,
And snoring in their nest;
Unheard, and un-espy'd,
Through key-holes we do glide;   10
Over tables, stools, and shelves.
We trip it with our fairy elves.

And, if the house be foul *
With platter, dish or bowl,
Up stairs we nimbly creep,   15
And find the sluts asleep:
There we pinch their armes and thighes;
None escapes, nor none espies.

But if the house be swept,
And from uncleanness kept,   20
We praise the household maid,
And duely she is paid:
For we use before we goe
To drop a tester¹ in her shoe.

Upon a mushroomes head   25
Our table-cloth we spread;
A grain of rye, or wheat,
Is manchet,² which we eat;
Pearly drops of dew we drink
In acorn cups fill'd to the brink.   30

The brains of nightingales,
With unctuous fat of snailes,

[* Puck's speech in *Midsummer Night's Dream* (act v. sc. 2)—

  " I am sent with broom before
    To sweep the dust behind the door,"

illustrates the delight of the fairies in cleanliness, which is dwelt
upon in this and the following song.

¹ tester or teston=sixpence.   ² best kind of white bread.]

Between two cockles stew'd,
Is meat that's easily chew'd;
Tailes of wormes, and marrow of mice   35
Do make a dish, that's wonderous nice.

The grashopper, gnat, and fly,
Serve for our minstrelsie;
Grace said, we dance a while,
And so the time beguile;   40
And if the moon doth hide her head,
The gloe-worm lights us home to bed.

On tops of dewie grasse
So nimbly do we passe,
The young and tender stalk   45
Ne'er bends when we do walk:
Yet in the morning may be seen
Where we the night before have been.

XXVI.

THE FAIRIES FAREWELL.

HIS humorous old song fell from the hand of the witty Dr. *Corbet* (afterwards bishop of Norwich, &c.) and is printed from his *Poëtica Stromata*, 1648, 12mo. (compared with the third edition of his poems, 1672.) It is there called, *A proper new Ballad, intitled, The Fairies Farewell, or God-a-mercy Will, to be sung or whistled to the tune of The Meddow brow, by the learned; by the unlearned, to the tune of Fortune.*

The departure of Fairies is here attributed to the abolition of monkery: Chaucer has, with equal humour, assigned a cause the very reverse, in his *Wife of Bath's Tale.*

" In olde dayes of the king Artour,
Of which that Bretons speken gret honour,
All was this lond fulfilled of faerie;
The elf-quene, with hire joly compagnie

Danced ful oft in many a grene mede.
This was the old opinion as I rede;
I speke of many hundred yeres ago;
But now can no man see non elves mo,
For now the grete charitee and prayeres
Of limitoures and other holy freres,
That serchen every land and every streme,
As thikke as motes in the sonne beme,
Blissing halles, chambres, kichenes, and boures,
Citees and burghes, castles high and toures,
Thropes and bernes, shepenes and dairies,
This maketh that ther ben no faeries:
For ther as wont to walken was an elf,
Ther walketh now the limitour himself,
In undermeles and in morweninges,
And sayth his Matines and his holy thinges,
As he goth in his limitatioun.
Women may now go safely up and doun,
In every bush, and under every tree,
Ther is non other incubus but he,
And he ne will don hem no dishonour."

Tyrwhitt's Chaucer, i. p. 255.

Dr. Richard Corbet, having been bishop of Oxford about three years, and afterwards as long bishop of Norwich, died in 1635, Ætat. 52.

AREWELL rewards and Fairies!
　　Good housewives now may say;
　For now foule sluts in dairies,
　　Doe fare as well as they:
And though they sweepe their hearths no less　5
　　Than mayds were wont to doe,
Yet who of late for cleaneliness
　　Finds sixe-pence in her shoe?

Lament, lament old Abbies,
　　The fairies lost command;　　　　　　　10
They did but change priests babies,
　　But some have chang'd your land:

And all your children stoln from thence
  Are now growne Puritanes,
Who live as changelings ever since,   15
  For love of your demaines.

At morning and at evening both
  You merry were and glad,
So little care of sleepe and sloth,
These prettie ladies had.   20
When Tom came home from labour,
  Or Ciss to milking rose,
Then merrily went their tabour,
  And nimbly went their toes.

Witness those rings and roundelayes   25
  Of theirs, which yet remaine;
Were footed in queene Maries dayes
  On many a grassy playne.
But since of late Elizabeth
  And later James came in;   30
They never danc'd on any heath,
  As when the time hath bin.

By which wee note the fairies
  Were of the old profession:
Their songs were *Ave Maries*,   35
  Their dances were procession.
But now, alas! they all are dead,
  Or gone beyond the seas,
Or farther for religion fled,
  Or else they take their ease.   40

A tell-tale in their company
  They never could endure;
And whoso kept not secretly
  Their mirth, was punish'd sure:

It was a just and christian deed   45
   To pinch such blacke and blue:
O how the common-welth doth need
   Such justices, as you!

Now they have left our quarters;
   A Register they have,   50
Who can preserve their charters;
   A man both wise and grave.
An hundred of their merry pranks
   By one that I could name
Are kept in store; con twenty thanks   55
   To William for the same.

To William Churne of Staffordshire
   Give laud and praises due,
Who every meale can mend your cheare
   With tales both old and true: 60
To William all give audience,
   And pray yee for his noddle:
For all the fairies evidence
   Were lost, if it were addle.

*** After these *Songs* on the *Fairies*, the reader may be curious to see the manner in which they were formerly invoked and bound to human service. In Ashmole's *Collection of MSS.* at Oxford (Num. 8259. 1406. 2), are the papers of some alchymist, which contain a variety of Incantations and Forms of Conjuring both *Fairies*, *Witches*, and *Demons*, principally, as it should seem, to assist him in his Great Work of transmuting Metals. Most of them are too impious to be reprinted: but the two following may be very innocently laughed at.

Whoever looks into Ben Jonson's *Alchymist*, will find that these impostors, among their other secrets, affected to have a power over *Fairies*: and that they were commonly expected to be seen in a christal glass appears from that extraordinary book, *The Relation of Dr. John Dee's actions with Spirits*, 1659, folio.

" *An excellent way* to gett a *Fayrie*. (For myself I call *Margarett Barrance;* but this will obteine any one that is not allready bownd.)

" FIRST, gett a broad square christall or Venice glasse, in length and breadth 3 inches. Then lay that glasse or christall in the bloud of a white henne, 3 Wednesdayes, or 3 Fridayes. Then take it out, and wash it with holy aq. and fumigate it. Then take 3 hazle sticks, or wands of an yeare groth: pill them fayre and white; and make ' them' soe longe, as you write the *Spiritts* name, or *Fayries* name, which you call, 3 times on every sticke being made flatt on one side. Then bury them under some hill, whereas you suppose *Fayries* haunt, the Wednesday before you call her: and the Friday followinge take them uppe, and call her at 8 or 3 or 10 of the clocke, which be good planetts and houres for that turne: but when you call, be in cleane life, and turne thy face towards the east. And when you have her, bind her to that stone or glasse."

" AN UNGUENT to annoynt under the Eyelids, and upon the Eyelids eveninge and morninge: but especially when you call; or find your sight not perfect.

" R. A pint of sallet-oyle, and put it into a viall glasse: but first wash it with rose-water, and marygold-water; the flowers 'to' be gathered towards the east. Wash it till the oyle come white; then put it into the glasse, *ut supra:* and then put thereto the budds of holyhocke, the flowers of marygold, the flowers or toppes of wild thime, the budds of young hazle: and the thime must be gathered neare the side of a hill where *Fayries* use to be: and ' take' the grasse of a fayrie throne, there. All these put into the oyle, into the glasse: and set it to dissolve 3 dayes in the sunne, and then keep it for thy use; *ut supra.*"

After this receipt for the unguent follows a form of incantation, wherein the alchymist conjures a fairy, named *Elaby Gathon*, to appear to him in that chrystal glass, meekly and mildly; to resolve him truly in all manner of questions; and to be obedient to all his commands, under pain of damnation, &c.

One of the vulgar opinions about fairies is, that they cannot be seen by human eyes, without a particular charm exerted in favour of the person who is to see them: and that they strike with blindness such as having the gift of seeing them, take notice of them *mal-à-propos.*

As to the hazle sticks mentioned above, they were to be probably of that species called the *witch hazle;* which received its name from this manner of applying it in incantations.

THE END OF BOOK THE SECOND.

RELIQUES OF ANCIENT POETRY, ETC.

SERIES THE THIRD.

BOOK III.

I.

THE BIRTH OF ST. GEORGE.

THE incidents in this, and the other ballad of *St. George and the Dragon*, are chiefly taken from the old story-book of the Seven Champions of Christendome; which, tho' now the play-thing of children, was once in high repute. Bp. Hall in his *Satires*, published in 1597, ranks

"St. George's sorell, and his cross of blood,"

among the most popular stories of his time: and an ingenious critic thinks that Spencer himself did not disdain to borrow hints from it; * tho' I much doubt whether this popular romance were written so early as the *Faery Queen*.

The author of this book of the *Seven Champions* was one Richard Johnson, who lived in the reigns of Elizabeth and James, as we collect from his other publications: viz.—*The nine worthies of London*: 1592, 4to.—*The pleasant walks of Moor fields*: 1607, 4to.—*A crown garland of Goulden Roses, gathered, &c.* 1612, 8vo. —*The life and death of Rob. Cecill, E. of Salisbury*: 1612, 4to.— *The Hist. of Tom of Lincoln*, 4to. is also by R. J. who likewise reprinted *Don Flores of Greece*, 4to.

The *Seven Champions*, tho' written in a wild inflated style, contains some strong Gothic painting; which seems, for the most part, copied from the metrical romances of former ages. At least the story of *St. George and the fair Sabra* is taken almost verbatim from the old poetical legend of *Syr Bevis of Hampton*.

This very antique poem was in great fame in Chaucer's time (see above, pag. 107.), and so continued till the introduction of printing, when it ran thro' several editions; two of which are in

---

* Mr. Warton. Vid. Observations on the *Fairy Queen*, 2 vol. 1762, 12mo. *passim*.

black letter, 4to. "imprinted by Wyllyam Copland," without date; containing great variations.

As a specimen of the poetic powers of this very old rhimist, and as a proof how closely the author of the *Seven Champions* has followed him, take a description of the dragon slain by sir Bevis.

> " — Whan the dragon, that foule is,
> Had a syght of syr Bevis,
> He cast up a loude cry,
> As it had thondred in the sky;
> He turned his bely towarde the son;
> It was greater than any tonne:
> His scales was bryghter then the glas,
> And harder they were than any bras:
> Betwene his shulder and his tayle,
> Was forty fote withoute fayle.
> He waltred out of his denne,
> And Bevis pricked his stede then,
> And to hym a spere he thraste
> That all to shyvers he it braste:
> The dragon then gan Bevis assayle,
> And smote syr Bevis with his tayle;
> Then downe went horse and man,
> And two rybbes of Bevis brused than."

After a long fight, at length, as the dragon was preparing to fly, sir Bevis

> " Hit him under the wynge,
> As he was in his flyenge,
> There he was tender without scale,
> And Bevis thought to be his bale.
> He smote after, as I you saye,
> With his good sword Morglaye.
> Up to the hiltes Morglay yode
> Through harte, lyver, bone, and bloude:
> To the ground fell the dragon,
> Great joye syr Bevis begon.
> Under the scales al on hight
> He smote off his head forth right,
> And put it on a spere: &c."
> Sign. K. iv.

Sir Bevis's dragon is evidently the parent of that in the *Seven Champions*, see chap. iii., viz. "The dragon no sooner had a sight of him (St. George) but he gave such a terrible peal, as though it had thundered in the elements. . . . Betwixt his shoulders and his

tail were fifty feet in distance, his scales glistering as bright as
silver, but far more hard than brass; his belly of the colour of
gold, but bigger than a tun. Thus weltered he from his den, &c.
. . . The champion . . . gave the dragon such a thrust with his
spear, that it shivered in a thousand pieces: whereat the furious
dragon so fiercely smote him with his venomous tail, that down
fell man and horse: in which fall two of St. George's ribs were so
bruised, &c.—At length . . . St. George smote the dragon under
the wing where it was tender without scale, whereby his good
sword Ascalon with an easie passage went to the very hilt through
both the dragon's heart, liver, bone, and blood.—Then St. George
—cut off the dragon's head and pitcht it upon the truncheon of a
spear, &c."

The *History of the Seven Champions*, being written just before
the decline of books of chivalry, was never, I believe, translated
into any foreign language: But *Le Roman de Beuves of Hantonne*
was published at Paris in 1502, 4to. Let. Gothique.

The learned Selden tell us, that about the time of the Norman
invasion was Bevis famous with the title of Earl of Southampton,
whose residence was at Duncton in Wiltshire; but he observes,
that the monkish enlargements of his story have made his very
existence doubted. See *Notes on Poly-Olbion, Song* iii.

This hath also been the case of *St. George* himself; whose
martial history is allowed to be apocryphal. But, to prove that
there really existed an orthodox saint of this name (altho' little o1
nothing, it seems, is known of his genuine story) is the subject of
*An Historical and Critical Inquiry into the Existence and Character
of St. George, &c.* By the Rev. J. Milner, F.S.A. 1792, 8vo.

The equestrian figure worn by the Knights of the Garter, has
been understood to be an emblem of the Christian warrior, in his
spiritual armour, vanquishing the old serpent.

But on this subject the inquisitive reader may consult *A Dissertation on the Original of the Equestrian Figure of the George and of
the Garter, ensigns of the most noble order of that name.* Illustrated
with copper-plates. By John Petingal, A.M., Fellow of the Society
of Antiquaries, London, 1753, 4to. This learned and curious work
the author of the *Historical and Critical Inquiry* would have done
well to have seen.

It cannot be denied, but that the following ballad is for the
most part modern: for which reason it would have been thrown
to the end of the volume, had not its subject procured it a place
here.

[In respect to the last paragraph, Ritson writes, "It may be
safely denied, however, that the least part of it is ancient."]

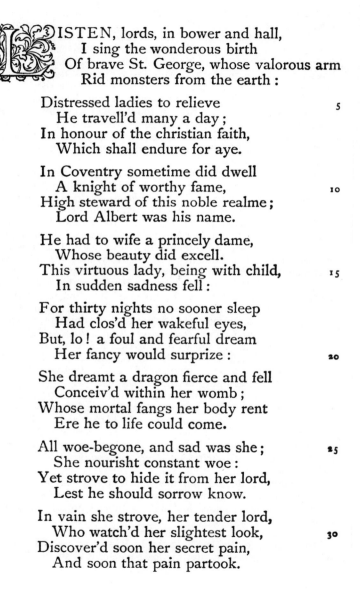

ISTEN, lords, in bower and hall,
    I sing the wonderous birth
Of brave St. George, whose valorous arm
    Rid monsters from the earth :

Distressed ladies to relieve   5
    He travell'd many a day ;
In honour of the christian faith,
    Which shall endure for aye.

In Coventry sometime did dwell
    A knight of worthy fame,   10
High steward of this noble realme ;
    Lord Albert was his name.

He had to wife a princely dame,
    Whose beauty did excell.
This virtuous lady, being with child,   15
    In sudden sadness fell :

For thirty nights no sooner sleep
    Had clos'd her wakeful eyes,
But, lo ! a foul and fearful dream
    Her fancy would surprize :   20

She dreamt a dragon fierce and fell
    Conceiv'd within her womb ;
Whose mortal fangs her body rent
    Ere he to life could come.

All woe-begone, and sad was she ;   25
    She nourisht constant woe :
Yet strove to hide it from her lord,
    Lest he should sorrow know.

In vain she strove, her tender lord,
    Who watch'd her slightest look,   30
Discover'd soon her secret pain,
    And soon that pain partook.

And when to him the fearful cause
   She weeping did impart,
With kindest speech he strove to heal   35
   The anguish of her heart.

Be comforted, my lady dear,
   Those pearly drops refrain;
Betide me weal, betide me woe,
   I'll try to ease thy pain.   40

And for this foul and fearful dream,
   That causeth all thy woe,
Trust me I'll travel far away
   But I'll the meaning knowe.

Then giving many a fond embrace,   45
   And shedding many a teare,
To the weïrd lady of the woods
   He purpos'd to repaire.

To the weïrd lady of the woods,
   Full long and many a day,   50
Thro' lonely shades, and thickets rough
   He winds his weary way.

At length he reach'd a dreary dell
   With dismal yews o'erhung;
Where cypress spred it's mournful boughs,   55
   And pois'nous nightshade sprung.

No chearful gleams here pierc'd the gloom,
   He hears no chearful sound;
But shrill night-ravens' yelling scream,
   And serpents hissing round.   60

The shriek of fiends, and damned ghosts
   Ran howling thro' his ear:
A chilling horror froze his heart,
   Tho' all unus'd to fear.

Three times he strives to win his way,   65
   And pierce those sickly dews :
Three times to bear his trembling corse
   His knocking knees refuse.

At length upon his beating breast
   He signs the holy crosse ;   70
And, rouzing up his wonted might,
   He treads th' unhallow'd mosse.

Beneath a pendant craggy cliff,
   All vaulted like a grave,
And opening in the solid rock,   75
   He found the inchanted cave.

An iron gate clos'd up the mouth,
   All hideous and forlorne ;
And, fasten'd by a silver chain,
   Near hung a brazed horne.   80

Then offering up a secret prayer,
   Three times he blowes amaine :
Three times a deepe and hollow sound
   Did answer him againe.

" Sir knight, thy lady beares a son,   85
   " Who, like a dragon bright,
" Shall prove most dreadful to his foes,
   " And terrible in fight.

" His name advanc'd in future times
   " On banners shall be worn :   90
" But lo ! thy lady's life must passe
   " Before he can be born."

All sore opprest with fear and doubt
   Long time lord Albert stood ;
At length he winds his doubtful way   95
   Back thro' the dreary wood.

Eager to clasp his lovely dame
  Then fast he travels back:
But when he reach'd his castle gate,
  His gate was hung with black.   100

In every court and hall he found
  A sullen silence reigne;
Save where, amid the lonely towers,
  He heard her maidens 'plaine;

And bitterly lament and weep,   105
  With many a grievous grone:
Then sore his bleeding heart misgave,
  His lady's life was gone.

With faultering step he enters in,
  Yet half affraid to goe;   110
With trembling voice asks why they grieve,
  Yet fears the cause to knowe.

" Three times the sun hath rose and set;"
  They said, then stopt to weep:
" Since heaven hath laid thy lady deare   115
  " In death's eternal sleep.

" For, ah! in travel sore she fell,
  " So sore that she must dye;
" Unless some shrewd and cunning leech
  " Could ease her presentlye.   120

" But when a cunning leech was fet,
  " Too soon declared he,
" She, or her babe must lose its life;
  " Both saved could not be.

" Now take my life, thy lady said,   125
  " My little infant save:
" And O commend me to my lord,
  " When I am laid in grave.

" O tell him how that precious babe
  " Cost him a tender wife :   130
" And teach my son to lisp her name,
  " Who died to save his life.

" Then calling still upon thy name,
  " And praying still for thee ;
" Without repining or complaint,   135
  " Her gentle soul did flee."

What tongue can paint lord Albret's woe,
  The bitter tears he shed,
The bitter pangs that wrung his heart,
  To find his lady dead ?   140

He beat his breast : he tore his hair ;
  And shedding many a tear,
At length he askt to see his son ;
  The son that cost so dear.

New sorrowe seiz'd the damsells all :   145
  At length they faultering say ;
" Alas ! my lord, how shall we tell ?
  " Thy son is stoln away.

" Fair as the sweetest flower of spring,
  " Such was his infant mien :   150
" And on his little body stampt
  " Three wonderous marks were seen :

" A blood-red cross was on his arm ;
  " A dragon on his breast :
" A little garter all of gold   155
  " Was round his leg exprest.

" Three carefull nurses we provide
  " Our little lord to keep :
" One gave him sucke, one gave him food,
  " And one did lull to sleep.   160

" But lo ! all in the dead of night,
  " We heard a fearful sound :
" Loud thunder clapt ; the castle shook ;
  " And lightning flasht around.

" Dead with affright at first we lay ;   165
  " But rousing up anon,
" We ran to see our little lord :
  " Our little lord was gone !

" But how or where we could not tell ;
  " For lying on the ground,   170
" In deep and magic slumbers laid,
  " The nurses there we found."

O grief on grief ! lord Albret said :
  No more his tongue cou'd say,
When falling in a deadly swoone,   175
  Long time he lifeless lay.

At length restor'd to life and sense
  He nourisht endless woe,
No future joy his heart could taste,
  No future comfort know.   180

So withers on the mountain top
  A fair and stately oake,
Whose vigorous arms are torne away,
  By some rude thunder-stroke.

At length his castle irksome grew,   185
  He loathes his wonted home ;
His native country he forsakes
  In foreign lands to roame.

There up and downe he wandered far,
  Clad in a palmer's gown ;   190
Till his brown locks grew white as wool,
  His beard as thistle down.

At length, all wearied, down in death
  He laid his reverend head.
Meantime amid the lonely wilds   195
  His litttle son was bred.

There the weïrd lady of the woods
  Had borne him far away,
And train'd him up in feates of armes,
  And every martial play.   200

***

II.

ST. GEORGE AND THE DRAGON.

HE following ballad is given (with some corrections)
from two ancient black-letter copies in the *Pepys Collection:* one of which is in 12mo., the other in folio.

[The story of *St. George and the Dragon* is found in many
forms in the northern languages.]

F Hector's deeds did Homer sing;
    And of the sack of stately Troy,
What griefs fair Helena did bring,
    Which was sir Paris' only joy:
And by my pen I will recite   5
St. George's deeds, and English knight.

Against the Sarazens so rude
    Fought he full long and many a day,
Where many gyants he subdu'd,
    In honour of the christian way: 10
And after many adventures past
To Egypt land he came at last.

Now, as the story plain doth tell,
　　Within that countrey there did rest
A dreadful dragon fierce and fell,　　　　15
　　Whereby they were full sore opprest;
Who by his poisonous breath each day,
Did many of the city slay.

The grief whereof did grow so great
　　Throughout the limits of the land,　　20
That they their wise-men did intreat
　　To shew their cunning out of hand;
What way they might this fiend destroy,
That did the countrey thus annoy.

The wise-men all before the king　　　　25
　　This answer fram'd incontinent;
The dragon none to death might bring
　　By any means they could invent:
His skin more hard than brass was found,
That sword nor spear could pierce nor wound.　30

When this the people understood,
　　They cryed out most piteouslye,
The dragon's breath infects their blood,
　　That every day in heaps they dye:
Among them such a plague it bred,　　　　35
The living scarce could bury the dead.

No means there were, as they could hear,
　　For to appease the dragon's rage,
But to present some virgin clear,
　　Whose blood his fury might asswage;　40
Each day he would a maiden eat,
For to allay his hunger great.

This thing by art the wise-men found,
　　Which truly must observed be;
Wherefore throughout the city round　　　45
　　A virgin pure of good degree

Was by the king's commission still
Taken up to serve the dragon's will.

Thus did the dragon every day
    Untimely crop some virgin flowr,   50
Till all the maids were worn away,
    And none were left him to devour :
Saving the king's fair daughter bright,
Her father's only heart's delight.

Then came the officers to the king   55
    That heavy message to declare,
Which did his heart with sorrow sting ;
    She is, quoth he, my kingdom's heir :
O let us all be poisoned here,
Ere she should die, that is my dear.   60

Then rose the people presently,
    And to the king in rage they went ;
They said his daughter dear should dye,
    The dragon's fury to prevent :
Our daughters all are dead, quoth they,   65
And have been made the dragon's prey :

And by their blood we rescued were,
    And thou hast sav'd thy life thereby ;
And now in sooth it is but faire,
    For us thy daughter so should die.   70
O save my daughter, said the king ;
And let ME feel the dragon's sting.

Then fell fair Sabra on her knee,
    And to her father dear did say,
O father, strive not thus for me,   75
    But let me be the dragon's prey ;
It may be, for my sake alone
This plague upon the land was thrown.

Tis better I should dye, she said,
    Than all your subjects perish quite;   80
Perhaps the dragon here was laid,
    For my offence to work his spite:
And after he hath suckt my gore,
Your land shall feel the grief no more.

What hast thou done, my daughter dear,   85
    For to deserve this heavy scourge?
It is my fault, as may appear,
    Which makes the gods our state to purge;
Then ought I die, to stint the strife,
And to preserve thy happy life.   90

Like mad-men, all the people cried,
    Thy death to us can do no good;
Our safety only doth abide
    In making her the dragon's food.
Lo! here I am, I come, quoth she,   95
Therefore do what you will with me.

Nay stay, dear daughter, quoth the queen,
    And as thou art a virgin bright,
That hast for vertue famous been,
    So let me cloath thee all in white;   100
And crown thy head with flowers sweet,
An ornament for virgins meet.

And when she was attired so,
    According to her mother's mind,
Unto the stake then did she go;   105
    To which her tender limbs they bind:
And being bound to stake a thrall
She bade farewell unto them all.

Farewell, my father dear, quoth she,
    And my sweet mother meek and mild;   110
Take you no thought nor weep for me,
    For you may have another child:

Since for my country's good I dye,
Death I receive most willinglye.

The king and queen and all their train   115
    With weeping eyes went then their way,
And let their daughter there remain,
    To be the hungry dragon's prey:
But as she did there weeping lye,
Behold St. George came riding by.   120

And seeing there a lady bright
    So rudely tyed unto a stake,
As well became a valiant knight,
    He straight to her his way did take:
Tell me, sweet maiden, then quoth he,   125
What caitif thus abuseth thee?

And, lo! by Christ his cross I vow,
    Which here is figured on my breast,
I will revenge it on his brow,
    And break my lance upon his chest: 130
And speaking thus whereas he stood,
The dragon issued from the wood.

The lady that did first espy
    The dreadful dragon coming so,
Unto St. George aloud did cry,   135
    And willed him away to go;
Here comes that cursed fiend, quoth she;
That soon will make an end of me.

St. George then looking round about,
    The fiery dragon soon espy'd,   140
And like a knight of courage stout,
    Against him did most fiercely ride;
And with such blows he did him greet,
He fell beneath his horse's feet.

For with his launce that was so strong,   145
    As he came gaping in his face,
In at his mouth he thrust along;
    For he could pierce no other place:
And thus within the lady's view
This mighty dragon straight he slew.   150

The savour of his poisoned breath
    Could do this holy knight no harm.
Thus he the lady sav'd from death,
    And home he led her by the arm;
Which when king Ptolemy did see,   155
There was great mirth and melody.

When as that valiant champion there
    Had slain the dragon in the field,
To court he brought the lady fair,
    Which to their hearts much joy did yield.   160
He in the court of Egypt staid
Till he most falsely was betray'd.

That lady dearly lov'd the knight,
    He counted her his only joy;   165
But when their love was brought to light
    It turn'd unto their great annoy:
Th' Morocco king was in the court,
Who to the orchard did resort,

Dayly to take the pleasant air,   170
    For pleasure sake he us'd to walk,
Under a wall he oft did hear
    St. George with lady Sabra talk:
Their love he shew'd unto the king,
Which to St. George great woe did bring.   175

Those kings together did devise
    To make the christian knight away,
With letters him in curteous wise
    They straightway sent to Persia:

But wrote to the sophy him to kill,   180
And treacherously his blood to spill.

Thus they for good did him reward
      With evil, and most subtilly
By much vile meanes they had regard
      To work his death most cruelly;   185
Who, as through Persia land he rode,
With zeal destroy'd each idol god.

For which offence he straight was thrown
      Into a dungeon dark and deep;
Where, when he thought his wrongs upon,   190
      He bitterly did wail and weep:
Yet like a knight of courage stout,
At length his way he digged out.

Three grooms of the king of Persia
      By night this valiant champion slew,   195
Though he had fasted many a day;
      And then away from thence he flew
On the best steed the sophy had;
Which when he knew he was full mad.

Towards Christendom he made his flight,   200
      But met a gyant by the way,
With whom in combat he did fight
      Most valiantly a summer's day:
Who yet, for all his bats of steel,
Was forc'd the sting of death to feel.   205

Back o'er the seas with many bands
      Of warlike souldiers soon he past,
Vowing upon those heathen lands
      To work revenge; which at the last,
Ere thrice three years were gone and spent,   210
He wrought unto his heart's content.

Save onely Egypt land he spar'd
    For Sabra bright her only sake,
And, ere for her he had regard,
    He meant a tryal kind to make: 215
Mean while the king o'ercome in field
Unto saint George did quickly yield.

Then straight Morocco's king he slew,
    And took fair Sabra to his wife,
But meant to try if she were true   220
    Ere with her he would lead his life:
And, tho' he had her in his train,
She did a virgin pure remain.

Toward England then that lovely dame
    The brave St. George conducted strait, 225
An eunuch also with them came,
    Who did upon the lady wait;
These three from Egypt went alone.
Now mark St. George's valour shown.

When as they in a forest were,   230
    The lady did desire to rest;
Mean while St. George to kill a deer,
    For their repast did think it best:
Leaving her with the eunuch there,
Whilst he did go to kill the deer.   235

But lo! all in his absence came
    Two hungry lyons fierce and fell,
And tore the eunuch on the same
    In pieces small, the truth to tell;
Down by the lady then they laid,   240
Whereby they shew'd, she was a maid.

But when he came from hunting back,
    And did behold this heavy chance,
Then for his lovely virgin's sake
    His courage strait he did advance,   245

And came into the lions sight,
Who ran at him with all their might.

Their rage did him no whit dismay,
   Who, like a stout and valiant knight,
Did both the hungry lyons slay   250
   Within the lady Sabra's sight:
Who all this while sad and demure,
There stood most like a virgin pure.

Now when St. George did surely know
   This lady was a virgin true,   255
His heart was glad, that erst was woe,
   And all his love did soon renew:
He set her on a palfrey steed,
And towards England came with speed.

Where being in short space arriv'd   260
   Unto his native dwelling-place;
Therein with his dear love he liv'd,
   And fortune did his nuptials grace:
They many years of joy did see,
And led their lives at Coventry.   265

III.

LOVE WILL FIND OUT THE WAY.

HIS excellent song is ancient: but we could only give it from a modern copy.

[Earlier editions of this spirited song are printed in Evans's *Old Ballads*, iii. 282 (1810), and Rimbault's *Little Book of Songs and Ballads*, p. 137. It is quoted in Brome's *Sparagus Garden*, acted in 1635, and Shirley's *Constant Maid* was republished in 1661, under the title of *Love will find out the Way*, by T. B.

Dr. Rimbault has the following note in his *Musical Illustrations*, "The old black-letter copy of this ballad is called ' *Truth's Integrity:*

or, *a curious Northerne Ditty,* called *Love will finde out the Way.* To a pleasant new Tune Printed at London for F. Coules, dwelling in the Old Bailey.' There is a second part consisting of six stanzas, which Percy has not reprinted. The tune is here given (translated from the *Tablature*) from *Musicks Recreation on the Lyra Viol,* published by Playford in 1652. It is also preserved in Forbes's *Cantus,* 1662; in *Musick's Delight on the Cithren,* 1666; and in D'Urfey's *Pills to Purge Melancholy,* 1719. The *Pepysian Collection* contains several ballads to this tune."

Mr. Chappell writes, "The air is still current, for in the summer of 1855, Mr. Jennings, Organist of All Saints' Church, Maidstone, noted it down from the wandering hop-pickers singing a song to it on their entrance into that town." *Popular Music,* vol. i. p. 304.]

OVER the mountains,
    And over the waves;
Under the fountains,
    And under the graves;
Under the floods that are deepest,   5
    Which Neptune obey;
Over rocks that are steepest,
    Love will find out the way.

Where there is no place
    For the glow-worm to lye;   10
Where there is no space
    For receipt of a fly;
Where the midge dares not venture,
    Lest herself fast she lay;
If love come, he will enter,   15
    And soon find out his way.

You may esteem him
    A child for his might;
Or you may deem him
    A coward from his flight;   20

But if she, whom love doth honour,
    Be conceal'd from the day,
Set a thousand guards upon her,
    Love will find out the way.

Some think to lose him,   25
    By having him confin'd;
And some do suppose him,
    Poor thing, to be blind;
But if ne'er so close ye wall him,
    Do the best that you may,   30
Blind love, if so ye call him,
    Will find out his way.

You may train the eagle
    To stoop to your fist;
Or you may inveigle   35
    The phenix of the east;
The lioness, ye may move her
    To give o'er her prey;
But you'll ne'er stop a lover:
    He will find out his way.

**

IV.

LORD THOMAS AND FAIR ANNET,

A Scottish Ballad,

SEEMS to be composed (not without improvements) out of two ancient English ones, printed in the former part of this volume. See book i. ballad xv. and book ii. ballad iv.—If this had been the original, the authors of those two ballads would hardly have adopted two such different stories: besides, this contains enlargements not to be found in either of the others. It is given with some corrections, from a MS. copy transmitted from Scotland.

[Jamieson prints a version of this ballad which was taken down from the recitation of Mrs. W. Arrot of Aberbrothick, and is entitled *Sweet Willie and Fair Annie.* He contends that it is "pure and entire," and expresses his opinion that the text of Percy's copy had been "adjusted" previous to its leaving Scotland.]

ORD Thomas and fair Annet
    Sate a' day on a hill;
    Whan night was cum, and sun was sett,
    They had not talkt their fill.

Lord Thomas said a word in jest,   5
    Fair Annet took it ill:
A'! I will nevir wed a wife
    Against my ain friends will.

Gif ye wull nevir wed a wife,
    A wife wull neir wed yee.   10
Sae he is hame to tell his mither,
    And knelt upon his knee:

O rede, O rede, mither, he says,
    A gude rede gie to mee:
O sall I tak the nut-browne bride,   15
    And let faire Annet bee?

The nut-browne bride haes gowd and gear,
    Fair Annet she has gat nane;
And the little beauty fair Annet has,
    O it wull soon be gane!   20

And he has till his brother gane:
    Now, brother, rede ye mee;
A' sall I marrie the nut browne bride,
    And let fair Annet bee?

The nut-browne bride has oxen, brother,   25
   The nut-browne bride has kye;
I wad hae ye marrie the nut-browne bride,
   And cast fair Annet bye.

Her oxen may dye i' the house, Billìe,
   And her kye into the byre;   30
And I sall hae nothing to my sell,
   Bot a fat fadge[1] by the fyre.

And he has till his sister gane:
   Now, sister, rede ye mee;
O sall I marrie the nut-browne bride,   35
   And set fair Annet free?

Ise rede ye tak fair Annet, Thomas,
   And let the browne bride alane;
Lest ye sould sigh and say, Alace!
   What is this we brought hame?   40

No, I will tak my mithers counsel,
   And marrie me owt o' hand;
And I will tak the nut-browne bride;
   Fair Annet may leive the land.

Up then rose fair Annets father   45
   Twa hours or it wer day,
And he is gane into the bower,
   Wherein fair Annet lay.

Rise up, rise up, fair Annet, he says,
   Put on your silken sheene;   50
Let us gae to St. Maries kirke,
   And see that rich weddeen.

My maides, gae to my dressing roome,
   And dress to me my hair;
Whair-eir yee laid a plait before,
   See yee lay ten times mair.

[1 bundle of sticks.]

My maids, gae to my dressing room,
    And dress to me my smock ;
The one half is o' the holland fine,
    The other o' needle-work. 60

The horse fair Annet rade upon,
    He amblit like the wind,
Wi' siller he was shod before,
    Wi' burning gowd behind.

Four and twenty siller bells 65
    Wer a' tyed till his mane,
And yae tift[1] o' the norland wind,
    They tinkled ane by ane.

Four and twenty gay gude knichts
    Rade by the fair Annets side, 70
And four and twenty fair ladies,
    As gin she had bin a bride.

And whan she cam to Maries kirk,
    She sat on Maries stean :
The cleading that fair Annet had on 75
    It skinkled in their een.

And whan she cam into the kirk,
    She shimmer'd like the sun ;
The belt that was about her waist,
    Was a' wi' pearles bedone. 80

She sat her by the nut-browne bride,
    And her een they wer sae clear,
Lord Thomas he clean forgat the bride,
    Whan fair Annet she drew near.

He had a rose into his hand, 85
    And he gave it kisses three,
And reaching by the nut-browne bride,
    Laid it on fair Annets knee

[1 gust of wind.]

Up than spak the nut-browne bride,
   She spak wi' meikle spite ;   90
And whair gat ye that rose-water,
   That does mak yee sae white ?

O I did get the rose-water,
   Whair ye wull neir get nane,
For I did get that very rose-water   95
   Into my mithers wame.

The bride she drew a long bodkin,
   Frae out her gay head-gear,
And strake fair Annet unto the heart,
   That word she nevir spak mair.   100

Lord Thomas he saw fair Annet wex pale,
   And marvelit what mote bee :
But whan he saw her dear hearts blude,
   A' wood-wroth[1] wexed hee.

He drew his dagger, that was sae sharp,   105
   That was sae sharp and meet,
And drave into the nut-browne bride,
   That fell deid at his feit.

Now stay for me, dear Annet, he sed,
   Now stay, my dear, he cry'd ;   110
Then strake the dagger untill his heart,
   And fell deid by her side.

Lord Thomas was buried without kirk-wa',
   Fair Annet within the quiere ;
And o' the tane thair grew a birk,   115
   The other a bonny briere.

And ay they grew, and ay they threw,
   As they wad faine be neare ;
And by this ye may ken right weil,
   They ware twa luvers deare.   120

[1 furiously enraged.]

V.

UNFADING BEAUTY.

THIS little beautiful sonnet is reprinted from a small volume of "*Poems* by *Thomas Carew*, Esq. one of the gentlemen of the privie-chamber, and sewer in ordinary to his majesty (Charles I.) Lond. 1640." This elegant, and almost-forgotten writer, whose poems have been deservedly revived, died in the prime of his age, in 1639.

In the original follows a third stanza; which, not being of general application, nor of equal merit, I have ventured to omit.

[Dr. Rimbault informs us that the original music was composed by Henry Lawes, and is included in his *Ayres and Dialogues for one, two and three Voyces*, 1653.]

HEE, that loves a rosie cheeke,
    Or a corall lip admires,
    Or from star-like eyes doth seeke
    Fuell to maintaine his fires,
As old time makes these decay,   5
So his flames must waste away.

But a smooth and stedfast mind,
    Gentle thoughts, and calme desires,
Hearts with equal love combin'd
    Kindle never-dying fires :   10
Where these are not I despise
Lovely cheekes, or lips, or eyes.
        *   *   *   *   *

VI.

GEORGE BARNWELL.

HE subject of this ballad is sufficiently popular from the modern play which is founded upon it. This was written by *George Lillo*, a jeweller of London, and first acted about 1730.—As for the ballad it was printed at least as early as the middle of the last century.

It is here given from three old printed copies, which exhibit a strange intermixture of Roman and black letter. It is also collated with another copy in the *Ashmole Collection* at Oxford, which is thus intitled, "An excellent ballad of *George Barnwell*, an apprentice of London, who . . . thrice robbed his master and murdered his uncle in Ludlow." The tune is *The Merchant*.

This tragical narrative seems to relate a real fact; but when it happened I have not been able to discover.

[Ritson writes as follows concerning certain improvements made by Percy in the following ballad (*Ancient Songs*, 1829, vol. ii. p. 165, note):—" Throughout this 'second part' (except in a single instance) the metre of the first line of each stanza is in the old editions lengthened by a couple of syllables, which are, occasionally at least, a manifest interpolation. The person also is for the most part changed from the first to the third, with evident impropriety. Dr. Percy has very ingeniously restored the measure by ejecting the superfluous syllables, and given consistency to the whole by the restoration of the proper person; and as it is now highly improbable that any further ancient copy will be found, and those which exist are manifestly corrupt, it seemed justifiable to adopt the judicious emendations of this ingenious editor."

Dr. Rimbault observes, " This curious tune (*The Merchant*) which has been quite overlooked by antiquaries, is found, together with the original ballad, *The Merchant and the Fiddler's Wife*, in D'Urfey's *Pills to Purge Melancholy*, vol. v. p. 77, edit. 1719."

The former great popularity of the story of the wicked young prentice is shown by James Smith's parody in the *Rejected Addresses* and Thackeray's caricature romance—*George de Barnwell.*]

The First Part.

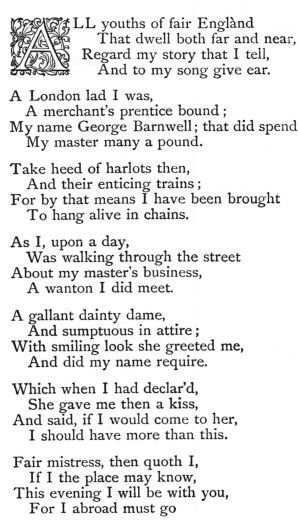

ALL youths of fair Englànd
   That dwell both far and near,
Regard my story that I tell,
   And to my song give ear.

A London lad I was,   5
   A merchant's prentice bound ;
My name George Barnwell; that did spend
   My master many a pound.

Take heed of harlots then,
   And their enticing trains ;   10
For by that means I have been brought
   To hang alive in chains.

As I, upon a day,
   Was walking through the street
About my master's business,   15
   A wanton I did meet.

A gallant dainty dame,
   And sumptuous in attire ;
With smiling look she greeted me,
   And did my name require.   20

Which when I had declar'd,
   She gave me then a kiss,
And said, if I would come to her,
   I should have more than this.

Fair mistress, then quoth I,   25
   If I the place may know,
This evening I will be with you,
   For I abroad must go

To gather monies in,
   That are my master's due :
And ere that I do home return,
   I'll come and visit you.
30

Good Barnwell, then quoth she,
   Do thou to Shoreditch come,
And ask for Mrs. Millwood's house,
   Next door unto the Gun.
35

And trust me on my truth,
   If thou keep touch with me,
My dearest friend, as my own heart
   Thou shalt right welcome be.
40

Thus parted we in peace,
   And home I passed right ;
Then went abroad, and gathered in,
   By six o'clock at night,

An hundred pound and one :
   With bag under my arm
I went to Mrs. Millwood's house,
   And thought on little harm ;
45

And knocking at the door,
   Straightway herself came down ;
Rustling in most brave attire,
   With hood and silken gown.
50

Who, through her beauty bright,
   So gloriously did shine,
That she amaz'd my dazzling eyes,
   She seemed so divine.
55

She took me by the hand,
   And with a modest grace,
Welcome, sweet Barnwell, then quoth she,
   Unto this homely place.
60

And since I have thee found
    As good as thy word to be:
A homely supper, ere we part,
    Thou shalt take here with me.

O pardon me, quoth I,   65
    Fair mistress, I you pray;
For why, out of my master's house,
    So long I dare not stay.

Alas, good Sir, she said,
    Are you so strictly ty'd,   70
You may not with your dearest friend
    One hour or two abide?

Faith, then the case is hard:
    If it be so, quoth she,
I would I were a prentice bound,   75
    To live along with thee:

Therefore, my dearest George,
    List well what I shall say,
And do not blame a woman much,
    Her fancy to bewray.   80

Let not affection's force
    Be counted lewd desire;
Nor think it not immodesty,
    I should thy love require.

With that she turn'd aside,   85
    And with a blushing red,
A mournful motion she bewray'd
    By hanging down her head.

A handkerchief she had,
    All wrought with silk and gold: 90
Which she to stay her trickling tears
    Before her eyes did hold.

This thing unto my sight
   Was wondrous rare and strange;
And in my soul and inward thought   95
   It wrought a sudden change:

That I so hardy grew,
   To take her by the hand:
Saying, Sweet mistress, why do you
   So dull and pensive stand?   100

Call me no mistress now,
   But Sarah, thy true friend,
Thy servant, Millwood, honouring thee,
   Until her life hath end.

If thou wouldst here alledge,   105
   Thou art in years a boy;
So was Adonis, yet was he
   Fair Venus' only joy.

Thus I, who ne'er before
   Of woman found such grace,
But seeing now so fair a dame   110
   Give me a kind embrace,

I supt with her that night,
   With joys that did abound;
And for the same paid presently,   115
   In money twice three pound.

An hundred kisses then,
   For my farewel she gave;
Crying, Sweet Barnwell, when shall I
   Again thy company have?   120

O stay not hence too long,
   Sweet George, have me in mind.
Her words bewicht my childishness,
   She uttered them so kind:

So that I made a vow,   125
  Next Sunday without fail,
With my sweet Sarah once again
  To tell some pleasant tale.

When she heard me say so,
  The tears fell from her eye;   130
O George, quoth she, if thou dost fail,
  Thy Sarah sure will dye.

Though long, yet loe! at last,
  The appointed day was come,
That I must with my Sarah meet;   135
  Having a mighty sum

Of money in my hand,*
  Unto her house went I,
Whereas my love upon her bed
  In saddest sort did lye.   140

What ails my heart's delight,
  My Sarah dear? quoth I;
Let not my love lament and grieve,
  Nor sighing pine, and die.

But tell me, dearest friend,   145
  What may thy woes amend,
And thou shalt lack no means of help,
  Though forty pound I spend.

With that she turn'd her head,
  And sickly thus did say,   150
Oh me, sweet George, my grief is great,
  Ten pound I have to pay

---

* The having a sum of money with him on Sunday, &c. shews
this narrative to have been penned before the civil wars: the strict
observance of the sabbath was owing to the change of manners
at that period.

Unto a cruel wretch;
　And God he knows, quoth she,
I have it not.　Tush, rise, I said,　　　155
　And take it here of me.

Ten pounds, nor ten times ten,
　Shall make my love decay.
Then from my bag into her lap,
　I cast ten pound straightway.　　　160

All blithe and pleasant then,
　To banqueting we go;
She proffered me to lye with her,
　And said it should be so.

And after that same time,　　　165
　I gave her store of coyn,
Yea, sometimes fifty pound at once;
　All which I did purloyn.

And thus I did pass on;
　Until my master then　　　170
Did call to have his reckoning in
　Cast up among his men.

The which when as I heard,
　I knew not what to say:
For well I knew that I was out　　　175
　Two hundred pound that day.

Then from my master straight
　I ran in secret sort;
And unto Sarah Millwood there
　My case I did report.　　　180

" But how she us'd this youth,
　In this his care and woe,
And all a strumpet's wiley ways,
　The SECOND PART may showe."

The Second Part.

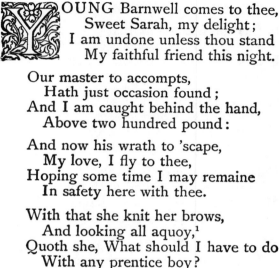OUNG Barnwell comes to thee,
   Sweet Sarah, my delight;
I am undone unless thou stand
   My faithful friend this night.

Our master to accompts,   5
   Hath just occasion found;
And I am caught behind the hand,
   Above two hundred pound:

And now his wrath to 'scape,
   My love, I fly to thee,   10
Hoping some time I may remaine
   In safety here with thee.

With that she knit her brows,
   And looking all aquoy,[1]
Quoth she, What should I have to do   15
   With any prentice boy?

And seeing you have purloyn'd
   Your master's goods away,
The case is bad, and therefore here
   You shall no longer stay.   20

Why, dear, thou knowst, I said,
   How all which I could get,
I gave it, and did spend it all
   Upon thee every whit.

Quoth she, Thou art a knave,   25
   To charge me in this sort,
Being a woman of credit fair,
   And known of good report:

[¹ coy, shy.]

Therefore I tell thee flat,
  Be packing with good speed;   30
I do defie thee from my heart,
  And scorn thy filthy deed.

Is this the friendship, that
  You did to me protest?
Is this the great affection, which   35
  You so to me exprest?

Now fie on subtle shrews!
  The best is, I may speed
To get a lodging any where,
  For money in my need.   40

False woman, now farewell,
  Whilst twenty pound doth last,
My anchor in some other haven
  With freedom I will cast.

When she perceiv'd by this,   45
  I had store of money there :
Stay, George, quoth she, thou art too quick :
  Why, man, I did but jeer :

Dost think for all my speech,
  That I would let thee go?   50
Faith no, said she, my love to thee
  I wiss is more than so.

You scorne a prentice boy,
  I heard you just now swear,
Wherefore I will not trouble you.——   55
  ——Nay, George, hark in thine ear;

Thou shalt not go to-night,
  What chance so e're befall :
But man we'll have a bed for thee,
  O else the devil take all.   60

So I by wiles bewitcht,
 And snar'd with fancy still,
Had then no power to 'get' away,
 Or to withstand her will.

For wine on wine I call'd,   65
 And cheer upon good cheer;
And nothing in the world I thought
 For Sarah's love too dear.

Whilst in her company,
 I had such merriment;   70
All, all too little I did think,
 That I upon her spent.

A fig for care and thought!
 When all my gold is gone,
In faith, my girl, we will have more,   75
 Whoever I light upon.

My father's rich, why then
 Should I want store of gold?
Nay with a father sure, quoth she,
 A son may well make bold.   80

I've a sister richly wed,
 I'll rob her ere I'll want.
Nay, then quoth Sarah, they may well
 Consider of your scant.

Nay, I an uncle have;   85
 At Ludlow he doth dwell :
He is a grazier, which in wealth
 Doth all the rest excell.

Ere I will live in lack,
 And have no coyn for thee :   90
I'll rob his house, and murder him,
 Why should you not ? quoth she :

Was I a man, ere I
  Would live in poor estate;
On father, friends, and all my kin,   95
  I would my talons grate.

For without money, George,
  A man is but a beast:
But bringing money, thou shalt be
  Always my welcome guest.   100

For shouldst thou be pursued
  With twenty hues and cryes,
And with a warrant searched for
  With Argus' hundred eyes,

Yet here thou shalt be safe;   105
  Such privy ways there be,
That if they sought an hundred years,
  They could not find out thee.

And so carousing both
  Their pleasures to content: 110
George Barnwell had in little space
  His money wholly spent.

Which done, to Ludlow straight
  He did provide to go,
To rob his wealthy uncle there;   115
  His minion would it so.

And once he thought to take
  His father by the way,
But that he fear'd his master had
  Took order for his stay*.   120

Unto his uncle then
  He rode with might and main,
Who with a welcome and good cheer,
  Did Barnwell entertain.

---

* *i.e.* for stopping, and apprehending him at his father's.

One fortnight's space he stayed, 125
    Until it chanced so,
His uncle with his cattle did
    Unto a market go.

His kinsman rode with him,
    Where he did see right plain, 130
Great store of money he had took :
    When coming home again,

Sudden within a wood,
    He struck his uncle down,
And beat his brains out of his head ; 135
    So sore he crackt his crown.

Then seizing fourscore pound,
    To London straight he hyed,
And unto Sarah Millwood all
    The cruell fact descryed. 140

Tush, 'tis no matter, George,
    So we the money have
To have good cheer in jolly sort,
    And deck us fine and brave.

Thus lived in filthy sort, 145
    Until their store was gone :
When means to get them any more,
    I wis, poor George, had none.

Therefore in railing sort,
    She thrust him out of door : 150
Which is the just reward of those,
    Who spend upon a whore.

O ! do me not disgrace
    In this my need, quoth he.
She call'd him thief and murderer, 155
    With all the spight might be :

To the constable she sent,
  To have him apprehended;
And shewed how far, in each degree,
  He had the laws offended.   160

When Barnwell saw her drift,
  To sea he got straightway;
Where fear and sting of conscience
  Continually on him lay.

Unto the lord mayor then,   165
  He did a letter write;
In which his own and Sarah's fault
  He did at large recite.

Whereby she seized was,
  And then to Ludlow sent: 170
Where she was judg'd, condemn'd, and hang'd,
  For murder incontinent.

There dyed this gallant quean,
  Such was her greatest gains:
For murder in Polonia,   175
  Was Barnwell hang'd in chains.

Lo! here's the end of youth,
  That after harlots haunt;
Who in the spoil of other men,
  About the streets do flaunt.   180

VII.

THE STEDFAST SHEPHERD.

HESE beautiful stanzas were written by *George Wither*, of whom some account was given in the former part of this volume ; see the song intitled, *The Shepherd's Resolution*, book ii. song xxi. In the first edition of this work only a small fragment of this sonnet was inserted. It was afterwards rendered more compleat and intire by the addition of five stanzas more, extracted from Wither's pastoral poem, intitled, *The Mistress of Philarete*, of which this song makes a part. It is now given still more correct and perfect by comparing it with another copy, printed by the author in his improved edition of *The Shepherd's Hunting*, 1620, 8vo.

[The Folio MS. (ed. Hales and Furnivall, vol. iii. p. 360) contains only the fifth and sixth stanzas slightly varied, which were printed in the first edition of the *Reliques*, with the title of *The Aspiring Shepherd*.]

ENCE away, thou Syren, leave me,
 Pish! unclaspe these wanton armes ;
Sugred words can ne'er deceive me,
 (Though thou prove a thousand
  charmes).
  Fie, fie, forbeare ;   5
  No common snare
Can ever my affection chaine :
  Thy painted baits,
  And poore deceits,
Are all bestowed on me in vaine. 10

I'me no slave to such, as you be ;
 Neither shall that snowy brest,
Rowling eye, and lip of ruby
 Ever robb me of my rest :

Goe, go display 15
Thy beautie's ray
To some more soone-enamour'd swaine;
Those common wiles
Of sighs and smiles
Are all bestowed on me in vaine. 20

I have elsewhere vowed a dutie;
Turne away thy tempting eye:
Shew not me a painted beautie;
These impostures I defie:
My spirit lothes 25
Where gawdy clothes
And fained othes may love obtaine:
I love her so,
Whose looke sweares No;
That all your labours will be vaine. 30

Can he prize the tainted posies,
Which on every brest are worne;
That may plucke the virgin roses
From their never-touched thorne?
I can goe rest 35
On her sweet brest,
That is the pride of Cynthia's traine:
Then stay thy tongue;
Thy mermaid song
Is all bestowed on me in vaine. 40

Hee's a foole, that basely dallies,
Where each peasant mates with him:
Shall I haunt the thronged vallies,
Whilst ther's noble hills to climbe?
No, no, though clownes 45
Are scar'd with frownes,
I know the best can but disdaine;
And those Ile prove:
So will thy love
Be all bestowed on me in vaine. 50

I doe scorne to vow a dutie,
    Where each lustfull lad may wooe :
Give me her, whose sun-like beautie
    Buzzards dare not soar unto :
        Shee, shee it is   55
        Affoords that blisse
    For which I would refuse no paine :
        But such as you,
        Fond fooles, adieu ;
    You seeke to captive me in vaine.   60

Leave me then, you Syrens, leave me ;
    Seeke no more to worke my harmes :
Craftie wiles cannot deceive me,
    Who am proofe against your charmes :
        You labour may   65
        To lead astray
    The heart, that constant shall remaine :
        And I the while
        Will sit and smile
    To see you spend your time in vaine.   7

VIII.

THE SPANISH VIRGIN, or EFFECTS
OF JEALOUSY.

HE subject of this ballad is taken from a folio collection
of tragical stories, intitled, *The theatre of God's judg-
ments,* by Dr. Beard and Dr. Taylor, 1642. Pt. ii. p. 89.
—The text is given (with corrections) from two copies;
one of them in black-letter in the Pepys collection. In this every
stanza is accompanied with the following distich by way of burden :

    " Oh jealousie ! thou art nurst in hell :
    Depart from hence, and therein dwell."

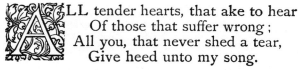LL tender hearts, that ake to hear
 Of those that suffer wrong;
All you, that never shed a tear,
 Give heed unto my song.

Fair Isabella's tragedy   5
 My tale doth far exceed:
Alas! that so much cruelty
 In female hearts should breed!

In Spain a lady liv'd of late,
 Who was of high degree;   10
Whose wayward temper did create
 Much woe and misery.

Strange jealousies so fill'd her head
 With many a vain surmize,
She thought her lord had wrong'd her bed, 15
 And did her love despise.

A gentlewoman passing fair
 Did on this lady wait;
With bravest dames she might compare;
 Her beauty was compleat.   20

Her lady cast a jealous eye
 Upon this gentle maid;
And taxt her with disloyaltye;
 And did her oft upbraid.

In silence still this maiden meek   25
 Her bitter taunts would bear,
While oft adown her lovely cheek
 Would steal the falling tear.

In vain in humble sort she strove
 Her fury to disarm;   30
As well the meekness of the dove
 The bloody hawke might charm.

Her lord of humour light and gay,
   And innocent the while,
As oft as she came in his way,   35
   Would on the damsell smile.

And oft before his lady's face,
   As thinking her her friend,
He would the maiden's modest grace
   And comeliness commend.   40

All which incens'd his lady so
   She burnt with wrath extreame;
At length the fire that long did glow,
   Burst forth into a flame.

For on a day it so befell,   45
   When he was gone from home,
The lady all with rage did swell,
   And to the damsell come.

And charging her with great offence,
   And many a grievous fault;   50
She bade her servants drag her thence,
   Into a dismal vault,

That lay beneath the common-shore:
   A dungeon dark and deep:
Where they were wont, in days of yore,   55
   Offenders great to keep.

There never light of chearful day
   Dispers'd the hideous gloom;
But dank and noisome vapours play
   Around the wretched room: 60

And adders, snakes, and toads therein,
   As afterwards was known,
Long in this loathsome vault had bin,
   And were to monsters grown.

Into this foul and fearful place,   65
   The fair one innocent
Was cast, before her lady's face;
   Her malice to content.

This maid no sooner enter'd is,
   But strait, alas! she hears   70
The toads to croak, and snakes to hiss:
   Then grievously she fears.

Soon from their holes the vipers creep,
   And fiercely her assail:
Which makes the damsel sorely weep,   75
   And her sad fate bewail.

With her fair hands she strives in vain
   Her body to defend:
With shrieks and cries she doth complain,
   But all is to no end.   80

A servant listning near the door,
   Struck with her doleful noise,
Strait ran his lady to implore;
   But she'll not hear his voice.

With bleeding heart he goes agen   85
   To mark the maiden's groans;
And plainly hears, within the den,
   How she herself bemoans.

Again he to his lady hies
   With all the haste he may: 90
She into furious passion flies,
   And orders him away.

Still back again does he return
   To hear her tender cries;
The virgin now had ceas'd to mourn;   95
   Which fill'd him with surprize.

In grief, and horror, and affright,
   He listens at the walls;
But finding all was silent quite,
   He to his lady calls.   100

Too sure, O lady, now quoth he,
   Your cruelty hath sped;
Make hast, for shame, and come and see;
   I fear the virgin's dead.

She starts to hear her sudden fate,   105
   And does with torches run :
But all her haste was now too late,
   For death his worst had done.

The door being open'd strait they found
   The virgin stretch'd along :   110
Two dreadful snakes had wrapt her round,
   Which her to death had stung.

One round her legs, her thighs, her waist
   Had twin'd his fatal wreath :
The other close her neck embrac'd,   115
   And stopt her gentle breath.

The snakes, being from her body thrust,
   Their bellies were so fill'd,
That with excess of blood they burst,
   Thus with their prey were kill'd.   120

The wicked lady at this sight,
   With horror strait ran mad;
So raving dy'd, as was most right,
   'Cause she no pity had.

Let me advise you, ladies all,   125
   Of jealousy beware :
It causeth many a one to fall,
   And is the devil's snare.

⁎

IX.

JEALOUSY TYRANT OF THE MIND.

 HIS Song is by *Dryden,* being inserted in his Tragi-
Comedy of *Love Triumphant,* &c.—On account of
the subject it is inserted here.

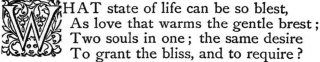HAT state of life can be so blest,
As love that warms the gentle brest;
Two souls in one; the same desire
To grant the bliss, and to require?
If in this heaven a hell we find,   5
        Tis all from thee,
        O Jealousie!
Thou tyrant, tyrant of the mind.

All other ills, though sharp they prove,
Serve to refine and perfect love :   10
In absence, or unkind disdaine,
Sweet hope relieves the lovers paine:
        But, oh, no cure but death we find
            To sett us free
            From jealousie,   15
Thou tyrant, tyrant of the mind.

False in thy glass all objects are,
Some sett too near, and some too far:
Thou art the fire of endless night,
The fire that burns, and gives no light.   20
        All torments of the damn'd we find
            In only thee,
            O Jealousie;
Thou tyrant, tyrant of the mind.

X.

CONSTANT PENELOPE.

HE ladies are indebted for the following notable documents to the Pepys collection, where the original is
preserved in black-letter, and is intitled, *A looking-
glass for ladies, or a mirrour for married women.* Tune
Queen Dido, or Troy town.

WHEN Greeks and Trojans fell at strife,
    And lords in armour bright were seen ;
When many a gallant lost his life
    About fair Hellen, beauty's queen ;
Ulysses, general so free,   5
Did leave his dear Penelope.

When she this wofull news did hear,
    That he would to the warrs of Troy ;
For grief she shed full many a tear,
    At parting from her only joy ;   10
Her ladies all about her came,
To comfort up this Grecian dame.

Ulysses, with a heavy heart,
    Unto her then did mildly say,
The time is come that we must part ;   15
    My honour calls me hence away ;
Yet in my absence, dearest, be
My constant wife, Penelope.

Let me no longer live, she sayd,
    Then to my lord I true remain ;   20
My honour shall not be betray'd
    Until I see my love again ;
For I will ever constant prove,
As is the loyal turtle-dove.

Thus did they part with heavy chear,   25
  And to the ships his way he took;
Her tender eyes dropt many a tear;
  Still casting many a longing look:
She saw him on the surges glide,
And unto Neptune thus she cry'd: 30

Thou god, whose power is in the deep,
  And rulest in the ocean main,
My loving lord in safety keep
  Till he return to me again:
That I his person may behold,   35
To me more precious far than gold.

Then straight the ships with nimble sails
  Were all convey'd out of her sight:
Her cruel fate she then bewails,
  Since she had lost her hearts delight.   40
Now shall my practice be, quoth she,
True vertue and humility.

My patience I will put in ure,[1]
  My charity I will extend;
Since for my woe there is no cure,
  The helpless now I will befriend: 45
The widow and the fatherless
I will relieve, when in distress.

Thus she continued year by year
  In doing good to every one;   50
Her fame was noised every where,
  To young and old the same was known,
That she no company would mind,
Who were to vanity inclin'd.

[1 use.]

Mean while Ulysses fought for fame,   55
  'Mongst Trojans hazarding his life:
Young gallants, hearing of her name,
  Came flocking for to tempt his wife:
For she was lovely, young, and fair,
No lady might with her compare.   60

With costly gifts and jewels fine,
  They did endeavour her to win;
With banquets and the choicest wine,
  For to allure her unto sin:
Most persons were of high degree,   65
Who courted fair Penelope.

With modesty and comely grace,
  Their wanton suits she did denye;
No tempting charms could e'er deface
  Her dearest husband's memorye;   70
But constant she would still remain,
Hopeing to see him once again.

Her book her dayly comfort was,
  And that she often did peruse;
She seldom looked in her glass;   75
  Powder and paint she ne'er would use.
I wish all ladies were as free
From pride, as was Penelope.

She in her needle took delight,
  And likewise in her spinning-wheel;   80
Her maids about her every night
  Did use the distaff, and the reel:
The spiders, that on rafters twine,
Scarce spin a thread more soft and fine.

Sometimes she would bewail the loss   85
  And absence of her dearest love:
Sometimes she thought the seas to cross,
  Her fortune on the waves to prove.

I fear my lord is slain, quoth she,
He stays so from Penelope.   90

At length the ten years siege of Troy
    Did end: in flames the city burn'd;
And to the Grecians was great joy,
    To see the towers to ashes turn'd:
Then came Ulysses home to see   95
His constant, dear, Penelope.

O blame her not if she was glad,
    When she her lord again had seen.
Thrice-welcome home, my dear, she said,
    A long time absent thou hast been: 100
The wars shall never more deprive
Me of my lord whilst I'm alive.

Fair ladies all example take;
    And hence a worthy lesson learn,
All youthful follies to forsake,   105
    And vice from virtue to discern:
And let all women strive to be,
As constant as Penelope.

XI.

TO LUCASTA, ON GOING TO THE WARS.

Y Col. Richard Lovelace: from the volume of his poems, intitled *Lucasta*, (Lond. 1649. 12mo.). The elegance of this writer's manner would be more admired, if it had somewhat more of simplicity.

[Percy's admirers would be glad to expunge the above unjust judgment. Some of Lovelace's poems may be affected, but that charge cannot be brought against these exquisite verses, the last two of which have become a world-famed quotation.]

ELL me not, sweet, I am unkinde,
    That from the nunnerie
Of thy chaste breast and quiet minde,
    To warre and armes I flie.

True, a new mistresse now I chase,   5
    The first foe in the field;
And with a stronger faith imbrace
    A sword, a horse, a shield.

Yet this inconstancy is such,
    As you too shall adore;   10
I could not love thee, deare, so much,
    Lov'd I not honour more.

XII.

VALENTINE AND URSINE.

HE old story-book of *Valentine and Orson* (which suggested the plan of this tale, but it is not strictly followed in it) was originally a translation from the French, being one of their earliest attempts at romance. See *Le Bibliothèque de Romans, &c.*

The circumstance of the bridge of bells is taken from the old metrical legend of Sir Bevis, and has also been copied in the *Seven Champions.* The original lines are,

> " Over the dyke a bridge there lay,
> That man and beest might passe away:
> Under the brydge were sixty belles;
> Right as the Romans telles;
> That there might no man passe in,
> But all they rang with a gyn."
> Sign. E. iv.

In the Editor's folio MS. was an old poem on this subject, in a wretched corrupt state, unworthy the press: from which were taken such particulars as could be adopted.

[The poem entitled *The Emperour and the Childe* in the Folio MS. (ed. Hales and Furnivall, vol. ii. p. 390) only suggested the subject of the present ballad.   It commences—

> Within the Grecyan land some time did dwell
> an Emperour, whose name did ffar excell;
> he tooke to wiffe the lady B[e]llefaunt,
> the only sister to the kinge of ffrance,
> with whome he liued in pleasure and delight
> vntill that ffortune came to worke them spighte.

There are no particular signs of " corruption," and the piece is probably superior to Percy's own effusion.

Percy's trumpery commencement is an echo of the beginning of the printed copies of *Sir Andrew Barton.*

The name Ursine, like that of Orson, is derived from Fr. *Ourson,* the diminutive of *Ours,* a bear (Latin, *ursus.*)]

Part the First.

THEN Flora 'gins to decke the fields
  With colours fresh and fine,
  Then holy clerkes their mattins sing
  To good Saint Valentine!

The king of France that morning fair   5
  He would a hunting ride :
To Artois forest prancing forth
  In all his princelye pride.

To grace his sports a courtly train
  Of gallant peers attend ;   10
And with their loud and cheerful cryes
  The hills and valleys rend.

Through the deep forest swift they pass,
  Through woods and thickets wild ;
When down within a lonely dell   15
  They found a new-born child ;

All in a scarlet kercher lay'd
  Of silk so fine and thin :
A golden mantle wrapt him round
  Pinn'd with a silver pin.   20

The sudden sight surpriz'd them all ;
  The courtiers gather'd round ;
They look, they call, the mother seek ;
  No mother could be found.

At length the king himself drew near,   25
  And as he gazing stands,
The pretty babe look'd up and smil'd,
  And stretch'd his little hands.

Now, by the rood, king Pepin says,
  This child is passing fair :   30
I wot he is of gentle blood ;
  Perhaps some prince's heir.

Goe bear him home unto my court
  With all the care ye may :
Let him be christen'd Valentine,   35
  In honour of this day :

And look me out some cunning nurse ;
  Well nurtur'd let him bee;
Nor ought be wanting that becomes
  A bairn of high degree.   40

They look'd him out a cunning nurse ;
  And nurtur'd well was hee ;
Nor ought was wanting that became
  A bairn of high degree.

Thus grewe the little Valentine   45
  Belov'd of king and peers ;
And shew'd in all he spake or did
  A wit beyond his years.

But chief in gallant feates of arms
   He did himself advance,   50
That ere he grewe to man's estate
   He had no peere in France.

And now the early downe began
   To shade his youthful chin ;
When Valentine was dubb'd a knight,   55
   That he might glory win.

A boon, a boon, my gracious liege,
   I beg a boon of thee!
The first adventure, that befalls,
   May be reserv'd for mee.   60

The first adventure shall be thine ;
   The king did smiling say.
Nor many days, when lo! there came
   Three palmers clad in graye.

Help, gracious lord, they weeping say'd ;   65
   And knelt, as it was meet :
From Artoys forest we be come,
   With weak and wearye feet.

Within those deep and drearye woods
   There wends a savage boy ;   70
Whose fierce and mortal rage doth yield
   Thy subjects dire annoy.

'Mong ruthless beares he sure was bred ;
   He lurks within their den :
With beares he lives; with beares he feeds;   75
   And drinks the blood of men.

To more than savage strength he joins
   A more than human skill :
For arms, ne cunning may suffice
   His cruel rage to still :   80

Up then rose sir Valentine,
    And claim'd that arduous deed.
Go forth and conquer, say'd the king,
    And great shall be thy meed.

Well mounted on a milk-white steed,   85
    His armour white as snow;
As well beseem'd a virgin knight,
    Who ne'er had fought a foe;

To Artoys forest he repairs
    With all the haste he may;   90
And soon he spies the savage youth
    A rending of his prey.

His unkempt hair all matted hung
    His shaggy shoulders round :
His eager eye all fiery glow'd :   95
    His face with fury frown'd.

Like eagles' talons grew his nails :
    His limbs were thick and strong;
And dreadful was the knotted oak
    He bare with him along.   100

Soon as sir Valentine approach'd,
    He starts with sudden spring;
And yelling forth a hideous howl,
    He made the forests ring.

As when a tyger fierce and fell   105
    Hath spyed a passing roe,
And leaps at once upon his throat;
    So sprung the savage foe;

So lightly leap'd with furious force
    The gentle knight to seize :   110
But met his tall uplifted spear,
    Which sunk him on his knees.

A second stroke so stiff and stern
   Had laid the savage low;
But springing up, he rais'd his club,   115
   And aim'd a dreadful blow.

The watchful warrior bent his head,
   And shun'd the coming stroke;
Upon his taper spear it fell,
   And all to shivers broke.   120

Then lighting nimbly from his steed,
   He drew his burnisht brand:
The savage quick as lightning flew
   To wrest it from his hand.

Three times he grasp'd the silver hilt;   125
   Three times he felt the blade;
Three times it fell with furious force;
   Three ghastly wounds it made.

Now with redoubled rage he roared;
   His eye-ball flash'd with fire;   130
Each hairy limb with fury shook;
   And all his heart was ire.

Then closing fast with furious gripe
   He clasp'd the champion round,
And with a strong and sudden twist   135
   He laid him on the ground.

But soon the knight, with active spring,
   O'erturn'd his hairy foe:
And now between their sturdy fists
   Past many a bruising blow.   140

They roll'd and grappled on the ground,
   And there they struggled long:
Skilful and active was the knight;
   The savage he was strong.

But brutal force and savage strength   145
  To art and skill must yield:
Sir Valentine at length prevail'd,
  And won the well-fought field.

Then binding strait his conquer'd foe
  Fast with an iron chain,   15
He tyes him to his horse's tail,
  And leads him o'er the plain.

To court his hairy captive soon
  Sir Valentine doth bring;
And kneeling downe upon his knee,   155
  Presents him to the king.

With loss of blood and loss of strength,
  The savage tamer grew;
And to sir Valentine became
  A servant try'd and true.   160

And 'cause with beares he erst was bred,
  Ursine they call his name;
A name which unto future times
  The Muses shall proclame.

PART THE SECOND.

IN high renown with prince and peere
  Now liv'd sir Valentine:
His high renown with prince and peere
  Made envious hearts repine.

It chanc'd the king upon a day   5
  Prepar'd a sumptuous feast:
And there came lords, and dainty dames,
  And many a noble guest.

Amid their cups, that freely flow'd,
    Their revelry, and mirth ;   10
A youthful knight tax'd Valentine
    Of base and doubtful birth.

The foul reproach, so grossly urg'd,
    His generous heart did wound :
And strait he vow'd he ne'er would rest   15
    Till he his parents found.

Then bidding king and peers adieu,
    Early one summer's day,
With faithful Ursine by his side,
    From court he took his way.   20

O'er hill and valley, moss and moor,
    For many a day they pass ;
At length upon a moated lake,
    They found a bridge of brass.

Beyond it rose a castle fair   25
    Y-built of marble stone :
The battlements were gilt with gold,
    And glittred in the sun.

Beneath the bridge, with strange device,
    A hundred bells were hung ;   30
That man, nor beast, might pass thereon,
    But strait their larum rung.

This quickly found the youthful pair,
    Who boldly crossing o'er,
The jangling sound bedeaft their ears,   35
    And rung from shore to shore.

Quick at the sound the castle gates
    Unlock'd and opened wide,
And strait a gyant huge and grim
    Stalk'd forth with stately pride.   40

Ver. 23. *i.e.* a lake that served for a moat to a castle.

Now yield you, caytiffs, to my will;
    He cried with hideous roar;
Or else the wolves shall eat your flesh,
    And ravens drink your gore.

Vain boaster, said the youthful knight,   45
    I scorn thy threats and thee :
I trust to force thy brazen gates,
    And set thy captives free.

Then putting spurs unto his steed,
    He aim'd a dreadful thrust :   50
The spear against the gyant glanc'd,
    And caus'd the blood to burst.

Mad and outrageous with the pain,
    He whirl'd his mace of steel :
The very wind of such a blow   55
    Had made the champion reel.

It haply mist; and now the knight
    His glittering sword display'd,
And riding round with whirlwind speed
    Oft made him feel the blade.   60

As when a large and monstrous oak
    Unceasing axes hew :
So fast around the gyant's limbs
    The blows quick-darting flew.

As when the boughs with hideous fall   65
    Some hapless woodman crush :
With such a force the enormous foe
    Did on the champion rush.

A fearful blow, alas! there came,
    Both horse and knight it took,   70
And laid them senseless in the dust;
    So fatal was the stroke.

Then smiling forth a hideous grin,
  The gyant strides in haste,
And, stooping, aims a second stroke: 75
  " Now caytiff breathe thy last!"

But ere it fell, two thundering blows
  Upon his scull descend :
From Ursine's knotty club they came,
  Who ran to save his friend.   80

Down sunk the gyant gaping wide,
  And rolling his grim eyes :
The hairy youth repeats his blows :
  He gasps, he groans, he dies.

Quickly sir Valentine reviv'd   85
  With Ursine's timely care :
And now to search the castle walls
  The venturous youths repair.

The blood and bones of murder'd knights
  They found where'er they came :   90
At length within a lonely cell
  They saw a mournful dame.

Her gentle eyes were dim'd with tears ;
  Her cheeks were pale with woe :
And long sir Valentine besought   95
  Her doleful tale to know.

" Alas ! young knight," she weeping said,
  " Condole my wretched fate :
A childless mother here you see ;
  A wife without a mate.   100

" These twenty winters here forlorn
  I've drawn my hated breath ;
Sole witness of a monster's crimes,
  And wishing aye for death.

" Know, I am sister of a king;   105
  And in my early years
Was married to a mighty prince,
  The fairest of his peers.

"With him I sweetly liv'd in love
  A twelvemonth and a day: 110
When, lo! a foul and treacherous priest
  Y-wrought our loves' decay.

" His seeming goodness wan him pow'r;
  He had his master's ear:
And long to me and all the world   115
  He did a saint appear.

" One day, when we were all alone,
  He proffer'd odious love:
The wretch with horrour I repuls'd,
  And from my presence drove.   120

" He feign'd remorse, and piteous beg'd
  His crime I'd not reveal:
Which, for his seeming penitence,
  I promis'd to conceal.

" With treason, villainy, and wrong   125
  My goodness he repay'd:
With jealous doubts he fill'd my lord,
  And me to woe betray'd.

" He hid a slave within my bed,
  Then rais'd a bitter cry.   130
My lord, possest with rage, condemn'd
  Me, all unheard, to dye.

" But 'cause I then was great with child,
  At length my life he spar'd;
But bade me instant quit the realme,   135
  One trusty knight my guard.

" Forth on my journey I depart,
  Opprest with grief and woe;
And tow'rds my brother's distant court,
  With breaking heart, I goe.   140

" Long time thro' sundry foreign lands
  We slowly pace along:
At length within a forest wild
  I fell in labour strong:

" And while the knight for succour sought, 145
  And left me there forlorn,
My childbed pains so fast increast
  Two lovely boys were born.

" The eldest fair, and smooth, as snow
  That tips the mountain hoar: 150
The younger's little body rough
  With hairs was cover'd o'er.

" But here afresh begin my woes:
  While tender care I took
To shield my eldest from the cold,   155
  And wrap him in my cloak;

" A prowling bear burst from the wood,
  And seiz'd my younger son:
Affection lent my weakness wings,
  And after them I run.   160

" But all forewearied, weak and spent,
  I quickly swoon'd away;
And there beneath the greenwood shade
  Long time I lifeless lay.

" At length the knight brought me relief, 165
  And rais'd me from the ground:
But neither of my pretty babes
  Could ever more be found.

"And, while in search we wander'd far,
　We met that gyant grim;　　　　　　170
Who ruthless slew my trusty knight,
　And bare me off with him.

"But charm'd by heav'n, or else my griefs,
　He offer'd me no wrong;
Save that within these lonely walls　　175
　I've been immur'd so long."

Now, surely, said the youthful knight,
　You are lady Bellisance,
Wife to the Grecian emperor:
　Your brother's king of France.　　　180

For in your royal brother's court
　Myself my breeding had;
Where oft the story of your woes
　Hath made my bosom sad.

If so, know your accuser's dead,　　　185
　And dying own'd his crime;
And long your lord hath sought you out
　Thro' every foreign clime.

And when no tidings he could learn
　Of his much-wronged wife,　　　　190
He vow'd thenceforth within his court
　To lead a hermit's life.

Now heaven is kind! the lady said;
　And dropt a joyful tear:
Shall I once more behold my lord?　　195
　That lord I love so dear?

But, madam, said sir Valentine,
　And knelt upon his knee;
Know you the cloak that wrapt your babe,
　If you the same should see?　　　　200

And pulling forth the cloth of gold,
  In which himself was found;
The lady gave a sudden shriek,
  And fainted on the ground.

But by his pious care reviv'd,   205
  His tale she heard anon;
And soon by other tokens found,
  He was indeed her son.

But who's this hairy youth? she said;
  He much resembles thee: 210
The bear devour'd my younger son,
  Or sure that son were he.

Madam, this youth with bears was bred,
  And rear'd within their den.
But recollect ye any mark   215
  To know you son agen?

Upon his little side, quoth she,
  Was stampt a bloody rose.
Here, lady, see the crimson mark
  Upon his body grows!   220

Then clasping both her new-found sons
  She bath'd their cheeks with tears;
And soon towards hèr brother's court
  Her joyful course she steers.

What pen can paint king Pepin's joy,   225
  His sister thus restor'd!
And soon a messenger was sent
  To cheer her drooping lord:

Who came in haste with all his peers,
  To fetch her home to Greece;   230
Where many happy years they reign'd
  In perfect love and peace.

To them sir Ursine did succeed,
  And long the scepter bare.
Sir Valentine he stay'd in France,   235
  And was his uncle's heir.

⁎

XIII.

THE DRAGON OF WANTLEY.

THIS humourous song (as a former Editor* has well observed) is to old metrical romances and ballads of chivalry, what *Don Quixote* is to prose narratives of that kind:—a lively satire on their extravagant fictions. But altho' the satire is thus general, the subject of this ballad is local and peculiar: so that many of the finest strokes of humour are lost for want of our knowing the minute circumstances to which they allude. Many of them can hardly now be recovered, altho' we have been fortunate enough to learn the general subject to which the satire referred, and shall detail the information, with which we have been favoured, at the end of this introduction.

In handling his subject, the Author has brought in most of the common incidents which occur in romance. The description of the dragon†—his outrages—the people flying to the knight for succour—his care in chusing his armour—his being drest for fight by a young damsel—and most of the circumstances of the battle and victory (allowing for the burlesque turn given to them) are what occur in every book of chivalry, whether in prose or verse.

If any one piece, more than other, is more particularly levelled at, it seems to be the old rhiming legend of sir Bevis. There a *Dragon* is attacked from a *Well* in a manner not very remote from this of the ballad :—

There was a well, so have I wynne,
And Bevis stumbled ryght therein.
*   *   *   *

Than was he glad without fayle,
And rested a whyle for his avayle ;

---

* Collection of Historical Ballads in 3 vol. 1727.
† See above, pp. 108, 216.

And dranke of that water his fyll;
And then he lepte out, with good wyll,
And with Morglay his brande
He assayled the dragon, I understande:
On the dragon he smote so faste,
Where that he hit the scales braste:
The dragon then faynted sore,
And cast a galon and more
Out of his mouthe of venim strong,
And on syr Bevis he it flong:
It was venymous y-wis.

This seems to be meant by the Dragon of Wantley's stink, ver. 110. As the politick knight's creeping out, and attacking the dragon, &c. seems evidently to allude to the following:

Bevis blessed himselfe and forth yode,
And lepte out with haste full good;
And Bevis unto the dragon gone is;
And the dragon also to Bevis.
Longe, and harde was that fyght
Betwene the dragon, and that knyght:
But ever whan syr Bevis was hurt sore,
He went to the well, and washed him thore;
He was as hole as any man,
Ever freshe as whan he began.
The dragon sawe it might not avayle
Besyde the well to hold batayle;
He thought he would, wyth some wyle,
Out of that place Bevis begyle;
He woulde have flowen then awaye,
But Bevis lepte after with good Morglaye,
And hyt him under the wynge,
As he was in his flyenge, &c.

Sign. M. jv. L. j. &c.

After all, perhaps the writer of this ballad was acquainted with the above incidents only thro' the medium of Spenser, who has assumed most of them in his *Faery Queen.* At least some particulars in the description of the Dragon, &c. seem evidently borowed from the latter. See book i. canto 11, where the Dragon's 'two wynges like sayls—huge long tayl—with stings—his cruel rending clawes—and yron teeth—his breath of smothering smoke and sulphur"—and the duration of the fight for upwards of two days, bear a great resemblance to passages in the following ballad; though it must be confessed that these particulars are common to all old writers of romance.

Altho' this ballad must have been written early in the last century, we have met with none but such as were comparatively modern copies. It is here printed from one in Roman letter, in the Pepys collection, collated with such others as could be procured.

A description of the supposed scene of this ballad, which was communicated to the Editor in 1767, is here given in the words of the relater:—

"In Yorkshire, 6 miles from Rotherham, is a village, called *Wortley*, the seat of the late *Wortley Montague*, Esq. About a mile from this village is a lodge, named *Warncliff Lodge*, but vulgarly called *Wantley*: here lies the scene of the song. I was there about forty years ago: and it being a woody rocky place, my friend made me clamber over rocks and stones, not telling me to what end, till I came to a sort of a cave; then asked my opinion of the place, and pointing to one end, says, Here lay the dragon killed by *Moor* of *Moor-hall*: here lay his head; here lay his tail; and the stones we came over on the hill, are those he could not crack; and yon white house you see half a mile off, is *Moor-hall.* I had dined at the lodge, and knew the man's name was *Matthew*, who was a keeper to Mr. Wortley, and, as he endeavoured to persuade me, was the same Matthew mentioned in the song: In the house is the picture of the Dragon and Moor of Moor-hall, and near it a well, which, says he, is the well described in the ballad."

Since the former editions of this humorous old song were printed, the following *Key to the Satire* hath been communicated by *Godfrey Bosville*, Esq. of Thorp, near Malton, in Yorkshire; who, in the most obliging manner, gave full permission to adjoin it to the poem.

Warncliffe Lodge, and *Warncliffe* Wood (vulgarly pronounced *Wantley*), are in the parish of Penniston, in Yorkshire. The rectory of Penniston was part of the dissolved monastery of St. Stephen's, Westminster; and was granted to the Duke of Norfolk's family: who therewith endowed an hospital, which he built at Sheffield, for women. The trustees let the impropriation of the great Tythes of Penniston to the Wortley family, who got a great deal by it, and wanted to get still more; for Mr. Nicholas Wortley attempted to take the tythes in kind, but Mr. Francis Bosville opposed him, and there was a decree in favour of the Modus in 37th Eliz. The vicarage of Penniston did not go along with the rectory, but with the copyhold rents, and was part of a large purchase made by Ralph Bosville, Esq. from Qu. Elizabeth, in the 2d year of her reign: and that part he sold in 12th Eliz. to his elder brother Godfrey, the father of Francis; who left it, with the rest of his estate, to his wife, for her life, and then to Ralph,

3d son of his uncle Ralph. The widow married Lyonel Rowlestone, lived eighteen years, and survived Ralph.

This premised, the ballad apparently relates to the law-suit
carried on concerning this claim of tythes made by the Wortley
family. " Houses and churches, were to him geese and turkeys : "
which are tytheable things, the dragon chose to live on. Sir
Francis Wortley, the son of Nicholas, attempted again to take
the tythes in kind : but the parishioners subscribed an agreement
to defend their Modus. And at the head of the agreement was
Lyonel Rowlestone, who is supposed to be one of " the Stones,
dear Jack, which the Dragon could not crack." The agreement
is still preserved in a large sheet of parchment, dated 1st of James I.,
and is full of names and seals, which might be meant by the coat
of armour, " with spikes all about, both within and without."
More of *More-hall* was either the attorney, or counsellor, who
conducted the suit. He is not distinctly remembered, but More-
hall is still extant at the very bottom of Wantley [Warncliff]
Wood, and lies so low, that it might be said to be in a well : as
the dragon's den [Warncliff Lodge] was at the top of the wood,
" with Matthew's house hard by it." The keepers belonging to
the Wortley family were named, for many generations, Matthew
Northall : the last of them left this lodge, within memory, to be
keeper to the Duke of Norfolk. The present owner of More-hall
still attends Mr. Bosville's Manor-Court at Oxspring, and pays a
rose a year. " More of More-hall, with nothing at all, slew the
Dragon of Wantley." He gave him, instead of tythes, so small a
Modus, that it was in effect nothing at all, and was slaying him
with a vengeance. " The poor children three," &c. cannot surely
mean the three sisters of Francis Bosville, who would have been
coheiresses, had he made no will ? The late Mr. Bosville had a
contest with the descendants of two of them, the late Sir Geo.
Saville's father, and Mr. Copley, about the presentation to Penniston, they supposing Francis had not the power to give this part
of the estate from the heirs at law ; but it was decided against
them. The dragon (Sir Francis Wortley) succeeded better with
his cousin Wordesworth, the freehold lord of the manor (for it is
the copyhold manor that belongs to Mr. Bosville) having per-
suaded him not to join the refractory parishioners, under a promise that he would let him his tythes cheap : and now the estates
of Wortley and Wordesworth are the only lands that pay tythes in
the parish.

N.B. " Two days and a night," mentioned in ver. 125, as the
duration of the combat, was probably that of the trial at law.

[In Gough's edition of Camden's *Britannia* we learn that " Sir
Thomas Wortley, who was knight of the body to Edward IV.,

Richard III., Henry VII. and VIII., built a lodge in his chace of Warncliffe, and had a house and park there, disparked in the Civil War."

Mr. Gilfillan has the following note in his edition of the *Reliques*, " A legend current in the Wortley family states the dragon to have been a formidable drinker, drunk dead by the chieftain of the opposite moors. Ellis thinks it was a wolf or some other fierce animal hunted down by More of More-hall." A writer in the *Notes and Queries* (3rd S. ix. 29), who signs himself " Fitzhopkins," expresses his disbelief in the above explanation communicated to Percy by Godfrey Bosville.]

LD stories tell how Hercules
    A dragon slew at Lerna,
    With seven heads, and fourteen eyes,
      To see and well discern-a :
But he had a club, this dragon to drub,   5
    Or he had ne'er done it, I warrant ye :
But More of More-Hall, with nothing at all,
    He slew the dragon of Wantley.

This dragon had two furious wings,
    Each one upon each shoulder ;   10
With a sting in his tayl as long as a flayl,
    Which made him bolder and bolder.
He had long claws, and in his jaws
    Four and forty teeth of iron ;
With a hide as tough, as any buff,   15
    Which did him round environ.

Have you not heard how the Trojan horse
    Held seventy men in his belly ?
This dragon was not quite so big,
    But very near, I'll tell ye.   20
Devoured he poor children three,
    That could not with him grapple ;
And at one sup he eat them up,
    As one would eat an apple.

All sorts of cattle this dragon did eat.   25
　　Some say he ate up trees,
And that the forests sure he would
　　Devour up by degrees :
For houses and churches were to him geese and
　　turkies ;
　　He ate all, and left none behind,   30
But some stones, dear Jack, that he could not crack,
　　Which on the hills you will find.

In Yorkshire, near fair Rotherham,[1]
　　The place I know it well ;
Some two or three miles, or thereabouts,   35
　　I vow I cannot tell.
But there is a hedge, just on the hill edge,
　　And Matthew's house hard by it ;
O there and then was this dragon's den,
　　You could not chuse but spy it.   40

Some say, this dragon was a witch ;
　　Some say, he was a devil,
For from his nose a smoke arose,
　　And with it burning snivel ;
Which he cast off, when he did cough,   45
　　In a well that he did stand by ;
Which made it look, just like a brook
　　Running with burning brandy.

Hard by a furious knight there dwelt,
　　Of whom all towns did ring ;   50
For he could wrestle, play at quarter-staff, kick,
　　cuff, and huff,
　　Call son of a whore, do any kind of thing :

Ver. 29. were to him gorse and birches. *Other Copies.*

[1 Wharncliffe is about six miles from Rotherham.]

By the tail and the main, with his hands twain
　　He swung a horse till he was dead;
And that which is stranger, he for very anger　　　55
　　Eat him all up but his head.

These children, as I am told, being eat;
　　Men, women, girls and boys,
Sighing and sobbing, came to his lodging,
　　And made a hideous noise:　　　60
O save us all, More of More-Hall,
　　Thou peerless knight of these woods;
Do but slay this dragon, who won't leave us a rag on,
　　We'll give thee all our goods.

Tut, tut, quoth he, no goods I want;　　　65
　　But I want, I want, in sooth,
A fair maid of sixteen, that's brisk, and keen,
　　With smiles about the mouth;
Hair black as sloe, skin white as snow,
　　With blushes her cheeks adorning;　　　70
To anoynt me o'er night, ere I go to fight,
　　And to dress me in the morning.

This being done, he did engage
　　To hew the dragon down;
But first he went, new armour to　　　75
　　Bespeak at Sheffield town;
With spikes all about, not within but without,
　　Of steel so sharp and strong;
Both behind and before, arms, legs, and all o'er
　　Some five or six inches long.　　　80

Had you but seen him in this dress,
　　How fierce he look'd and how big,
You would have thought him for to be
　　Some Egyptian porcupig:

He frighted all, cats, dogs, and all,   85
 Each cow, each horse, and each hog :
For fear they did flee, for they took him to be
 Some strange outlandish hedge-hog.

 To see this fight, all people then
  Got up on trees and houses,   90
 On churches some, and chimneys too ;
  But these put on their trowses,
Not to spoil their hose. As soon as he rose,
 To make him strong and mighty,
He drank by the tale, six pots of ale, 95
 And a quart of aqua-vitæ.

 It is not strength that always wins,
  For wit doth strength excell ;
 Which made our cunning champion
  Creep down into a well ;   100
Where he did think, this dragon would drink,
 And so he did in truth ;
And as he stoop'd low, he rose up and cry'd, boh !
 And hit him in the mouth.

 O, quoth the dragon, pox take thee, come out, 105
  Thou disturb'st me in my drink :
 And then he turn'd, and s . . . at him ;
  Good lack how he did stink !
Beshrew thy soul, thy body's foul,
 Thy dung smells not like balsam ; 110
Thou son of a whore, thou stink'st so sore.
 Sure thy diet is unwholesome.

 Our politick knight, on the other side,
  Crept out upon the brink,
 And gave the dragon such a douse, 115
  He knew not what to think :
By cock, quoth he, say you so : do you see ?
 And then at him he let fly

With hand and with foot, and so they went to't ;
And the word it was, Hey boys, hey ! 120

Your words, quoth the dragon, I don't under-
    stand :
  Then to it they fell at all,
Like two wild boars so fierce, if I may,
  Compare great things with small.
Two days and a night, with this dragon did fight 125
Our champion on the ground ;
Tho' their strength it was great, their skill it was
    neat,
  They never had one wound.

At length the hard earth began to quake,
  The dragon gave him a knock, 130
Which made him to reel, and straitway he thought,
  To lift him as high as a rock,
And thence let him fall.   But More of More-Hall,
  Like a valiant son of Mars,
As he came like a lout, so he turn'd him about, 135
  And hit him a kick on the a . . .

Oh, quoth the dragon, with a deep sigh,
  And turn'd six times together,
Sobbing and tearing, cursing and swearing
  Out of his throat of leather ; 140
More of More-Hall ! O thou rascàl !
  Would I had seen thee never ;
With the thing at thy foot, thou hast prick'd my
    a . . gut,
  And I'm quite undone for ever.

Murder, murder, the dragon cry'd, 145
  Alack, alack, for grief ;
Had you but mist that place, you could
  Have done me no mischief.

Then his head he shaked, trembled and quaked,
  And down he laid and cry'd ;   150
First on one knee, then on back tumbled he,
  So groan'd, kickt, s . . ., and dy'd.

XIV.

ST. GEORGE FOR ENGLAND.

THE FIRST PART.

S the former song is in ridicule of the extravagant incidents in old ballads and metrical romances ; so this is
a burlesque of their style ; particularly of the rambling
transitions and wild accumulations of unconnected
parts, so frequent in many of them.

This ballad is given from an old black-letter copy in the Pepys
collection, "imprinted at London, 1612." It is more ancient
than many of the preceding ; but we place it here for the sake
of connecting it with the *Second Part.*

[*Saint George that, O! did break the dragon's heart* is one of the
ballads offered for sale by Nightingale, the ballad-singer in Ben
Jonson's comedy of *Bartholomew Fair* (act ii. sc. 1), and according
to Fielding's Tom Jones, *St. George, he was for England*, was one
of Squire Western's favourite tunes.

This ballad is printed in several collections, and Mr. Chappell
notices a modernization subscribed S. S. and "printed for W.
Gilbertson in Giltspur Street," about 1659, which commences—

       "What need we brag or boast at all
       Of Arthur and his knights."]

HY doe you boast of Arthur and his
      knightes,
    Knowing 'well' how many men have en-
      dured fightes ?
For besides king Arthur, and Lancelot du lake,
  Or sir Tristram de Lionel, that fought for ladies
    sake ;

Read in old histories, and there you shall see
How St. George, St. George the dragon made to
flee.
St. George he was for England; St. Dennis was for
France;
Sing, *Honi soit qui mal y pense.*

Mark our father Abraham, when first he resckued
Lot
Onely with his household, what conquest there he
got:
David was elected a prophet and a king,
He slew the great Goliah, with a stone within a
sling:
Yet these were not knightes of the table round;
Nor St. George, St. George, who the dragon did
confound.
St. George he was for England; St. Dennis was for
France;
Sing, *Honi soit qui mal y pense.*

Jephthah and Gideon did lead their men to fight,
They conquered the Amorites, and put them all to
flight:
Hercules his labours 'were' on the plaines of Basse;
And Sampson slew a thousand with the jawbone of
an asse,
And eke he threw a temple downe, and did a
mighty spoyle:
But St. George, St. George he did the dragon foyle.
St. George he was for England; St. Dennis was for
France;
Sing, *Honi soit qui mal y pense.*

The warres of ancient monarchs it were too long to
tell,
And likewise of the Romans, how farre they did
excell;

Hannyball and Scipio in many a fielde did fighte :
Orlando Furioso he was a worthy knighte :
Remus and Romulus, were they that Rome did
    builde :
But St. George, St. George the dragon made to
    yielde.
St. George he was for England; St. Dennis was for
    France ;
    Sing, *Honi soit qui mal y pense.*

The noble Alphonso, that was the Spanish king,
The order of the red scarffes and bandrolles in did
    bring :*
He had a troope of mighty knightes, when first he
    did begin,
Which sought adventures farre and neare, that con-
    quest they might win :
The ranks of the Pagans he often put to flight :
But St. George, St. George did with the dragon fight.
St. George he was for England ; St. Dennis was for
    France ;
    Sing, *Honi soit qui mal y pense.*

Many 'knights' have fought with proud Tamber-
    laine.
Cutlax the Dane, great warres he did maintaine :
Rowland of Beame, and good ' sir ' Olivere
In the forest of Acon slew both woolfe and beare :
Besides that noble Hollander, ' sir ' Goward with
    the bill :
But St. George, St. George the dragon's blood did
    spill.

---

* This probably alludes to " An Ancient Order of Knighthood,
called the Order of the Band, instituted by Don Alphonsus, king
of Spain, . . . to wear a red riband of three fingers breadth," &c.
See Ames *Typog.* p. 327.

St. George he was for England ; St. Dennis was for
  France ;
  Sing, *Honi soit qui mal y pense.*

Valentine and Orson were of king Pepin's blood :
Alfride and Henry they were brave knightes and
  good :
The four sons of Aymon, that follow'd Charlemaine:
Sir Hughon of Burdeaux, and Godfrey of Bullaine :
These were all French knightes that lived in that
  age :
But St. George, St. George the dragon did assuage.
St. George he was for England ; St. Dennis was for
  France ;
  Sing, *Honi soit qui mal y pense.*

Bevis conquered Ascapart, and after slew the boare,
And then he crost beyond the seas to combat with
  the moore :
Sir Isenbras, and Eglamore they were knightes
  most bold ;
And good Sir John Mandeville of travel much hath
  told :
There were many English knights that Pagans did
  convert :
But St. George, St. George pluckt out the dragon's
  heart.
St. George he was for England ; St. Dennis was for
  France ;
  Sing, *Honi soit qui mal y pense.*

The noble earl of Warwick, that was call'd sir Guy,
The infidels and pagans stoutlie did defie ;
He slew the giant Brandimore, and after was the death
Of that most ghastly dun cowe, the divell of Duns-
  more heath ;
Besides his noble deeds all done beyond the seas :
But St. George, St. George the dragon did appease.

St. George he was for England ; St. Dennis was for
   France ;
   Sing, *Honi soit qui mal y pense.*

Richard Cœur-de-lion erst king of this land,
He the lion gored with his naked hand :*
The false duke of Austria nothing did he feare ;
But his son he killed with a boxe on the eare ;
Besides his famous actes done in the holy lande :
But St. George, St. George the dragon did with-
   stande.
St. George he was for England ; St. Dennis was for
   France ;
   Sing, *Honi soit qui mal y pense.*

Henry the fifth he conquered all France,
And quartered their arms, his honour to advance :
He their cities razed, and threw their castles downe,
And his head he honoured with a double crowne :
He thumped the French-men, and after home he
   came :
But St. George, St. George he did the dragon tame.
St. George he was for England ; St. Dennis was for
   France ;
   Sing, *Honi soit qui mal y pense.*

St. David of Wales the Welsh-men much advance :
St. Jaques of Spaine, that never yet broke lance :
St. Patricke of Ireland, which was St. Georges boy,
Seven yeares he kept his horse, and then stole him
   away :
For which knavish act, as slaves they doe remaine :
But St. George, St. George the dragon he hath
   slaine.

---

* Alluding to the fabulous exploits attributed to this king in
the old romances.   See the dissertation affixed to this volume.

St. George he was for England ; St. Dennis was for
France ;
Sing, *Honi soit qui mal y pense.*

XV.

ST. GEORGE FOR ENGLAND.

The Second Part

AS written by JOHN GRUBB, M.A. of Christ Church,
Oxford. The occasion of its being composed is said
to have been as follows. A set of gentlemen of the
university had formed themselves into a club, all the
members of which were to be of the name of *George:* Their anni-
versary feast was to be held on *St. George's* day. Our author
solicited strongly to be admitted ; but his name being unfortunately
John, this disqualification was dispensed with only upon this con-
dition, that he would compose a song in honour of their Patron
Saint, and would every year produce one or more new stanzas,
to be sung on their annual festival. This gave birth to the following humorous performance, the several stanzas of which were
the produce of many successive anniversaries.*

This diverting poem was long handed about in manuscript, at
length a friend of *Grubb's* undertook to get it printed, who, not
keeping pace with the impatience of his friends, was addressed in
the following whimsical macaronic lines, which, in such a collection
as this, may not improperly accompany the poem itself.

Expostulatiuncula, sive *Querimoniuncula* ad *Antonium* [*Atherton*]
ob Poema *Johannis Grubb*, Viri τοῦ πάνυ ingeniosissimi in lucem
nondum editi.

Toni! Tune sines divina poemata Grubbi
Intomb'd in secret thus still to remain any longer,
Τοὔνομα σου shall last, Ὦ Γρυββε διαμπερες αει,
Grubbe tuum nomen vivet dum nobilis ale-a

* To this circumstance it is owing that the editor has never met
with two copies, in which the stanzas are arranged alike, he has

Efficit heroas, dignamque heroe puellam.
Est genus heroum, quos nobilis efficit alea-a
Qui pro niperkin clamant, quaternque liquoris
Quem vocitant Homines Brandy, Superi Cherry-brandy.
Sæpe illi longcut, vel small-cut flare Tobacco
Sunt soliti pipos. Ast si generosior herba
(Per varios casus, per tot discrimina rerum)
Mundungus desit, tum non funcare recusant
Brown-paper tostâ, vel quod fit arundine bed-mat.
Hic labor, hoc opus est heroum ascendere sedes!
Ast ego quo rapiar! quo me feret entheus ardor
Grubbe, tui memorem? Divinum expande poema.
Quæ mora? quæ ratio est, quin Grubbi protinus anser
Virgilii, Flaccique simul canat inter olores?

At length the importunity of his friends prevailed, and Mr. Grubb's song was published at Oxford, under the following title:

The British Heroes.

A New Poem in honour of St. George,

By Mr. *John Grubb,*

School-master of Christ-Church,

Oxon. 1688.

Favete linguis: carmina non prius
Audita, musarum sucerdos
Canto.—   HOR.

Sold by Henry Clements. Oxon.

HE story of king Arthur old
　　Is very memorable,
　　The number of his valiant knights,
　　And roundness of his table:
The knights around his table in   5
　A circle sate d'ye see:
And altogether made up one
　Large hoop of chivalry.

therefore thrown them into what appeared the most natural order. The verses are properly long Alexandrines, but the narrowness of the page made it necessary to subdivide them: they are here printed with many improvements.

He had a sword, both broad and sharp,
  Y-clepd Caliburn,   10
Would cut a flint more easily,
  Than pen-knife cuts a corn;
As case-knife does a capon carve,
  So would it carve a rock,
And split a man at single slash,   15
  From noddle down to nock.
As Roman Augur's steel of yore
  Dissected Tarquin's riddle,
So this would cut both conjurer
  And whetstone thro' the middle.   20
He was the cream of Brecknock,
  And flower of all the Welsh:
But George he did the dragon fell,
  And gave him a plaguy squelsh.[1]
St. George he was for England; St. Dennis was for
  France;   25
Sing, *Honi soit qui mal y pense.*

Pendragon, like his father Jove,
  Was fed with milk of goat;
And like him made a noble shield
  Of she-goat's shaggy coat: 30
On top of burnisht helmet he
  Did wear a crest of leeks;
And onions' heads, whose dreadful nod
  Drew tears down hostile cheeks.
Itch, and Welsh blood did make him hot,   35
  And very prone to ire;
H' was ting'd with brimstone, like a match,
  And would as soon take fire.
As brimstone he took inwardly
  When scurf gave him occasion,   40
His postern puff of wind was a
  Sulphureous exhalation.

[¹ blow.]

The Briton never tergivers'd,
  But was for adverse drubbing,
And never turn'd his back to aught,   45
  But to a post for scrubbing.
His sword would serve for battle, or
  For dinner, if you please;
When it had slain a Cheshire man,
  'Twould toast a Cheshire cheese.   50
He wounded, and, in their own blood,
  Did anabaptize Pagans:
But George he made the dragon an
  Example to all dragons.
St. George he was for England; St. Dennis was for
  France;   55
  Sing, *Honi soit qui mal y pense.*

Brave Warwick Guy, at dinner time,
  Challeng'd a gyant savage;
And streight came out the unweildy lout
  Brim-full of wrath and cabbage: 60
He had a phiz of latitude,
  And was full thick i' th' middle;
The chekes of puffed trumpeter,
  And paunch of squire Beadle.*
But the knight fell'd him, like an oak,   65
  And did upon his back tread;
The valiant knight his weazon cut,
  And Atropos his packthread.
Besides he fought with a dun cow,
  As say the poets witty,   70
A dreadful dun, and horned too,
  Like dun of Oxford city:
The fervent dog-days made her mad,
  By causing heat of weather,

---

* Men of bulk answerable to their places, as is well known at Oxford.

Syrius and Procyon baited her,   75
  As bull-dogs did her father:
Grafiers, nor butchers this fell beast,
  E'er of her frolick hindered;
John Dosset* she'd knock down as flat,
  As John knocks down her kindred: 8
Her heels would lay ye all along,
  And kick into a swoon;
Frewin's† cow-heels keep up your corpse,
  But hers would beat you down.
She vanquisht many a sturdy wight,   85
  And proud was of the honour;
Was pufft by mauling butchers so,
  As if themselves had blown her.
At once she kickt, and pusht at Guy,
  But all that would not fright him;   90
Who wav'd his winyard o'er sir-loyn,
  As if he'd gone to knight him.
He let her blood, frenzy to cure,
  And eke he did her gall rip;
His trenchant blade, like cook's long spit,   95
  Ran thro' the monster's bald-rib:
He rear'd up the vast crooked rib,
  Instead of arch triumphal:
But George hit th' dragon such a pelt,
  As made him on his bum fall.   100
St. George he was for England; St. Dennis was for
    France;
Sing, *Honi soit qui mal y pense.*

Tamerlain, with Tartarian bow,
  The Turkish squadrons slew;
And fetch'd the pagan crescent down,   105
  With half-moon made of yew:

---

* A butcher that then served the college.
† A cook, who on fast nights was famous for selling cow-heel
and tripe.

His trusty bow proud Turks did gall,
 With showers of arrows thick,
And bow-strings, without strangling, sent
 Grand Viziers to old Nick :   110
Much turbants, and much Pagan pates
 He made to humble in dust ;
And heads of Saracens he fixt
 On spear, as on a sign-post :
He coop'd in cage Bajazet the prop 115
 Of Mahomet's religion,
As if 't been the whispering bird,
 That prompted him ; the pigeon.
In Turkey leather scabbard, he
 Did sheathe his blade so trenchant : 120
But George he swinged the dragon's tail,
 And cut off every inch on't.
St. George he was for England ; St. Dennis was for
 France ;
 Sing, *Honi soit qui mal y pense.*

The amazon Thalestris was   125
 Both beautiful, and bold ;
She sear'd her breasts with iron hot,
 And bang'd her foes with cold.
Her hand was like the tool, wherewith
 Jove keeps proud mortals under : 130
It shone just like his lightning,
 And batter'd like his thunder.
Her eye darts lightning, that would blast
 The proudest he that swagger'd,
And melt the rapier of his soul,   135
 In its corporeal scabbard.
Her beauty, and her drum to foes
 Did cause amazement double ;
As timorous larks amazed are
 With light, and with a low-bell : 140

With beauty, and that lapland-charm,*
    Poor men she did bewitch all;
Still a blind whining lover had,
    As Pallas had her scrich-owl.
She kept the chastness of a nun   145
    In armour, as in cloyster:
But George undid the dragon just
    As you'd undo an oister.
St. George he was for England; St. Dennis was for
    France;
Sing, *Honi soit qui mal y pense.*   150

Stout Hercules, was offspring of
    Great Jove, and fair Alcmene:
One part of him celestial was,
    One part of him terrene.
To scale the hero's cradle walls   155
    Two fiery snakes combin'd,
And, curling into swaddling cloaths,
    About the infant twin'd:
But he put out these dragons' fires,
    And did their hissing stop;   160
As red-hot iron with hissing noise
    Is quencht in blacksmith's shop.
He cleans'd a stable, and rubb'd down
    The horses of new-comers;
And out of horse-dung he rais'd fame,   165
    As Tom Wrench† does cucumbers.
He made a river help him through;
    Alpheus was under-groom;
The stream, disgust at office mean,
    Ran murmuring thro' the room: 170
This liquid ostler to prevent
    Being tired with that long work,

---

* The drum.
† Who kept Paradise gardens at Oxford.

His father Neptune's trident took,
    Instead of three-tooth'd dung-fork.
This Hercules, as soldier, and   175
    As spinster, could take pains;
His club would sometimes spin ye flax,
    And sometimes knock out brains:
H' was forc'd to spin his miss a shift
    By Juno's wrath and hér-spite;   180
Fair Omphale whipt him to his wheel,
    As cook whips barking turn-spit.
From man, or churn he well knew how
    To get him lasting fame:
He'd pound a giant, till the blood,   185
    And milk till butter came.
Often he fought with huge battoon,
    And oftentimes he boxed;
Tapt a fresh monster once a month,
    As Hervey* doth fresh hogshead.   190
He gave Anteus such a hug,
    As wrestlers give in Cornwall:
But George he did the dragon kill,
    As dead as any door-nail.
St. George he was for England; St. Dennis was for
    France;   195
    Sing, *Honi soit qui mal y pense.*

The Gemini, sprung from an egg,
    Were put into a cradle:
Their brains with knocks and bottled ale,
    Were often-times full addle: 200
And, scarcely hatch'd, these sons of him,
    That hurls the bolt trisulcate,
With helmet-shell on tender head,
    Did tustle with red-ey'd pole-cat.

---

* A noted drawer at the Mermaid tavern in Oxford.

Castor a horseman, Pollux tho'   205
   A boxer was, I wist :
The one was fam'd for iron heel ;
   Th' other for leaden fist.
Pollux to shew he was god,
   When he was in a passion   210
With fist made noses fall down flat
   By way of adoration :

This fist, as sure as French disease,
   Demolish'd noses' ridges :
He like a certain lord * was famd'   215
   For breaking down of bridges.
Castor the flame of fiery steed,
   With well-spur'd boots took down ;
As men, with leathern buckets, quench
   A fire in country town.   220
His famous horse, that liv'd on oats,
   Is sung on oaten quill ;
By bards' immortal provender
   The nag surviveth still.
This shelly brood on none but knaves   225
   Employ'd their brisk artillery :
And flew as naturally at rogues,
   As eggs at thief in pillory.†
Much sweat they spent in furious fight,
   Much blood they did effund :   230
Their whites they vented thro' the pores ;
   Their yolks thro' gaping wound :

---

* Lord Lovelace broke down the bridges about Oxford, at the beginning of the Revolution. See on this subject a Ballad in Smith's Peoms, p. 102. London, 1713.

† It has been suggested by an ingenious correspondent that this was a popular subject at that time :—

     Not carted bawd, or Dan de Foe,
     In wooden ruff ere bluster'd so.
                Smith's Poems, p. 117.

Then both were cleans'd from blood and dust
　　To make a heavenly sign;
The lads were, like their armour, scowr'd,　　235
　　And then hung up to shine;
Such were the heavenly double-Dicks,
　　The sons of Jove and Tyndar:
But George he cut the dragon up,
　　As he had bin duck or windar.[1]　　240
St. George he was for England; St. Dennis was for
　　France;
　　Sing, *Honi soit qui mal y pense.*

Gorgon a twisted adder wore
　　For knot upon her shoulder:
She kemb'd her hissing periwig,　　245
　　And curling snakes did powder.
These snakes they made stiff changelings
　　Of all the folks they hist on;
They turned barbars into hones,
　　And masons into free-stone:　　250
Sworded magnetic Amazon
　　Her shield to load-stone changes;
Then amorous sword by magic belt
　　Clung fast unto her haunches.
This shield long village did protect,　　255
　　And kept the army from-town,
And chang'd the bullies into rocks,
　　That came t' invade Long-Compton.*
She post-diluvian stores unmans,
　　And Pyrrha's work unravels;　　260
And stares Deucalion's hardy boys
　　Into their primitive pebbles.

---

* See the account of Rolricht Stones, in Dr. Plott's *Hist. of Oxfordshire.*

[[1] perhaps a contraction of windhover, a kind of hawk.]

Red noses she to rubies turns,
  And noddles into bricks :
But George made dragon laxative ;   265
  And gave him a bloody flix.
St. George he was for England ; St. Dennis was for
    France ;
  Sing, *Honi soit qui mal y pense.*

By boar-spear Meleager got,
  An everlasting name,   270
And out of haunch of basted swine,
  He hew'd eternal fame.
This beast each hero's trouzers ript,
  And rudely shew'd his bare-breech,
Prickt but the wem, and out there came   275
  Heroic guts and garbadge.
Legs were secur'd by iron boots
  No more, than peas by peascods :
Brass helmets, with inclosed sculls,
  Wou'd crackle in's mouth like chest-
    nuts.   280
His tawny hairs erected were
  By rage, that was resistless ;
And wrath, instead of cobler's wax,
  Did stiffen his rising bristles.
His tusk lay'd dogs so dead asleep,   285
  Nor horn, nor whip cou'd wake 'um :
It made them vent both their last blood,
  And their last album-grecum.
But the knight gor'd him with his spear,
  To make of him a tame one,   290
And arrows thick, instead of cloves,
  He stuck in monster's gammon.
For monumental pillar, that
  His victory might be known,
He rais'd up, in cylindric form,   295
  A collar of the brawn.

He sent his shade to shades below,
 In Stygian mud to wallow:
And eke the stout St. George eftsoon,
 He made the dragon follow.   300
St. George he was for England; St. Dennis was for
  France;
 Sing, *Honi soit qui mal y pense.*

Achilles of old Chiron learnt
 The great horse for to ride;
H' was taught by th' Centaur's rational part,   305
 The hinnible to bestride.
Bright silver feet, and shining face
 Had that stout hero's mother;
As rapier's silver'd at one end,
 And wounds you at the other.   310
Her feet were bright, his feet were swift,
 As hawk pursuing sparrow:
Her's had the metal, his the speed
 Of Braburn's* silver arrow.
Thetis to double pedagogue   315
 Commits her dearest boy;
Who bred him from a slender twig
 To be the scourge of Troy:
But ere he lash't the Trojans, h' was
 In Stygian waters steept;   320
As birch is soaked first in piss,
 When boys are to be whipt.
With skin exceeding hard, he rose
 From lake, so black and muddy,
As lobsters from the ocean rise,   325
 With shell about their body:
And, as from lobster's broken claw,
 Pick out the fish you might:

---

* Braburn, a gentleman commoner of Lincoln college, gave a silver arrow to be shot for by the archers of the university of Oxford.

So might you from one unshell'd heel
    Dig pieces of the knight.   330
His myrmidons robb'd Priam's barns
    And hen-roosts, says the song;
Carried away both corn and eggs,
    Like ants from whence they sprung.
Himself tore Hector's pantaloons,   335
    And sent him down bare-breech'd
To pedant Radamanthus, in
    A posture to be switch'd.
But George he made the dragon look,
    As if he had been bewitch'd.   340
St. George he was for England; St. Dennis was for
    France;
    Sing, *Honi soit qui mal y pense.*

Full fatal to the Romans was
    The Carthaginian Hanni-
bal; him I mean, who gave them such   345
    A devilish thump at Cannæ:
Moors thick, as goats on Penmenmure,
    Stood on the Alpes's front:
Their one-eyed guide,* like blinking mole,
    Bor'd thro' the hindring mount: 350
Who, baffled by the massy rock,
    Took vinegar for relief;
Like plowmen, when they hew their way
    Thro' stubborn rump of beef.
As dancing louts from humid toes   355
    Cast atoms of ill favour
To blinking Hyatt,† when on vile crowd
    He merriment does endeavour,

---

* Hannibal had but one eye.
† A one-eyed fellow, who pretended to make fiddles, as well as play on them; well known at that time in Oxford.

And saws from suffering timber out
  Some wretched tune to quiver :   360
So Romans slunk and squeak'd at sight
  Of Affrican carnivor.
The tawny surface of his phiz
  Did serve instead of vizzard :
But George he made the dragon have   365
  A grumbling in his gizzard.
St. George he was for England ; St. Dennis was for
      France ;
  Sing, *Honi soit qui mal y pense.*

The valour of Domitian,
  It must not be forgotten ;   370
Who from the jaws of worm-blowing flies,
  Protected veal and mutton.
A squadron of flies errant,
  Against the foe appears ;
With regiments of buzzing knights,   375
  And swarms of volunteers :
The warlike wasp encourag'd 'em,
  With animating hum ;
And the loud brazen hornet next,
  He was their kettle-drum :   380
The Spanish don Cantharido
  Did him most sorely pester,
And rais'd on skin of vent'rous knight
  Full many a plaguy blister.
A bee whipt thro' his button hole,   385
  As thro' key hole a witch,
And stabb'd him with her little tuck
  Drawn out of scabbard breech :
But the undaunted knight lifts up
  An arm both big and brawny,   390
And slasht her so, that here lay head,
  And there lay bag and honey :

Then 'mongst the rout he flew as swift,
  As weapon made by Cyclops,
And bravely quell'd seditious buz,   395
  By dint of massy fly-flops.
Surviving flies do curses breathe,
  And maggots too at Cæsar :
But George he shav'd the dragon's beard,
  And Askelon* was his razor.   400
St. George he was for England ; St. Dennis was for
    France ;
  Sing, *Honi soit qui mal y pense.*

John Grubb, the facetious writer of the foregoing song, makes a distinguished figure among the Oxford wits so humorously enu-merated in the following distich :

Alma nover genuit célebres Rhedycina poetas
Bub, Stubb, Grubb, Crabb, Trap, Young, Carey, Tickel, Evans.

These were Bub Dodington (the late lord Melcombe), Dr. Stubbes, our poet *Grubb*, Mr. Crabb, Dr. Trapp the poetry-professor, Dr. Edw. Young, the author of Night-Thoughts, Walter Carey, Thomas Tickel, Esq., and Dr. Evans the epigrammatist.

As for our poet *Grubb*, all that we can learn further of him is contained in a few extracts from the University Register, and from his epitaph. It appears from the former that he was matricu-lated in 1667, being the son of John Grubb, " *de Acton Burnel in comitatu Salop. pauperis.*" He took his degree of Bachelor of Arts, June 28, 1671 : and became Master of Arts, June 28, 1675. He was appointed Head Master of the Grammar School at Christ Church : and afterwards chosen into the same employment at Gloucester, where he died in 1697, as appears from his monument in the church of St. Mary de Crypt in Gloucester, which is inscribed with the following epitaph :—

H. S. E.
Johannes Grubb, A. M.
Natus apud Acton Burnel in agro Salopiensi
Anno Dom. 1645.

---

* The name of St. George's sword.

Cujus variam in linguis notitiam,
et felicem erudiendis pueris industriam,
gratâ adhuc memoriâ testatur Oxonium :
Ibi enim Ædi Christi initiatus,
artes excoluit ;
Pueros ad easdem mox excolendas
accuratè formavit :
Huc demum
unanimi omnium consensu accitus,
eandem suscepit provinciam,
quam feliciter adeo absolvit,
ut nihil optandum sit
nisi ut diutius nobis interfuisset :
Fuit enim
propter festivam ingenij suavitatem,
simplicem morum candorem, et
præcipuam erga cognatos benevolentiam,
omnibus desideratissimus.
Obiit 2do die Aprilis, Anno Dni. 1697.
Ætatis suæ 51.

XVI.

MARGARET'S GHOST.

HIS ballad, which appeared in some of the public news-papers in or before the year 1724, came from the pen of David Mallet, Esq. who in the edition of his poems, 3 vols. 1759, informs us that the plan was suggested by the four verses quoted above in page 124, which he supposed to be the beginning of some ballad now lost.

"These lines, says he, naked of ornament and simple, as they are, struck my fancy ; and bringing fresh into my mind an unhappy adventure much talked of formerly, gave birth to the following poem, which was written many years ago."

The two introductory lines (and one or two others elsewhere) had originally more of the ballad simplicity, viz.

"When all was wrapt in dark midnight,
And all were fast asleep," &c.

In a late publication, intitled, *The Friends*, &c. Lond. 1773, 2 vols. 12mo. (in the first volume, p. 71) is inserted a copy of the foregoing ballad, with very great variations, which the editor of that work contends was the original; and that Mallet adopted it for his own and altered it, as here given.—But the superior beauty and simplicity of the present copy, gives it so much more the air of an original, that it will rather be believed that some transcriber altered it from Mallet's, and adapted the lines to his own taste; than which nothing is more common in popular songs and ballads.

[This ballad, more generally known as *William and Margaret*, is supposed to have been printed for the first time in Aaron Hill's *Plain Dealer* (No. 36, July 24, 1724), when the author was a very young man   Hill introduced it to the reader as the work of an old poet, and wrote, "I am sorry I am not able to acquaint my readers with his name to whom we owe this melancholy piece of finished poetry under the humble title of a ballad." In the following month the editor announced that "he had discovered the author to be still alive." The verses were probably written in 1723, in the August of which year Mallet left Scotland, for Allan Ramsay, in his *Stanzas to Mr. David Mallock on his departure from Scotland*, alludes to them :—

> "But he that could, in tender strains,
>   Raise Margaret's plaining shade,
> And paints distress that chills the veins,
>   While William's crimes are red."

The ballad at once became popular, and was printed in several collections, undergoing many alterations for the worse by the way. Sundry attempts were made to rob Mallet of the credit of his song. Besides the one mentioned above by Percy, Captain Thompson, the editor of Andrew Marvell's Works, claimed it for Marvell, but this claim was even more ridiculous than those he set up against Addison and Watts. Although Mallet doubtless knew the ballads *Fair Margaret and Sweet William* (book ii. No. 4) and *Sweet William's Ghost* (No. 6), he is said to have founded his own upon a true story which came under his observation. A daughter of Professor James Gregory of St. Andrews, and afterwards of Edinburgh, was seduced by a son of Sir William Sharp of Strathyrum, who had promised to marry her, but heartlessly deserted her.

The ballad has been extravagantly praised : Ritson observes, "It may be questioned whether any English writer has produced so fine a ballad as *William and Margaret*." Percy describes it as one of the most beautiful ballads in our own or any other language; and Allan Ramsay writes, "I know not where to seek a finer mixture of pathos and terror in the whole range of Gothic romance." Scott, on the other hand, was of opinion that "The ballad, though the best of Mallet's writing, is certainly inferior to the original, which I presume to be the very fine and terrific old Scottish tale, beginning

'There came a ghost to Margaret's door.'"

The extreme popularity of the poem is seen by the various parodies, one of which, *Watty and Madge*, is printed in Ramsay's *Tea Table Miscellany* (vol. iii.). It commences—

"'Twas at the shining mid-day hour,"

and each succeeding verse is parodied in the same manner. Vincent Browne imitated the original in Latin verse, and a German version was published as *Wilhelm und Gretchen*.

Mallet was a native of Crieff in Perthshire, and is believed to have been born in the year 1702. He was sometime tutor to the Montrose family, through whose influence he was introduced into public life. He changed his name from Malloch to Mallet when he settled in London, and in 1742 he was appointed Under Secretary to the Prince of Wales. He died on the 21st of April, 1765. Mallet is a writer little cared for now, but he can hardly be said to be neglected, for in 1857 Mr. Frederick Dinsdale published an illustrated edition of his Ballads and Songs, chiefly made up of copious notes on *William and Margaret* and *Edwin and Emma*.]

WAS at the silent solemn hour,
    When night and morning meet;
  In glided Margaret's grimly ghost,
    And stood at William's feet.

Her face was like an April morn,   5
    Clad in a wintry cloud :
And clay-cold was her lily hand,
    That held her sable shroud.

So shall the fairest face appear,
    When youth and years are flown :   10
Such is the robe that kings must wear,
    When death has reft their crown.

Her bloom was like the springing flower,
   That sips the silver dew;
The rose was budded in her cheek,   15
   Just opening to the view.

But love had, like the canker worm,
   Consum'd her early prime :
The rose grew pale, and left her cheek;
   She dy'd before her time.   20

"Awake!" she cry'd, "thy true love calls,
   Come from her midnight grave ;
Now let thy pity hear the maid,
   Thy love refus'd to save.

" This is the dark and dreary hour,   25
   When injur'd ghosts complain ;
Now yawning graves give up their dead,
   To haunt the faithless swain.

" Bethink thee, William, of thy fault,
   Thy pledge, and broken oath :   30
And give me back my maiden vow,
   And give me back my troth.

" Why did you promise love to me,
   And not that promise keep ?
Why did you swear mine eyes were bright,   35
   Yet leave those eyes to weep ?

" How could you say my face was fair,
   And yet that face forsake ?
How could you win my virgin heart,
   Yet leave that heart to break ?   40

" Why did you say my lip was sweet,
   And made the scarlet pale ?
And why did I, young witless maid,
   Believe the flattering tale ?

" That face, alas ! no more is fair ;   45
    These lips no longer red :
Dark are my eyes, now clos'd in death,
    And every charm is fled.

" The hungry worm my sister is ;
    This winding-sheet I wear :   50
And cold and weary lasts our night,
    Till that last morn appear.

" But hark ! the cock has warn'd me hence !
    A long and last adieu !
Come see, false man, how low she lies,   55
    Who dy'd for love of you."

The lark sung loud ; the morning smil'd,
    With beams of rosy red :
Pale William shook in ev'ry limb,
    And raving left his bed.   60

He hyed him to the fatal place,
    Where Margaret's body lay ;
And stretch'd him on the grass-green turf,
    That wrapt her breathless clay :

And thrice he call'd on Margaret's name,   65
    And thrice he wept full sore :
Then laid his cheek to her cold grave,
    And word spake never more.

XVII.

LUCY AND COLIN

AS written by Thomas Tickell, Esq. the celebrated friend
of Mr. Addison, and editor of his works. He was son
of a clergyman in the north of England, had his educa-
tion at Queen's college, Oxon, was under secretary to
Mr. Addison and Mr. Craggs, when successively secretaries of

state; and was lastly (in June, 1724) appointed secretary to the
Lords Justices in Ireland, which place he held till his death in
1740.* He acquired Mr. Addison's patronage by a poem in praise
of the opera of *Rosamond*, written while he was at the University.

It is a tradition in Ireland, that the song was written at Castle-
town, in the county of Kildare, at the request of the then Mrs.
Conolly—probably on some event recent in that neighbourhood.

[Gray called *Lucy and Colin* " the prettiest" ballad in the world,
although he was not partial to Tickell's other poems.

The fine old melody given by Dr. Rimbault for this ballad is
taken from " *The Merry Musician; or a Cure for the Spleen;* being a collection of the most diverting Songs and pleasant Ballads
set to Musick," 1716.]

F Leinster, fam'd for maidens fair,
    Bright Lucy was the grace;
  Nor e'er did Liffy's limpid stream
    Reflect so fair a face.

Till luckless love, and pining care   5
  Impair'd her rosy hue,
Her coral lip, and damask cheek,
  And eyes of glossy blue.

Oh ! have you seen a lily pale,
  When beating rains descend ?   10
So droop'd the slow-consuming maid ;
  Her life now near its end.

By Lucy warn'd, of flattering swains
  Take heed, ye easy fair :
Of vengeance due to broken vows,   15
  Ye perjured swains, beware.

Three times, all in the dead of night,
  A bell was heard to ring;
And at her window, shrieking thrice,
  The raven flap'd his wing.   20

[* Born 1686.]

Too well the love-lorn maiden knew
   That solemn boding sound;
And thus, in dying words, bespoke
   The virgins weeping round.

" I hear a voice, you cannot hear,   25
   Which says I must not stay :
I see a hand, you cannot see,
   Which beckons me away.

" By a false heart, and broken vows,
   In early youth I die.   30
Am I to blame, because his bride
   Is thrice as rich as I ?

" Ah Colin ! give not her thy vows;
   Vows due to me alone :
Nor thou, fond maid, receive his kiss,   35
   Nor think him all thy own.

" To-morrow in the church to wed,
   Impatient, both prepare ;
But know, fond maid, and know, false man,
   That Lucy will be there,   40

" Then, bear my corse ; ye comrades, bear,
   The bridegroom blithe to meet ;
He in his wedding-trim so gay,
   I in my winding-sheet."

She spoke, she dy'd ;—her corse was borne,   45
   The bridegroom blithe to meet ;
He in his wedding-trim so gay,
   She in her winding-sheet.

Then what were perjur'd Colin's thoughts ?
   How were those nuptials kept ?   50
The bride-men flock'd round Lucy dead,
   And all the village wept.

Confusion, shame, remorse, despair
    At once his bosom swell :
The damps of death bedew'd his brow,
    He shook, he groan'd, he fell.

From the vain bride (ah bride no more !)
    The varying crimson fled,
When, stretch'd before her rival's corse,
    She saw her husband dead.

Then to his Lucy's new-made grave,
    Convey'd by trembling swains,
One mould with her, beneath one sod,
    For ever now remains.

Oft at their grave the constant hind
    And plighted maid are seen ;
With garlands gay, and true-love knots
    They deck the sacred green.

But, swain forsworn, whoe'er thou art,
    This hallow'd spot forbear ;   70
Remember Colin's dreadful fate,
    And fear to meet him there.

XVIII.

THE BOY AND THE MANTLE,

AS REVISED AND ALTERED BY A MODERN HAND.

MR. WARTON, in his ingenious *Observations on Spenser*, has given his opinion, that the fiction of the *Boy and the Mantle* is taken from an old French piece intitled *Le court mantel*, quoted by M. de St. Palaye in his curious *Mémoires sur l'ancienne Chevalerie*, Paris, 1759, 2 tom. 12mo., who tells us the story resembles that of Ariosto's inchanted cup. 'Tis possible our English poet may have taken the hint of this subject from that old French romance, but he does not appear to have copied it in the manner of execution; to which (if one may judge from the specimen given in the *Mémoires*) that of the ballad does not bear the least resemblance. After all, 'tis most likely that all the old stories concerning K. Arthur are originally of British growth, and that what the French and other southern nations have of this kind, were at first exported from this island. See *Mémoires de l'Acad. des Inscrip.* tom. xx. p. 352.

(Since this volume was printed off, the *Fabliaux ou Contes*, 1781, 5 tom. 12mo., of *M. le Grand*, have come to hand: and in tom. i. p. 54, he hath printed a modern version of the old tale *Le Court Mantel*, under a new title *Le Manteau maltaillé;* which contains the story of this ballad much enlarged, so far as regards the *Mantle;* but without any mention of the *Knife*, or the *Horn*.)

[See book i. No. 1, for the original of this ballad.]

N Carleile dwelt king Arthur,
  A prince of passing might;
 And there maintain'd his table round,
  Beset with many a knight.

And there he kept his Christmas   5
  With mirth and princely cheare,
When, lo! a straunge and cunning boy
  Before him did appeare.

A kirtle and a mantle
  This boy had him upon,   10
With brooches, rings, and owches[1]
  Full daintily bedone.

He had a sarke[2] of silk
  About his middle meet;
And thus, with seemly curtesy,   15
  He did king Arthur greet.

[[1] bosses or buttons of gold.   [2] shirt.]

" God speed thee, brave king Arthur,
 Thus feasting in thy bowre.
And Guenever thy goodly queen,
 That fair and peerlesse flowre.   20

" Ye gallant lords, and lordings,
 I wish you all take heed,
Lest, what ye deem a blooming rose
 Should prove a cankred weed."

Then straitway from his bosome   25
 A little wand he drew ;
And with it eke a mantle
 Of wondrous shepe, and hew.

" Now have thou here, king Arthur,
 Have this here of mee,   30
And give unto thy comely queen,
 All-shapen as you see.

" No wife it shall become,
 That once hath been to blame."
Then every knight in Arthur's court   35
 Slye glaunced at his dame.

And first came lady Guenever,
 The mantle she must trye.
This dame, she was new-fangled,
 And of a roving eye.   40

When she had tane the mantle,
 And all was with it cladde,
From top to toe it shiver'd down,
 As tho' with sheers beshradde.

One while it was too long,   45
 Another while too short,
And wrinkled on her shoulders
 In most unseemly sort.

Now green, now red it seemed,
 Then all of sable hue.   50
" Beshrew me, quoth king Arthur,
 I think thou beest not true."

Down she threw the mantle,
 Ne longer would not stay ;
But storming like a fury,   55
 To her chamber flung away.

She curst the whoreson weaver,
 That had the mantle wrought :
And doubly curst the froward impe,
 Who thither had it brought. 60

" I had rather live in desarts
 Beneath the green-wood tree :
Than here, base king, among thy groomes,
 The sport of them and thee."

Sir Kay call'd forth his lady, 65
 And bade her to come near :
" Yet dame, if thou be guilty,
 I pray thee now forbear."

This lady, pertly gigling,
 With forward step came on, 70
And boldly to the little boy
 With fearless face is gone.

When she had tane the mantle,
 With purpose for to wear :
It shrunk up to her shoulder, 75
 And left her b**side bare.

Then every merry knight,
 That was in Arthur's court,
Gib'd, and laught, and flouted,
 To see that pleasant sport. 80

Down she threw the mantle,
　No longer bold or gay,
But with a face all pale and wan,
　To her chamber slunk away.

Then forth came an old knight, 85
　A pattering o'er his creed;
And proffer'd to the little boy
　Five nobles to his meed;

" And all the time of Christmass
　Plumb-porridge shall be thine, 90
If thou wilt let my lady fair
　Within the mantle shine."

A saint his lady seemed,
　With step demure, and slow,
And gravely to the mantle 95
　With mincing pace doth goe,

When she the same had taken,
　That was so fine and thin,
It shrivell'd all about her,
　And show'd her dainty skin. 100

Ah! little did HER mincing,
　Or HIS long prayers bestead;
She had no more hung on her,
　Than a tassel and a thread.

Down she threwe the mantle, 105
　With terror and dismay,
And, with a face of scarlet,
　To her chamber hyed away.

Sir Cradock call'd his lady,
　And bade her to come neare: 110
" Come win this mantle, lady,
　And do me credit here.

"Come win this mantle, lady,
    For now it shall be thine,
If thou hast never done amiss,   115
    Sith first I made thee mine."

The lady gently blushing,
    With modest grace came on,
And now to trye this wondrous charm
    Courageously is gone.   120

When she had tane the mantle,
    And put it on her backe,
About the hem it seemed
    To wrinkle and to cracke.

"Lye still, shee cried, O mantle!   125
    And shame me not for nought,
I'll freely own whate'er amiss,
    Or blameful I have wrought.

"Once I kist Sir Cradocke
    Beneathe the green wood tree :   130
Once I kist Sir Cradocke's mouth
    Before he married me."

When thus she had her shriven,
    And her worst fault had told,
The mantle soon became her   135
    Right comely as it shold.

Most rich and fair of colour,
    Like gold it glittering shone :
And much the knights in Arthur's court
    Admir'd her every one.   140

Then towards king Arthur's table
    The boy he turn'd his eye :
Where stood a boar's-head garnished
    With bayes and rosemarye.

When thrice he o'er the boar's head   145
  His little wand had drawne,
Quoth he, " There's never a cuckold's knife,
  Can carve this head of brawne."

Then some their whittles rubbed
  On whetstone, and on hone :   150
Some threwe them under the table,
  And swore that they had none.

Sir Cradock had a little knife
  Of steel and iron made ;
And in an instant thro' the skull   155
  He thrust the shining blade.

He thrust the shining blade
  Full easily and fast :
And every knight in Arthur's court
  A morsel had to taste.   160

The boy brought forth a horne,
  All golden was the rim :
Said he, " No cuckolde ever can
  Set mouth unto the brim.

" No cuckold can this little horne   165
  Lift fairly to his head ;
But or on this, or that side,
  He shall the liquor shed."

Some shed it on their shoulder,
  Some shed it on their thigh ;   170
And hee that could not hit his mouth,
  Was sure to hit his eye.

Thus he, that was a cuckold,
  Was known of every man :
But Cradock lifted easily,   175
  And wan the golden can.

Thus boar's head, horn and mantle
  Were this fair couple's meed :
And all such constant lovers,
  God send them well to speed.   180

Then down in rage came Guenever,
  And thus could spightful say,
" Sir Cradock's wife most wrongfully
  Hath borne the prize away.

" See yonder shameless woman,   185
  That makes herselfe so clean :
Yet from her pillow taken
  Thrice five gallants have been.

" Priests, clarkes, and wedded men
  Have her lewd pillow prest :   19
Yet she the wondrous prize forsooth
  Must beare from all the rest."

Then bespake the little boy,
  Who had the same in hold :
" Chastize thy wife, king Arthur,   195
  Of speech she is too bold :

" Of speech she is too bold,
  Of carriage all too free ;
Sir king, she hath within thy hall
  A cuckold made of thee.   200

" All frolick light and wanton
  She hath her carriage borne :
And given thee for a kingly crown
  To wear a cuckold's horne."

           ⁎

⁎ The Rev. Evan Evans, editor of the specimens of *Welsh Poetry*, 4to. affirmed that the *Boy and the Mantle* is taken from what is related in some of the old Welsh MSS. of Tegan Earfron, one of King Arthur's mistresses.   She is said to have possessed a mantle that would not fit any immodest or incontinent woman ;

this, (which, the old writers say, was reckoned among the curiosities of Britain) is frequently alluded to by the old Welsh Bards.

Carleile, so often mentioned in the ballads of K. Arthur, the editor once thought might probably be a corruption of *Caer-leon,* an ancient British city on the river Uske, in Monmouthshire, which was one of the places of K. Arthur's chief residence; but he is now convinced, that it is no other than *Carlisle,* in Cumberland; the old English minstrels, being most of them northern men, naturally represented the hero of romance as residing in the north: And many of the places mentioned in the old ballads are still to be found there: As *Tearne-Wadling,* &c.

Near Penrith is still seen a large circle, surrounded by a mound of earth, which retains the name of Arthur's Round Table.

[For a full statement of the claims of the "North" to be considered as the home of King Arthur, see J. S. Stuart Glennie's Essay on *Arthurian Localities,* in the edition of the Prose Romance of *Merlin,* published by the Early English Text Society.]

XIX.

THE ANCIENT FRAGMENT OF THE MARRIAGE OF SIR GAWAINE.*

THE second poem in this volume, intitled *The Marriage of Sir Gawaine,* having been offered to the reader with large conjectural supplements and corrections, the old fragment itself is here literally and exactly printed from the editor's folio MS. with all its defects, inaccuracies, and errata; that such austere antiquaries, as complain that the ancient copies have not been always rigidly adhered to, may see how unfit for publication many of the pieces would have been, if all the blunders, corruptions, and nonsense of illiterate reciters and transcribers had been superstitiously retained, without some attempt to correct and emend them.

This ballad had most unfortunately suffered by having half of every leaf in this part of the MS. torn away; and, as about nine

---

* [Printed for the first time in the fourth edition.]

stanzas generally occur in the half page now remaining, it is concluded, that the other half contained nearly the same number of
stanzas.

[The following poem is printed in Hales' and Furnivall's edition
of the MS., vol. i. p. 105.]

INGE Arthur liues in merry Carleile,
   & seemely is to see,
   & there he hath wth him Queene Genev^r,
   y^t bride soe bright of blee.

And there he hath wth him Queene Genever,
y^t bride soe bright in bower,
& all his barons about him stoode
y^t were both stiffe & stowre.

The K. kept a royall Christmasse
of mirth & great honor,
& when . . .

   [*About Nine Stanzas wanting.*]

And bring me word what thing it is
y^t a woman most desire.
this shalbe thy ransome, Arthur, he sayes
for Ile haue noe other hier.

K. Arthur then held vp his hand
according thene as was the law ;
he tooke his leaue of the baron there,
& homward can he draw.

And when he came to Merry Carlile,
to his chamber he is gone,
& ther came to him his Cozen Sr Gawaine
as he did make his mone.

And there came to him his Cozen Sr Gawaine
y^t was a curteous knight,
why sigh you soe sore vnckle Arthur, he said
or who hath done thee vnright.

O peace, o peace, thou gentle Gawaine,
y^t faire may thee beffall,
for if thou knew my sighing soe deepe,
thou wold not meruaile att all ;

ffor when I came to tearne wadling,
a bold barron there I fand,

wth a great club vpon his backe,
standing stiffe & strong ;

And he asked me wether I wold fight,
or from him I shold be gone,
o[r] else I must him a ransome pay
& soe dep't him from.

To fight wth him I saw noe cause,
me thought it was not meet,
ffor he was stiffe & strong wth all,
his strokes were nothing sweete.

Therfor this is my ransome, Gawaine
I ought to him to pay
I must come againe, as I am sworne,
vpon the Newyeers day.

And I must bring him word what thing it is
        [*About Nine Stanzas wanting.*]

Then king Arthur drest him for to ryde
in one soe rich array
toward the foresaid Tearne wadling,
y^t he might keepe his day.

And as he rode over a more,
hee see a lady where shee sate
betwixt an oke & a greene hollen[1] :
she was cladd in red scarlett.

Then there as shold have stood her mouth,
then there was sett her eye
the other was in her forhead fast
the way that she might see.

Her nose was crooked & turnd outward,
her mouth stood foule a wry;
a worse formed lady then shee was,
neuer man saw wth his eye.

To halch[2] vpon him, k. Arthur
this lady was full faine
but k. Arthur had forgott his lesson
what he shold say againe

[1 holly. 2 salute.]

What knight art thou, the lady sayd,
that wilt not speake to me?
of me be thou nothing dismayd
tho I be vgly to see;

for I haue halched you curteouslye,
& you will not me againe,
yett I may happen S^r knight, shee said
to ease thee of thy paine.

Giue thou ease me, lady, he said
or helpe me any thing,
thou shalt haue gentle Gawaine, my cozen
& marry him wth a ring.

Why, if I helpe thee not, thou noble k. Arthur
of thy owne hearts desiringe,
of gentle Gawaine . . . .

[*About Nine Stanzas wanting.*]

And when he came to the tearne wadling
the baron there cold he fimde*
wth a great weapon on his backe,
standing stiffe & stronge

And then he tooke k. Arthur's letters in his hands
& away he cold them fling,
& then he puld out a good browne sword,
& cryd himselfe a k.

And he sayd, I haue thee & thy land, Arthur
to doe as it pleaseth me,
for this is not thy ransome sure,
therfore yeeld thee to mee.

And then bespoke him noble Arthur,
& bad him hold his hands,
& give me leave to speake my mind
in defence of all my land.

He said as I came over a More,
I see a lady where shee sate
betweene an oke & a green hollen;
shee was clad in red scarlett;

---

* Sic MS. = finde.

And she says a woman will haue her will,
& this is all her cheefe desire :
doe me right as thou art a baron of sckill,
this is thy ransome & and all thy hyer.

He sayes an early vengeance light on her,
she walkes on yonder more ;
it was my sister that told thee this
& she is a misshappen hore.

But heer Ile make mine avow[1] to god
to do her an euill turne,
for an euer I may thate fowle theefe get,
in a fyer I will her burne.

[*About Nine Stanzas wanting.*]

THE 2d PART.

IR Lancelott & s[r] Steven bold
they rode wth them that day,
and the formost of the company
there rode the steward Kay,

Soe did S[r] Banier & S[r] Bore
S[r] Garrett wth them soe gay,
soe did S[r] Tristeram y[t] gentle k[t],
to the forrest fresh & gay

And when he came to the greene forrest
vnderneath a greene holly tree
their sate that lady in red scarlet
y[t] vnseemly was to see.

S[r] Kay beheld this Ladys face,
& looked vppon her smire[2]
whosoeuer kisses this lady, he sayes
of his kisse he standes in feare.

S[r] Kay beheld the lady againe,
& looked vpon her snout,
whosoeuer kisses this lady, he saies,
of his kisse he stands in doubt.

[[1] my vow.   [2] qy. for swire = neck.]

Peace coz. Kay, then said Sr Gawaine
amend thee of thy life ;
for there is a knight amongst us all
y^t must marry her to his wife.

What, wedd her to wiffe, then said Sr Kay,
in the diuells name anon,
gett me a wiffe where ere I may,
for I had rather be slaine.

Then soome tooke vp their hawkes in hast
& some tooke vp their hounds,
& some sware they wold not marry her
for Citty nor for towne.

And then be spake him noble k. Arthur,
& sware there by this day,
for a litle foule sight and misliking

[*About Nine Stanzas wanting.*]

Then shee said choose thee gentle Gawaine,
truth as I doe say,
wether thou wilt haue me in this liknesse
in the night or else in the day.

And then bespake him Gentle Gawaine,
wth one soe mild of moode,
sayes, well I know what I wold say,
god grant it may be good.

To haue thee fowle in the night
when I wth thee shold play ;
yet I had rather, if I might
haue thee fowle in the day.

What, when Lords goe wth ther seires,* shee said
both to the Ale & wine
alas then I must hyde my selfe,
I must not goe withinne.

And then bespake him gentle gawaine,
said, Lady thats but a skill ;
And because thou art my owne lady,
thou shalt haue all thy will.

---

* Sic in MS. pro *feires*, i. e. Mates.

Then she said, blesed be thou gentle Gawain
this day y^t I thee see,
for as thou see me att this time,
from hencforth I wilbe:

My father was an old knight,
& yett it chanced soe
that he marryed a younge lady
y^t brought me to this woe.

Shee witched me, being a faire young Lady,
to the greene forrest to dwell,
& there I must walke in womans liknesse,
most like a feend of hell.

She witched my brother to a Carlist B . . . .
[About Nine Stanzas wanting.]

that looked soe foule & that was wont
on the wild more to goe.

Come kisse her, Brother Kay, then said Sr Gawaine,
& amend the of thy liffe ;
I sweare this is the same lady
y^t I marryed to my wiffe.

Sr Kay kissed that lady bright,
standing vpon his ffeete ;
he swore, as he was trew knight,
the spice was neuer soe sweete.

Well, Coz. Gawaine, sayes Sr Kay,
thy chance is fallen arright,
for thou hast gotten one of the fairest maids
I euer saw wth my sight.

It is my fortune, said Sr Gawaine ;
for my Vnckle Arthurs sake
I am glad as grasse wold be of raine,
great Ioy that I may take.

Sr Gawaine tooke the lady by the one arme,
Sr Kay tooke her by the tother,
they led her straight to k. Arthur
as they were brother & brother.

K. Arthur welcomed them there all,
& soe did lady Geneuer his queene,
wth all the knights of the round table
most seemly to be seene.

K. Arthur beheld that lady faire
that was soe faire & bright,
he thanked christ in trinity
for Sr Gawaine that gentle knight;

Soe did the knights, both more and lesse,
reioyced all that day
for the good chance y^t hapened was
to Sr Gawaine & his lady gay.   *Finis.*

THE END OF THE THIRD BOOK.

APPENDIX I.

THE WANTON WIFE OF BATH.

APPENDIX I.

THE WANTON WIFE OF BATH.

ROM an ancient copy in black-print, in the Pepys Collection. Mr. Addison has pronounced this an excellent ballad: see the *Spectator*, No. 248.

[This ballad was printed in the third volume of the first edition of the *Reliques*, Book ii. No. 12, but was afterwards expunged by Percy. Professor Child gives the following references in his collection of *English and Scottish Ballads*, vol. viii. p. 152:—
"The same story circulates among the peasantry of England and Scotland in the form of a penny tract or chap-book, *Notices of Popular Histories*, p. 16, (*Percy Soc.* vol. xxiii.); *Notes and Queries*, New Series, vol. iii. p. 49. This jest is an old one. Mr. Halli-well refers to a fabliau in Barbazan's Collection, which contains the groundwork of this piece, *Du Vilain qui Conquist Paradis par Plait*, Meon's ed. iv. 114."]

N Bath a wanton wife did dwelle,
    As Chaucer he doth write;
Who did in pleasure spend her dayes;
    And many a fond delight.

Upon a time sore sicke she was   5
    And at the length did dye;
And then her soul at heaven gate,
    Did knocke most mightilye.

First Adam came unto the gate :
  Who knocketh there? quoth hee   10
I am the wife of Bath, she sayd,
  And faine would come to thee.

Thou art a sinner, Adam sayd,
  And here no place shalt have.
And so art thou, I trowe, quoth shee,   15
  ' and eke a' doting knave.

I will come in, in spight, she sayd,
  Of all such churles as thee ;
Thou wert the causer of our woe,
  Our paine and misery ;   20

And first broke God's commandiments,
  In pleasure of thy wife.
When Adam heard her tell this tale,
  He ranne away for life.

Then downe came Jacob at the gate,   25
  And bids her packe to hell,
Thou false deceiving knave, quoth she
  Thou mayst be there as well.

For thou deceiv'dst thy father deare,
  And thine own brother too.   30
Away ' slunk' Jacob presently,
  And made no more adoo.

She knockes again with might and maine,
  And Lot he chides her straite,
How now, quoth she, thou drunken ass,   35
  Who bade thee here to prate ?

With thy two daughters thou didst lye,
  On them two bastardes got.
And thus most tauntingly she chaft
  Against poor silly Lot.   40

Ver. 16. Now gip you, *P.*

Who calleth there, quoth Judith then,
   With such shrill sounding notes?
This fine minkes surely came not here,
   Quoth she, for cutting throats.

Good Lord, how Judith blush'd for shame,   45
   When she heard her say soe!
King David hearing of the same,
   He to the gate would goe.

Quoth David, who knockes there so loud,
   And maketh all this strife;   50
You were more kinde, good sir, she sayd,
   Unto Uriah's wife.

And when thy servant thou didst cause
   In battle to be slaine;
Thou causedst far more strife than I,   55
   Who would come here so faine.

The woman's mad, quoth Solomon,
   That thus doth taunt a king.
Not half so mad as you, she sayd,
   I trowe in manye a thing.   60

Thou hadst seven hundred wives at once,
   For whom thou didst provide;
And yet God wot, three hundred whores
   Thou must maintaine beside:

And they made thee forsake thy God,   65
   And worship stockes and stones;
Besides the charge they put thee to
   In breeding of young bones.

Hadst thou not bin beside thy wits,
   Thou wouldst not thus have ventur'd;   70
And therefore I do marvel much,
   How thou this place hast enter'd.

I never heard, quoth Jonas then,
    So vile a scold as this.
Thou whore-son run-away, quoth she,   75
    Thou diddest more amiss.

' They say,' quoth Thomas, women's tongues,
    Of aspen-leaves are made.
Thou unbelieving wretch, quoth she,
    All is not true that's sayd.   80

When Mary Magdalen heard her then,
    She came unto the gate.
Quoth she, good woman, you must think
    Upon your former state.

No sinner enters in this place   85
    Quoth Mary Magdalene.   Then
'Twere ill for you, fair mistress mine,
    She answered her agen :

You for your honestye, quoth she,
    Had once been ston'd to death ;   9
Had not our Saviour Christ come by,
    And written on the earth.

It was not by your occupation,
    You are become divine :
I hope my soul in Christ his passion,   95
    Shall be as safe as thine.

Uprose the good apostle Paul,
    And to this wife he cryed,
Except thou shake thy sins away,
    Thou here shalt be denyed.   100

Remember, Paul, what thou hast done,
    All through a lewd desire :
How thou didst persecute God's church,
    With wrath as hot as fire.

Ver. 77. I think, *P.*

Then up starts Peter at the last,   105
    And to the gate he hies :
Fond fool, quoth he, knock not so fast,
    Thou weariest Christ with cries.

Peter, said she, content thyselfe,
    For mercye may be won,   110
I never did deny my Christ,
    As thou thyselfe hast done.

When as our Saviour Christ heard this,
    With heavenly angels bright,
He comes unto this sinful soul,   115
    Who trembled at his sight.

Of him for mercye she did crave.
    Quoth he, thou hast refus'd
My proffer'd grace, and mercy both,
    And much my name abus'd.   120

Sore have I sinned, Lord, she sayd,
    And spent my time in vaine,
But bring me like a wandring sheepe
    Into thy flocke againe.

O Lord my God, I will amend   125
    My former wicked vice :
The thief for one poor silly word,
    Past into Paradise.

My lawes and my commandments,
    Saith Christ, were known to thee ;   130
But of the same in any wise,
    Not yet one word did yee.

I grant the same, O Lord, quoth she ;
    Most lewdly did I live :
But yet the loving father did   135
    His prodigal son forgive.

So I forgive thy soul, he sayd,
  Through thy repenting crye ;
Come enter then into my joy,
  I will not thee denye.   140

APPENDIX II.

ON THE ANCIENT METRICAL ROMANCES, &c.

I.

THE first attempts at composition among all barbarous nations are ever found to be poetry and song. The praises of their gods, and the achievements of their heroes, are usually chanted at their festival meetings. These are the first rudiments of history. It is in this manner that the savages of North America preserve the memory of past events (*a*): and the same method is known to have prevailed among our Saxon ancestors before they quitted their German forests (*b*). The ancient Britons had their Bards, and the Gothic nations their Scalds or popular poets (*c*), whose business it was to record the victories of their warriors, and the genealogies of their princes, in a kind of narrative songs, which were committed to memory, and delivered down from one reciter to another. So long as poetry continued a distinct profession, and

---

(*a*) Vid. *Lasiteau, Moeurs de Sauvages*, t. ii. Dr. Browne's *Hist. of the Rise and Progress of Poetry*.

(*b*) "Germani celebrant carminibus antiquis (quod unum apud illos memoriæ et annalium genus est) Tuistonem," &c. *Tacit. Germ.* c. ii.

(*c*) *Barth. Antiq. Dan.* lib. i. cap. x. *Wormii Literatura Runica*, ad finem.

while the Bard, or Scald, was a regular and stated
officer in the prince's court, these men are thought
to have performed the functions of the historian
pretty faithfully; for though their narrations would
be apt to receive a good deal of embellishment, they
are supposed to have had at the bottom so much of
truth as to serve for the basis of more regular annals.
At least succeeding historians have taken up with
the relations of these rude men, and for the want of
more authentic records, have agreed to allow them
the credit of true history (*d*).

After letters began to prevail, and history assumed
a more stable form, by being committed to plain
simple prose ; these songs of the Scalds or Bards
began to be more amusing than useful. And in proportion as it became their business chiefly to entertain and delight, they gave more and more into
embellishment, and set off their recitals with such
marvellous fictions, as were calculated to captivate
gross and ignorant minds. Thus began stories of
adventures with giants and dragons, and witches
and enchanters, and all the monstrous extravagances
of wild imagination, unguided by judgment, and un-
corrected by art (*e*).

This seems to be the true origin of that species of
romance, which so long celebrated feats of chivalry,
and which at first in metre, and afterwards in prose,
was the entertainment of our ancestors, in common
with their contemporaries on the continent, till the
satire of Cervantes, or rather the increase of knowledge and classical literature, drove them off the

---

(*d*) See *Northern Antiquities, or a Description of the Manners,
Customs, &c., of the ancient Danes and other Northern Nations,
translated from the Fr. of M. Mallet*, 1770, 2 vols. 8vo. (vol. i.
p. 49, &c.)

(*e*) *Vid. infra*, pp. 341, 342, &c.

stage to make room for a more refined species of fiction, under the name of French Romances, copied from the Greek (*f*).

That our old romances of chivalry may be derived in a lineal descent from the ancient historical songs of the Gothic Bards and Scalds, will be shown below, and indeed appears the more evident, as many of those songs are still preserved in the north, which exhibit all the seeds of chivalry before it became a solemn institution (*g*). "Chivalry, as a distinct military order, conferred in the way of investiture, and accompanied with the solemnity of an oath, and other ceremonies," was of later date, and sprung out of the feudal constitution, as an elegant writer has clearly shown (*h*). But the ideas of chivalry prevailed long before in all the Gothic nations, and may be discovered as in embriyo in the customs, manners, and opinions of every branch of that people (*i*). That fondness of going in quest of adventures, that spirit of challenging to single combat, and that respectful complaisance shewn to the fair sex, (so different from the manners of the Greeks and Romans), all are of Gothic origin, and may be traced up to the earliest times among all the northern nations (*k*). These existed long before the feudal ages, though they were called forth and strengthened in a peculiar manner under that constitution, and at length arrived to their full maturity in the times of the Crusades, so replete with romantic adventures (*l*).

(*f*) Viz. *Astræa, Cassandra, Clelia,* &c.

(*g*) Mallet. vid. *Northern Antiquities,* vol. i. p. 318, &c.; vol. ii. p. 234, &c.

(*h*) *Letters concerning Chivalry,* 8vo. 1763.

(*i*) (*k*) Mallet.

(*l*) The seeds of chivalry sprung up so naturally out of the original manners and opinions of the northern nations, that it is

Even the common arbitrary fictions of romance were (as is hinted above) most of them familiar to the ancient Scalds of the North, long before the time of the Crusades. They believed the existence of giants and dwarfs (*m*) ; they entertained opinions not unlike the more modern notion of fairies (*n*), they were strongly possessed with the belief of spells and inchantment (*o*), and were fond of inventing combats with dragons and monsters (*p*).

The opinion therefore seems very untenable, which some learned and ingenious men have entertained, that the turn for chivalry, and the taste for that species of romantic fiction were caught by the Spaniards from the Arabians or Moors after their invasion of Spain, and from the Spaniards transmitted to the

---

not credible they arose so late as after the establishment of the Feudal System, much less the Crusades. Nor, again, that the romances of chivalry were transmitted to other nations, through the Spaniards, from the Moors and Arabians. Had this been the case the first French romances of chivalry would have been on Moorish, or at least Spanish subjects : whereas the most ancient stories of this kind, whether in prose or verse, whether in Italian, French, English, &c., are chiefly on the subjects of Charlemagne and the Paladins, or of our British Arthur and his Knights of the Round Table, &c., being evidently borrowed from the fabulous chronicles of the supposed Archbishop Turpin and of Jeffery of Monmouth. Not but some of the oldest and most popular French romances are also on Norman subjects, as *Richard Sans-peur*, *Robert le Diable*, &c., whereas I do not recollect so much as one in which the scene is laid in Spain, much less among the Moors, or descriptive of Mahometan manners. Even in *Amadis de Gaul*, said to have been the first romance printed in Spain, the scene is laid in Gaul and Britain ; and the manners are French : which plainly shews from what school this species of fabling was learnt and transmitted to the southern nations of Europe.

(*m*) Mallet. *North. Antiquities*, vol. i. p. 36 ; vol. ii. *passim*.
(*n*) *Olaus Verelius, Herv. Saga*, pp. 44, 45.   Hickes's *Thesaur.* vol. ii. p. 311.   *Northern Antiquities*, vol. ii. *passim*.
(*o*) *Ibid.* vol. i. pp. 69, 374, &c.; vol. ii. p. 216, &c.
(*p*) Rollof's *Saga*, c. 35, &c.

bards of Armorica (*q*), and thus diffused through Britain, France, Italy, Germany, and the North. For it seems utterly incredible, that one rude people should adopt a peculiar taste and manner of writing

---

(*q*) It is peculiarly unfortunate that such as maintain this opinion are obliged to take their first step from the Moorish provinces in Spain, without one intermediate resting place, to Armorica or Bretagne, the province in France from them most remote, not more in situation than in the manners, habits, and language of its Welsh inhabitants, which are allowed to have been derived from this island, as must have been their traditions, songs, and fables ; being doubtless all of Celtic original. See p. 3 of the *Dissertation on the Origin of Romantic Fiction in Europe,* prefixed to Mr. Tho. Warton's *History of English Poetry,* vol. i. 1774, 4to. If any pen could have supported this darling hypothesis of Dr. Warburton that of this ingenious critic would have effected it. But under the general term Oriental, he seems to consider the ancient inhabitants of the north and the south of Asia, as having all the same manners, traditions, and fables ; and because the secluded people of Arabia took the lead under the religion and empire of Mahomet, therefore everything must be derived from them to the Northern Asiatics in the remotest ages, &c. With as much reason under the word Occidental, we might represent the early traditions and fables of the north and south of Europe to have been the same ; and that the Gothic mythology of Scandinavia, the Druidic or Celtic of Gaul and Britain, differed not from the classic of Greece and Rome.

There is not room here for a full examination of the minuter arguments, or rather slight coincidences, by which our agreeable dissertator endeavours to maintain and defend this favourite opinion of Dr. W., who has been himself so completely confuted by Mr. Tyrwhitt. (See his notes on *Love's Labour Lost,* &c.) But some of his positions it will be sufficient to mention : such as the referring the Gog and Magog, which our old Christian bards might have had from Scripture, to the *Jaguiouge* and *Magiouge* of the Arabians and Persians, &c. (p. 13). That "we may venture to affirm that this (Geoffrey of Monmouth's) Chronicle, supposed to contain the ideas of the Welsh bards, entirely consists of Arabian inventions" (p. 13). And that, "as Geoffrey's history is the grand repository of the acts of Arthur, so a fabulous history ascribed to Turpin is the ground-work of all the chimerical legends which have been related concerning the conquests of Charlemagne and his twelve peers. Its subject is the expulsion of the Saracens

or thinking from another, without borrowing at the same time any of their particular stories and fables, without appearing to know anything of their heroes, history, laws, and religion. When the Romans began to adopt and imitate the Grecian literature, they immediately naturalized all the Grecian fables, histories, and religious stories; which became as familiar to the poets of Rome, as of Greece itself. Whereas all the old writers of chivalry, and of that species of romance, whether in prose or verse, whether of the Northern nations, or of Britain, France, and Italy, not excepting Spain itself (*r*), appear utterly unacquainted with whatever relates to the Mahometan

---

from Spain, and it is filled with fictions evidently congenial to those which characterize Geoffrey's History " (p. 17). That is, as he afterwards expresses it, "lavishly decorated by the Arabian fablers " (p. 58). We should hardly have expected that the Arabian fablers would have been lavish in decorating a history of their enemy : but what is singular, as an instance and proof of this Arabian origin of the fictions of Turpin, a passage is quoted from his fourth chapter, which I shall beg leave to offer, as affording decisive evidence, that they could not possibly be derived from a Mahometan source. Sc. " The Christians under Charlemagne are said to have found in Spain a golden idol, or image of Mahomet, as high as a bird can fly—it was framed by Mahomet himself ot the purest metal, who, by his knowledge in necromancy, had sealed up within it a legion of diabolical spirits. It held in its hand a prodigious club ; and the Saracens had a prophetic tradition, that this club should fall from the hand of the image in that year when a certain king should be born in France, &c." (*vid.* p. 18, note.)

(*r*) The little narrative songs on Morisco subjects, which the Spaniards have at present in great abundance, and which they call peculiarly *romances*, (see vol. i. book iii. no. xvi. &c.), have nothing in common with their proper romances (or histories) of chivalry, which they call *Historias de Cavallerias ;* these are evidently imitations of the French, and shew a great ignorance of Moorish manners : and with regard to the Morisco, or song *romances*, they do not seem of very great antiquity ; few of them appear, from their subjects, much earlier than the reduction of Granada, in the fifteenth century : from which period, I believe, may be plainly

nations. Thus with regard to their religion, they constantly represent them as worshipping idols, as paying adoration to a golden image of Mahomet, or else they confound them with the ancient pagans, &c. And indeed in all other respects they are so grossly ignorant of the customs, manners, and opinions of every branch of that people, especially of their heroes, champions, and local stories, as almost amounts to a demonstration that they did not imitate them in their songs or romances : for as to dragons, serpents, necromancies, &c., why should these be thought only derived from the Moors in Spain so late as after the eighth century ? since notions of this kind appear too familiar to the northern Scalds, and enter too deeply into all the northern mythology, to have been transmitted to the unlettered Scandinavians, from so distant a country, at so late a period. If they may not be allowed to have brought these opinions with them in their original migrations from the north of Asia, they will be far more likely to have borrowed them from the Latin poets after the Roman conquests in Gaul, Britain, Germany, &c. For, I believe one may challenge the maintainers of this opinion, to produce any Arabian poem or history, that could possibly have been then known in Spain, which resembles the old Gothic romances of chivalry half so much as the Metamorphoses of Ovid.

But we well know that the Scythian nations situate in the countries about Pontus, Colchis, and the Euxine sea, were in all times infamous for their magic arts : and as Odin and his followers are said to have come precisely from those parts of Asia ; we can readily account for the prevalence of fictions of

---

traced among the Spanish writers, a more perfect knowledge of Moorish customs, &c.

this sort among the Gothic nations of the North, without fetching them from the Moors in Spain; who for many centuries after their irruption, lived in a state of such constant hostility with the unsubdued Spanish Christians, whom they chiefly pent up in the mountains, as gave them no chance of learning their music, poetry, or stories; and this, together with the religious hatred of the latter for their cruel invaders, will account for the utter ignorance of the old Spanish romancers in whatever relates to the Mahometan nations, although so nearly their own neighbours.

On the other hand, from the local customs and situations, from the known manners and opinions of the Gothic nations in the north, we can easily account for all the ideas of chivalry and its peculiar fictions (*s*). For, not to mention their distinguished respect for the fair sex, so different from the manners of the Mahometan nations (*t*), their national and domestic history so naturally assumes all the wonders of this species of fabling, that almost all their historical narratives appear regular romances. One might refer in proof of this to the old northern Sagas in general: but to give a particular instance it will be sufficient to produce the history of King Regner Lodbrog, a celebrated warrior and pirate, who reigned in Denmark about the year 800 (*u*). This hero signalized his youth by an exploit of gallantry. A Swedish prince had a beautiful daughter whom he intrusted (probably during some expedition) to the care of one of his officers, assigning a strong castle for their defence. The officer fell in love with his ward, and detained her in his castle, spite of all the

---

(*s*) See *Northern Antiquities*, passim.   (*t*) *Ibid.*
(*u*) *Saxon Gram.* p. 152, 153. Mallet, *North. Antiq.* vol. i. p. 321.

efforts of her father.   Upon this he published a pro-
clamation through all the neighbouring countries,
that whoever would conquer the ravisher and rescue
the lady should have her in marriage.   Of all that
undertook the adventure, Regner alone was so happy
as to achieve it: he delivered the fair captive, and
obtained her for his prize.   It happened that the
name of this discourteous officer was Orme, which in
the Islandic language signifies serpent: Wherefore
the Scalds, to give the more poetical turn to the adventure, represent the lady as detained from her
father by a dreadful dragon, and that Regner slew
the monster to set her at liberty.   This fabulous
account of the exploit is given in a poem still extant,
which is even ascribed to Regner himself, who was a
celebrated poet; and which records all the valiant
achievements of his life (x).

With marvelous embellishments of this kind the
Scalds early began to decorate their narratives: and
they were the more lavish of these, in proportion as
they departed from their original institution, but it
was a long time before they thought of delivering a
set of personages and adventures wholly feigned.
Of the great multitude of romantic tales still preserved in the libraries of the North, most of them
are supposed to have had some foundation in truth,
and the more ancient they are, the more they are
believed to be connected with true history (y).

It was not probably till after the historian and the
bard had been long disunited, that the latter ventured at pure fiction.   At length when their business
was no longer to instruct or inform, but merely to
amuse, it was no longer needful for them to adhere

(x) See a translation of this poem, among *Five pieces of Runic
Poetry*, printed for Dodsley, 1764, 8vo.

(y) *Vid.* Mallet, *Northern Antiquities*, passim.

to truth.   Then succeeded fabulous songs and romances in verse, which for a long time prevailed in
France and England before they had books of chivalry in prose.   Yet in both these countries the
minstrels still retained so much of their original institution, as frequently to make true events the subject of their songs (z) ; and indeed, as during the
barbarous ages, the regular histories were almost all
written in Latin by the monks, the memory of events
was preserved and propagated among the ignorant
laity by scarce any other means than the popular
songs of the minstrels.

II.   The inhabitants of Sweden, Denmark, and
Norway, being the latest converts to Christianity,
retained their original manners and opinions longer
than the other nations of Gothic race : and therefore they have preserved more of the genuine compositions of their ancient poets, than their southern
neighbours.   Hence the progress, among them, from
poetical history to poetical fiction is very discernible :
they have some old pieces, that are in effect complete Romances of Chivalry (a).   They have also
(as hath been observed) a multitude of Sagas (b) or
histories on romantic subjects, containing a mixture
of prose and verse, of various dates, some of them
written since the times of the Crusades, others long
before : but their narratives in verse only are esteemed
the more ancient.

(z) The editor's MS. contains a multitude of poems of this
latter kind.   It was probably from this custom of the minstrels
that some of our first historians wrote their chronicles in verse, as
Rob. of Gloucester, Harding, &c.

(a) See a specimen in 2d vol. of *Northern Antiquities*, &c.,
p. 248, &c.

(b) *Eccardi Hist. Stud. Etym.* 1711, p. 179, &c.   Hickes's
Thesaur. vol. ii. p. 314.

Now as the irruption of the Normans (*c*) into France under Rollo did not take place till towards the beginning of the tenth century, at which time the Scaldic art was arrived to the highest perfection in Rollo's native country, we can easily trace the descent of the French and English romances of chivalry from the Northern Sagas. That conqueror doubtless carried many Scalds with him from the north, who transmitted their skill to their children and successors. These adopting the religion, opinions, and language of the new country, substituted the heroes of Christendom instead of those of their pagan ancestors, and began to celebrate the feats of Charlemagne, Roland, and Oliver; whose true history they set off and embellished with the Scaldic figments of dwarfs, giants, dragons, and enchantments. The first mention we have in song of those heroes of chivalry is in the mouth of a Norman warrior at the conquest of England (*d*) : and this circumstance alone would sufficiently account for the propagation of this kind of romantic poems among the French and English.

But this is not all ; it is very certain, that both the Anglo-Saxons and the Franks had brought with them, at their first emigrations into Britain and Gaul, the same fondness for the ancient songs of their ancestors, which prevailed among the other Gothic tribes (*e*), and that all their first annals were transmitted in these popular oral poems. This fondness they even retained long after their conversion to Christianity, as we learn from the examples of

---

(*c*) *i.e.* Northern men, being chiefly emigrants from Norway, Denmark, &c.

(*d*) See the account of Taillefer in vol. i. Essay, and Note.

(*e*) " Ipsa Carmina memoriæ mandabant, & prælia inituri decantabant ; qua memoria tam fortium gestorum a majoribus patratorum ad imitationem animus adderetur."—*Jornandes de Gothis.*

Charlemagne and Alfred (*f*). Now poetry, being thus the transmitter of facts, would as easily learn to blend them with fictions in France and England, as she is known to have done in the north, and that much sooner, for the reasons before assigned (*g*). This, together with the example and influence of the Normans, will easily account to us, why the first romances of chivalry that appeared both in England and France (*h*) were composed in metre, as a rude kind of epic songs. In both kingdoms tales in verse were usually sung by minstrels to the harp on festival occasions: and doubtless both nations derived their relish for this sort of entertainment from their Teutonic ancestors, without either of them borrowing it from the other. Among both people narrative songs on true or fictitious subjects had evidently obtained from the earliest times. But the professed romances of chivalry seem to have been first composed in France, where also they had their name.

The Latin tongue, as is observed by an ingenious

(*f*) *Eginhartus de Carolo magno.* "Item barbara, & antiquissima carmina, quibus veterum regum actus & bella canebantur, scripsit."—c. 29.

Asserius de Ælfredo magno. "Rex inter bella, &c. . . . . Saxonicos libros recitare, & *maxime carmina Saxonica* memoriter discere, aliis imperare, & solus assidue pro viribus, studiosissime non desinebat."—Ed. 1722, 8vo. p. 43.

(*g*) See above, pp. 340, 347.

(*h*) The romances on the subject of Perceval, San Graal, Lancelot du Lac, Tristan, &c., were among the first that appeared in the French language in prose, yet these were originally composed in metre: the editor has in his possession a very old French MS. in verse, containing *L'ancien Roman de Perceval,* and metrical copies of the others may be found in the libraries of the curious. See a note of Wanley's in *Harl. Catalog. Num.* 2252, p. 49, &c. Nicholson's *Eng. Hist. Library,* 3rd ed. p. 91, &c. See also a curious collection of old French romances, with Mr. Wanley's account of this sort of pieces, in *Harl. MSS. Catal.* 978, 106.

writer (*i*), ceased to be spoken in France about the ninth century, and was succeeded by what was called the Romance tongue, a mixture of the language of the Franks and bad Latin. As the songs of chivalry became the most popular compositions in that language, they were emphatically called Romans or Romants; though this name was at first given to any piece of poetry. The romances of chivalry can be traced as early as the eleventh century (*k*). I know not if the *Roman de Brut* written in 1155, was such: but if it was, it was by no means the first poem of the kind; others more ancient are still extant (*l*). And we have already seen, that, in the preceding century, when the Normans marched down to the battle of Hastings, they animated themselves, by singing (in some popular romance or ballad) the exploits of Roland and the other heroes of chivalry (*m*).

So early as this I cannot trace the songs of chivalry in English. The most ancient I have seen, is that

---

(*i*) The author of the *Essay on the Genius of Pope*, p. 282.

(*k*) *Ibid.* p. 283. *Hist. Lit.* tom. 6, 7.

(*l*) *Voir Preface aux* " Fabliaux & Contes des Poetes François des xii. xiii. xiv. & xv. siècles, &c., Paris, 1756, 3 tom. 12mo." (a very curious work).

(*m*) *Vid. supra,* note (*d*), vol. i. Essay, &c. *Et vide* Rapin, Carte, &c. This song of *Roland* (whatever it was) continued for some centuries to be usually sung by the French in their marches, if we may believe a modern French writer. " Un jour qu'on chantoit la *Chanson de Roland,* comme c'etoit l'usage dans les marches. Il y a long temps, dit il (John K. of France, who died in 1364), qu'on ne voit plus de Rolands parmi les François. On y verroit encore des Rolands, lui répondit un vieux capitaine, s'ils avoient un Charlemagne à leur tête." *Vid.* tom. iii. p. 202, *des Essaies Hist. sur Paris, de M. de Saintefoix:* who gives as his authority, Boethius in *Hist. Scotorum.* This author, however, speaks of the complaint and repartee, as made in an Assembly of the States (*vocato senatu*), and not upon any march, &c. *Vid.* Boeth. lib. xv. fol. 327. Ed. Paris, 1574.

of Hornechild described below, which seems not older than the twelfth century.   However, as this rather resembles the Saxon poetry than the French, it is not certain that the first English romances were translated from that language.* We have seen above, that a propensity to this kind of fiction prevailed among all the Gothic nations(*n*); and, though after the Norman Conquest, this country abounded with French romances, or with translations from the French, there is good reason to believe, that the English had original pieces of their own.

The stories of King Arthur and his Round Table, may be reasonably supposed of the growth of this island; both the French and the Armoricans probably had them from Britain(*o*).   The stories of Guy and Bevis, with some others, were probably the invention of English minstrels(*p*).   On the other hand, the English procured translations of such romances as were most current in France; and in the list given at the conclusion of these remarks, many are doubtless of French original.

---

* See on this subject, vol. i. note, s. 2, p. 404; and in note G g, p. 424, &c.

(*n*) The first romances of chivalry among the Germans were in metre : they have some very ancient narrative songs (which they call *Lieder*) not only on the fabulous heroes of their own country, but also on those of France and Britain, as Tristram, Arthur, Gawain, and the knights *von der Tafel-ronde* (*vid.* Goldasti Not. in *Eginhart. Vit. Car. Mag.* 4to. 1711, p. 207.)

(*o*) The Welsh have still some very old romances about K. Arthur; but as these are in prose, they are not probably their first pieces that were composed on that subject.

(*p*) It is most credible that these stories were originally of English invention, even if the only pieces now extant should be found to be translations from the French.   What now pass for the French originals were probably only amplifications, or enlargements of the old English story.   That the French romances borrowed some things from the English, appears from the word *termagant*.

The first prose books of chivalry that appeared in
our language, were those printed by Caxton (*q*); at
least, these are the first I have been able to discover, and these are all translations from the French.
Whereas romances of this kind had been long current in metre, and were so generally admired in the
time of Chaucer, that his rhyme of Sir Thopas was
evidently written to ridicule and burlesque them(*r*).

He expressly mentions several of them by name
in a stanza, which I have had occasion to quote more
than once in this volume:

> " Men speken of Romaunces of pris
> Of Horn-Child, and of Ipotis
>   Of Bevis, and Sire Guy
> Of Sire Libeux, and Pleindamour,
> But Sire Thopas, he bereth the flour
>   Of real chevalrie " (*s*).

Most, if not all of these are still extant in MS. in
some or other of our libraries, as I shall shew in the
conclusion of this slight essay, where I shall give a
list of such metrical histories and romances as have
fallen under my observation.

As many of these contain a considerable portion
of poetic merit, and throw great light on the manners
and opinions of former times, it were to be wished
that some of the best of them were rescued from

(*q*) *Recuyel of the Hystoryes of Troy*, 1471 ; *Godfroye of Boloyne*,
1481 ; *Le Morte de Arthur*, 1485 ; *The Life of Charlemagne*, 1485,
&c. As the old minstrelsy wore out, prose books of chivalry
became more admired, especially after the Spanish romances began
to be translated into English towards the end of Q. Elizabeth's
reign : then the most popular metrical romances began to be
reduced into prose, as *Sir Guy*, *Bevis*, &c.

(*r*) See extract from a letter, written by the editor of these
volumes, in Mr. Warton's *Observations*, vol. ii. p. 139.

(*s*) *Canterbury Tales* (Tyrwhitt's edit.), vol. ii. p. 238. In all
the former editions which I have seen the name at the end of the
fourth line is *Blandamoure*.

oblivion. A judicious collection of them accurately published with proper illustrations, would be an important accession to our stock of ancient English literature. Many of them exhibit no mean attempts at epic poetry, and though full of the exploded fictions of chivalry, frequently display great descriptive and inventive powers in the bards, who composed them. They are at least generally equal to any other poetry of the same age. They cannot indeed be put in competition with the nervous productions of so universal and commanding a genius as Chaucer, but they have a simplicity that makes them be read with less interruption, and be more easily understood: and they are far more spirited and entertaining than the tedious allegories of Gower, or the dull and prolix legends of Lydgate. Yet, while so much stress was laid upon the writings of these last, by such as treat of English poetry, the old metrical romances, though far more popular in their time, were hardly known to exist. But it has happened unluckily, that the antiquaries, who have revived the works of our ancient writers, have been for the most part men void of taste and genius, and therefore have always fastidiously rejected the old poetical romances, because founded on fictitious or popular subjects, while they have been careful to grub up every petty fragment of the most dull and insipid rhymist, whose merit it was to deform morality, or obscure true history. Should the publick encourage the revival of some of those ancient epic songs of chivalry, they would frequently see the rich ore of an Ariosto or a Tasso, though buried it may be among the rubbish and dross of barbarous times.

Such a publication would answer many important uses: It would throw new light on the rise and progress of English poetry, the history of which can be but imperfectly understood, if these are neglected:

It would also serve to illustrate innumerable passages in our ancient classic poets, which without their help must be for ever obscure. For, not to mention Chaucer and Spencer, who abound with perpetual allusions to them, I shall give an instance or two from Shakespeare, by way of specimen of their use.

In his play of *King John* our great dramatic poet alludes to an exploit of Richard I. which the reader will in vain look for in any true history. Faulconbridge says to his mother, act i. sc. 1.

> " Needs must you lay your heart at his dispose . . .
> Against whose furie and unmatched force,
> The awlesse lion could not wage the fight,
> Nor keepe his princely heart from Richard's hand :
> He that perforce robs Lions of their hearts
> May easily winne a woman's : "

The fact here referred to, is to be traced to its source only in the old romance of *Richard Ceur de Lyon* (*t*), in which his encounter with a lion makes a very shining figure. I shall give a large extract from this poem, as a specimen of the manner of these old rhapsodists, and to shew that they did not in their fictions neglect the proper means to produce the ends, as was afterwards so childishly done in the prose books of chivalry.

The poet tells us, that Richard, in his return from the Holy Land, having been discovered in the habit of "a palmer in Almayne," and apprehended as a spy, was by the king thrown into prison. Wardrewe, the king's son, hearing of Richard's great strength, desires the jailor to let him have a sight of his prisoners. Richard being the foremost, Wardrewe asks

---

(*t*) Dr. Grey has shewn that the same story is alluded to in Rastell's *Chronicle:* as it was doubtless originally had from the romance, this is proof that the old metrical romances throw light on our first writers in prose : many of our ancient historians have recorded the fictions of romance.

him, "if he dare stand a buffet from his hand?" and that on the morrow he shall return him another. Richard consents, and receives a blow that staggers him. On the morrow, having previously waxed his hands, he waits his antagonist's arrival. Wardrewe accordingly, proceeds the story, "held forth as a trewe man," and Richard gave him such a blow on the cheek, as broke his jaw-bone, and killed him on the spot. The king, to revenge the death of his son, orders, by the advice of one Eldrede, that a lion, kept purposely from food, shall be turned loose upon Richard. But the king's daughter having fallen in love with him, tells him of her father's resolution, and at his request procures him forty ells of white silk "kerchers;" and here the description of the combat begins:

> " The kever-chefes (*u*) he toke on honde,
> And aboute his arme he wonde;
> And thought in that ylke while,
> To slee the lyon with some gyle.
> And syngle in a kyrtyll he stode,
> And abode the lyon fyers and wode,
> With that came the jaylere,
> And other men that wyth him were,
> And the lyon them amonge;
> His pawes were stiffe and stronge.
> The chambre dore they undone,
> And the lyon to them is gone.
> Rycharde sayd, Helpe lorde Jesu!
> The lyon made to hym venu,
> And wolde hym have all to rente:
> Kynge Rycharde besyde hym glente (*v*)
> The lyon on the breste hym spurned,
> That aboute he tourned.
> The lyon was hongry and megre,
> And bette his tayle to be egre;
> He loked aboute as he were madde;
> Abrode he all his pawes spradde.

(*u*) *i.e.* handkerchiefs. Here we have the etymology of the word, viz. *Couvre le Chef.*"   (*v*) *i.e.* slipt aside.

He cryed lowde, and yaned (*w*) wyde.
Kynge Rycharde bethought hym that tyde
What hym was beste, and to hym sterte,
In at the throte his honde he gerte,
And hente out the herte with his honde,
Lounge and all that he there fonde.
The lyon fell deed to the grounde:
Rycharde felte no wem (*x*), ne wounde.
He fell on his knees on that place,
And thanked Jesu of his grace."

*   *   *   *   *

What follows is not so well, and therefore I shall extract no more of this poem.—For the above feat the author tells us, the king was deservedly called

" Stronge Rycharde Cure de Lyowne."

That distich which Shakespeare puts in the mouth of his madman in *K. Lear*, act iii. sc. 4.

" Mice and Rats and such small deere
Have been Tom's food for seven long yeare,"

has excited the attention of the critics. Instead of *deere*, one of them would substitute *geer;* and another *cheer* (*y*). But the ancient reading is established by the old romance of Sir Bevis, which Shakespeare had doubtless often heard sung to the harp. This distich is part of a description there given of the hardships suffered by Bevis, when confined for seven years in a dungeon:

" Rattes and myse and such small dere
Was his meate that seven yere."—Sign. F. iii.

III. In different parts of this work, the reader will find various extracts from these old poetical legends; to which I refer him for farther examples of their style and metre. To complete this subject,

---

(*w*) *i.e.* yawned.   (*x*) *i.e.* hurt.
(*y*) Dr. Warburton.—Dr. Grey.

it will be proper at least to give one specimen of their skill in distributing and conducting their fable, by which it will be seen that nature and common sense had supplied to these old simple bards the want of critical art, and taught them some of the most essential rules of epic poetry.—I shall select the romance of *Libius Disconius*(*a*), as being one of those mentioned by Chaucer, and either shorter or more intelligible than the others he has quoted.

If an epic poem may be defined, (*b*) "A fable related by a poet, to excite admiration, and inspire virtue, by representing the action of some one hero, favoured by heaven, who executes a great design, in spite of all the obstacles that oppose him :" I know not why we should withold the name of Epic Poem from the piece which I am about to analyse.

My copy is divided into IX. Parts or Cantos, the several arguments of which are as follows.

Part I.

Opens with a short exordium to bespeak attention : the hero is described ; a natural son of Sir Gawain a celebrated knight of king Arthur's court, who being brought up in a forest by his mother, is kept ignorant of his name and descent. He early exhibits marks of his courage, by killing a knight in single combat, who encountered him as he was hunting. This inspires him with a desire of seeking adventures : therefore cloathing himself in his enemy's armour, he goes to K. Arthur's court, to request the order of knighthood. His request granted, he obtains a promise

---

(*a*) So it is intitled in the editor's MS. But the true title is *Le Beaux Disconus*, or the Fair Unknown. See a note on the *Canterbury Tales*, vol. iv. p. 333.

(*b*) Vid. *Discours sur la Poesie Epique*, prefixed to *Télémaque*.

of having the first adventure assigned him that shall offer.—A damsel named Ellen, attended by a dwarf, comes to implore K. Arthur's assistance, to rescue a young princess, "the Lady of Sinadone" their mistress, who is detained from her rights, and confined in prison. The adventure is claimed by the young knight Sir Lybius : the king assents ; the messengers are dissatisfied, and object to his youth; but are forced to acquiesce. And here the first book closes with a description of the ceremony of equipping him forth.

PART II.

Sir Lybius sets out on the adventure: he is derided by the dwarf and the damsel on account of his youth: they come to the bridge of Perill, which none can pass without encountering a knight called William de la Braunch. Sir Lybius is challenged : they just with their spears : De la Braunch is dismounted : the battle is renewed on foot: Sir William's sword breaks : he yields. Sir Lybius makes him swear to go and present himself to K. Arthur, as the first-fruits of his valour. The conquered knight sets out for K. Arthur's court: is met by three knights, his kinsmen ; who, informed of his disgrace, vow revenge, and pursue the conqueror. The next day they overtake him : the eldest of the three attacks Sir Lybius ; but is overthrown to the ground. The two other brothers assault him : Sir Lybius is wounded ; yet cuts off the second brother's arm : the third yields ; Sir Lybius sends them all to K. Arthur. In the third evening he is awaked by the dwarf, who has discovered a fire in the wood.

PART III.

Sir Lybius arms himself, and leaps on horseback: he finds two giants roasting a wild boar, who have a fair lady their captive. Sir Lybius, by favour of the night, runs one of them through with his spear: is assaulted by the other: a fierce battle ensues: he cuts off the giant's arm, and at length his head. The rescued lady (an Earl's daughter) tells him her story; and leads him to her father's castle; who entertains him with a great feast; and presents him at parting with a suit of armour and a steed. He sends the giant's head to K. Arthur.

Part IV.

Sir Lybius, maid Ellen, and the dwarf, renew their journey: they see a castle stuck round with human heads; and are informed it belongs to a knight called Sir Gefferon, who, in honour of his lemman or mistress, challenges all comers: He that can produce a fairer lady, is to be rewarded with a milk-white faulcon, but if overcome, to lose his head. Sir Lybius spends the night in the adjoining town: In the morning goes to challenge the faulcon. The knights exchange their gloves: they agree to just in the market place: the lady and maid Ellen are placed aloft in chairs: their dresses: the superior beauty of Sir Gefferon's mistress described: the ceremonies previous to the combat. They engage: the combat described at large: Sir Gefferon is incurably hurt; and carried home on his shield. Sir Lybius sends the faulcon to K. Arthur; and receives back a large present in florins. He stays 40 days to be cured of his wounds, which he spends in feasting with the neighbouring lords.

Part V.

Sir Lybius proceeds for Sinadone: in the forest he meets a knight hunting, called Sir Otes de Lisle: maid Ellen charmed with a very beautiful dog, begs

Sir Lybius to bestow him upon her: Sir Otes meets them, and claims his dog: is refused: being unarmed he rides to his castle, and summons his followers: they go in quest of Sir Lybius: a battle ensues: he is still victorious, and forces Sir Otes to follow the other conquered knights to K. Arthur.

PART VI.

Sir Lybius comes to a fair city and castle by a riverside, beset round with pavilions or tents: he is informed, in the castle is a beautiful lady besieged by a giant named Maugys, who keeps the bridge, and will let none pass without doing him homage: this Lybius refuses: a battle ensues: the giant described: the several incidents of the battle; which lasts a whole summer's day; the giant is wounded: put to flight; slain. The citizens come out in procession to meet their deliverer: the lady invites him into her castle: falls in love with him; and seduces him to her embraces. He forgets the princess of Sinadone, and stays with this bewitching lady a twelvemonth. This fair sorceress, like another Alcina, intoxicates him with all kinds of sensual pleasure; and detains him from the pursuit of honour.

PART VII.

Maid Ellen by chance gets an opportunity of speaking to him; and upbraids him with his vice and folly: he is filled with remorse, and escapes the same evening. At length he arrives at the city and castle of Sinadone: Is given to understand that he must challenge the constable of the castle to single combat, before he can be received as a guest. They just: the constable is worsted: Sir Lybius is feasted in the castle: he declares his

intention of delivering their lady; and inquires the
particulars of her history. "Two necromancers have
built a fine palace by sorcery, and there keep her inchanted, till she will surrender her duchy to them,
and yield to such base conditions as they would
impose."

Part VIII.

Early on the morrow Sir Lybius sets out for the
inchanted palace. He alights in the court: enters
the hall: the wonders of which are described in
strong Gothic painting. He sits down at the high
table: on a sudden all the lights are quenched: it
thunders, and lightens; the palace shakes; the walls
fall in pieces about his ears. He is dismayed and
confounded: but presently hears horses neigh, and
is challenged to single combat by the sorcerers.
He gets to his steed: a battle ensues, with various
turns of fortune: he loses his weapon; but gets a
sword from one of the necromancers, and wounds
the other with it: the edge of the sword being
secretly poisoned, the wound proves mortal.

Part IX.

He goes up to the surviving sorcerer, who is carried away from him by inchantment: at length he
finds him, and cuts off his head; he returns to the
palace to deliver the lady; but cannot find her: as
he is lamenting, a window opens, through which
enters a horrible serpent with wings and a woman's
face: it coils round his neck and kisses him; then
is suddenly converted into a very beautiful lady.
She tells him she is the Lady of Sinadone, and was
so inchanted, till she might kiss Sir Gawain, or some
one of his blood: that he has dissolved the charm,
and that herself and her dominions may be his re-

ward. The knight (whose descent is by this means discovered) joyfully accepts the offer; makes her his bride, and then sets out with her for King Arthur's court.

Such is the fable of this ancient piece: which the reader may observe, is as regular in its conduct, as any of the finest poems of classical antiquity. If the execution, particularly as to the diction and sentiments, were but equal to the plan, it would be a capital performance; but this is such as might be expected in rude and ignorant times, and in barbarous unpolished language.

IV. I shall conclude this prolix account, with a list of such old metrical romances as are still extant; beginning with those mentioned by Chaucer.

1. The romance of *Horne Childe* is preserved in the British Musenm, where it is intitled þe ȝeste of kyng Horne. See Catalog. Harl. MSS. 2253, p. 70. The language is almost Saxon, yet from the mention in it of Sarazens, it appears to have been written after some of the Crusades. It begins thus:

> " All heo ben blyþe
> þat to my sonȝ ylyþe:
> A sonȝ ychulle ou sinȝ
> Of Allof þe ȝode kynȝe," (*a*) &c.

Another copy of this poem, but greatly altered, and somewhat modernized, is preserved in the Advocates Library at Edinburgh, in a MS. quarto volume of old English poetry [W. 4. 1.] Num. XXXIV. in seven leaves or folios (*b*), intitled, *Horn-child and Maiden Rinivel*, and beginning thus:

(*a*) *i.e.* May all they be blithe that to my song listen: A song I shall you sing, Of Allof the good king, &c.

(*b*) In each full page of this volume are forty-four lines, when the poem is in long metre: and eighty-eight when the metre is short, and the page in two columns.

" Mi leve frende dere,
Herken and ye may here."

2. The poem of *Ipotis* (or *Ypotis*) is preserved in
the Cotton Library, Calig. A. 2, fo. 77, but is rather
a religious legend, than a romance. Its beginning is,

" He þat wyll of wysdome here
Herkeneth nowe ye may here
Of a tale of holy wryte
Seynt Jon the Evangelyste wytnesseth hyt."

3. The romance of Sir *Guy* was written before
that of Bevis, being quoted in it (*c*). An account of
this old poem is given above, p. 107. To which it
may be added, that the two complete copies in MS.
are preserved at Cambridge, the one in the public
library (*d*), the other in that of Caius College, Class
A. 8.—In Ames's Typog. p. 153, may be seen the
first lines of the printed copy.— The first MS.
begins,

" Sythe the tyme that God was borne."

4. *Guy and Colbronde*, an old romance in three
parts, is preserved in the Editor's folio MS. (p. 349.)
[printed edition, vol. ii. p. 527.] It is in stanzas of
six lines, the first of which may be seen in vol. ii. p.
175, beginning thus :

" When meate and drinke is great plentye."

In the Edinburgh MS. (mentioned above) are two
ancient poems on the subject of *Guy of Warwick* :
viz. Num. XVIII. containing 26 leaves, and XX.
59 leaves. Both these have unfortunately the be-

(*c*) Sign. K. 2. b.
(*d*) For this and most of the following, which are mentioned as
preserved in the Public Library, I refer the reader to the *Oxon
Catalogue of MSS.*, 1697, vol. ii. p. 394 ; in Appendix to Bp.
More's MSS. No. 690, 33, since given to the University of Cambridge.

ginnings wanting, otherwise they would perhaps be found to be different copies of one or both the preceding articles.

5. From the same MS. I can add another article to this list, viz. the romance of *Rembrun* son of Sir Guy; being Num. XXI. in 9 leaves : this is properly a continuation of the History of *Guy :* and in Art. 3, the Hist. of Rembrun follows that of Guy as a necessary part of it. This Edinburgh romance of Rembrun begins thus :

> " Jesu that erst of mighte most
> Fader and sone and Holy Ghost."

Before I quit the subject of Sir Guy, I must observe, that if we may believe Dugdale in his *Baronage* (vol. i. p. 243, col. 2), the fame of our English Champion had in the time of Henry IV. travelled as far as the East, and was no less popular among the Sarazens, than here in the West among the nations of Christendom. In that reign a Lord Beauchamp travelling to Jerusalem was kindly received by a noble person, the Soldan's Lieutenant, who hearing he was descended from the famous Guy of Warwick, " whose story they had in books of their own language," invited him to his palace ; and royally feasting him, presented him three precious stones of great value, besides divers cloaths of silk and gold given to his servants.

6. The romance of *Syr Bevis* is described in page 216 of this vol. Two manuscript copies of this poem are extant at Cambridge, viz., in the public library (*e*), and in that of Caius Coll. Class A. 9. (5.)—The first of these begins,

> " Lordyngs lystenyth grete and smale."

(*e*) No. 690, § 31. Vid. *Catalog. MSS.* p. 394.

There is also a copy of this romance of *Sir Bevis of Hamptoun*, in the Edinburgh MS. Numb. XXII. consisting of twenty-five leaves, and beginning thus :

"Lordinges herkneth to mi tale,
Is merier than the nightengale."

The printed copies begin different from both, viz.,

"Lysten, Lordinges, and hold you styl."

7. *Libeaux* (*Libeaus*, or *Lybius*) *Disconius* is preserved in the Editor's folio MS. (page 317) [pr. ed. vol. ii. p. 415], where the first stanza is,

"Jesus Christ christen kinge,
And his mother that sweete thinge,
Helpe them at their neede,
That will listen to my tale,
Of a Knight I will you tell,
A doughtye man of deede."

An older copy is preserved in the Cotton Library (Calig. A. 2. fol. 40) but containing such innumerable variations, that it is apparently a different translation of some old French original, which will account for the title of *Le Beaux Disconus*, or the Fair Unknown. The first line is,

"Jesu Christ our Savyour."

As for *Pleindamour*, or *Blandamoure*, no romance with this title has been discovered ; but as the word *Blaundemere* occurs in the romance of *Libius Disconius*, in the Editor's folio MS. p. 319 [pr. ed. vol. ii. p. 420], he thought the name of *Blandamoure* (which was in all the editions of Chaucer he had then seen) might have some reference to this. But *Pleindamour*, the name restored by Mr. Tyrwhitt, is more remote.

8. *Le Morte Arthure* is among the Harl. MSS. 2252, § 49. This is judged to be a translation from the French ; Mr. Wanley thinks it no older than the

time of Henry VII., but it seems to be quoted in Syr Bevis, (Sign. K. ij. b.)   It begins,

> " Lordinges, that are lesse and deare."

In the library of Bennet Coll. Cambridge, No. 351, is a MS. intitled in the catalogue *Acta Arthuris Metrico Anglicano*, but I know not its contents.

9. In the Editor's folio MS. are many songs and romances about King Arthur and his knights, some of which are very imperfect, as *King Arthur and the King of Cornwall* (page 24) [pr. ed. vol. i. p. 61], in stanzas of four lines, beginning,

> " ' Come here,' my cozen Gawaine so gay."

The Turke and Gawain (p. 38) [pr. ed. vol. i. p. 90], in stanzas of six lines beginning thus :

> " Listen lords great and small," *

but these are so imperfect that I do not make distinct articles of them.   See also in this volume, Book I. No. I., II., IV., V.

In the same MS. p. 203 [pr. ed. vol. ii. p. 58], is the *Greene Knight*, in two parts, relating a curious adventure of Sir Gawain, in stanzas of six lines, beginning thus :—

> " List: wen Arthur he was k : "

10. *The Carle of Carlisle* is another romantic tale about Sir Gawain, in the same MS. p. 448 [pr. ed. vol. iii. p. 277], in distichs :

> " Listen : to me a litle stond."

In all these old poems the same set of knights are always represented with the same manners and

---

* In the former editions, after the above, followed mention of a fragment in the same MS., intitled, *Sir Lionel*, in distichs (p. 32) [pr. ed. vol. i. p. 75]; but this being only a short ballad, and not relating to K. Arthur, is here omitted.

characters; which seem to have been as well known, and as distinctly marked among our ancestors, as Homer's Heroes were among the Greeks : for, as *Ulysses* is always represented crafty, *Achilles* irascible, and *Ajax* rough; so *Sir Gawain* is ever courteous and gentle, *Sir Kay* rugged and disobliging, &c. " *Sir Gawain with his olde curtesie* " is mentioned by Chaucer as noted to a proverb, in his *Squire's Tale. Canterb. Tales,* vol. ii. p. 104.

11. *Syr Launfal,* an excellent old romance concerning another of King Arthur's knights, is preserved in the Cotton Library, Calig. A 2, f. 33. This is a translation from the French (*f*), made by one *Thomas Chestre,* who is supposed to have lived in the reign of Henry VI. (See Tanner's Biblioth.) It is in stanzas of six lines, and begins,

> " Be douyty Artours dawes."

The above was afterwards altered by some minstrel into the romance of *Sir Lambewell,* in three parts, under which title it was more generally known (*g*). This is the Editor's folio MS. p. 60 [pr. ed. vol. i. p. 144], beginning thus :

> " Doughty in king Arthures dayes."

12. *Eger and Grime,* in six parts (in the Editor's folio MS. p. 124) [pr. ed. vol. i. p. 354], is a well invented tale of chivalry, scarce inferior to any of Ariosto's. This which was inadvertently omitted in the former editions of this list, is in distichs, and begins thus :

> " It fell sometimes in the Land of Beame."

(*f*) The French original is preserved among the Harl. MSS. No. 978, § 112, *Lanval.*

(*g*) See Laneham's *Letter concern. Q. Eliz. entertainment at Killingworth,* 1575, 12mo. p. 34.

13. The romance of *Merline*, in nine parts (preserved in the same folio MS. p. 145 [pr. ed. vol. i. p. 422]), gives a curious account of the birth, parentage, and juvenile adventures of this famous British Prophet. In this poem the *Saxons* are called *Sarazens;* and the thrusting the rebel angels out of heaven is attributed to "*oure Lady.*" It is in distichs and begins thus:

> " He that made with his hand."

There is an old romance *Of Arthour and of Merlin*, in the Edinburgh MS. of old English poems : I know not whether it has anything in common with this last mentioned. It is in the volume numbered xxiii. and extends through fifty-five leaves. The two first lines are:

> " Jesu Crist, heven king
> Al ous graunt gode ending."

14. *Sir Isenbras* (or as it is in the MS. copies, *Sir Isumbras*), is quoted in Chaucer's *R. of Thopas*, v. 6. Among Mr. Garrick's old plays is a printed copy; of which an account has been already given in vol. i. book iii. No. vii. It is preserved in MS. in the Library of Caius Coll. Camb., Class A. 9 (2), and also in the Cotton Library, Calig. A. 12 (f. 128). This is extremely different from the printed copy. E. g.

> " God þat made both erþe and hevene."

15. *Emarè*, a very curious and ancient romance, is preserved in the same vol. of the Cotton Library, f. 69. It is in stanzas of six lines, and begins thus:

> "Jesu þat ys kyng in trone."

16. *Chevelere assigne*, or The Knight of the Swan, preserved in the Cotton Library, has been already described in vol. ii. Appendix, *Essay on P. Plowman's Metre*, &c., as hath also

17. *The Sege of Jērlam* (or Jerusalem), which seems to have been written after the other, and may not improperly be classed among the romances; as may also the following, which is preserved in the same volume, viz.,

18. *Owaine Myles* (fol. 90), giving an account of the wonders of St. Patrick's Purgatory. This is a translation into verse of the story related in Mat. Paris's *Hist.* (sub. Ann. 1153.) It is in distichs beginning thus :

> "God þat ys so full of myght."

In the same manuscript are three or four other narrative poems, which might be reckoned among the romances, but being rather religious legends, I shall barely mention them; as *Tundale,* f. 17 ; *Trentale Sci Gregorii,* f. 84 ; *Jerome,* f. 133 ; *Eustache,* f. 136.

19. *Octavian imperator,* an ancient romance of chivalry, is in the same vol. of the Cotton Library, f. 20. Notwithstanding the name, this old poem has nothing in common with the history of the Roman Emperors. It is in a very peculiar kind of stanza, whereof 1, 2, 3, & 5 rhyme together, as do the 4 and 6. It begins thus :

> "Ihesu þat was with spere ystonge."

In the public library at Cambridge (*h*), is a poem with the same title, and begins very differently :

> "Lyttyll and mykyll, olde and yonge."

20. *Eglamour of Artas* (or *Artoys*) is preserved in the same vol. with the foregoing, both in the Cotton Library and Public Library at Cambridge. It is also in the Editor's folio MS. p. 295 [pr. ed.

(*h*) No. 690. (30.) *Vid. Oxon. Catalog. MSS.* p. 394.

vol. ii. p. 341], where it is divided into six parts. A printed copy in the Bodleian Library, C. 39. Art. Seld., and also among Mr. Garrick's old plays, K. vol. x. It is in distichs, and begins thus:

> " Ihesu Crist of heven kyng."

21. *Syr Triamore* (in stanzas of six lines) is preserved in MS. in the Editor's volume, p. 210 [pr. ed. vol. ii. p. 80], and in the Public Library at Cambridge (690, § 29. Vid. Cat. MSS. p. 394.) Two printed copies are extant in the Bodleian Library, and among Mr. Garrick's plays in the same volumes with the last article. Both the editor's MS. and the printed copy begin,

> " Nowe Jesu Chryste our heven kynge."

The Cambridge copy thus:

> " Heven blys that all shall wynne."

22. *Sir Degree* (*Degare*, or *Degore*, which last seems the true title) in five parts, in distichs, is preserved in the Editor's folio MS. p. 371 [pr. ed. vol. iii. p. 20], and in the Public Library at Cambridge (ubi supra). A printed copy is in the Bod. Library C. 39. Art. Seld. and among Mr. Garrick's plays, K. vol. ix. The Editor's MS. and the printed copies begin,

> " Lordinges, and you wyl holde you styl."

The Cambridge MS. has it,

> " Lystenyth, lordyngis, gente and fre."

23. *Ipomydon* (or *Chylde Ipomydon*), is preserved among the Harl. MSS. 2252 (44). It is in distichs, and begins,

> " Mekely, lordyngis, gentylle and fre."

In the library of Lincoln Cathedral, K k. 3, 10, is

an old imperfect printed copy, wanting the whole first sheet A.

24. *The Squyr of Lowe degre*, is one of those bur-lesqued by Chaucer in his Rhyme of Thopas (*i*). Mr. Garrick has a printed copy of this, among his old plays, K. vol. ix. It begins,

> " It was a squyer of lowe degre,
> That loved the kings daughter of Hungre."

25. *Historye of K. Richard Cure* [*Cœur*] *de Lyon.* (Impr. W. de Worde, 1528, 4to.) is preserved in the Bodleian Library, C. 39, Art. Selden. A frag-ment of it is also remaining in the Edinburgh MS. of old English poems ; No. xxxvi. in two leaves. A large extract from this romance has been given already above, p. 356. Richard was the peculiar patron of Chivalry, and favourite of the old minstrels and troubadours. See Warton's *Observ.* vol. i. p. 29, vol. ii. p. 40.

26. Of the following I have only seen No. 27, but I believe they may all be referred to the class of romances.

The *Knight of Courtesy and the Lady of Faguel* (Bodl. Lib. C. 39. Art. Sheld. a printed copy). This Mr. Warton thinks is the story of Coucy's Heart, related in Fauchet, and in Howel's Letters. (v. i. s. 6, L. 20, see Wart. *Obs.* v. ii. p. 40). The Editor has seen a very beautiful old ballad on this subject in French.

27. The four following are all preserved in the MS. so often referred to in the Public Library at Cambridge, (690. Appendix to Bp. More's MSS. in Cat. MSS. tom. ii. p. 394), viz., *The Lay of Erle of*

(*i*) This is alluded to by Shakespeare in his *Hen. V.* (Act v.), where Fluellyn tells Pistol, he will make him a squire of low degree, when he means, to knock him down.

Tholouse (No. 27), of which the Editor hath also a copy from " Cod. MSS. Mus. Ashmol. Oxon." The first line of both is,

> " Jesu Chryste in Trynyte."

28. *Roberd Kynge of Cysyll* (or Sicily) shewing the fall of pride. Of this there is also a copy among the Harl. MSS. 1703 (3). The Cambridge MS. begins,

> " Princis that be prowde in prese."

29. *Le bone Florence of Rome*, beginning thus:

> " As ferre as men ride or gone."

30. *Dioclesian the Emperour*, beginning,

> " Sum tyme ther was a noble man."

31. The two knightly brothers *Amys and Amelion* (among the Harl MSS. 2386, §. 42) is an old romance of chivalry, as is also, I believe, the fragment of the *Lady Belesant, the Duke of Lombardy's fair daughter*, mentioned in the same article. See the catalog. vol. ii.

32. In the Edinburgh MS. so often referred to (preserved in the Advocates Library, W. 4. i.) might probably be found some other articles to add to this list, as well as other copies of some of the pieces mentioned in it, for the whole volume contains not fewer than thirty-seven poems or romances, some of them very long. But as many of them have lost the beginnings, which have been cut out for the sake of the illuminations, and as I have not had an opportunity of examining the MS. myself, I shall be content to mention only the articles that follow (*k*): viz.

(*k*) Some of these I give, though mutilated and divested of their titles, because they may enable a curious inquirer to complete or improve other copies.

An old romance about *Rouland* (not I believe the famous Paladine, but a champion named *Rouland Louth;* query) being in the volume, No. xxvii. in five leaves, and wants the beginning.

33. Another romance that seems to be a kind of continuation of this last, intitled, *Otuel a Knight*, (No. xxviii. in eleven leaves and a half). The two first lines are,

> " Herkneth both yinge and old,
> That willen heren of battailes bold."

34. *The King of Tars* (No. iv. in five leaves and a half; it is also in the Bodleyan Library, MS. Vernon, f. 304) beginning thus :

> " Herkneth to me bothe eld and ying
> For Maries love that swete thing."

35. A tale or romance (No. i. two leaves), that wants both beginning and end. The first lines now remaining are,

> " Th Erl him graunted his will y-wis. that the knicht him haden
>   y told.
> The Baronnis that were of mikle pris. befor him thay weren
>   y-cald."

36. Another mutilated tale or romance (No. iii. four leaves). The first lines at present are,

> "To Mr. Steward wil y gon. and tellen him the sothe of the
> Reseyved bestow sone anon. gif you will serve and with hir be."

37. A mutilated tale or romance (No. xi. in thirteen leaves). The two first lines that occur are,

> " That riche Dooke his fest gan hold
> With Erls and with Baronns bold."

I cannot conclude my account of this curious manuscript, without acknowledging that I was indebted to the friendship of the Rev. Dr. Blair, the ingenious professor of Belles Lettres, in the University of Edinburgh, for whatever I learned of its contents, and for the important additions it enabled me to make to the foregoing list.

To the preceding articles two ancient metrical romances in the Scottish dialect may now be added, which are published in Pinkerton's *Scottish Poems*, reprinted "from scarce editions," Lond. 1792, in 3 vols. 8vo. viz.

38. *Gawan and Gologras*, a metrical romance; from an edition printed at Edinburgh, 1508, 8vo. beginning :—

> " In the tyme of Arthur, as trew men me tald."

It is in stanzas of thirteen lines.

39. *Sir Gawan and Sir Galaron of Galloway*, a metrical romance, in the same stanzas as No. 38, from an ancient MS. beginning thus :

> "In the tyme of Arthur an aunter (*l*) betydde
> By the Turnwathelan, as the boke tells ;
> Whan he to Carlele was comen, and conqueror kyd," &c.

Both these (which exhibit the union of the old alliterative metre, with rhyme, &c., and in the termination of each stanza the short triplets of the Turnament of Tottenham), are judged to be as old as the time of our K. Henry VI., being apparently the production of an old poet, thus mentioned by Dunbar, in his *Lament for the Deth of the Makkaris*:

> " Clerk of Tranent eik he hes take,
> That made the aventers of Sir Gawane."

It will scarce be necessary to remind the reader, that *Turnewathelan* is evidently *Tearne-Wadling*,

---

(*l*) *i.e.* adventure.

celebrated in the old ballad of the *Marriage of Sir Gawaine.* See pp. 14 and 325 of this volume.

Many new references, and perhaps some additional articles might be added to the foregoing list from Mr. Warton's *History of English Poetry*, 3 vols. 4to. and from the notes to Mr. Tyrwhitt's improved edition of *Chaucer's Canterbury Tales*, &c. in 5 vols. 8vo. which have been published since this Essay, &c. was first composed; but it will be sufficient once for all to refer the curious reader to those popular works.

The reader will also see many interesting particulars on the subject of these volumes, as well as on most points of general literature, in Sir John Hawkins's curious *History of Music*, &c., in 5 volumes, 4to., as also in Dr. Burney's *Hist.* &c. in 4 vols. 4to.

[Much has been written upon the subject of this Essay since Percy's time, but no exhaustive work has yet appeared. The reader may consult W. C. Hazlitt's new edition of Warton's *History*, 1871; Ellis's *Specimens of Early English Metrical Romances*, new edition, by J. O. Halliwell, 1848; Dunlop's *History of Fiction;* J. M. Ludlow's *Popular Epics of the Middle Ages, Norse, German, and Carlovingian Cycles*, 1865; G. W. Cox and E. H. Jones's *Popular Romances of the Middle Ages*, 1871; and also the prefaces of the various old English romances printed by the Percy, Camden, and Early English Text Societies; and by the Abbotsford, Bannatyne, and Roxburghe Clubs.]

GLOSSARY

TO THE THREE VOLUMES.

THIS is an amalgamation of the three original glossaries, with large additions and alterations, and the introduction of references. It has not, however, been thought necessary to refer to every passage in which a particular word may occur.

Percy's explanatory notes are marked with the letter P.

Many words which appear in a slightly varied form from the present spelling are not included in this glossary.

A', *all.*
A, *at.*
A, i. 27, *of.* Watter a Twyde, i. 25, *water of Tweed.*
Abacke, *back.*
Abenche, i. 409, *on a bench.*
Able, i. 87, *fit, suitable.*
Abone, i. 24 ; aboon, i. 323 ; aboone, i. 101 ; aboun, i. 32, *above.*
Aboven ous, ii. 8, *above us.*
Abowght, i. 40, *about.*
Abraide, i. 168, *abroad.*
Abuve, ii. 83, *in the uplands.*
Abye, iii. 31, *suffer, pay for, expiate.*

Acton, i. 72, *a quilted leather jacket, worn under the coat of mail.* Fr. hacqueton.
Advoutry, ii. 136, *adultery.*
Aff, ii. 70, *off.*
Affore, i. 269 ; afore, ii. 115, *before.*
Aft, i. 321, *oft.*
Agayne, i. 121, *against.*
Ageyn, i. 119, *against.*
Agone, ii. 41, *gone.*
Ahte, ii. 11, *ought.*
Aik, iii. 147, *oak.*
Ail, ii. 84, *trouble.*
Ain, i. 102, *own.*
Aith, ii. 70, *oath.*

Al, ii. 9, *albeit, although.*
Al gife, *although.*
Alace, iii. 236, *alas.*
Alane, ii. 83, *alone.*
Alemaigne, ii. 7, *Germany.*
Allgyf, i. 125, *although.*
Almaine, iii. 110, *Germany.*
Alyes, ii. 33, *always.*
Amang, ii. 20, *among.*
Amangis, ii. 81, *amongst.*
Amblit, iii. 237, *ambled.*
Among, ii. 35, *at intervals, some-times.*
An, *and.*
An, i. 60, *if.*
Ancyent, i. 271, *flag, banner, stan-dard.*
And, *if,* but and, i. 27 ; *but if;* and youe, *if you.*
And but, ii. 15, *and unless.*
Ane, i. 30, ii. 118, *one, an, a.*
Anes, ii. 112, *once,* ii. 109. (?)
Angel, ii. 176, *a gold coin varying in value from* 6s. 8d. *to* 10s.
Ann, ii. 69, *if*
Anneuche, ii. 81, *enough.*
Annoy, ii. 211, *trouble.*
Ant, ii. 7, *and.*
Aplyht, al aplyht, ii. 14, *entirely.*
Aquoy, iii. 247, *coy, shy.*
Ar, ii. 24, *are.*
Aras, i. 24, *arrows.*
Archeborde, ii. 193, 203, *side of the ship?* See Hach-borde.
Arcir, i. 103, *archer.*
Argabushe, ii. 53, *harquebuse, an old-fashioned kind of musket.*
Arrand, i. 80, *errand.*
Arros, i. 28, *arrows.*
Ase, ii. 8, *as.*
Aslake, ii. 37, *abate.*
Assay, i. 80, *essay,* assayed, ii. 44.
Assoyld, i. 179, *absolved.*
Astate, i. 119, *estate.*
Astonied, iii. 34, *astonished, stunned.*
Astound, i. 207, *stunned.*
Ath, i. 25, *of the.*
Att me, i. 276, *from me.*
Attour, ii. 81 ; attowre, ii. 84, 86, *over.*
Au, iii. 75, *all.*
Auld, i. 83, 101, ii. 68, *old.*

Aule, i. 308, *awl.*
Aureat, i. 123, *golden.*
Austerne, i. 285, *stern, austere.*
Avaunce, ii. 49, *advance.*
Avow, iii. 327 ; avowe, i. 23, 34, 47, 172 ; ii. 23, 58, *vow.*
Aw, iii. 145, *all.*
Awa', ii. 69, *away.*
Awin, ii. 133, *own.*
Awne, i. 121, 274, *own.*
Axed, i. 129, *asked.*
Ay, ii. 70, *ever ;* also *ah ! alas !*
Ayein, ii. 12, *against.*
Ayont the ingle, ii. 68, *beyond the fire. The fire was in the middle of the room.*
   " In the west of Scotland, at this present time, in many cottages, they pile their peats and turfs upon stones in the middle of the room. There is a hole above the fire in the ridge of the house to let the smoke out at. In some places are cottage-houses, from the front of which a very wide chimney projects like a bow-window : the fire is in a grate, like a malt-kiln grate, round which the people sit : sometimes they draw this grate into the middle of the room." (Mr. Lambe.) P.

Ba', i. 59, *ball.*
Bacheleere, i. 64, 78, *knight ;* bachelary, ii. 28 ; bachelery, ii. 23, *company of bachelors.*
Badena, iii. 93, *delayed not.*
Baile, i. 122, *bale, evil, mischief, misery, trouble.*
Bairn, ii. 70 ; bairne, i. 59, *child.*
Baith, i. 143, 321, *both.*
Bale, i. 108, 280, ii. 8, 59, *evil, hurt, mischief, misery ;* baleful, i. 136.
Balow, ii. 211 (a nursery term), *hush, lullaby.*
Balys bete, i. 35, *remedy our evils.*
Ban, ii. 70, *curse.*
Band, i. 70, 148, *bond, covenant.*
Bandrolles, iii. 290, *streamers, little flags.*
Bane, i. 29, *bone.*
Banket, ii. 225, *banquet.*

Banning, ii. 212, *cursing.*
Barker, ii. 96, *dealer in bark.*
Barne, i. 26, *child, man, person.*
Barrow hogge, i. 214, *gelded hog.*
Basnete, i. 29, basnite, i. 28, bassonett, i. 48, *helmet.*
Bason, *helmet.*
Batchilere, i. 68, *knight.*
Bathe, i. 30, *both.*
Bats, ii. 21, *cudgels.*
Bauld, i. 321, *bold.*
Bauzen's skinne, i. 308. *Sheepskin gloves with the wool on the inside.*
Bayard, ii. 22, *a noted horse in the old romances.*
Be, ii. 9, *by.*
Beanes, ii. 203, *beams.*
Bearing arowe, i. 176, *an arrow that carries well.*
Bed, ii. 13, *bade.*
Bede, ii. 21, 23, *bid, offer, engage.*
Bedeaft, iii. 272, *deafened.*
Bedeene, ii. 57, iii. 11, *immediately.*
Bedight, i. 132, *bedecked.*
Bedone, iii. 6, 237, *wrought, made-up, ornamented.*
Beere, i. 50, iii. 42, *bier.*
Beforn, i. 321 ; beforne, i. 29, 65, *before.*
Begilde, ii. 76 ; begylde, ii. 44, *beguiled, deceived.*
Beheard, i. 114, *heard.*
Behove, i. 180, *behoof.*
Beir, i. 84 ; beire, ii. 212, *bear.*
Belive, i. 115 ; belyfe, i. 173, *immediately, presently, shortly.*
Ben, ii. 15, 16, iii. 208, *been, be, are.*
Ben, ii. 70, *within doors, the inner room.*
  (The "but" is the outer room. "A but and a ben" is a house containing two rooms.)
Bene, ii. 16, *bean, an expression of contempt.*
Benison, i. 322, *blessing.*
Bent, bents, *long coarse grass,* i. 24, 25, 28 ; *also wild fields,* i. 41, 43, 65, 78.
Beoth, ii. 11, *be, are.*
Ber, ii. 13, *bare.*
Ber the prys, ii. 11, *bare the prize.*
Berne, i. 41, *man.*

Bernes, iii. 208, *barns.*
Berys, ii. 21, *beareth.*
Beseeme, *become.*
Besene, ii. 25, *dressed.*
Beshradde, iii. 317, *cut into shreds.*
Besmirche, *to soil, discolour.*
Bespake, iii. 158, *spoke.*
Besprent, ii. 52, *besprinkled.*
Beste, *beest, art.*
Beste, i. 189, *beast.*
Bested, *abode.*
Bestis, i. 122, *beasts.*
Bestrawghted, i. 189, *distracted.*
Besy, i. 129, *busy.*
Bet, *better.*
Beth, i. 284, *be, is, are.*
Bett, ii. 63, *lighted.* A.S. bétan fyr, *to make or light a fire.*
Bette, iii. 356, *did beat.*
Beuche, ii. 391, *bough.*
Bewray, ii. 179, *discover.*
Bi mi leautè, ii. 7, *by my loyalty, honesty.*
Bickarte, i. 24, *skirmished ;* also *swiftly* coursed.
  Mr. Lambe also interprets "Bickering," by rattling, *e.g.*,

And on that slee Ulysses head
Sad curses down does BICKER.
         Translat. of Ovid. P.

Bide at hame, iii. 97, *remain at home.*
Biilt, ii. 63, *built.*
Bil, i. 168, *pike or halbert.*
Bille, i. 282, 289, ii. 143, *writing.*
Biqueth, ii. 12, *bequeath.*
Bird, iii. 94, *child, term of affection usually applied to a woman.*
Birk, ii. 363, iii. 238, *birch-tree.*
Blak, ii. 21 ; blake, ii. 21, *black.*
Blan, i. 269 ; blane, i. 30 ; blanne, i. 68, 91, 275, ii. 144, *lingered, stopped.*
Blaw, i. 145, iii. 147, *blow ;* blawing, iii. 147, *blowing.*
Blaze, ii. 260, *emblazon, display.*
Blee, i. 72, ii. 56, *colour, complexion.*
Bleid, iii. 94, *bleed ;* bleids, ii. 116, *bleeds.*
Blend, iii. 55 ; blent, iii. 51, *blended.*
Blent, *ceased.*

Blink, ii. 120, *a glimpse of light.*
Blinkan, iii. 123, *twinkling.*
Blinks, iii. 74, *twinkles, sparkles.*
Blinne, iii. 46, *cease, give over.*
Blissing, iii. 208, *blessing.*
Blist, i. 310, *blessed.*
Blude, i. 34, *blood;* blude reid, i. 100, *blood red.*
Bluid, i. 59, 83, *blood;* bluidy, i. 144, *bloody;* reid bluid, *red blood,* i. 146.
Blyth, ii. 68, *joyous, sprightly.*
Blyth, iii. 74, *joy, sprightliness.*
Blyve, i. 175, *instantly.*
Bode, i. 120, *abode, stayed.*
Boist, boisteris, *boast, boasters.*
Boke, ii. 16, *book.*
Bollys, ii. 21, *bowls.*
Boltes, *shafts, arrows.*
Bomen, i. 24, *bowmen.*
Bonny, iii. 147, *handsome, comely.*
Bonys, ii. 22, *bones.* Rounde bonys, ii. 22.
Bookes-man, iii. 52, *clerk, secretary.*
Boot, ii. 97; boote, i. 109, 115, 136, ii. 59; boots, iii. 154, *gain, advantage, help, assistance.*
Bore, iii. 112, *boar.*
Bore, iii. 40, *born.*
Borowe, i. 162, *to redeem.*
Borrow, i. 275; borrowe, i. 269, *pledge, surety.*
Bost, ii. 24; boste, i. 122, *pride; boast,* ii. 8.
Bot, ii. 60, *but.*
Bot, ii. 109, *without;* bot and, i. 144, *and also;* bot dreid, *without dread, or certainly;* bot gif, ii. 83, *unless.*
Bots, iii. 186, *a worm troublesome to horses.*
Bougill, i. 147, *bugle-horn, hunting-horn.*
Boun, i. 146, *ready.*
Bowen, ii. 44, *ready.*
Bower, iii. 125, 126, 131, *parlour, chamber.*
Bower-window, iii. 125, *chamber window.*
Bowne, i. 63, 77, ii. 94, *ready;* bowned, *prepared;* bowne ye, i. 107, *prepare ye, get ready;*

bowne to dine, *going to dine.* Bowne *is a common word in the North for "going,"* e.g. Where are you bowne to? *Where are you going to?* P.
Bow're-woman, iii. 96, *chambermaid.*
Bowyn, i. 41, *ready.*
Bowynd, i. 40, *prepared.*
Bowys, i. 28, *bows.*
Brade, ii. 107, 112, *broad.*
Brae, iii. 147, *the brow or side of a hill, a declivity.* Braes of Yarrow, ii. 363, *hilly banks of the river Yarrow.*
Braid, *broad.*
Braid, i. 100, *open.*
Brand, i. 83, 96; brande, i. 25, 30, 40, 48, 67, *sword.*
Brast, i. 66, 168, ii. 56, 98, iii. 61, *burst.*
Braw, ii. 227, *brave.*
Braw, ii. 69, *bravely, handsomely.*
Brayd attowre the bent, ii. 84, *hastened over the field.*
Brayn-pannes, ii. 25, *skulls.*
Bread, ii. 192, *breadth.*
Bred, i. 43, *broad.*
Breeden, i. 108, *breed.*
Breere, i. 111, *briar.*
Bren, i. 80, 145; brenn, ii. 57, *burn.*
Brenand drake, ii. 23, *fiery dragon.*
Brenn, i. 144; brenne, i. 73, 159, *burn;* brent, i. 160, ii. 55, iii. 87, *burnt;* brenning, ii. 142, *burning.*
Brest, i. 29, *breast.*
Brest, ii. 21, *burst.*
Brether, i. 87, *brethren.*
Bridal (bride-ale), *nuptial feast.*
Brigue, iii. 95; briggs, iii. 92, *bridge.*
Brimme, ii. 257, *public, universally known;* A.-S. bryme.
Britled, iii. 12, *carved.*
Broche, ii. 22, *any ornamental trinket. Stone buckles of silver or gold with which gentlemen and ladies clasp their shirt-bosoms, and handkerchiefs, are called in the North* broches, *from the* Fr. broche, *a spit.* P.

Brocht, ii. 85, *brought.*
Broder, ii. 360, *brother.*
Broding, i. 64, 78, *pricking.*
Broht, ii. 13; brohte, ii. 8, *brought.*
Bronde, i. 49, *sword.*
Brooche, brouche, *a spit, a bodkin.*
Brooke, *enjoy;* and I brook, i. 34, *if I enjoy.*
Brouke hur wyth wynne, ii. 20, *enjoy her with pleasure.*
Browd, i. 24, *broad.*
Broyt, ii. 21, *brought.*
Bryttlynge, i. 25, *cutting up, quartering, carving.*
Buen, ii. 12; bueth, ii. 13, *been, be, are.*
Buff, i. 150, *arm, dress.*
Bugle, i. 65, 78, *bugle horn, hunting horn (being the horn of a* bugle *or wild bull).*
Buik, *book.*
Buit, ii. 81, *help.*
Burgens, ii. 383, *buds, young shoots.*
Burn, iii. 147, bourne, *brook.*
Bushment, i. 122, *ambush, snare.*
Busk, i. 146, *dress, deck;* busk ye, i. 107, ii. 363, *dress ye;* busk and boun, i. 146, *make yourselves ready to go;* buske them blyve, i. 175, *get them ready instantly;* buskit, i. 143, *dressed;* buskt them, i. 122, *prepared themselves, made themselves ready.*
But, *without;* but let, *without hindrance.*
But, i. 75, ii. 144, *unless;* but an, i. 144, *unless;* but yf, ii. 23, *unless.*
Bute, ii. 83, *boot, good, advantage.*
Butt, ii. 70, *the outer room.* See Ben.
By three, *of three.*
Byde, ii. 83, *stay.*
Bydys, i. 28, *bides, abides.*
Bye, *buy, pay for.*
Byears, i. 33, beeres, *biers.*
Byhynde, ii. 19, *behind.*
Byre, iii. 236, *cow-house.*
Byste, i. 41, *beest, art.*

Ca', iii. 93, *call.*
Caddis, i. 376, *worsted ribbon.*

Cadgily, ii. 68, *merrily, cheerfully.*
Caitif, iii. 228; caitive, ii. 135, *wretch.*
Cales, ii. 243, *Cadiz.*
Calliver, *a large pistol or blunderbuss.*
Camscho, iii. 385. (Glossary— *Eldridge*) *grim.*
Can, i. 44, 77, ii. 24, 70; cane, i. 47, *gan, began.*
Can, ii. 37, *know.*
Canna, iii. 123; cannae, i. 59, 146, *cannot.*
Cannes, *wooden cups, bowls.*
Cantabanqui, i. 374, *ballad-singers, singers on benches.*
Cantells, ii. 23, *pieces, corners.*
Canty, ii. 69, *cheerful, chatty.*
Capul, ii. 24, *a poor horse;* capulys, ii. 24, *horses.*
Capull hyde, i. 107, 114, *horse hide.*
Carle, ii. 68, iii. 123, *clown, a strong, hale old man.*
Carlish, i. 133, iii. 14, *churlish, discourteous.*
Carlist, iii. 329, *churlish?*
Carp, ii. 136; carpe, ii. 19, *to speak, recite,* also *to censure,* i. 33, *complain.*
Carpyng, ii. 20, *tumult.*
Cast, i. 26, *mean, intend.*
Caste, ii. 128, *stratagem.*
Catives, ii. 302, *wretches.*
Cau, ii. 71, *call.*
Cauld, i. 143, ii. 68, *cold.*
Causey, ii. 139, *causeway.*
Cawte and kene, i. 44, *cautious and active.*
Cent, i. 130, *scent.*
Cetywall, i. 307, *setiwall, the herb valerian, or mountain spikenard.*
Cham, ii. 288, *I am, in Somersetshire dialect.*
Chanteclere, i. 307, *the cock.*
Chap, iii. 93, 95, *knock.*
Charke-bord, ii. 203? same as archeborde, *side of the ship?* See Hach-borde.
Chayme, ii. 74, *Cain,* or *Ham.*
Chays, i. 26, *chase.*
Che, ii. 286, *I, in Somersetshire dialect.*

Cheare, ii. 216, *chair.*
Checke, i. 301, *to stop, to chide.*
Cheefe, *the upper part of the scutcheon in heraldry.*
Cheffe, i. 28, *chief;* cheffest, iii. 44, *chiefest.*
Cheften, i. 28, *chieftain.*
Cheis, *choose.*
Chevaliers, *knights.*
Cheveron, ii. 25, *upper part of the scutcheon in heraldry.*
Chevy Chase, i. 19, *Cheviot chase or hunt.* See same contraction in Tividale.
Chield, *fellow.*
Child, iii. 58, *knight.*
Children, i. 66, 77, *knights.*
Chill, ii. 286, *I will, in Somersetshire dialect.*
Cholde, y-cholde, ii. 12, *I would.*
Choul'd, ii. 287, *I would, in Som. dialect.*
Christentie, christentye, i. 92, ii. 61; christianté, i. 31, *Christendom.*
Church-ale, iii. 198, *a wake or feast in commemoration of the dedication of a church.*
Chyf, chyfe, *chief.*
Chylded, ii. 382, *brought forth, was delivered.*
Chylder, ii. 25, *children's.*
Chyviat chays, i. 26. (See Chevy Chase.)
Claiths, ii. 69, *clothes.*
Clattered, *beat so as to rattle.*
Clawde, *clawed, tore, scratched;* figuratively, *beat.*
Clead, ii. 69, *clad, clothe;* cleading, iii. 237, *clothing.*
Cleaped, i. 306, *called, named.*
Cled, iii. 147, *clad, clothed.*
Clepe, ii. 13, *call;* cleped, ii. 14, *called.*
Cliding, iii. 97, *clothing.*
Clin, i. 155, *contraction of Clement.*
Clough, i. 155, *a broken cliff.*
Clout, i. 197, *a cloth to strain milk through;* *rag,* ii. 71;
Clout, ii. 100, *mend.*
Clowch, *clutch, grasp.*
Clymme, ii. 74, *climb.*

Coate, i. 309, *cot, cottage.*
Cockers, i. 308, *a sort of buskins or short boots fastened with laces or buttons, worn by farmers or shepherds.* Cokers, *fishermen's boots* (Littleton's Dict.)
Cog, iii. 203, *to lie, cheat.*
Cohorted, ii. 382, *incited, exhorted.*
Cokenay, ii. 28, explained by Percy to be a diminutive of cook, from the Latin coquinator, or coquinarius; it really means *a lean chicken.*
Cold, ii. 232; colde, ii. 55, *could.*
Cold, iii. 6, *knew,* where I cold be; i. 286, *where I was.*
Cold rost, *nothing to the purpose.*
Cole, iii. 108, *coal.*
Coleyne, iii. 33, *Cologne steel.*
Collayne, i. 48, *Cologne steel.*
Com, ii. 12; come, ii. 21, *came;* comen, i. 89; commen, i. 33, *come.*
Con, ii. 27, *can.*
Con fare, *went, passed.*
Con springe, ii. 11, *spread abroad.*
Con twenty thanks, iii. 210, *give twenty thanks.*
Confeterd, i. 120, *confederated.*
Confound, i. 218, *destroy.*
Contray, ii. 19, *country.*
Cop, ii. 9, *head, the top of anything.*
Coppell, ii. 21, *name of a hen.*
Cordiwin, i. 318, *originally Spanish or Cordovan leather, afterwards commoner leather.*
Cors, ii. 21, *body.*
Cors, i. 26, *curse.*
Corsiare, i. 30, *courser, steed.*
Coste, ii. 30, *coast, side, region.*
Cote, i. 303; cott, iii. 183, *cottage.*
Cote, iii. 53, *coat.*
Cotydyallye, ii. 381, *daily, every day.*
Could bear, ii. 137, did *bare.*
Could be, *was.*
Could dye, *died.*
Could his good, *knew what was good for him.*

Could weip, *wept.*
Coulde, *cold.*
Counsayl, *secret.*
Countie, i. 303, *count, earl.*
Coupe, i. 300, *coop, or a pen for poultry.*
Courtas, ii. 82, *courteous.*
Courteys, ii. 46, *courteous.*
Courtnalls, iii. 182, *courtiers.*
Couth, i. 306, *could.*
Couthen, ii. 13, *knew.*
Cowde, i. 44, *could.*
Coyntrie, i. 308, *Coventry.*
Cramasie, iii. 75, 147, *crimson.*
Crancke, i. 307, *exultingly.*
Cranion, iii. 198, *skull.*
Crech, ii. 27. This word is incorrectly explained in the text as *crutch.* It is really a form of the French *crèche*, a crib or manger. It occurs as *cracche* in the "Promptorium Parv." (1440).
Crepyls, ii. 24, *cripples.*
Cricke, i. 196, *properly an ant, but used for any small insect.*
Crinkle, iii. 10, *run in and out, run into flexures, wrinkle.*
Cristes cors, *Christ's corse.*
Croche, ii. 312, *crouch.*
Croft, ii. 22, *inclosure near a house.*
Crois, ii. 13 ; croiz, ii. 12, *cross.*
Crook, ii. 70, *twist, wrinkle, distort;* crook my knee, ii. 71, *make lame my knee.* They say in the North "the horse is crookit," *i.e.* lame ; the "horse crooks," *i.e.* goes lame. P.
Crouneth, ii. 12, *crown ye.*
Crowch, i. 180, *crutch.*
Crown, i. 26, *head.*
Crowt, iii. 10, *to pucker up, draw close together.* (Another form of crowd.)
Crumpling, ii. 257, *crooked, horned.*
Cryance, i. 65, 66, 78, *fear.*
Cule, ii. 229, *cool.*
Cum, i. 28, 59, 101, 143 ; ii. 132, *come, came.*
Cummer, ii. 133, *gossip, friend;* Fr. commère, compère.
Cure, ii. 76, *care, heed, regard.*

Dale, *deal;* bot gif I dale, ii. 83, *unless I share.*
Dampned, i. 161, *damned, condemned.*
Dan, *an ancient title of respect,* from Lat. Dominus.
Danske, ii. 254, *Denmark.*
Dare, ii. 360, *their;* ii. 361, *there.*
Darh, ii. 14, *need.*
Darr'd, ii. 118, *hit.*
Dart the tree, ii. 115, *hit the tree.*
Dat, ii. 360, *that.*
Daunger halt, ii. 16, *fear holdeth.*
Dawes, iii. 368, *days.*
Dawkin, ii. 19, diminutive of David.
De, ii. 360, *the.*
De, i. 26, 30, *die.*
Dealan, iii. 134, *dealing.*
Deare, ii. 308, *hurt.*
Deare, iii. 82, *dearly.*
Deas, iii. *the high table in a hall.* F. dais, a canopy.
Ded, ii. 26 ; dede, i. 30, *dead.*
Dede is do, ii. 36, *deed is done.*
Dee, iii. 99, *die.*
Deemed, iii. 52 ; deemedst, ii 217, *doomed, judged;* thus in the Isle of Man judges are called Deemsters. P.
Deere, ii. 304, *hurt, mischief.*
Deerely, ii. 194, iii. 27 ; *preciously, richly.*
Default, i. 303, *neglect.*
Deid, ii. 83, *dead;* deid bell, iii. 134, *passing bell.*
Deid, i. 101, 147, *deed.*
Deip, i. 60 ; *deep.*
Deir, i. 83, 101 ; *dear.*
Deir, iii. 96, *dearly.*
Deir, ii. 82, *hurt, trouble.*
Deie, ii. 35, *deal, bit.*
Dele, ii. 45, *to deal.*
Dell, *deal, part;* every dell, *every part.*
Delt, iii. 119, *dealt.*
Dem, ii. 361, *them.*
Demaines, iii. 209, *demesnes, estates.*
Deme, ii. 265, *judged, doomed.*
Denay, i. 217, *deny, refuse.*
Dent, ii. 21, *a dint, blow.*
Deol, ii. 13, *dole, grief.*

Depart, ii. 37, *separate;* departing, ii. 84, *dividing.*
Depured, i. 129, *purified, run clear.*
Deray, ii. 28, *confusion.*
Dere, ii. 20, *dear,* also *hurt.*
Dere, ii. 19, *dire or sad.* A.-S. derian, to hurt. " My dearest foe"—*Hamlet.*
Dere, iii. 357, *wild animals.*
Derked, ii. 37, *darkened.*
Dern, ii. 82, *secret;* I'dern, ii. 83, *in secret.*
Descreeve, i. 63, *describe;* descrying, iii. 168, *describing.*
Devys, ii. 12, *devise, the act of bequeathal by will.*
Dey, ii. 361, *they.*
Dey, i. 33 ; deye, ii. 12, *die.*
Did off, i. 114, *took off;* did on, iii. 65, *put on.*
Dight, i. 63, 74 ; dighte, ii. 162, *decked, dressed, prepared, wrought, fitted out, done.*
Diht, ii. 11, *wrought;* ii. 12, *sent.*
Dill, ii. 82, *share.*
Dill, *still, calm, mitigate.*
Dill, i. 63, 77, 78, *dole, grief, pain, sorrow;* dill I drye, i. 64, *pain I suffer;* dill was dight, *grief was upon him.*
Dinge, iii. 51, *knock, beat.*
Dis, *this.*
Discreeve, i. 77, *describe, or discover.*
Disna, iii. 123, *does not.*
Disteynyd, i. 124, *stained.*
Distrere, iii. 108, *the horse ridden by a knight in the tournament.*
Do, ii. 36, *done.*
Dochter, i. 59, 145, ii. 68, *daughter.*
Dois, i. 59, 83, *does.*
Dois, *days.*
Dol, ii. 13 ; dole, i. 63, 137, 292, *dole, grief, sorrow.*
Doleful dumps, i. 188, 261, *sorrowful gloom or heaviness of heart.*
Dolours, *dolorous, mournful.*
Don, iii. 208, *do.*
Don, ii. 23, *be made.*
Done roun, ii. 80, *run down.*
Dosend, iii. 123, *dosing, drowsy, torpid, benumbed.*

Doth, dothe, doeth, *do.*
Doubt, iii. 327, *fear.*
Doubteous, *doubtful.*
Dough, ii. 360, *though.*
Doughty, iii. 26 ; doughtye, i. 305; dowghtye, i. 40 ; *formidable.*
Doughete, i. 28, *a doughty man.*
Dounae, i. 60, *cannot.*
Dout, ii. 23, *fear.*
Doute, i. 167, *doubt.*
Doutted, i. 123, *redoubted, feared.*
Douyty, *doughty.*
Doy-trogh, ii. 24, *dough trough, a kneading trough.*
Doys, i. 34, *does.*
Doyter, ii. 20, *daughter.*
Drake ; brenand drake, ii. 23, *burning, fire-breathing dragon.*
Drap, *drop;* draping, ii. 114, drapping, iii. 97, *dropping.*
Dre, i. 31, 83, *suffer.*
Dreid, ii. 82, *dread.*
Dreips, i. 146, *drips, drops.*
Dreiry, iii. 100, *dreary.*
Drieps, iii. 146, *drips, drops.*
Drie, i. 144, *suffer;* ill, i. 284 ; *undergo,* i. 83.
Drighnes, i. 119, *dryness.*
Drogh, ii. 26, *drew.*
Drovyers, i. 254, *drovers, cattle-drivers.*
Drye, i. 49, 64, 78, *suffer, endure.*
Dryng, ii. 8, *drink.*
Duble dyse, *double or false dice.*
Dude, ii. 7, *did;* dudest, ii. 9, *didst.*
Duel, ii. 11, *grief.*
Dughty, ii. 19, 26, *doughty;* dughtynesse of dent, ii. 21, *sturdiness of blows.*
Dule, i. 83, 145, *dole, grief, sorrow;* dulefu', ii. 69, *doleful.*
Dumps, i. 188, 261, ii. 69, *heaviness of heart.*
Dwellan, iii. 134, *dwelling.*
Dy, *die;* dyan, iii. 134, *dying.*
Dyd on, i. 159, *put on;* dyd off, i. 164, *doffed, put off.*
Dyght, i. 30, *dressed, put on.*
Dyht, ii. 14, *to dispose, order.*
Dynt, i. 30, dynte, i. 31, dyntes, i. 32, *dint, blow, stroke.*
Dystrayne, ii. 37, *afflict.*
Dyyt, ii. 24, *dight, dressed.*

Eame, *uncle.*
Eard, *earth.*
Earn, ii. 70, *to curdle, make cheese.*
Eathe, i. 273, *easy.*
Eather, iii. 100, *either.*
Eche, ii. 246, *each.*
Ee, i. 101, 178, ii. 60 ; een, i. 320, *eye, eyes.*
Eene, iii. 75, *even.*
Effund, iii. 301, *pour forth.*
Eftsoon, iii. 304, *in a short time.*
Egge, ii. 259, *to urge on.*
Eik, ii. 83, *also.*
Eiked, ii. 85, *added, enlarged.*
Ein, i. 145, *even.*
Eir, i. 101, 146, 320, *ever.*
Eise, ii. 212, *ease.*
Eke, ii. 13, *also.*
Eldridge, i. 64, 78, *wild, hideous, ghostly, lonesome, uninhabited.*

" In the ballad of *Sir Cauline* we have ' Eldridge Hills,' p. 65, ' Eldridge Knight,' p. 65, ' Eldridge Sword,' p. 67. So Gawin Douglas calls the Cyclops the ' Elriche Brethir,' *i.e.* brethren (b. ii. p. 91, l. 16), and in his Prologue to b. vii. (p. 202, l. 3) he thus describes the Night-Owl :—

" ' Laithely of forme, with crukit camscho beik,
" ' Ugsome to here was his wyld *elrische* skreik.'

" In Bannatyne's MS. Poems (fol. 135, in the Advocate's Library at Edinburgh) is a whimsical rhapsody of a deceased old woman travelling in the other world ; in which

" ' Scho wanderit, and yeid by, to an *Elrich* well.'

" In the Glossary to G. Douglas, Elriche, &c. is explained by ' Wild, hideous : Lat. *Trux, immanis;*' but it seems to imply somewhat more, as in Allan Ramsay's Glossaries." P.

Elke, *each.*
Elles, ii. 20, *else.*
Ellumynynge, i. 123, *embellishing*
Elyconys, i. 119, *Helicon's.*

Elvish, *peevish, fantastical.*
Eme, i. 44, ii. 9, *uncle, kinsman.*
Endyed, i. 123, *dyed.*
Ene, eyn, *eyes.*
Ene, *even.*
Enharpid, i. 123, *hooked or edged.*
Enkankered, *cankered.*
Enouch, iii. 100, *enough.*
Enowe, i. 275, *enough.*
Ensue, ii. 43, *follow.*
Entendement, ii. 382, *understanding.*
Entent, ii. 49, *intent.*
Ententifly, ii. 382, *to the intent, purposely.*
Envie ; envye, i. 42, *malice, ill-will, injury.*
Er, ii. 20, 26, *are.*
Ere, ii. 36, 42, *ear.*
Erlys, ii. 47 ; erlés, iii. 94, *earls.*
Erst, i. 83, *heretofore.*
Etermynable, i. 126, *interminable, unlimited.*
Ettled, ii. 116, *aimed.*
Evanished, iii. 133, *vanished.*
Everych, ii. 27, *every;* everych-one, i. 156 ; iii. 108, *every one.*
Ew-bughts, iii. 74, *pens for milch-ewes.*
Eyen, i. 72 ; eyn, ii. 15 ; eyne, i. 132, *eyes.*
Ezar, iii. 97, *maple.*

Fa', i. 84, 146, *fall ;* fa's, iii. 123, *falls.*
Fach, i. 33, feche, *fetch.*
Fader, iii. 365; fadir, i. 83; fatheris, *father, father's.*
Fadge, iii. 236, *a bundle of sticks, a thick loaf of bread, coarse heap of stuff.*
Fadom, i. 102, *fathom.*
Fae, ii. 109, *foe.*
Fain, ii. 69 ; faine, i. 164, 287 ; fayne, i. 157, *glad, fond, well pleased;* faine of fighte, i. 92, *fond of fighting.*
Fair of feir, *of a fair and health-ful look;* perhaps, far off (free from) fear. P.
Falds, iii. 123, *thou foldest.*
Fallan, iii. 133, *falling.*
Fals, ii. 212, *false.*

Falser, iii. 161, *a deceiver, hypo-crite.*

Falsing, ii. 61, *dealing in false-hood.*

Fand, iii. 324, *found.*

Fang, ii. 26, *make off.*

Fann'd, ii. 246, *found.*

Fannes, *instruments for winnow-ing corn.*

Fantacy, ii. 136 ; fantasye, ii. 160, *fancy.*

Farden, i. 72, *flashed.*

Fare, i. 84, ii. 21, *go forth, pass, travel.*

Fare, *the price of a passage, shot, reckoning.*

Farley, i. 107, *strange.*

Fauht, i. 122, *fought.*

Fauld, ii. 85, *field.*

Fauyt, ii. 30, *fought.*

Fawkon, i. 42, *falcon.*

Fawn, iii. 122, *fallen.*

Fawte, i. 122, *fought.*

Fay, i. 178 ; faye, i. 106, *faith.*

Fayrere, ii. 45, *fairer.*

Faytors, i. 215, *deceivers, dissem-blers, cheats.*

Fe, i. 178, *fee, reward*, also *bribe.*
Applied to lands and tene-ments which are held by per-petual right, and by acknow-ledgment of superiority to a higher lord.

Feare. In feare, ii. 149, *company.*

Feat, i. 300, *nice, neat.*

Featously, i. 306, *neatly, dexter-ously.*

Fedyrs, ii. 22, *feathers.*

Fee, ii. 140, *property.*

Feere, i. 63, 76, *mate, companion.*

Feill, ii. 86, *fail (?).*

Feil, fele, *many.*

Feirs, ii. 114, *companions.*

Feir, i. 101, ii. 82 ; feire, ii. 212, *fear.*

Feit, i. 84, 102, *feet.*

Felawe, ii. 44, *fellow.*

Feld, ii. 25, *field.*

Fell, i. 65, 78 ; ii. 19, *furious, fierce, keen,* i. 306.

Fell, ii. 25, *hide.*

Feloy, ii. 25, *fellow.*

Fend, ii. 21 ; fende, ii. 59, *defend.*

Fendys pray, i. 125, *the prey of the fiends.*

Fere, ii. 36, *fear.*

Fere, i. 64, 68, 73, 156, ii. 20, *mate,* play-feres, i. 59, *play-fellows.*

Ferly, ii. 19, *wonder;* also *wonder-fully,* ii. 25.

Ferlyng, ii. 8, *furlong.*

Ferr, i. 62, *far.*

Fersly, i. 160, *fiercely.*

Fesaunt, i. 42, *pheasant.*

Fest, ii. 27, *feast.*

Fet, ii. 128, iii. 193 ; fett, i. 286 ; fette, i. 50, 68, *fetched;* deepe-fette, i. 76, *deep-drawn.*

Fethe, i. 29, *faith.*

Fettle, i. 116 ; fetteled, i. 108 ; fettled, i. 113, 116, *prepared, addressed, made ready.*

Fey, ii. 118, *predestinated to some misfortune.*

Feyytyng, ii. 19, *fighting.*

Fie, ii. 82, *sheep or cattle.*

Fier, i. 149, *fire.*

Filde, *field.*

Filinge, iii. 63, *defiling*

Fillan, iii. 134, *filling.*

Finaunce, i. 125, *fine, forfeiture.*

Find frost, *find mischance or dis-aster.*

Firth, ii. 85, *copse, wood.*

Fit, i. 27 ; fitt, ii. 177 ; fytte, i. 44, *part or division of a song.*
Fitts, *i.e.* divisions or parts in music, are alluded to in "Troilus and Cressida," act. iii. sc. 1. (See Steevens's note.) P.

Fit, *foot, feet;* a fit, ii. 70, *on foot.*

Flatred, ii. 25, *slit.*

Flayne, iii. 25, *flayed.*

Flearing, i. 215, *sneering.*

Flee, iii. 97, *fly.*

Fles, ii. 24, *fleece.*

Fleyke, ii. 134, *a large kind of hurdle;* cows are frequently milked in hovels made of fleyks.

Flindars, iii. 97, *pieces, splinters.*

Flix, iii. *flux.*

Flote, i. 201.
To flote is to flete or fleet, to flit, to change position easily, to move away quickly; as fleeting moments, flitting birds.

Flote and flete are two forms of the same word; and flutter bears the same relation to flote that flitter does to flete.

In the Roxburghe copy of the ballad of *Willow, Willow* this word is printed as " fleet." (Roxb. Ballads, ed. Chappell, part i. p. 172.)

Flout, ii. 179; floute, i. 197, *to sneer;* fflouting, i. 289.

Flowan, ii. 364, *flowing.*

Flude, ii. 364, *flood.*

Flyte, i. 196, 281, 288, *to contend with words, scold.*

Fole, iii. 108, *foal.*

Fonde, ii. 12, *contrive, endeavour, try.*

Foo, i. 50, *foe.*

Fooder, ii. 66, *wine tun;* Germ. *fuder.*

For, *on account of.*

For but, ii. 146, *unless.*

Forbode, *commandment.*

Force, no force, *no matter.*

Forced, ii. 76, *regarded, heeded.*

Forefend, i. 268 ; forfend, ii. 97, *prevent, defend, avert, hinder.*

Forewearied, *over-wearied.*

Forfeebled, ii. 107, *enfeebled.*

For-fought, ii. 25, *over-fought.*

Fors, ii. 21, *strength.*

Fors. I do no fors, ii. 16, *I don't care.*

Forsede, i. 122, *heeded, regarded.*

Forst, ii. 76, *regarded.*

Forthynketh, i. 174, *repenteth, vexeth, troubleth.*

Forthy, *therefore.*

Forwarde, i. 44, *van.*

Forewatcht, ii. 77, *over-wakeful, kept awake.*

Fosters of the fe, i. 175, *foresters of the king's demesnes.*

Fot pot, ii. 9, *with his foot push on.*

Fote, i. 49, *foot.*

Fou, i. 147, iii. 75 ; fow, iii. 99, *full,* also *fuddled.*

Fowkin, ii. 22, *crepitus ventris.*

Fox't, *drunk.*

Frae, i. 144, *from.*

Fraemang, ii. 107, *from among.*

Fraid, i. 323, *afraid.*

Freake, i. 31, *man, person, human creature.*

Freake, *a whim or maggot.*

Freckys, i. 29, *men.*

Freers, ii. 128 ; fryars, *friars.*

Freits, i. 146, *ill omens, ill-luck.*

Freke, i. 49, ii. 25, *man;* frekys, ii. 25, *men.*

Freyke, ii. 135, *humour, freak.*

Freyke, i. 29, *strong man.*

Freyned, ii. 134, *asked;* freyned that freake, ii. 134, *asked that man.*

Frie, ii. 82 ; *free.*

Fro, i. 159 ; froe, i. 106, 139, *from.*

Fruward, *forward.*

Furth, ii. 21, *forth.*

Fuyson, i. 123 ; foyson, *plenty,* also *substance.*

Fyer, ii. 55, 105, *fire;* fyerye, iii. 118, *fiery.*

Fyers, *fierce.*

Fyhte, ii. 12, *fight.*

Fykkill, i. 123, *fickle.*

Fyl'd, iii. 147, *defiled.*

Fyll, i. 121, *fell.*

Ga, ii. 24 ; *go;* gais, ii. 83, *goes.*

Ga, ii. 113, *gave.*

Gaberlunyie, ii. 71, *a wallet;* gaberlunyie man, ii. 67, *a tinker, beggar, one who carried a wallet.*

Gade, iii. 122, *went.*

Gadelyngys, ii. 20, *gadders, idle fellows.*

Gaderyd, ii. 27, *gathered.*

Gadryng, ii. 22, *gathering.*

Gae, ii. 70, *gave.*

Gae, i. 143; gaes, ii. 69, *go, goes.*

Gaed, ii. 69, *went.*

Gair, ii. 86, *strip of land.*

Gair, i. 59, *geer, dress.*

Gait, iii. 95, *gate.*

Galliard, ii. 162, *a sprightly kind of dance.*

Gamon, i. 67, *to make game, to sport.* A.-S. gamenian *jocari.*

Gan, i. 63, 129, 309, ii. 68, *began.*

Gan, i. 30 ; gane, i. 30, ii. 69, *gone.*

Gang, i. 83, ii. 69, *go.*

Ganyde, i. 28, *gained.*

Gar, ii. 70; iii. 94, gare, garre, i. 44, *make, cause, force,* &c.; gars, i. 321, *makes.*

Gard, iii. 97; garde, i. 28; garred, garr'd, ii. 117; gart, iii. 97, *made.*

Gargeyld, i. 128, from *gargouille, the spout of a gutter.* The tower was adorned with spouts cut in the figures of greyhounds, lions, &c.

Garland, i. 111, *the ring within which the prick or mark was set to be shot at.*

Garth, ii. 391, *garden, yard.*

Gat, i. 146, *got.*

Gate, i. 108, *way.*

Gaup, ii. 139 *gapes, waits.*

Gear, i. 322, iii. 122, *goods, effects, stuff.*

Gederede ys host, ii. 8, *gathered his host.*

Geere, i. 274, 288, *property.*

Gef, ii. 31, *give.*

Geid, *gave.*

Geir, ii. 69, *gear, property.*

Gerte, iii. 357, *pierced.*

Gesse, ii. 49, *guess.*

Gest, ii. 85, *act, feat, story, history.*

Gettyng, i. 43, *booty.*

Geud, i. 103, *good.*

Geve, ii. 53, *give.*

Gibed, *jeered.*

Gi', i. 145; gie, i. 145, *give*; gied, i. 321, *gave.*

Giff, i. 322; giffe, ii. 57, *if.*

Gilderoy, i. 320, *red boy* (or gillie); Gaelic, *Gille ruadh* (pronounced *roy*).

Gillore, ii. 361, *plenty.*

Gimp, ii. 110, *neat, slender.*

Gin, i. 60, iii. 74, *if.*

Gin, iii. 203; Ginn, iii. 53; *engine, contrivance.*

Gins, ii. 53, *begins.*

Give, ii. 237; *if.*

Glave, ii. 115, *sword.*

Glede, i. 26, *a red-hot coal.*

Glent, i. 24, *glanced.*

Glente, iii. 356, *slipped aside.*

Gleyinge, i. 408, *minstrelsy.*

Glist, ii. 110, *glistered.*

Glose, i. 120, *gloss over.*

Glowr, iii. 75, *stare* or *frown.*

Gloze, iii. 203, *canting, dissimulation, fair outside.*

God before, *God be thy guide,* a form of blessing.

So in Shakespeare's "King Hen. V." (A. iii. sc. 8) the King says:—

"My army's but a weak and sickly guard;
Yet, God before, tell him we will come on." P.

Gode, ii. 21, *good.*

Gods-pennie, ii. 140, *earnest money.*

Gon, ii. 21, *began.*

Gone, *go.*

Good, *a good deal.*

Good-e'ens, ii. 68, *good evenings.*

Good-se peny, ii. 147, *earnest money.*

Gorget, ii. 57, *the dress of the neck.*

Gorrel-bellyed, ii. 346, *pot-bellied.*

Gowan, ii. 364, *the common yellow crowfoot or gold cup, daisy.*

Gowd, i. 145, iii. 75, *gold;* gowden glist, ii. 110, *shone like gold;* gowden graith'd, ii. 230, *caparisoned with golden accoutrements.*

Graine, i. 158, i. 197, *scarlet.*

Graith'd, ii. 230, *caparisoned.*

Gramarye, i. 91; grammarye, i. 92, *grammar, abstruse learning.*

Gramercy, i. 173; gramercye, ii. 95, *I thank you.* Fr. grandmercie.

Graunge; peakish graunge, i. 299, *a lone country house.*

Graythed, ii. 21, *made ready.*

Gre, ii. 21, *prize.*

Grea-hondes, i. 24, *grey-hounds.*

Grece, i. 129, *step, flight of steps.*

Greece, *fat;* hart of greece, i. 170, *a fat hart.* Fr. graisse.

Greet, iii. 100, *weep.*

Grein, iii. 75, *green.*

Gresse, i. 43, iii. 62, *grass.*

Gret, ii. 12, *grieved.*

Greves, i. 24, *groves, bushes.*

Grippel, ii. 254, *griping, tenacious, miserly.*

Grone, iii. *groan.*

Ground-wa', i. 145, *groundwall.*

Growynde, i. 48, 49, *ground.*

Grownes, ii. 256, *grounds.*

Growte, ii. 256. In Northampton-shire is a kind of small beer extracted from the malt after the strength has been drawn off. In Devon it is a kind of sweet ale medicated with eggs, said to be a Danish liquor. (Growte is a kind of fare much used by Danish sailors, being boiled groats, *i.e.* hulled oats, or else shelled barley, served up very thick, and butter added to it.— *Mr. Lambe.*) P.

Grype, ii. 57, *a griffin.*

Grysely groned, i. 49, *dreadfully groaned.*

Gude, ii. 70, 82, *good.*

Guerdon, iii. 18, *reward.*

Guid, i. 83, *good.*

Gule, iii. 7, *red.*

Gyb, ii. 22, *nickname of Gilbert.*

Gybe, ii. 257, *jibe, jest, joke;* gybing, ii. 260.

Gyle, gyles, *guile, guiles.*

Gyn, ii. 9, *engine, contrivance.*

Gyrd, ii. 22, *girded, lashed.*

Gyrdyl, ii. 22, *girdle.*

Gyse, *guise, form, fashion.*

Ha, i. 196, *has;* hae, ii. 71, *have;* haes, iii. 235, *has.*

Ha', i. 84, iii. 94, *hall;* ha's, ii. 109, *halls.*

Habbe ase he brew, ii. 8, *have as he brews.*

Habergeon, *a lesser coat of mail.*

Hable, i. 121, *able.*

Hach-borde, ii. 193, *probably that part of the bulwark of the ship which is removed to form the gangway or entrance on board, —in fact, the "hatch"—(or half-door) "board."*

Haif, ii. 82, *have.*

Haggis, ii. 132, *a sheep's stomach stuffed with a pudding made of mince-meat, &c.*

Hail, ii. 83, *healthful.*

Hair, ii. 81, 86, *hoar or grey.*

Halch, iii. 325, *salute.*

Halched, i. 280, *saluted, embraced, fell on his neck.*

Halesome, ii. 142, *wholesome healthy.*

Halse, iii. 75, *the neck, throat.*

Halt, ii. 16, *holdeth.*

Ham, ii. 21, *them.*

Hame, i. 143, *home;* hameward, ii. 84, *homeward.*

Han, ii. 13, *have.*

Handbow, *the long-bow or common bow, as distinguished from the cross-bow.*

Hap, i. 255; happ, iii. 138; happe, i. 283, *fortune;* hap, i. 287, *chance, happen,* i. 303.

Hard, ii. 312, *heard.*

Hare . . . swerdes, ii. 8, *their . . swords.*

Harflue, ii. 30, *Harfleur.*

Harlocke, i. 307, *perhaps charlock, or wild rape, which bears a yellow flower, and grows among corn, &c.*

Harneis, i. 273, *armour.*

Harnisine, ii. 112, *harness, armour.*

Harrowe, i. 280, *harass.*

Harowed, i. 164, *harassed, disturbed.*

Hart, iii. 128, *heart;* hartes, i. 50; harts, i. 138; hartis, i. 147.

Hartely, ii. 38, *earnestly.*

Hartly lust, i. 124, *hearty desire.*

Harwos, ii. 27, *harrows.*

Haryed, i. 41, 22, *pillaged.*

Hastarddis, i. 120, *perhaps hasty, rash fellows, or upstarts.*

Hatcht, ii. 77, *seized.*

Hauld, i. 143, *hold.*

Hauss bone, iii. 75, *the neck bone (halse bone), a phrase for the neck.*

Have owre, i. 102, *half over.*

Haves, ii. 20, *effects, substance, riches.*

Haveth, ii. 8, *has.*

Haviour, i. 304, *behaviour.*

Hawberke, i. 66, *a coat of mail, consisting of iron rings, &c.*

Hawkin, ii. 19, *diminutive of Harry, from Halkin.*

Haylle, i. 43, *hale, strong.*

He, i. 171, *hie, hasten.*

He, i. 24, *high.*

Heal, i. 29, *hail.*

Hear, i. 103, *here.*
Heare, ii. 77 ; heares, *hair, hairs.*
Heathynesse, iii. 40, *heathen-dom.*
Heawying, i. 31, *hewing, hacking.*
Hech, ii. 27, *hatch, half door of a cottage* (sometimes spelt heck).
 " Dogs leap the hatch," *King Lear,* act. iii. sc. 6.
 " 'He'll have to ride the *hatch*' is a familiar phrase about Looe, and signifies ' He'll be brought to trial.' It is generally used jocosely in the case of any loud professor of religion who has been ' overtaken in a fault ;' and the idea is that his trial will be the ordeal of attempting to ride or sit on the top or narrow edge of a hatch or half-door, when if he maintain his seat he will be pronounced innocent, if he fall he is guilty. If he fall inwards (*i.e.* within the room or building), he will be pardoned, but if he fall outwards, he will be excommunicated." W. Pengelly (*Devonshire Association Report,* vol. vii. p. 488).
Hecht to lay thee law, *promised (engaged) to lay the low.*
Hed, hede, *head;* hedys, ii. 25, *heads.*
Hede, ii. 12, *had.*
Hede, *hied.*
Hee, i. 42, *high.*
Heele, i. 291, *he will.*
Hees, ii. 70, *he is.*
Heght, ii. 117, *promised.*
Heiding hill, ii. 231, *the heading (or beheading) hill.* The place of execution was anciently an artificial hillock.
Heigh, iii. 94, *high.*
Heil, ii. 81, *health.*
Heir, ii. 83, *here;* also *hear;* herid, iii. 96, *heard.*
Hele, ii. 42, *health.*
Helen, ii. 15, *heal.*
Helpeth, ii. 12, *help ye.*
Hem, ii. 13, *them.*
Hend, i. 72, i. 74, 80, *kind, gentle, courteous.*

Henne, ii. 8, *hence.*
Hent, ii. 26, *laid hold of.*
Hepps and hawes, ii. 284, *hips and haws.*
Herault, ii. 59, *herald.*
Her, ii. 393, *hear.*
Her, ii. 35, *their.*
Here, ii. 42, *hair.*
Herkneth, ii. 7, *hearken ye.*
Herry, ii. 19, *Harry.*
Hert, i. 59, *heart.*
Hes, ii. 80, *has.*
Hest, *hast.*
Hest, i. 67, *command, injunction.*
Het, ii. 346, *heated.*
Hete, ii. 41, *heat.*
Hether, *hither.*
Hether, *heather, heath.*
Hett, iii. 6, *bid, call, command.*
Heuch, ii. 86, *rock or steep hill.*
Hevede, ii. 9, *had, hadst;* hevedest, ii. 12.
Hevenriche, ii. 12, *heavenly.*
Hewberke, i. 72, *coat of mail.*
Hewkes, iii. 26, *party-coloured coats of the heralds.*
Hewyns in to, *hewn in two.*
Hey-day guise, iii. 204, *rustic dances, a corruption of "heyde-gies."*
Heynd, ii. 82, *gentle, obliging.*
Heyye, ii. 13, *high.*
Hi, hie, *he.*
Hicht, a-hicht, *on height.*
Hie, i. 32, *high;* hier, ii. 169, *higher; hire,* iii. 324.
Hight, i. 29, 270, 286, *promise, promised, engaged,* also *named, called.*
Hilt, ii. 98, *taken off, flayed.*
Hinch boys, *pages of honour.*
Hind, ii. 70, *behind.*
Hinde, i. 32, *gentle.*
Hings, iii. 97, *hangs.*
Hinnible, iii. 304, *horse,* or *pony.*
Hinny, ii. 84, *honey.*
Hip, iii. 99, *the berry which contains the stones or seeds of the dog-rose.*
Hir, i. 143 ; hire, iii. 207, *her;* hir lain, iii. 95, *herself alone.*
Hird, ii. 81, *herd.*
Hirsel, i. 143, *herself.*

Hit, ii. 13, *it;* hit be write, ii. 12, *it be written.*

Hode, i. 164, *hood, cap.*

Holden, ii. 14, *hold.*

Hole, i. 124, 126, iii. 280, *whole.*

Hollen, iii. 325, *holly.*

Holp, i. 120, *help;* holpe, iii. 32, *helped.*

Holt, ii. 140, *wood.*

Holtes, i. 42, *woods, groves.* In Norfolk a plantation of cherry-trees is called a " cherry holt." P.

Holtis hair, ii. 81, 86, *hoary or grey woods or heaths.*
" Holtes seems evidently to signify hills in the following passage from Turberville's " Songs and Sonnets," 12mo. 1567, fol. 56 :—
" Yee that frequent the hilles, And highest Holtes of all ; Assist me with your skilfull quilles, And listen when I call."

" As also in this other verse of an ancient poet :—
" Underneath the Holtes so hoar." P.

Holy, *wholly.*

Holy-rode, ii. 22, *holy cross;* holye rood, ii. 56.

Honde, *hand;* honden wrynge, ii. 11, *hands wring.*

Hondert, i. 50, *hundred.*

Hondrith, i. 24, 25, 30, 32, 34, *hundred.*

Hong, ii. 77 ; honge, i. 161, *hang;* hung, i. 308.

Hooly, iii. 134, *slowly, gently.*

Hophalt, *limping, hopping, and halting.*

Hore, iii. 327, *whore.*

Hount, i. 26, *hunt.*

Houzle, ii. 60, *give the sacrament.*

Hoved, i. 129, *heaved; hovered,* i. 43.

Howers, ii. 234, *hours.*

Huche, ii. 81, *wood, or a shed.*

Hud, ii. 23, *proper name.*

Hue, ii. 12, *she.* A.-S. heo ; refers to huerte, which is feminine. It is an interesting example of the continuance of a grammatical gender in English.

Huerte trewe, ii. 11, *true heart.*

Huggle, iii. 72, *hug, clasp.*

Hull, i. 307, *hill.*

Hur, ii. 20 ; hurr, ii. 24, *her.*

Hye, i. 136, *high, highest;* hyest, ii. 59 ; hyer, iii. 63, *hire.*

Hyght, i. 44, *promised or engaged.*

Hyght, *high ;* on hyght, i. 41, 47, *aloud.*

Hyllys, i. 32, *hills.*

Hynd out o'er, ii. 115, *over the country.*

Hyp-halte, ii. 27, *lame in the hip.*

Hyrdyllys, ii. 27, *hurdles.*

Hys, ii. 20, *his.*

Hyssylton, ii. 19, *Islington.*

Hyt, hytt, ii. 49, *it.*

Hyyt, ii. 20, *promised.*

I-clipped, i. 129, *called.*

I-feth, i. 29, *in faith.*

I-lore, ii. 13, *lost.*

I-strike, ii. 16, *stricken, struck.*

I-trowe, *verily.*

I-tuned, *tuned.*

I-ween, *verily.*

I-wis, i. 276, *verily;* I-wys, i. 68, 70.

I-wot, *verily.*

Ich, ii. 286, *I ;* ich biqueth, ii. 12, *I bequeath.*

Ich, ii. 22; icha, ii. 25, *each.*

Ide, iii. 72, *I would.*

Ild, ii. 69, *I'd, I would.*

Ile, i. 196, *I'll, I will.*

Illfardly, ii. 70, *ill-favouredly, uglily.*

Ilk, *same ;* this ilk, *this same.*

Ilk on, ii. 21, *each one ;* ilka, ilke, *every;* ilka ane, iii. 122, *every one.*

Im, i. 103, *him.*

Ime, i. 198, ii. 57, *I am.*

Incontinent, iii. 187, *forthwith.*

In fere, ii. 36, *together, in company.*

Ingle, ii. 68, *fire.*

Inogh, ii. 26, *enough;* inoughe, ii. 147, *enough.*

Into, iii. 238, *in.*

Intres, i. 129, *entrance, admittance.*

Irke, ii. 148, *angry.*

Is, i. 149, ii. 8, *his.*
Ise, ii. 211, iii. 236, *I shall.*
I'st, i. 289, 292, *I'll.*
It's neir, *it shall never.*
Iye, i. 432, *eye.*

Janglers, ii. 85, *talkative persons, wranglers, tell-tales.*
Jear, ii. 118, *derision.*
Jetted, iii. 186, *strutted, or went proudly.*
Jille, iii. 77, *used here as a man's name.*
Jimp, i. 145, *slender.*
Jo, i. 320, ii. 132, *sweetheart, friend,* contraction of *joy.*
Jogelers, i. 441, *jugglers.*
Jow, iii. 134, *single stroke in tolling.*
Juncates, iii. 202, *junket, curds and clouted cream.*
Jupe, ii. 116, *an upper garment.*

Kall, i. 125, *call.*
Kame, iii. 147, *comb;* kameing, iii. 97, *combing.*
Kan, i. 123, 430, *can.*
Kantle, iii. 26, *piece, corner.*
Karlis of kynde, i. 120, *churls by nature.*
Kauk, ii. 71, *chalk.*
Kauld, i. 103, *called.*
Keel, ii. 71, *ruddle.*
Keepe, i. 309, ii. 256, *care, heed.* So in the old play of " Hick Scorner," "I keepe not to clymbe so hye;" *i.e.* I study not, care not, &c.
Keip, ii. 82, *keep;* ii. 84, *watch.*
Keipand, ii. 82, *keeping.*
Kell, iii. 101, *net for a woman's hair.*
Kembe, iii. 100, 186, *to comb;* kembing, iii. 102, *combing;* kemb'd, iii. 302, *combed.*
Kempe, i. 90, 94, ii. 183, *soldier, warrior.*
Kemperye man, i. 94, *soldier, fighting man.*
    " *Germanis* Camp, *Exercitum, aut Locum ubi Exercitus castrametatur, significat : inde ipsis Vir Castrensis et Militaris* kemffer, *et* kempher, *et* kemper,

et kimber, *et* kamper, *pro varietate dialectorum, vocatur : Vocabulum hoc nostro sermone nondum penitus exolevit ; Norfolcienses enim plebeio et proletario sermone dicunt* 'He is a kemper old man, *i.e. Senex Vegetus est :'* Hinc Cimbris *suum nomen :* ' kimber *enim Homo bellicosus, pugil, robustus miles, &c. significat.'* Sheringham de Anglor. gentis. orig. pag. 57. *Rectius autem Lazius* [apud eundem, p. 49]. ' Cimbros *a bello quod* kamff, *et Saxonice* kamp *nuncupatos crediderim : unde bellatores viri* Die Kempffer, Die Kemper.' " P.
Kems, i. 102, *combs.*
Ken, ii. 69, *know;* kens, iii. 122, *knows;* kenst, i. 196, *knowest.*
Kend, ii. 70, *knew;* known, iii. 99; kenn'd, ii. 365.
Kene, ii. 15, *keen.*
Kepand, ii. 81, *keeping.*
Kepers, i. 181. " Those that watch by the corpse shall tye up my winding-sheet." P.
Kester, i. 276, *nickname for Christopher.*
Kever chefes, *kerchiefs* or *head covers.* (See vol. 3, p. 356.)
Kexis, ii. 27, *elder sticks used for candles.*
Kilted, iii. 132, *tucked up.*
Kind, *nature.* To carp is our kind, *it is natural for us to talk of;* of hir kind, ii. 154, *of her family.*
Kirk, iii. 75; kirke, i. 137, *church;* kirk wa', iii. 238, *church wall,* or *churchyard wall;* kirkyard, i. 243, iii. 132, *churchyard.*
Kirns to kirn, ii. 70, *churns to churn.*
Kirtle, i. 222, *a petticoat, a woman's gown.*
Kist, ii. 69, *chest.*
Kit, i. 123, *cut.*
Knave, *servant.*
Knaw, ii. 82, *know.*
Knellan, iii. 134, *knelling, ringing the knell.*

Knicht, iii. 237, *knight.*
Knight's fe, *such a portion of land as required the possessor to serve with man and horse.*
Knowles, *knolls, little hills.*
Knyled, i. 32, *knelt.*
Kowarde, i. 46, *coward.*
Kowe, ii. 21, *cow.*
Kuntrey, i. 124, *country.*
Kurteis, i. 125, *courteous.*
Kyd, ii. 21, *shown.*
Kye, ii. 134, *kine, cows.*
Kyrtel, ii. 42; kyrtell, i. 65, *petticoat, gown, a man's under garment.*
"Bale, in his 'Actes of Eng. Votaries' (part ii. fol. 53), uses the word Kyrtle to signify a monk's frock. He says, Roger, Earl of Shrewsbury, when he was dying, sent 'to Clunyake, in France, for the kyrtle of holy Hugh the abbot there,' &c." P.
Kythe, i. 427, *make appear, show, declare.*
Kythed, *appeared.*

Laigh, ii. 117, *low.*
Laith, i. 101, ii. 70, *loth.*
Laithly, *loathsome, hideous.*
Laitl, i. 103, *little.*
Lamb's wool, iii. 183, *a liquor composed of ale and roasted apples.*
Lane, lain, *lone;* her lane, ii. 69; hir lain, iii. 95, *alone by herself.*
Lang, i. 101, ii. 20, *long.*
Lang'd, ii. 107, *longed.*
Langsome, i. 321, *long, tedious.*
Lap, iii. 93, 95, *leaped.*
Largesse, iii. 26, *gift, liberality.*
Lasse, ii. 13, *less.*
Late, ii. 47, *let.*
Latte, ii. 12, *hinder.*
Lauch, i. 101, *laugh;* lauched, i. 101, *laughed.*
Launde, i. 170, *clear space in a forest.*
Lawlands, ii. 227, *lowlands.*
Lay, i. 79, *law.*
Layde, i. 291, *lady.*
Layden, i. 66, *laid.*
Layland, i. 66, 67, 79, *green sward.*

Laylands, i. 73, *lands in general.*
Layne, lain, *laid.*
Layne, i. 45, 46, *deceive, break one's word.*
Lazar, ii. 55, *leper.*
Leal, ii. 69, *loyal, honest, true.*
Leane, *conceal, hide.*
Lear'd, i. 307, *pastured.*
Lease, *lying, falsehood;* withouten lease, i. 170, *verily, without lying.*
Lease, iii. 102, *leash, thong, cord.*
Leasynge, *lying, falsehood.*
Leaute, ii. 7, *loyalty.*
Lee, ii. 68, *lea, field, pasture.*
Lee, iii. 96, *lie.*
Leeche, i. 63, 75, 77, *physician.*
Leechinge, i. 63; leedginge, i. 77, *doctoring, medicinal care.*
Leek, *phrase of contempt.*
Leel, ii. 112, *true.*
Leer, *look.*
Leeve London, i. 273, iii. 101, *dear London.*
Leever, i. 160, *sooner.*
Leeveth, i. 88, *believeth.*
Lefe, i. 173, *dear.*
Lefe, *leave;* leves, *leaves.*
Leffe, leefe, *dear.*
Leid, iii. 96, *lyed.*
Leil, ii. 85, *loyal, true.*
Leir, ii. 82, *learn;* lere, i. 306, *learning.*
Leive, i. 84, iii. 236, *leave.*
Leman, i. 186, 327; leiman, i. 301; lemman, iii. 97, *lover, mistress.*
Lemster wooll, i. 307, *Leominster wool.*
Lene, ii. 13, *give.*
Lenger, i. 64, ii. 20, *longer.*
Lengeth in, *resideth in.*
Lere, i. 72, *face, countenance, complexion.*
Lese, ii. 26, *lose.*
Lesynge, i. 174; *leasing, lying, falsehood.*
Let, i. 24, *hinder;* lett, ii. 85, *hindrance.*
Lett, i. 93, *left or let be opened.*
Lettest, i. 74, *hinderest, detainest.*
Letteth, i. 168, *hindereth.*
Lettyng, i. 172, *hindrance, without delay.*

Leugh, ii. 118; leuche, ii. 81, *laughed.*

Leve, ii. 38, *remain.*

Lever, i. 46, 71, 75, 173, *rather;* lever than, ii. 39, *rather then.*

Leves and bowes, ii. 42, *leaves and boughs.*

Lewd, i. 308; leud, ii. 134, *ignorant, scandalous.*

Ley, iii. 123, *lay.*

Leyke, ii. 135, *play.*

Leyre, lere, *learning, lore.*

Libbard, *leopard;* libbard's bane, iii. 198, *the herb wolfbane.*

Lichtly, iii. 147, *lightly, easily.*

Lig, i. 144, iii. 70, *lie;* ligge, ii. 11; liggd, ii. 83, *lay.*

Lightfoote, iii. 182, *venison.*

Lightile, i. 161, *quickly.*

Lightsome, i. 65, *cheerful, sprightly.*

Limber, ii. 260, *supple, flexible.*

Limitoures, iii. 208, *friars licensed to beg within certain limits.*

Limitatioun, iii. 208, *a certain precinct allowed to a limitour.*

Lingell, i. 308, *a thread of hemp rubbed with resin, &c., used by rustics for mending their shoes.*

Lire, *flesh, complexion.*

List, i. 256; lith, ii. 11, *lieth.*

Lith, i. 156; lithe, i. 268; lythe, *attend, hearken, listen.*

Lither, i. 94, iii. 47, *idle, lazy, naughty, worthless, wicked.*

Live-lang, iii. 132, *live-long.*

Liver, i. 282, *deliver.*

Liverance, i. 282, 289, *deliverance (money or a pledge for delivering you up).*

Livor, i. 289, *deliver.*

Load; lay on load, i. 74, *give blows.*

Lodly, ii. 63; lodlye, ii. 56, *loathsome.*

Loe, ii. 70, iii. 99, *love;* lo'ed, iii. 98, *loved.*

Logeyng, i. 43, *lodging.*

Loht, ii. 9; be the luef, be the loht, *whether you like it or loathe it.*

Loke, i. 308, *lock of wool.*

Lokyd, ii. 73; lokyde, i. 25, *looked.*

Lome, ii. 63, *man, object.*

Lond, iii. 207, *land.*

Longes, i. 218, *belongs;* longeth, ii. 43, *belongeth.*

Longs, i. 30, *lungs.*

Looket, i. 149, *looked.*

Loone, ii. 145, *idle fellow.*

Looset, i. 115, *loosed.*

Lope, i. 65, 80, ii. 217, *leapt.*

Lore, ii. 9, 13, *teaching, lesson, doctrine, learning.*

Lore, *lost.*

Lorrel, i. 441, *a sorry, worthless person.*

Losel, ii. 134, 145, *the same as Lorrel.*

Lothly, ii. 142, *loathsome.*

"The adverbial terminations *-some* and *-ly* were applied indifferently by our old writers : thus, as we have *lothly* for *loathsome* above, so we have *ugsome* in a sense not very remote from *ugly* in Lord Surrey's version of Æn. 2nd, viz.—

"'In every place the ugsome sightes I saw' (p. 29)." P.

Loud and still, ii. 82, *openly and secretly.*

Lough, i. 95, *laugh;* lought, ii. 282, *laughed.*

Loun, i. 322, *loon, rascal.*

Lounge, iii. 357, *lung.*

Lourd, iii. 100, *rather (?)*

Lout, ii. 117; loute, ii. 26, *stoop.*

Louted, i. 72; lowtede, *bowed, did obeisance.*

Lowe, i. 114, *a little hill.*

Lowne, i. 198, *rascal.*

Lowns, ii. 113, *blazes.*

Lowttede, i. 120, *crouched.*

Lude, ii. 82, *loved.*

Lued, i. 323, *loved.*

Luef, ii. 9, *love.*

Lues, iii. 75, *loves, love.*

Lugh, ii. 26, *laughed.*

Luik, i. 146, *look;* luiks, i. 146, *looks;* luikt, ii. 229, *looked.*

Luivt, ii. 82, *loved.*

Lung, ii. 28, *long.*

Lurden, i. 163; lurdeyne, *sluggard, drone.*

Lust, ii. 42, *desire.*

Luve, i. 320, *love;* luver, ii. 212, *lover.*

Luvely, i. 143, *lovely.*

Lyan, iii. 134, *lying.*
Lyard, ii. 9, *grey; a name given to a horse from its grey colour, as Bayard from bay.*
Lyff, ii. 49, *life.*
Lyk, i. 28; lyke, ii. 38, *like.*
Lynde, i. 168; lyne, i. 112, *the lime-tree.*
Lys, ii. 12, *lies.*
Lystenyth, iii. 371, *listen.*
Lyth, i. 306, *easy, gentle, pliant, flexible, lithesome.*
Lyvar, i. 30, *liver*
Lyven na more, *live no more, no longer.*
Lyyt, ii. 27, *light;* lyytly, ii. 26, *lightly*

Mad, ii. 24, *made.*
Mahound, i. 88, *Mahomet.*
Maining, ii. 211, *moaning.*
Mair, ii. 84, *more, most.*
Maist, i. 42, *mayest.*
Mait, iii. 99, *might, may.*
Majeste, maist, mayeste, *may'st.*
Makes, i. 50, ii. 78, *mates.*
Making, *versifying.*
Makys, i. 33, *mates.*
    "As the words make and mate were, in some cases, used promiscuously by ancient writers, so the words cake and cate seem to have been applied with the same indifference; this will illustrate that common English proverb, 'to turn cat (*i.e.* cate) in pan.' A pancake is in Northamptonshire still called a pancate." P.
Male, i. 28, *coat of mail;* shirt of male, ii. 233.
Manchet, iii. 206, *best kind of white bread*
Mane, i. 26, *man.*
Mangonel, ii. 8, *a military engine used for discharging great stones, arrows, &c., before the invention of gunpowder.*
March perti, i. 33; march partes, i. 34, *in the parts lying upon the marches.*
March-pine, i. 306; marchpane, *a kind of biscuit.*

Mare ii. 25, *more.*
Margarite, ii. 328, *a pearl.*
Mark, *a coin, in value* 13s. 4d.
Marke hym to the Trenité, *commit himself to God.*
Marrow, ii. 109, 363, *match, or equal companion.*
Mart, ii. 82, *marred, hurt, damaged.*
Marvelit, iii. 238, *marvelled.*
Mast, maste, *may'st.*
Masterye, i. 110; maystery, i. 176, *a trial of skill.*
Maugre, ii. 8; mauger, i. 23, *in spite of.*
Maugre, ii. 83, *ill will.*
Maun, i. 84, 143, 145, *must.*
Mavis, iii. 97, *a thrush.*
Mawt, iii. 123, *malt.*
May, i. 63, 113; maye, i. 46, *maid.*
Mayne, i. 122, *force, strength.*
Mayne, *a horse's mane.*
Mayny, i. 120, *a company.*
Maze, *a labyrinth, anything entangled or intricate.*
    "On the top of Catherine-hill, Winchester (the usual play-place of the school), was a very perplexed and winding path, running in a very small space over a great deal of ground, called a Miz-Maze. The senior boys obliged the juniors to tread it, to prevent the figure from being lost, as I am informed by an ingenious correspondent." P.
Mazer, iii. 97, *drinking cup of maple.*
Me, *men;* me con, ii. 13, *men began.*
Me-thuncketh, ii. 11, *methinks.*
Meane, ii. 259, *moderate, middle-sized.*
Meany, i. 24, 25, *retinue, train, company.*
Mease, ii. 119, *soften, mollify.*
Meed, meede, i. 74, iii. 22, *reward.*
Meet, iii. 132, *even.*
Meid, *mood.*
Meikle, iii. 238, *much.*
Meit, iii. 95, *meat.*
Meit, ii. 83, 115, *meet, fit, proper.*
Mekyl, ii. 21, *much.*
Mell, ii. 260, *honey.*

Mell, *meddle, mingle.*
Meniveere, i. 308, *a species of fur.*
Mense the faught, ii. 116, *to measure the battle.*
  " To give to the mense is to give above the measure. Twelve and one to the mense is common with children in their play." P.
Menzie, ii. 113, *retinue, company.*
Merch, ii. 115, *march.*
Merchis, i. 34, *marches.*
Merth, merthe, ii. 31, *mirth.*
Messager, ii. 12, *messenger.*
Mete, i. 180, *meet, fit, proper.*
Mewe, ii. 254, *confinement.*
Micht, ii. 230, *might.*
Mickle, i. 65, 66, 72, 76, 137, 306, *much, great.*
Midge, iii. 233, *a small insect, a kind of gnat.*
Mids, ii. 77, *midst.*
Minged, i. 66, 79, *mentioned.*
Minny, ii. 69, *mother.*
Mirk, ii. 120 ; mirkie, iii. 154, *dark, black.*
Mirry, i. 101, 143, ii. 82, *merry;* mirriest, ii. 391, *merriest.*
Mirry-land toune, i. 59
Misconster, ii. 349, *misconstrue.*
Misdoubt, i. 302, *suspect, doubt.*
Miskaryed, *miscarried.*
Misken, i. 197, *mistake.*
Mister, *to need.*
Mith, iii. 45, *might.*
Mither, i. 60, 83, 145, *mother.*
Mo, i. 30, 161, ii. 16 ; moe, ii. 289, *more.*
Moche, ii. 47, *much.*
Mode, *mood.*
Moder, i. 126, *mother.*
Moiening, ii. 382, *by means of.*
Mome, ii. 258, *blockhead.*
Mon, ii. 11, *man.*
Mone, ii. 37, *moon.*
Mone lyyt, ii. 25, *moonlight.*
Mone, ii. 35, iii. 127, *moan.*
Monand, iii. 64, *moaning, bemoaning.*
Monnynday, i. 24, 34, *Monday.*
Mony, ii. 8, 13, 68, *many.*
More, iii. 17, " originally and properly signified *a hill* (from A.-S.

mor, *mons*), but the hills of the north being generally full of bogs, a moor came to signify boggy, marshy, ground in general." P.
Mores and the fenne, ii. 8, *hill and dale;* mores brodinge, i. 64, 78, *wide moors.*
Morne, i. 101 ; to morn, ii. 20, 83, *on the morrow, in the morning*
Mornyng, ii. 49, *mourning.*
Morwenynges, iii. 208, *mornings.*
Mort, i. 25, *dead stag.*
Most, *must.*
Mot, i. 121, 126, *may.*
Mote, i. 157, *might;* mote I thee, ii. 97, *may I thrive.*
Mou, ii. 70, *mouth.*
Mought, i. 68, 169, 308, *might may it,* ii. 302.
Mowe, ii. 13, 31, *may.*
Muchele bost, ii. 8, *great boast.*
Mude, ii. 82, *mood.*
Muid, i. 147, *mood.*
Mulne, ii. 8, *mill.*
Mun, i. 63, 66, *must.*
Mure, mures, *wild downs, heaths, &c.*
Murn, ii. 85 ; murnd, ii. 86 ; murnit, ii. 81 ; murnt, ii. 84 ; murning, ii. 83, *mourn, mourned, mourning.*
Muve, ii. 366, *move;* muvit, ii. 39, *moved.*
Mykel, i. 46, *great.*
Myllan, i. 29, *Milan steel.*
Myn, ii. 12, *my.*
Myne-ye-ple, i. 28, *probably a corruption of manople, a large gauntlet.*
Myrry, *merry.*
Mysuryd, i. 123, *misused, applied to a bad purpose.*
Myyt, ii. 26, *might;* myyty, *mighty.*

Na, ii. 12 ; nae, *no, not, none.*
Naebody, ii. 139, *nobody.*
Naithing, ii. 70, *nothing.*
Nane, i. 320, ii. 70, iii. 75, *none.*
Nappy, iii. 182, *strong, as ale.*
Nar, i. 25, 27, nare, i. 30, *nor.*
Nat, i. 143, ii. 35, *not.*

Natheless, ii. 264, *nevertheless.*

N' availeth not, ii. 16, *availeth not.*

Ne, ii. 12, *no, nor, not.*

Near, ner, nere, *ne'er, never.*

Neat, *oxen, cows, large cattle;* neates leather, ii. 100, *cowhide.*

Neatherd, *a keeper of cattle.*

Neatresse, ii. 259, *female keeper of cattle.*

Nee, i. 71, 178, *nigh.*

Neigh him neare, i. 94, *approach him near.*

Neir, i. 146, *ne'er, never.*

Neire, ii. 212; nere, *near.*

Nemped, i. 409, *named.*

Nere, ii. 135; ne were, *were it not for.*

Nest, ii. 12, *next, nearest.*

Nethar, *neither.*

Neven, i. 396, *name.*

New fangle, iii. 7, *new-fangled, fond of novelty.*

Nicht, ii. 85, *night.*

Nicked him of naye, i. 88, *nicked him with a refusal.*

Nipt, *pinched.*

No, *not.*

Noble, *a gold coin in value twenty groats, or 6s. 8d.*

Noblès, i. 120, *nobleness.*

Nocht, ii. 83, *not.*

Nock, iii. 295, *the posteriors.*

Nollys, ii. 21, *noddles, heads.*

Nom, ii. 12, *took.*

Nome, ii. 11, *name.*

Non, ii. 16, *none.*

None, i. 25, 31, ii. 37, *noon.*

Nones, ii. 27, *nonce.*

Nonys, ii. 22, *nonce or occasion.*

Norland, iii. 237, *northern.*

Norse, *Norway.*

Norss menzie, ii. 114, *the Norse army.*

North-gales, iii. 26, *North Wales.*

Nou, ii. 9, *now.*

Nourice, *nurse.*

Nout, ii. 8, *nought,* also *not,* ii. 14.

Nowght, *nought.*

Nowls, *noddles, heads.*

Noye, ii. 26, *hurt.*

Noyt, ii. 24, *nought, not.*

Ny, ii. 49; nye, i. 136, *nigh;* nyest, ii. 59, *nighest.*

Nyyt, ii. 27, *night.*

O, ii. 8, *one;* O', iii. 99, *of;* O, ii. 9, *on.*

O wow, ii. 68, *an exclamation.*

Obraid, iii. 99, *upbraid.*

Occupied, i. 121, *used.*

Ocht, *ought.*

Off, ii. 177, *of.*

Oloft, ii. 25, *on horseback.*

On, ii. 49, *one, an.*

On loft, ii. 22, *aloft.*

Onfowghten, unfoughten, *unfought.*

Ony, ii. 84, *any.*

Onys, ii, 23, *once.*

Opon, ii. 8, *upon.*

Or, ii. 42, *before ever.*

Ore, iii. 128, *over.*

Orisons, *prayers.*

Ost, i. 28, ii. 24, iii. 36; oste, i. 42, 43, 44; ooste, i. 272, *host.*

Osterne, i. 291, *austere.*

Oth, othe, iii. 49, *oath.*

Ou, ii. 12, *you.*

Ous, ii. 8, *us.*

Out-owr, i. 147, *quite over, over.*

Outbrayd, ii. 45, *drew out, unsheathed.*

Outhorne, i. 167, *the summoning to arms by the sound of a horn.*

Outrake, i. 285, 292, *an out ride or expedition; to raik is to go fast.*

"Outrake is a common term among shepherds. When their sheep have a free passage from enclosed pastures into open and airy grounds they call it a good outrake." (Mr. Lambe.) P.

Owar, i. 31, *hour.*

Oware of none, i. 25, *hour of noon.*

Owches, iii. 316, *bosses.*

Owre, i. 144, ii. 70; *over, o'er; ere,* i. 101.

Owreword, iii. 124, *the last word, burden of a song.*

Pa, i. 59.

Packing, i. 121, *dealing.*

Pall, i. 89; palle, i. 71, *a cloak or robe of state.*

Palmer, iii. 113, *a pilgrim who, having been in the Holy Land, carried a palm branch in his hand.*

Paramour, i. 310, *gallant, lover; mistress,* ii. 45.

Pardè, ii. 41 ; perdie, *verily* (par Dieu).

Paregall, i. 124, *equal.*

Parle, iii. 36, *speak or parley.*

Parti, party ; a parti, i. 26, *apart or aside.*

Partynere, ii. 41, *partner.*

Pat, ii. 132, *pot.*

Pattering, iii. 9, "*murmuring, mumbling, from the manner in which the Paternoster was anciently hurried over in a low inarticulate voice.*" P.

Pauky, ii. 68, *shrewd, cunning, sly.*

Paves, i. 121, *a pavice, a large shield that covered the whole body.* Fr. pavois.

Pavilliane, *pavilion, tent.*

Pay, i. 173, *liking, satisfaction.*

Paynim, i. 65, 88, iii. 41, *pagan.*

Peakish, i. 299, *rude, simple;* peakish hull, i. 307, *perhaps the Derbyshire Peak.*

Peare, i. 80, *peer, equal.*

Pearlins, iii. 75, *coarse sort of bone-lace.*

Pece, *piece of cannon.*

Pee, i. 148, *piece.*

Peere, i. 73, 77, *equal.*

Pees, ii. 7, *peace.*

Pele, ii. 24, *a baker's long-handled shovel.*

Penon, *a banner or streamer borne at the top of a lance.*

Pentarchye, ii. 345, *five heads.*

Perchmine, *parchment.*

Perde, i. 187, *verily.*

Perelous, parlous, *perilous, dangerous.*

Perfay, ii. 85, *verily.*

Perfight, i. 123, *perfect;* perfightly, i. 124, *perfectly.*

Perfytte, i. 272, *perfect.*

Perkyn, ii. 20, *diminutive of Peter.*

Perlese, i. 125, *peerless.*

Perte, i. 50, *part, side.*

Pertyd, i. 28, *parted, divided.*

Pese, ii. 45, *peace.*

Petye, i. 50, ii. 73, *pity.*

Peyn, ii. 16, *pain.*

Peyses, i. 48, *pieces.*

Peysse, i. 44, *peace.*

Peyters, ii. 13, *Peter's.*

Philomele, iii. 81, *the nightingale.*

Piece, *a little.*

Pil'd, *peeled, bald.*

Pine, i. 196, *famish, starve.*

Pinner, ii. 337, *pinder, or impounder of cattle.*

Pious chanson, i. 183, *a godly song or ballad.*

"Mr. Rowe's Edition of Shakespeare has 'The first Row of the Rubrick ;' which has been supposed by Dr. Warburton to refer to the red-lettered titles of old ballads. In the large collection made by Mr. Pepys, I do not remember to have seen one single ballad with its title printed in red letters." P.

Pipl, i. 103, *people.*

Playand, ii. 115, *playing.*

Play-feres, i. 59, *play-fellows.*

Playning, i. 243, *complaining.*

Plein, iii. 123, *complain.*

Pleis, ii. 82, *please.*

Plett, ii. 112, *plaited.*

Pley, i. 59, ii. 83, *play.*

Pleyn, ii. 16, *complain.*

Plyyt, ii. 27, *plight.*

Plowmell, ii. 25, *a small wooden hammer occasionally fixed to the plough.*

Poll-cat, *cant word for a prostitute.*

Pollys, ii. 21, *polls, heads.*

Pompal, i. 233, *proud, pompous.*

Popingay, i. 308, *a parrot.*

Porcupig, iii. 285, *porcupine.*

Portingale, iii. 50, *Portugal.*

Portingalls, ii. 198, *Portuguese.*

Portres, *porteress.*

Poterner, iii. 7, *probably a pouch or bag.*

Pottle, iii. 187, *a measure of two quarts.*

Poudered, ii. 23, *a term in heraldry for sprinkled over.*

Pow'd, i. 59, *pulled.*

Powlls, *polls, heads.*

Pownes, i. 300, *pounds.*

Praat, ii. 360, *prate.*

Pray, i. 125, *prey.*
Prayse-folk, ii. 27, *singing men and women.*
Preas, iii. 26, *press.*
Prece, i. 160, *crowd, press;* preced, i. 167, 171, *pressed.*
Prest, i. 205, ii. 21, *ready;* prestly, i. 171 ; prestlye, i. 72, *readily, quickly.*
Prickes, i. 111, *mark in the centre of the target.*
Pricke-wande, *pole set up for a mark.*
Pricked, i. 68, *spurred on, hasted.*
Priefe, ii. 96, *prove.*
Priving, ii. 70, *proving, testing.*
Prove, ii. 46, *proof.*
Prude, ii. 8, *pride.*
Prycke, i. 175, *the mark, commonly a hazel wand.*
Prycked, i. 43, *spurred.*
Pryme, i. 156, *daybreak, or six o'clock in the morning.*
Prys, ii. 11, *prize.*
Pu, i. 145, *pull.*
Puing, ii. 363, *pulling.*
Puissant, iii. 110, *strong, powerful.*
Purfell, iii. 25, *ornament, or border of embroidery.*
Purfelled, iii. 25, *embroidered.*
Purvayed, ii. 45, *provided.*
Putry, iii. 6, *whoredom.*
Pyght, i. 43, *pitched.*

Quadrant, *four-square.*
Quaint, ii. 257, *nice, fantastical.*
Quarry, i. 255, *the slaughtered game in hunting or hawking.*
Quat, ii. 116, *quitted.*
Quay, iii. 75, *a young heifer, called a whie in Yorkshire.*
Quean, iii. 21, 203, 252, *a sorry, base woman, a slut.*
Quel, ii. 135, *cruel, murderous.*
Quelch, *a blow or bang.*
Quere, i. 124, *quire, choir.*
Quest, i. 165, *inquest.*
Quha, i. 101, *who.*
Quhair, ii. 82, *where.*
Quhair-eir, ii. 84, *wherever.*
Quhan, i. 144, iii. 75, *when.*
Quhaneir, iii. 75, *whenever.*
Quhar, i. 100, *where.*

Quhat, i. 143, *what.*
Quhatten, i. 83, *what.*
Quhen, i. 143, ii. 82, *when.*
Quhilk, ii. 116, *which.*
Quhy, i. 145, *why.*
Quhyle, ii. 83, *while.*
Quick, iii. 53, *alive, living.*
Quiere, ii. 288, *choir.*
Quillets, ii. 283, *quibbles.*
Quiristers, ii. 166, *choristers.*
Quitt, ii. 311, *requite.*
Quo, ii. 69, *quoth.*
Quyle, ii. 84, *while.*
Quyrry, i. 25, *quarry of slaughtered game.*
Quyt, ii. 85, *quite.*
Quyte, i. 34, *requited.*
Qwyknit, ii. 131, *quickened, restored to life.*

Rade, i. 147, *rode.*
Rae, ii. 24, *roe.*
Raigne, ii. 253, *reign.*
Raik, *to go apace;* raik on raw, ii. 82, *extend in a row.*
Raise, ii. 69, *rose.*
Rampire, ii. 52, *rampart.*
Ranted, ii. 68, *made merry.*
Rashing, i. 208, *the old hunting term for the stroke made by a wild boar with his fangs.*
Raught, *reached, gained, obtained.*
Raw, ii. 82, *row.*
Rawstye, i. 116, *damp* (?)
Rayt, ii. 26, *raught or reached.*
Reachles, i. 113, *careless.*
Read, ii. 148 ; reade, ii. 144, *advice;* reade me, i. 87, *advise me.*
Rea'me, ii. 287, *realm.*
Reane, i. 34, *rain.*
Rearing, i. 88, *leaning against.*
Reas, i. 24, *raise.*
Reave, i. 89, 322, *bereave.*
Reckt, i. 143, *regarded.*
Reckyn, ii. 20, *reckon.*
Red, i. 101, *read.*
Redd, i. 79, *advise.*
Reddyl, ii. 23, *riddle or sieve.*
Rede, iii. 208 ; redde, ii. 13, *read.*
Rede, i. 41, 66, iii. 94, *advise;* rede I can, ii. 37, *advice I know*

Rede, i. 48, *guessed.*
Redouted, i. 120, *dreaded.*
Redresse, ii. 78, *care, labour.*
Redyn, ii. 23, *moved.*
Reek, i. 145, *smoke.*
Reev, ii. 17 ; reeve, iii. 179, *bailiff.*
Refe, ii. 20, *bailiff.*
Refe, *bereave.*
Reft, ii. 26, *bereft.*
Register, iii. 210, *the officer who keeps the public register.*
Reid, ii. 83, *advise.*
Reid, i. 59, 83, 146, *red;* reid roan, i. 83, *red roan.*
Reivs, ii. 83, *bereavest.*
Rekeles, i. 42, *regardless, rash.*
Remeid, ii. 83, *remedy.*
Renisht, i. 88, *harnessed.*
Renn, i. 196 ; renne, i. 160, ii. 89, *run.*
Renneth, iii. 108, *runneth;* renning, ii. 142, *running.*
Renyed, i. 122, *refused.*
Reporte, ii. 124, *refer.*
Rescous, ii. 40, *rescues;* rescew, ii. 175, *rescue.*
Reve, ii. 23, *bereave, deprive.*
Revers, ii. 114, *robbers, pirates, rovers.*
Rew, ii. 82, *take pity.*
Rew, iii. 98 ; rewe, i. 70, ii. 46, *regret;* reweth, ii. 9, *regrets;* rewyth, i. 42, *regrets.*
Rewth, i. 174, *ruth, pity.*
Riall, *royal.*
Richt, i. 101, *right.*
Riddle, *vulgar idiom for unriddle, or corruption of reade, to advise.*
Rin, i. 147 ; rinn, i. 60, *run;* rins, i. 59, *runs;* rinnes, i. 42, *runs.*
Rise, *shoot, bush, shrub.*
Rive, i. 244, *rend;* rives, i. 284 ; *rends.*
Rive, ii. 386, *rife, abounding.*
Roche, i. 128, *rock.*
Rofe, ii. 41, *roof.*
Roke, i. 48, *steam or smoke.*
Ronne, *ran;* roone, *run.*
Roo, i. 42, *roe.*
Roode, i. 76, *cross, crucifix.*
Rood loft, *the place in the church where the images were set up.*
Room, i. 84, *large.*

Roun, ii. 80, *run.*
Route, i. 158, *company.*
Route, iii. 108, *go about, travel.*
Routhe, i. 122, *ruth, pity.*
Row, i. 145 ; rowd, i. 60, 146, *roll, rolled.*
Rowght, i. 45 ; rowte, ii. 26, *rout.*
Rowyned, *round.*
Rowned, rownyd, *whispered.*
Rudd, iii. 8, *red, ruddy;* rud-red, iii. 22.
Rude, ii. 82 ; *rood, cross.*
Ruell bones, ii. 22.
Rues, *pitieth.*
Rugged, ii. 27, *pulled with violence.*
Runnagate, ii. 294, *runaway.*
Rushy gair, ii. 86, *rushy strip of land.*
Ruthe, ii. 46, *pity, woe.*
Ryal, ii. 30 ; ryall, i. 45, 129, *royal.*
Ryd, iii. 36, *rode;* rydand, ii. 22, *riding.*
Ryde, i. 91, *for ryse (?)*
Rydere, i. 178, *ranger.*
Ryghtwes, i. 427, *righteous.*
Ryhte, ii. 9, *right.*
Rynde, i. 46, *rent, flayed.*
Ryschys, ii. 27, *rushes.*
Rywe, ii. 30, *rue.*
Ryyt, ii. 20, *right;* even, ii. 23.

Sa, i. 144, ii. 26 ; sae, i. 144, *so.*
Safer, *sapphire.*
Saft, ii. 110, *soft;* saftly, ii. 107, *softly.*
Saif, i. 144, *safe.*
Saim, iii. 99, *same.*
Sair, i. 60, 147, *sore.*
Saisede, ii. 8, *seized.*
Sall, i. 60, 84, 143, *shall.*
Salvage, iii. 117, *savage.*
Sar, i. 31, *sore.*
Sarke, iii. 95, *shirt;* shift, i. 321.
Sat, i. 31, *set.*
Sauls, ii. 114, *souls.*
Saut, iii. 99, *salt.*
Saw, say, *speech, discourse.*
Say, i. 30, *saw.*
Saye, iii. 64, *essay, attempt.*
Say us no harme, *say no ill of us.*
Say'n, ii. 69, *saying.*
Scant, i. 90, 321, *scarce.*
Scath, i. 65, *hurt, injury.*

Schadow, ii. 25, *shadow*.
Schal, ii. 20; schall, i. 42, *shall*.
Schapen, ii. 24, *shaped*.
Schapped, i. 48, *swapped* (?), *i.e. smote*.
Scharpe, i. 46, 48, *sharp*.
Schatred, ii. 25, *shattered*.
Schaw, ii. 82, *show*.
Sche, i. 42, ii. 24, *she*.
Schene, *sheen*, also *brightness*.
Schepeskynnes, ii. 21, *sheepskins*.
Schip, i. 100, *ship;* schiples, *shipless*.
Scho, i. 59, ii. 20, *she*.
Schone, i. 41, *shone*.
Schoone, i. 101, *shoes*.
Schoote, i. 45, *shot, let go*.
Schowte, i. 47; schowtte, *shout*.
Schrill, *shrill*.
Schuke, *shook*.
Schuld, ii. 20 ; **schulde, i.** 46, *should*.
Schulder, ii. 27, *shoulder*.
Sckill, iii. 327, *skill*.
Sckirmish, ii. 236, *skirmish*.
Sckore, ii. 236, *score*.
Sclat, ii. 16, *slate*.
Scomfet, ii. 23, *discomfit*.
Scorke, i. 259, *struck*.
Scot, ii. 9, *tax, revenue;* also *shot, reckoning*, ii. 20.
See, ii. 8, *sea*.
Sed, iii. 47, *said*.
Seely, ii. 174; seelie, iii. 68, *poor, simple*.
Seignour, ii. 135, *Lord*.
Seik, i. 60, *seek*.
Seires, iii. 328, *for feires, i.e. mates*.
Sek-ful, ii. 22, *sackful*.
Sel, iii. 96 ; sell, iii. 123, *self*.
Selcouthe, ii. 391, *strange*.
Selven, ii. 32, *self*.
Selver, ii. 8, *silver*.
Sely, ii. 53, *simple*.
Semblyd, i. 25, *assembled*.
Sen, i. 34, ii. 83, iii. 95, *since*.
Seneschall, *steward*.
Senvy, *mustard seed*. Fr. senevé.
Serrett, i. 79, *closed fist* (?)
Sertayne, i. 48, *certain;* sertenly, i. 49, 50, *certainly*.
Sese, ii. 49, *seize*.

Setywall, *the herb valerian*.
Sey, iii. 75, *a kind of woollen stuff*.
Sey yow, ii. 15, *say to you;* I sey yow soth, ii. 16, *I tell you truth*.
Sey'd, ii. 114, *tried*.
Sey'd, *saw*.
Seyde, ii. 12, *said*.
Sha' na bide, ii. 116, *shall not endure*.
Shaint, ii. 360, *saint*.
Shave ; be shave, ii. 77, *be shaven*.
Shaw, ii. 114, *show;* shaw'd, ii. 110, *showed*.
Shaws, i. 106, *little woods*.
Shear, i. 24, *entirely*.
Sheede, iii. 12, *shed*.
Sheel, ii. 98 ; sheele, i. 88, 294, *she'll, she will*.
Sheene, i. 87, 106 ; iii. 236, *bright, brightness, beauty*. Germ. *schön*.
Shees, ii. 70, *she is*.
Sheeve, ii. 256, *shive, a great slice of bread*.
Sheip, ii. 82, *sheep;* sheips heid, ii. 132, *sheep's head*.
Sheits, i. 145, *sheets*.
Sheld, ii. 70, *she would*.
Shent, i. 72, 171, *disgraced; abashed*, ii. 49; *confounded*, ii. 84.
Shepenes, iii. 208, *cowhouses, sheep pens*. A.-S. scypen.
Shield bone, *the blade bone*, a common phrase in the north.
Shill, ii. 111, *shrill*.
Shimmer'd, iii. 237, *glittered; shimmering*, ii. 142, *shining by glances, glittering*.
Sho, ii. 49, *she*.
Shoen, ii. 100, *shoes*.
Shold, sholde, *should*.
Shoone, i. 243, 320 ; iii. 47, *shoes*.
Shope, iii. 54, *shaped*.
Shorte, ii. 43, *shorten*.
Shote, ii. 40, *shoot*.
Shott, ii. 149, *reckoning*.
Shoul, ii. 360, *soul*.
Shradds, i. 106, *twigs*.
Shreeven, iii. 10, *shriven, confessed*.
Shreward, ii. 9, *a male shrew*.

Shrive, ii. 60, *confess ; hear confession,* ii. 166.
Shroggs, i. 111, *shrubs, thorns, briars.*
Shuld, iii. 147 ; shulde, i. 32, *should.*
Shullen, *shall.*
Shunted, ii. 137, *shunned.*
Shuntyng, ii. 19, *recreation, diversion, sport.*
Shyars, i. 24, *shires.*
Shynand, ii. 113, *shining.*
Sib, *kin, akin.*
Sic, i. 84 ; sich, i. 327, *such.*
Sich, ii. 84, *sigh ;* sichit, ii. 81, sicht, ii. 86, *sighed.*
Sicht, ii. 114, *sight.*
Sick-like, iii. 123, *such like.*
Side, i. 375, *long.*
Sied, i. 147, *saw.*
Sigh clout, i. 197, *a cloth to strain milk through.*
Sighan, iii. 134, *sighing.*
Sik, i. 144 ; sike, i. 320, *such.*
Siker, i. 323, *secure, surely, certainly.*
Silk, iii. 100, *such.*
Siller, ii. 230 ; iii. 97, *silver.*
Silly, i. 192 ; ii. 68, *simple.*
Silven, iii. 100, *silver.*
Sindle, ii. 115, *seldom.*
Sist, iii. 55, *sighed.*
Sith, i. 68, 133, *since.*
Sitten, iii. 99, *sat.*
Sitteth, ii. 7, *sit ye.*
Skaith, ii. 115, *scath, harm, mischief.*
Skinker, *one that serves drink.*
Skinkled, iii. 237, *glittered.*
Skore, i. 28, *score.*
Slade, i. 108, *a breadth of greensward between ploughlands or woods.*
Slaited, iii. 98, *wiped.*
Slatred, ii. 25, *broke into splinters.*
Slaw, i. 308, *slew.*
Slaw, ii. 107, *slow.*
Sle, i. 15, *slay ;* sleest, slayest, i. 123.
Slee, ii. 69, *sly.*
Slean, i. 31, 33, 34, *slain.*
Sleath, iii. 108, *slayeth.*
Slein, ii. 70, *slain.*

Sleip, i. 60 ; sleipe, ii. 211, *sleep.*
Sleive, iii. 95, *sleeve.*
Slo, i. 120 ; sloe, i. 69, *slay.*
Slode, i. 66, 79, *slit, split.*
Slone, i. 49, 67, *slain.*
Sloughe, i. 28, *slew.*
Sma', i. 145, *small ; little,* iii. 95.
Smire, iii. 327 (? for swire = neck).
Smithers, i. 145, *smothers.*
Snae, iii. 97 ; snaw, ii. 69, *snow.*
Soar, i. 31, *sore.*
Sodenly, ii. 15, *suddenly.*
Solacious, i. 130 ; *affording solace.*
Soldan, i. 73, 74, 80 ; sowdan, i. 96, *sultan.*
Soll, i. 34, *soul.*
Son, ii. 23, *soon ;* sone, ii. 44, *soon.*
Sond, ii. 26, *sending, present*
Sone, ii. 41, *soon.*
Soothe, ii. 55, *truth, true.*
Sort, i. 122, 126, *set, company.*
Soth, i. 43, 49, 50, 51 ; ii. 16 ; iii. 30, *truth, true.*
Sothe, i. 27, *south.*
Sould, ii. 69, *should.*
Souldan, iii. 110, *sultan.*
Souling, ii. 257, *victualling.*
　Sowle is still used in the north for anything eaten with bread. P.
Souse, iii. 181, *the head, feet and ears of swine boiled and pickled for eating.*
Souter, i. 416, *psaltry.*
Sowne, ii. 52, *sound.*
Sowre, *sour.*
Sowre, *sore.*
Sowter, i. 416, *a shoemaker.*
Soy, i. 320, *silk.*
Spack, ii. 230 ; iii. 96, *spake.*
Spec, ii. 13, *spake.*
Speere, ii. 144 ; speered, ii. 144, *sparred, fastened, shut.*
　So in an old "Treatyse agaynst Pestilence, &c. 4to Emprynted by Wynkyn de Worde :" we are exhorted to " Spere [i.e. shut or bar] the wyndowes ayenst the south." fol. 5. P.
Speid, iii. 94, *speed.*
Speik, iii. 96, *speak.*

Speir, ii. 69 ; iii. 95, *ask, inquire.*
So Chaucer, in his Rhyme of
Sir Thopas—

—— " He foughte north and
south,
And oft he spired with his
mouth."

i.e. " inquired." Not spied, as
in the new edit. of Cant. Tales,
vol. ii. p. 234. P.
Speir, iii. 98, *spear.*
Spek, ii. 12, *spoke;* speken, iii.
207, *speak.*
Spence, ii. 52 ; spens, ii. 21, *ex-
pense.*
Spendyd, *grasped.*
Spill, i. 196, iii. 51 ; spille, i. 75,
spoil, kill.
Spillan, iii. 134, *spilling.*
Spindles and whorles, ii. 71, *the
instruments used for spinning
in Scotland instead of spinning-
wheels.*

" The Rock, Spindles, and
Whorles are very much used
in Scotland and the northern
parts of Northumberland at
this time. The thread for
shoemakers, and even some
linen webs, and all the twine
of which the Tweed salmon-
nets are made, are spun upon
spindles. They are said to make
a more even and smooth thread
than spinning-wheels." (*Mr.
Lambe.*) P.
Spittle, ii. 282, *hospital.*
Splene ; on the splene, ii. 46, *in
haste.*
Spole, ii. 198, *shoulder.*
Sporeles, ii. 9, *spurless, without
spurs.*
Sprente, i. 29, *spurted out, sprung
out.*
Sprite, iii. 132, *spirit.*
Spurging, iii. 197, *drivelling froth.*
Spurn, i. 34, *a kick.*
Spylt, i. 123, *spoiled, destroyed.*
Squelsh, iii. 295, *a blow or bang.*
Squyer, ii. 44 ; squyere, ii. 44,
squire.
Stalworth, ii. 19, *stout.*

Stalwurthlye, i. 41, *stoutly.*
Stane, i. 145, *stone.*
Starke, i. 72, *stout, strong.*
Startopes, ii. 256, *buskins or half
boots.*
Stean, i. 103, iii. 99, *stone.*
Stede, ii. 23, *place.*
Steid, i. 83, iii. 98, *steed.*
Steill, ii. 131, *steel.*
Steir, ii. 83, *stir.*
Stel, ii. 8, *steel.*
Stele, ii. 46, *steal.*
Sterne, i. 28, *fierce ones.*
Sterris, *stars.*
Sterte, i. 69, 73, *start;* sterted, iii.
15, *started.*
Sterve, ii. 16, *die, perish.*
Steven, i. 115, iii. 26, *voice, sound.*
Steven, i. 111, *time.*
Stint, i. 68, 133, 273, *stop, stopped.*
Stond, ii. 26, *stand.*
Stonderes, *standers by.*
Stonds, i. 44, *stands.*
Stound, i. 165, *hour.*
Stounde, i. 48, *time; for awhile,*
ii. 11.
Stoup, ii. 117, *stoop.*
Stoup of weir, ii. 115, *a pillar of
war.*
Stour, i. 31, 96 ; stower, i. 66,
iii. 26 ; stowre, i. 49, 74, 168,
iii. 14, *strong, fierce, stir, fight.*
This word is applied in the
North to signify dust agitated
and put in motion, as by the
sweeping of a room, &c. P.
Stown, ii. 69, *stolen.*
Stra, ii. 24 ; strae, ii. 69, iii. 98,
straw.
Strake, ii. 117, *struck.*
Strekene, i. 29, *stricken, struck.*
Stret, *street.*
Strick, i. 322, *strict.*
Strike, *stricken.*
Stroke, i. 28 ; stroken, i. 228,
struck.
Strout, iii. 119, *strut.*
Stude, i. 143, iii. 95, *stood.*
Styntyde, i. 30, *stinted, stayed,
stopped.*
Styrande, i. 40, *stirring.*
Styrt, ii. 26, *started.*
Suar, i. 28, 30, *sure.*

Suld, ii. 21, *should.*
Sum, i. 83, 146, ii. 25, *some.*
Summere, iii. 108, *a sumpter horse.*
Sumpters, i. 302, *horses that carry clothes, furniture, &c.*
Sune, *soon.*
Surmount, iii. 172, *surpass.*
Suore bi ys chyn, ii. 9, *sworn by his chin.*
Supprised, i. 124, *overpowered.*
Suraunce, ii. 49, *assurance.*
Suthe, ii. 386, *soon, quickly.*
Swa, ii. 24, *so.*
Swage, ii. 342, *assuage;* swaged, ii. 180, *assuaged.*
Swapte, i. 29; swapped, i. 48, *struck violently, exchanged blows.*
Sware, ii. 12, ii. 361, *swearing, oath.*
Swarned, ij. 206, *climbed.*
Swarved, ii. 197, *climbed, swarmed.*
    To swarm, in the midland counties, is to draw oneself up a tree or any other thing, clinging to it with the legs and arms. P.
Swat, i. 29, *did sweat.*
Swear, *sware.*
Swearde, ii. 128, *sword.*
Sweaven, i. 106, ii. 63; sweven, ii. 56, *a dream.*
Sweere, iii. 21, *neck.*
Sweit, iii. 74; swete, ii. 19, *sweet;* sweitly, ii. 212, *sweetly.*
Swepyls, ii. 25, "a swepyl is that staff of the flail with which the corn is beaten out. Vulg. a supple (called in the midland counties a swindgell, where the other part is termed the hand-staff)." P.
Swerdes, ii. 8, *swords.*
Swiche, i. 430, *such.*
Swith, i. 96, ii. 119, *quickly, instantly, at once.*
Swound, i. 240, 296, ii. 179, *swoon*
Swyke, *sigh.*
Swynkers, ii. 19, *labourers.*
Swyppyng, ii. 25, *striking fast.*
Swyving, ii. 8, *wenching, lechery.*
Sych, ii. 19, *such.*
Syd, *side;* on sydis shear, i. 25, *on all sides.*

Syn, ii. 16, *since.*
Syne, i. 43, ii. 114, iii. 147, *then, afterwards.*
Syns, *since.*
Syschemell, ii. 74, *Ishmael.*
Syth, ii. 38, *since.*
Syyt, ii. 27, *sight.*

Taiken, ii. 118, *taken.*
Tain, iii. 94; taine, i. 59, *taken.*
Tane, i. 289, ii. 193, *taken.*
Tane, iii. 238, *the one.*
Tarbox, ii. 256, *box containing tar for anointing sores in sheep, &c.*
Targe, ii. 53, *target, shield.*
Tauld, ii. 109, *told.*
Tayne, i. 50, *taken.*
Te, ii. 7, *to;* te-knowe, ii. 11, *to know;* te-make, *to make.*
Te-he, ii. 26, *interjection of laughing.*
Tear, i. 34, *tearing or pulling.*
Teene, i. 162, *vexation;* i. 284, 291, *injury;* iii. 194, *trouble;* teenefu, i. 147, *wrathful.*
Teene, i. 77, *vex.*
Teir, i. 101, *tear.*
Tene, i. 120, *wrath.*
Tenebrus, i. 128, *dark.*
Tent, ii. 83, *heed.*
Termagaunt, i. 85, 96, *the god of the Saracens.*
    The old French Romancers, who had corrupted *Termagant* into *Tervagant,* couple it with the name of Mahomet as constantly as ours; thus in the old *Roman de Blanchardin,*

" Cy guerpison tuit Apolin,
Et Mahomet et *Tervagant.*"

Hence La Fontaine, with great humour, in his Tale, intituled *La Fiancée du Roy de Garbe,* says,

" Et reniant Mahom, Jupin, et
    Tervagant,
Avec maint autre Dieu non
    moins extravagant."
—*Mem. de l'Acad. des Inscript.* tom. 20, 4to. p. 352.

    As *Termagant* is evidently of Anglo-Saxon derivation and can only be explained from the elements of that language, its being corrupted by the old French Romancers proves that they borrowed some things from ours. P.

Terrene, iii. 299, *earthly.*

Terry, ii. 19, *Thierry, or a diminutive of Terence.*

Tester, iii. 206, *teston, or sixpence.*

Tha, ii. 26, *them.*

Thah, ii. 7, *though.*

Thair, ii. 82, iii. 99, *there.*

Tham, ii. 21 ; thame, i. 84, 102, 146, *them.*

Than, i. 145, 206, *then.*

Thanns, ii. 25, *thence.*

Thay, i. 321, *they.*

Thaym, ii. 23, *them.*

Thayr, ii. 21, *their.*

The, *they ;* the wear, i. 29, *they were.*

The, i. 189, ii. 13, *thee.*

The God, ii. 30, *contraction for the* he (i.e. *high*) God. P.

Thear, i. 33, *there ;* i. 29, *their.*

Theder, ii. 19 ; thedyr, ii. 28, *thither.*

Thee, ii. 97, *thrive ;* so mote I thee, ii. 97, *so may I thrive.* So in Chaucer, *Cant. Tales,* vol. i. p. 308, " God let him never *the.*" P.

Then, *than.*

Ther, ii. 21 ; there i. 289, *their.*

Ther, ii. 23, *where.*

Thes, ii. 19, *these.*

Thether, i. 41, *thither.*

They, i. 78, *the.*

Theyther-ward, *thitherward, towards that place.*

Thie, *thy.*

Thii, ii. 386, *they.*

Thilke, ii. 14, *this.*

Thir, ii. 69, *this, these ;* thir towmonds, ii. 82, *these twelve months.*

Tho, i. 207, *then ; those,* ii. 39.

Thocht, iii. 94, *thought.*

Thole, ii. 119, *suffer.*

Thore, ii. 13, *there.*

Thorow, ii. 30 ; thorrow, i. 291, *through ;* thorowout, ii. 15, *throughout*

Thouse, i. 198, *thou art ; thou shalt,* iii. 131.

Thoust, i. 289, *thou shalt or shouldst.*

Thowe, *thou.*

Thrall, i. 297, ii. 79, *captive ; captivity,* i. 75, 135 ; ii. 256.

Thrang, ii. 115, *throng ; close,* ii. 69.

Thraste, iii. 216, *thrust.*

Thrawis, *throes.*

Thrawn, ii. 115, *thrown.*

Threape, i. 198, *to argue, to affirm or assert in a positive overbearing manner.*

Threven, ii. 133, *thrived.*

Threw, ii. 214, *drew.*

Threw, iii. 238, *thrived.*

Thrie, *three.*

Thrif, *thrive.*

Thrild upon a pinn, iii. 47, *twirled or twisted the door pin.*

Thrittè, i. 34, *thirty ;* thritti thousent, ii. 7, *thirty thousand.*

Thronge, i. 163, *hastened.*

Thropes, iii. 208, *villages.*

Through - girt, ii. 78, *pierced through.*

Throw, iii. 134, *through.*

Thruch, throuch, *through.*

Thrughe, *through.*

Thrustand, ii. 23, *thrusting.*

Thryes, ii. 23, *thrice.*

Thrysse, i. 47, *thrice.*

Thud, ii. 119, *dull sound.*

Tickle, ii. 299, *uncertain.*

Tift, iii. 237, *puff of wind.*

Till, i. 33, 65, 143, ii. 82, *unto.*

Till, i. 94, *entice.*

Timkin, *diminutive of Timothy.*

Tine, i. 64, *lose ;* tint, i. 71 ; ii. 363, *lost.*

Tirled at the pin, iii. 131, *twirled or twisted the door pin.*

Tividale, i. 25, *Tevioidale.*

To, *too, two.*

Tokenyng, ii. 22, *token.*

Tomkyn, ii. 19, *diminutive of Thomas.*

To-flatred, ii. 25, *slit.*

To-rente, iii. 356, *rent.*

To-schatred, ii. 25, *shattered.*

To-slatered, ii. 25, *splintered.*

Tone, i. 42, 87, iii. 103, *the one.*
Too-fall, ii. 365, *twilight.*
"Toofall of the night" seems to be an image drawn from a suspended canopy, so let fall as to cover what is below. (*Mr. Lambe.*) P.
Tooken, i. 274, *took.*
Tor, *a tower;* also *a high pointed rock or hill.*
Torn, i. 187, *turn.*
Tothar, i. 31, *the other.*
Tother, i. 87, *the other.*
Toun, i. 143 ; town, i. 321, *dwelling-house.*
Tow, i. 145, *to let down with a rope;* towd, i. 146, *let down.*
Tow, i. 106 ; towe, i. 31, 87, *two.*
Towmonds, ii. 82, *twelve months.*
Towyn, i. 41, *town.*
Traitorye, i. 283, 289, ii. 309 ; traytery, ii. 224, *treason.*
Tre, i. 28, ii. 13, *wood;* i. 30, *staff.*
Tree, i. 291, *ill.*
Trewest, ii. 11, *truest.*
Treytory, i. 124, *treachery.*
Trichard, ii. 7, *treacherous.*
Tricthen (should be trichen), ii. 7, *deceive.*
Triest furth, iii. 94, *draw forth to an assignation.*
Trifulcate, *three forked, three pointed.*
Trippand, ii. 27, *tripping.*
Trim, i. 191, *exact.*
Troate, ii. 360, *throat.*
Trogh, ii. 24, *trough.*
Trone. yn trone, i. 43, *enthroned.*
Troth, iii. 131, *truth, faith, fidelity;* trothles, i. 201, *faithless.*
Trough, trouth, *troth.*
Trouth plyyt, ii. 27, *truth plight.*
Trow, ii. 95, *true.*
Trow, iii. 96 ; trowe, i. 270, *believe, trust,* also *verily.*
Trumped, *boasted, told bragging lies;* a trump, *a lie.*
Tuik, i. 322, *took.*
Tuke gude keip, ii. 84, *took good watch.*
Tull, i. 320; for till, *to.*
Tup, ii. 257, *ram.*
Turn, such turn, *such an occasion.*

Turnes a crab, ii. 258, *roasts a crab apple.*
Tush, ii. 57, *tusk.*
Twa, i. 320 ; ii. 26, *two.*
Twatling, iii. 187, *trifling.*
Twaw, i. 27, *two.*
Twayne, ii. 37, *two.*
Twin'd, i. 59, *parted in two.*
Twirtle twist, ii. 112, *twirled twist.*
Twyes, ii. 23, *twice.*
Tyb, ii. 20, *the diminutive of Isabel.*
Tyll. com the tyll, i. 42, *come unto thee.*
Tyrry, ii. 26. See *Terry.*

Uch, ii. 14, *each.*
Ugsome, *shocking, horrible.*
'Um, iii. 333, *them.*
Unbethought, iii. 51, for *bethought.*
Undermeles, iii. 208, *afternoons.*
Undight, i. 309, *undecked.*
Unfeeled, *opened,* a term in falconry.
Unhap, ii. 77, *mishap.*
Unkempt, ii. 77, *uncombed.*
Unmacklye, i. 73, 80, *mis-shapen.*
Unmufit, *undisturbed.*
Unright, ii. 191, *wrong.*
Unsett steven, i. 111, *unappointed time, unexpectedly.*
Unsonsie, ii. 116, *unlucky, unfortunate.*
Untill, iii. 49 ; untyll, i. 162, *unto.*
Upo, ii. 70, *upon.*
Ure, iii. 262, *use.*
Uthers, ii. 86, *others.*

Vaints, ii. 289, *faints.*
Vair, ii. 286, *fair.*
Valeies, ii. 41, *valleys.*
Vart, ii. 286, *fart.*
Vazen, ii. 286, for *faith.*
Vellow, ii. 286 ; vellowe, ii. 287, *fellow.*
Venge, ii. 117, *revenge.*
Venu, iii. 356, *approach, coming.*
Verament, i. 25, 28, *truly.*
Vices, i. 129, *devices.*
Vilane, *rascally.*
Vitayle, ii. 42, *victual.*
Vive, ii. 386, *five.*

Vools, ii. 288, *fools;* voolish, ii. 288, *foolish.*
Vor, ii. 286, *for.*
Vorty, ii. 287, *forty.*
Vourteen, ii. 287, *fourteen.*
Voyded, i. 166, *quitted, left the place.*
Vrier, ii. 286, *friar.*

Wa, i. 142, 143, ii. 109, iii. 93, 95, *wall.*
Wache, i. 43, *a spy.*
Wad, i. 60, 145, 321, *would.*
Wadded, iii. 7, *light-blue or woad-coloured.*
Wadna, ii. 13, *would not.*
Wae, i. 83, 320, *woe;* waefo', iii. 100 ; waefu', ii. 110, *woeful.*
Wae worth, i. 145, 322, *woe betide.*
Wald, i. 145 ; walde, iii. 94, *would.*
Walker, iii. 8, *a fuller of cloth.*
Walowit, ii. 119, *faded, withered.*
Waltering, i. 75, ii. 119, *weltering;* waltred, *tumbled or rolled about.*
Waly, iii. 147, *an interjection of lamentation.*
Wame, iii. 238, *womb, belly.*
Wan, i. 72, 244 ; ii. 26, *won.*
Wan near, ii. 120, *drew near.*
Wane, i. 29, *the same as* ane, *one, so* wone *is one.*

In fol. 355 of Bannatyne's MS. is a short fragment, in which "wane" is used for "ane" or "one," viz.:—

"Amongst the monsters that we find,
There's *wane* belovved of wo-man-kind,
Renowned for antiquity,
From Adame drivs his pedi-gree." P.

The word wane in the text, however, is probably a mis-reading for mane.
Wanrufe, ii. 83, *uneasy.*
War, i. 25, *aware.*
War ant wys, ii. 11, *wary and wise.*
Ward, ii. 120, *watch, sentinel, warder.*

Warde, iii. 97, *advise, forewarn.*
Ware, i. 43, 107, 158, *aware.*
Ware, i. 306, *wore.*
Ware, iii. 238, *were.*
Warke, *work.*
Warld, ii. 85, *world;* warldis, i. 84, *worlds.*
Waryd, ii. 20, *accursed.*
Waryson, i. 46, *reward.*
Wassel, iii. 27, *drinking, good cheer.*
Wat, i. 322, ii. 68, *wet.*
Wat, i. 27, *know.*
Wate, iii. 97, *blamed.* (Preterite of *wyte,* to blame.)
Wauld, iii. 95, *would.*
Wayde, *waved.*
Wayed, iii. 195, *weighed.*
Weal, i. 33, *wail.*
Weale, *well.*
Wear, i. 29, *were.*
Wear-in, iii. 74, *drive in gently.*
Wearifu', ii. 70, *wearisome, trouble-some, tiresome, disturbing.*
Weddeen, iii. 236, *wedding.*
Wedder, ii. 83, *weather.*
Wede, ii. 21, *clothing.*
Wedous, i. 33, *widows.*
Wee, ii. 69, *little.*
Weede, iii. 59, *clothing, dress;* weeds, i. 88, 246, *garments.*
Weell, iii. 51, *we'll, we will.*
Weel, ii. 132 ; weele, i. 150, *well.*
Weel-faur'd, ii. 139, *well-fa-voured.*
Weene, i. 193, *think;* ween'd, i. 143 ; weened, ii. 80 ; weende, ii. 96, *thought.*
Weete, i. 101, ii. 216, *wet.*
Weet, ii. 95, *know.*
Weids, ii. 364, *cloathing.*
Weil, i. 145, *well.*
Weip, i. 60 ; weipe, ii. 211, *weep.*
Weir, ii. 115, *war.*
Weird, iii. 224, *witch-like.*
Weit, ii. 231, *wet.*
Wel longe, ii. 13, *very long.*
Wel-awaye, iii. 128, *an interjec-tion of grief.*
Weldynge, *ruling.*
Wele, ii. 24, *well.*
Welkin, iii. 201, *the sky.*
Wem, iii. 303, *spot.*

Wem, iii. 357, *hurt.*
Weme, i. 284, 291, *hollow.*
Wend, i. 156, ii. 13, *go.*
Wend, ii. 85 ; wende, i. 170, *thought;* wende do, ii. 8, *thought to do.*
Wenden, ii. 12, *go.*
Went, i. 164, *thought.*
Wer, iii. 134, *were.*
Wereth, *defendeth.*
Werke, i. 163, 306, *work.*
Werre, ii. 11, *war.*
Werryed, ii. 65, *worried.*
Wes, ii. 8, *was.*
Westlin, ii. 120, *western.*
Westlings, *whistling.*
Wete, i. 31, *wet.*
Wether, iii. 328, *whether.*
Wex, iii. 238, *wax, grow.*
Wha, ii. 71, *who.*
Whair, ii. 69, *where;* whair-eir, ii. 212, *wherever.*
Wham, ii. 11, *whom.*
Whan, i. 318, *when.*
Whang, ii. 70, *a large slice.*
Wheder, ii. 37, *whither.*
Whelyng, ii. 49, *wheeling.*
Whig, i. 299, ii. 256, *sour whey, buttermilk.*
While, *until.*
Whilk, ii. 71, *which.*
Whirry, iii. 202, *laugh.*
Whittles, *knives.*
Whoard, i. 214, *hoard.*
Whorles (see spindles).
Whyll, i. 48, *while.*
Whyllys, i. 30, *whilst.*
Wi', ii. 68, *with*
Wight, i. 63, 65, 72, 191, *man, human being*
Wight, i. 107, 288, *strong, lusty.*
Wightlye, i. 64, 78, *swiftly, vigorously.*
Wighty, i. 106, 147 ; wightye, i. 161, *strong, active.*
Wild-worme, iii. 30, 36, *serpent.*
Wildings, ii. 257, *wild or crab apples.*
Wilfull, i. 110, *ignorant.*
Windar, iii. 302, *a kind of hawk.*
Windling, *winding.*
Winna, iii. 96 ; winnae, i. 59, 144, *will not.*

Winyard, iii. 297, *long knife or short cutlass.*
Winsome, i. 323, ii. 70, 363, *agreeable, engaging.*
Wirk, ii. 83, *do.*
Wis, i. 269, *know;* wist, i. 72, iii. 148, *knew.*
Witchd, iii. 24, *bewitched.*
Withouten, i. 126; withowtten, i. 41; withowghten, i. 40, 43, *without.*
Wive, ii. 255, *marry.*
Wo, ii. 81, 86, *woe.*
Wobster, ii. 131, *webster, weaver.*
Wod, ii. 82 ; wode, i. 122, 160, 163, *mad, wild.*
Wod, iii. 94 ; wode, i. 156, ii. 37, *wood.*
Wodewarde, ii. 43, *towards the wood.*
Woe-man, *a sorrowful man.*
Woe worth, ii. 215, *woe be to thee.*
Wolden, i. 274, *would.*
Woll, ii. 24, *wool.*
Wolle, ii. 38, *will.*
Won, ii. 49, *wont, usage.*
Won'd, i. 306, *dwelt.*
Wonde, wounde, *winded.*
Wonders, *wondrous.*
Wondersly, i. 125, *wondrously.*
Wone, i. 31, *one.*
Wonne, *dwell.*
Woo, i. 28, *woe.*
Wood, i. 145, ii. 145 ; woode, iii. 57, *mad, furious.*
Wood-wroth, iii. 238, *furiously enraged.*
Woodweele, i. 106, *the golden ouzle, a bird of the thrush kind.*
Worm, iii. 30, 36, *serpent.*
Worship, i. 121, *honour.*
Worshipfully frended, *of worshipful friends.*
Wot, i. 69 ; wott, ii. 139, *know;* wotes, i. 219, *knows.*
Wouche, i. 28, *mischief, wrong.*
Wowe, i. 300, *woo.*
Wow, iii. 75, *who.*
Wow, ii. 22, *vow.*
Wrack, i. 296 ; wracke, iii. 41, *wreck, ruin, destruction;* wracked, iii. 117, *wrecked.*
Wrang, i. 147, *wrung.*
Wrange, i. 41, *wrong.*

Wreake, ii. 135, *pursue revenge-fully.*
Wrench, ii. 81, 86, *wretchedness.*
Wringe, i. 122, *to contend with violence.*
Writhe, i. 286, *writhed, twisted.*
Wroken, i. 106, 147, *revenged.*
Wrong, i. 166, *wrung.*
Wrotyn, ii. 22, *wrought.*
Wrouyt, ii. 30, *wrought.*
Wry, ii. 49, *turn aside.*
Wul, i. 83, 143 ; wull, iii. 235, *will.*
Wych, i. 44, *which.*
Wyld, i. 24, *wild deer.*
Wynn ther haye, i. 40, *gather in their hay.*
Wynne, i. 43, ii. 20, *joy, pleasure.*
Wynne, iii. 279, *heard.*
Wynnen, ii. 12, *win, gain.*
Wyrch wyselyer, ii. 24, *work more wisely.*
Wysse, ii. 12, 14, *teach, govern,*
Wyst, ii. 26 ; wyste, i. 25, *knew.*
Wyt, *know;* wyt wold I, ii. 20, *know would I.*
Wyte, iii. 97, *blame.*

Y, ii. 12, *I;* y singe, ii. 11, *I sing.*
Y-beare, ii. 57, *bear;* y-boren, ii. 8, *borne.*
Y-bent, *bent.*
Y-built, iii. 272, *built.*
Y-cald, iii. 374, *called.*
Y-chesyled, i. 129, *chiselled.*
Y-cleped, i. 326, *named, called.*
Y-con'd, i. 306, *taught, instructed.*
Y-core, ii. 12, *chosen.*
Y-fere, ii. 76, *together.*
Y-founde, ii. 13, *found.*
Y-mad, ii. 13, *made.*
Y-picking, i. 307, *picking, culling,*
Y-slaw, i. 175, *slain.*
Y-told, iii. 374, *told.*
Y-were, i. 87, *were.*
Y-wis, i. 132 ; ii. 12, *verily.*
Y-wonne, ii. 13, *won.*
Y-wrought, i. 306; iii. 275, *wrought.*
Y-yote, ii. 14, *cast.*
Yae, iii. 237, *each.*
Yalping, ii. 170, *yelping.*
Yaned, iii. 357, *yawned.*

Yate, i. 92 ; iii. 62, *gate;* yates, i. 144.
Yave, i. 272, *gave.*
Ych, i. 31, 48 ; ycha, ii. 23, *each, every.*
Ych, ii. 26, *same.*
Ycholde, ii. 12, *I would.*
Ychone, i. 49, *each one.*
Ychulle, iii. 363, *I shall.*
Ydle, *idle.*
Yeaning, ii. 257, *bringing forth young.*
Yearded, ii. 384, *buried, earthed.*
Yeats, iii. 93, *gates.*
Yebent, i. 28, *bent.*
Yede, ii. 21, 44, *went.*
Yee, *eye.*
Yef, ii. 12, *if.*
Yeid, ii. 81, *went.*
Yeir, i. 101, *year.*
Yeme, ii. 12, *take care of, govern.*
Yender, *yonder.*
Yenoughe, i. 28, 34, *enough.*
Yent, ii. 11, *through.*
Yerarchy, i. 126, *hierarchy.*
Yerle, i. 26, 28, 29, 48, *earl;* yerlle, i. 40, 44, 49.
Yerly, i. 24, *early.*
Yerly, i. 440, *yearly.*
Ye's, ii. 132 ; ye'se, iii. 134, *ye shall.*
Yestreen, ii. 111, *last evening.*
Yet, ii. 20, *still.*
Yf, ii. 23, *though.*
Ygnoraunce, i. 441, *ignorance.*
Ying, iii. 374 ; yinge, iii. 374, *young.*
Yit, *yet.*
Ylk, ii. 13, *same.*
Yll, ii. 36, *ill.*
Ylythe, *listen.*
Yn, ii. 9, *house.*
Yngglishe, i. 28, 47, 50, *English.*
Ynglonde, i. 27, 32, 34, 43, *England.*
Ynough, i. 155, *enough.*
Yode, iii. 67, *went.*
Yond, i. 285 ; ii. 191 ; yonds, i. 291, *yonder.*
Yong, i. 271 ; yonge, ii. 38, *young.*
Youd, iii. 48, *went.*
Youle, i. 274, 290, *you will.*
Your lane, iii. 94, *alone, by your-self.*

Youst, i. 290, *you will.*
Yow, ii. 16, *you.*
Ys, i. 189 ; ii. 14, *is;* ii. 12, *his.*
Yt, *it.*
Yth, i. 25, *in the.*
Yule, ii. 229, *Christmas.*

[In several of the poems Percy used the letter z to represent the Anglo-Saxon character ȝ, but as this is incorrect, and, moreover, gives rise to a very frequent mispronunciation, the z has been replaced by y in this edition, and several words have therefore been left out that occurred in the original glossary.]

Zacring bell, ii. 288, *sacring bell,* a little bell rung to give notice of the elevation of the host.   P.

Zaints, ii. 289, *saints.*
Zaw, ii. 290, *saw.*
Zay, ii. 287, *say.*
Zee, ii. 286, *see;* zeene, ii. 287. *seen.*
Zelf, ii. 287, *self.*
Zet, ii. 289, *set.*
Zhall, ii. 288, *shall.*
Zhowe, ii. 288, *show.*
Zinging, ii. 289, *singing.*
Zmell, ii. 286, *smell.*
Zo, ii. 289, *so.*
Zold, ii. 287, *sold.*
Zometimes, ii. 286, *sometimes.*
Zon, ii. 290, *son.*
Zorrow, ii. 289, *sorrow.*
Zorts, ii. 286, *sorts.*
Zubtil, ii. 290, *subtil.*
Zuch, ii. 288, *such.*
Zure, ii. 288, *sure.*
Zweet, ii. 289, *sweet.*

INDEX

TO THE THREE VOLUMES.

The Titles of the various Poems included in the *Reliques* are distinguished
from the other entries by being printed in italics.

CATALOGUE OF DOVER BOOKS

Literature, History of Literature

ARISTOTLE'S THEORY OF POETRY AND THE FINE ARTS, edited by S. H. Butcher. The celebrated Butcher translation of this great classic faced, page by page, with the complete Greek text. A 300 page introduction discussing Aristotle's ideas and their influence in the history of thought and literature, and covering art and nature, imitation as an aesthetic form, poetic truth, art and morality, tragedy, comedy, and similar topics. Modern Aristotelian criticism discussed by John Gassner. lxxvi + 421pp. 5⅜ x 8.   T42 Paperbound **$2.00**

INTRODUCTIONS TO ENGLISH LITERATURE, edited by B. Dobrée. Goes far beyond ordinary histories, ranging from the 7th century up to 1914 (to the 1940's in some cases.) The first half of each volume is a specific detailed study of historical and economic background of the period and a general survey of poetry and prose, including trends of thought, influences, etc. The second and larger half is devoted to a detailed study of more than 5000 poets, novelists, dramatists; also economists, historians, biographers, religious writers, philosophers, travellers, and scientists of literary stature, with dates, lists of major works and their dates, keypoint critical bibliography, and evaluating comments. The most compendious bibliographic and literary aid within its price range.

Vol. I. THE BEGINNINGS OF ENGLISH LITERATURE TO SKELTON, (1509), W. L. Renwick, H. Orton. 450pp. 5⅛ x 7⅞.   T75 Clothbound **$4.50**

Vol. II. THE ENGLISH RENAISSANCE, 1510-1688, V. de Sola Pinto. 381pp. 5⅛ x 7⅞.
                              T76 Clothbound **$4.50**

Vol. III. AUGUSTANS AND ROMANTICS, 1689-1830, H. Dyson, J. Butt. 320pp. 5⅛ x 7⅞.
                              T77 Clothbound **$4.50**

Vol. IV. THE VICTORIANS AND AFTER, 1830-1940's, E. Batho, B. Dobrée. 360pp. 5⅛ x 7⅞.
                              T78 Clothbound **$4.50**

EPIC AND ROMANCE, W. P. Ker. Written by one of the foremost authorities on medieval literature, this is the standard survey of medieval epic and romance. It covers Teutonic epics, Icelandic sagas, Beowulf, French chansons de geste, the Roman de Troie, and many other important works of literature. It is an excellent account for a body of literature whose beauty and value has only recently come to be recognized. Index. xxiv + 398pp. 5⅜ x 8.
                              T355 Paperbound **$2.00**

THE POPULAR BALLAD, F. B. Gummere. Most useful factual introduction; fund of descriptive material; quotes, cites over 260 ballads. Examines, from folkloristic view, structure; choral, ritual elements; meter, diction, fusion; effects of tradition, editors; almost every other aspect of border, riddle, kinship, sea, ribald, supernatural, etc., ballads. Bibliography. 2 indexes. 374pp. 5⅜ x 8.   T548 Paperbound **$1.85**

MASTERS OF THE DRAMA, John Gassner. The most comprehensive history of the drama in print, covering drama in every important tradition from the Greeks to the Near East, China, Japan, Medieval Europe, England, Russia, Italy, Spain, Germany, and dozens of other drama producing nations. This unsurpassed reading and reference work encompasses more than 800 dramatists and over 2000 plays, with biographical material, plot summaries, theatre history, etc. "Has no competitors in its field," THEATRE ARTS. "Best of its kind in English," NEW REPUBLIC. Exhaustive 35 page bibliography. 77 photographs and drawings. Deluxe edition with reinforced cloth binding, headbands, stained top. xxii + 890pp. 5⅜ x 8.   T100 Clothbound **$6.95**

THE DEVELOPMENT OF DRAMATIC ART, D. C. Stuart. The basic work on the growth of Western drama from primitive beginnings to Eugene O'Neill, covering over 2500 years. Not a mere listing or survey, but a thorough analysis of changes, origins of style, and influences in each period; dramatic conventions, social pressures, choice of material, plot devices, stock situations, etc.; secular and religious works of all nations and epochs. "Generous and thoroughly documented researches," Outlook. "Solid studies of influences and playwrights and periods," London Times. Index. Bibliography. xi + 679pp. 5⅜ x 8.
                              T693 Paperbound **$2.75**

A SOURCE BOOK IN THEATRICAL HISTORY (SOURCES OF THEATRICAL HISTORY), A. M. Nagler. Over 2000 years of actors, directors, designers, critics, and spectators speak for themselves in this potpourri of writings selected from the great and formative periods of western drama. On-the-spot descriptions of masks, costumes, makeup, rehearsals, special effects, acting methods, backstage squabbles, theatres, etc. Contemporary glimpses of Molière rehearsing his company, an exhortation to a Roman audience to buy refreshments and keep quiet, Goethe's rules for actors, Belasco telling of $6500 he spent building a river, Restoration actors being told to avoid "lewd, obscene, or indecent postures," and much more. Each selection has an introduction by Prof. Nagler. This extraordinary, lively collection is ideal as a source of otherwise difficult to obtain material, as well as a fine book for browsing. Over 80 illustrations. 10 diagrams. xxiii + 611pp. 5⅜ x 8.   T515 Paperbound **$3.00**

CATALOGUE OF DOVER BOOKS

WORLD DRAMA, B. H. Clark. The dramatic creativity of a score of ages and eras — all in two handy compact volumes. Over ⅓ of this material is unavailable in any other current edition! 46 plays from Ancient Greece, Rome, Medieval Europe, France, Germany, Italy, England, Russia, Scandinavia; India, China, Japan, etc. — including classic authors like Aeschylus, Sophocles, Euripides, Aristophanes, Plautus, Marlowe, Jonson, Farquhar, Goldsmith, Cervantes, Molière, Dumas, Goethe, Schiller, Ibsen, and many others. This creative collection avoids hackneyed material and includes only completely first-rate works which are relatively little known or difficult to obtain. "The most comprehensive collection of important plays from all literature available in English," SAT. REV. OF LITERATURE. Introduction. Reading lists. 2 volumes. 1364pp. 5⅜ x 8.
Vol. 1, T57 Paperbound **$2.50**
Vol. 2, T59 Paperbound **$2.50**

MASTERPIECES OF THE RUSSIAN DRAMA, edited with introduction by G. R. Noyes. This only comprehensive anthology of Russian drama ever published in English offers complete texts, in 1st-rate modern translations, of 12 plays covering 200 years. Vol. 1: "The Young Hopeful," Fonvisin; "Wit Works Woe," Griboyedov; "The Inspector General," Gogol; "A Month in the Country," Turgenev; "The Poor Bride," Ostrovsky; "A Bitter Fate," Pisemsky. Vol. 2: "The Death of Ivan the Terrible," Alexey Tolstoy "The Power of Darkness," Lev Tolstoy; "The Lower Depths," Gorky; "The Cherry Orchard," Chekhov; "Professor Storitsyn," Andreyev; "Mystery Bouffe," Mayakovsky. Bibliography. Total of 902pp. 5⅜ x 8.
Vol. 1 T647 Paperbound **$2.25**
Vol. 2 T648 Paperbound **$2.00**

EUGENE O'NEILL: THE MAN AND HIS PLAYS, B. H. Clark. Introduction to O'Neill's life and work. Clark analyzes each play from the early THE WEB to the recently produced MOON FOR THE MISBEGOTTEN and THE ICEMAN COMETH revealing the environmental and dramatic influences necessary for a complete understanding of these important works. Bibliography. Appendices. Index. ix + 182pp. 5⅜ x 8. T379 Paperbound **$1.35**

THE HEART OF THOREAU'S JOURNALS, edited by O. Shepard. The best general selection from Thoreau's voluminous (and rare) journals. This intimate record of thoughts and observations reveals the full Thoreau and his intellectual development more accurately than any of his published works: self-conflict between the scientific observer and the poet, reflections on transcendental philosophy, involvement in the tragedies of neighbors and national causes, etc. New preface, notes, introductions. xii + 228pp. 5⅜ x 8. T741 Paperbound **$1.50**

H. D. THOREAU: A WRITER'S JOURNAL, edited by L. Stapleton. A unique new selection from the Journals concentrating on Thoreau's growth as a conscious literary artist, the ideals and purposes of his art. Most of the material has never before appeared outside of the complete 14-volume edition. Contains vital insights on Thoreau's projected book on Concord, thoughts on the nature of men and government, indignation with slavery, sources of inspiration, goals in life. Index. xxxiii + 234pp. 5⅜ x 8. T678 Paperbound **$1.65**

THE HEART OF EMERSON'S JOURNALS, edited by Bliss Perry. Best of these revealing Journals, originally 10 volumes, presented in a one volume edition. Talks with Channing, Hawthorne, Thoreau, and Bronson Alcott; impressions of Webster, Everett, John Brown, and Lincoln; records of moments of sudden understanding, vision, and solitary ecstasy. "The essays do not reveal the power of Emerson's mind . . . as do these hasty and informal writings," N.Y. Times. Preface by Bliss Perry. Index. xiii + 357pp. 5⅜ x 8. T477 Paperbound **$1.85**

FOUNDERS OF THE MIDDLE AGES, E. K. Rand. This is the best non-technical discussion of the transformation of Latin pagan culture into medieval civilization. Covering such figures as Tertullian, Gregory, Jerome, Boethius, Augustine, the Neoplatonists, and many other literary men, educators, classicists, and humanists, this book is a storehouse of information presented clearly and simply for the intelligent non-specialist. "Thoughtful, beautifully written," AMERICAN HISTORICAL REVIEW. "Extraordinarily accurate," Richard McKeon, THE NATION. ix + 365pp. 5⅜ x 8. T369 Paperbound **$2.00**

PLAY-MAKING: A MANUAL OF CRAFTSMANSHIP, William Archer. With an extensive, new introduction by John Gassner, Yale Univ. The permanently essential requirements of solid play construction are set down in clear, practical language: theme, exposition, foreshadowing, tension, obligatory scene, peripety, dialogue, character, psychology, other topics. This book has been one of the most influential elements in the modern theatre, and almost everything said on the subject since is contained explicitly or implicitly within its covers. Bibliography. Index. xlii + 277pp. 5⅜ x 8. T651 Paperbound **$1.75**

HAMBURG DRAMATURGY, G. E. Lessing. One of the most brilliant of German playwrights of the eighteenth-century age of criticism analyzes the complex of theory and tradition that constitutes the world of theater. These 104 essays on aesthetic theory helped demolish the regime of French classicism, opening the door to psychological and social realism, romanticism. Subjects include the original functions of tragedy; drama as the rational world; the meaning of pity and fear, pity and fear as means for purgation and other Aristotelian concepts; genius and creative force; interdependence of poet's language and actor's interpretation; truth and authenticity; etc. A basic and enlightening study for anyone interested in aesthetics and ideas, from the philosopher to the theatergoer. Introduction by Prof. Victor Lange. xxii + 265pp. 4½ x 6⅜. T32 Paperbound **$1.45**

Social Sciences

SOCIAL THOUGHT FROM LORE TO SCIENCE, H. E. Barnes and H. Becker. An immense survey of sociological thought and ways of viewing, studying, planning, and reforming society from earliest times to the present. Includes thought on society of preliterate peoples, ancient non-Western cultures, and every great movement in Europe, America, and modern Japan. Analyzes hundreds of great thinkers: Plato, Augustine, Bodin, Vico, Montesquieu, Herder, Comte, Marx, etc. Weighs the contributions of utopians, sophists, fascists and communists; economists, jurists, philosophers, ecclesiastics, and every 19th and 20th century school of scientific sociology, anthropology, and social psychology throughout the world. Combines topical, chronological, and regional approaches, treating the evolution of social thought as a process rather than as a series of mere topics. "Impressive accuracy, competence, and discrimination . . . easily the best single survey," Nation. Thoroughly revised, with new material up to 1960. 2 indexes. Over 2200 bibliographical notes. Three volume set. Total of 1586pp. 5⅜ x 8.

T901 Vol I   Paperbound **$2.50**
T902 Vol II   Paperbound **$2.50**
T903 Vol III Paperbound **$2.50**
The set **$7.50**

FOLKWAYS, William Graham Sumner. A classic of sociology, a searching and thorough examination of patterns of behaviour from primitive, ancient Greek and Judaic, Medieval Christian, African, Oriental, Melanesian, Australian, Islamic, to modern Western societies. Thousands of illustrations of social, sexual, and religious customs, mores, laws, and institutions. Hundreds of categories: Labor, Wealth, Abortion, Primitive Justice, Life Policy, Slavery, Cannibalism, Uncleanness and the Evil Eye, etc. Will extend the horizon of every reader by showing the relativism of his own culture. Prefatory note by A. G. Keller. Introduction by William Lyon Phelps. Bibliography. Index. xiii + 692pp. 5⅜ x 8.   T508 Paperbound **$2.49**

PRIMITIVE RELIGION, P. Radin. A thorough treatment by a noted anthropologist of the nature and origin of man's belief in the supernatural and the influences that have shaped religious expression in primitive societies. Ranging from the Arunta, Ashanti, Aztec, Bushman, Crow, Fijian, etc., of Africa, Australia, Pacific Islands, the Arctic, North and South America, Prof. Radin integrates modern psychology, comparative religion, and economic thought with first-hand accounts gathered by himself and other scholars of primitive initiations, training of the shaman, and other fascinating topics. "Excellent," NATURE (London). Unabridged reissue of 1st edition. New author's preface. Bibliographic notes. Index. x + 322pp. 5⅜ x 8.
T393 Paperbound **$2.00**

PRIMITIVE MAN AS PHILOSOPHER, P. Radin. A standard anthropological work covering primitive thought on such topics as the purpose of life, marital relations, freedom of thought, symbolism, death, resignation, the nature of reality, personality, gods, and many others. Drawn from factual material gathered from the Winnebago, Oglala Sioux, Maori, Baganda, Batak, Zuni, among others, it does not distort ideas by removing them from context but interprets strictly within the original framework. Extensive selections of original primitive documents. Bibliography. Index. xviii + 402pp. 5⅜ x 8.   T392 Paperbound **$2.25**

A TREATISE ON SOCIOLOGY, THE MIND AND SOCIETY, Vilfredo Pareto. This treatise on human society is one of the great classics of modern sociology. First published in 1916, its careful catalogue of the innumerable manifestations of non-logical human conduct (Book One); the theory of "residues," leading to the premise that sentiment not logic determines human behavior (Book Two), and of "derivations," beliefs derived from desires (Book Three); and the general description of society made up of non-elite and elite, consisting of "foxes" who live by cunning and "lions" who live by force, stirred great controversy. But Pareto's passion for isolation and classification of elements and factors, and his allegiance to scientific method as the key tool for scrutinizing the human situation made his a truly twentieth-century mind and his work a catalytic influence on certain later social commentators. These four volumes (bound as two) require no special training to be appreciated and any reader who wishes to gain a complete understanding of modern sociological theory, regardless of special field of interest, will find them a must. Reprint of revised (corrected) printing of original edition. Translated by Andrew Bongiorno and Arthur Livingston. Index. Bibliography. Appendix containing index-summary of theorems. 48 diagrams. Four volumes bound as two. Total of 2063pp. 5⅜ x 8½.   The set Clothbound **$15.00**

THE POLISH PEASANT IN EUROPE AND AMERICA, William I. Thomas, Florian Znaniecki. A seminal sociological study of peasant primary groups (family and community) and the disruptions produced by a new industrial system and immigration to America. The peasant's family, class system, religious and aesthetic attitudes, and economic life are minutely examined and analyzed in hundreds of pages of primary documentation, particularly letters between family members. The disorientation caused by new environments is scrutinized in detail (a 312-page autobiography of an immigrant is especially valuable and revealing) in an attempt to find common experiences and reactions. The famous "Methodological Note" sets forth the principles which guided the authors. When out of print this set has sold for as much as $50. 2nd revised edition. 2 vols. Vol. 1: xv + 1115pp. Vol. 2: 1135pp. Index. 6 x 9.
T478 Clothbound 2 vol. set **$12.50**

Chess, Checkers, Games, Go

THE ADVENTURE OF CHESS, Edward Lasker. A lively history of chess, from its ancient beginnings in the Indian 4-handed game of Chaturanga, through to the great players of our day, as told by one of America's finest masters. He introduces such unusual sidelights and amusing oddities as Maelzel's chess-playing automaton that beat Napoleon 3 times. Major discussion of chess-playing machines and personal memories of Nimzovich, Capablanca, etc. 5-page chess primer. 11 illustrations, 53 diagrams. 296pp. 5⅜ x 8. S510 Paperbound **$1.75**

A TREASURY OF CHESS LORE, edited by Fred Reinfeld. A delightful collection of anecdotes, short stories, aphorisms by and about the masters, poems, accounts of games and tournaments, photography. Hundreds of humorous, pithy, satirical, wise, and historical episodes, comments, and word portraits. A fascinating "must" for chess players; revealing and perhaps seductive to those who wonder what their friends see in the game. 48 photographs (14 full page plates) 12 diagrams. xi + 306pp. 5⅜ x 8. T458 Paperbound **$1.75**

HOW DO YOU PLAY CHESS? by Fred Reinfeld. A prominent expert covers every basic rule of chess for the beginner in 86 questions and answers: moves, powers of pieces, rationale behind moves, how to play forcefully, history of chess, and much more. Bibliography of chess publications. 11 board diagrams. 48 pages. **FREE**

THE PLEASURES OF CHESS, Assiac. Internationally known British writer, influential chess columnist, writes wittily about wide variety of chess subjects: Anderssen's "Immortal Game;" only game in which both opponents resigned at once; psychological tactics of Reshevsky, Lasker; varieties played by masters for relaxation, such as "losing chess;" sacrificial orgies; etc. These anecdotes, witty observations will give you fresh appreciation of game. 43 problems. 150 diagrams. 139pp. 5⅜ x 8. T597 Paperbound **$1.25**

WIN AT CHESS, F. Reinfeld. 300 practical chess situations from actual tournament play to sharpen your chess eye and test your skill. Traps, sacrifices, mates, winning combinations, subtle exchanges, show you how to WIN AT CHESS. Short notes and tables of solutions and alternative moves help you evaluate your progress. Learn to think ahead playing the "crucial moments" of historic games. 300 diagrams. Notes and solutions. Formerly titled CHESS QUIZ. vi + 120pp. 5⅜ x 8. T438 Paperbound **$1.00**

THE ART OF CHESS, James Mason. An unabridged reprinting of the latest revised edition of the most famous general study of chess ever written. Also included, a complete supplement by Fred Reinfeld, "How Do You Play Chess?", invaluable to beginners for its lively question and answer method. Mason, an early 20th century master, teaches the beginning and intermediate player more than 90 openings, middle game, end game, how to see more moves ahead, to plan purposefully, attack, sacrifice, defend, exchange, and govern general strategy. Supplement. 448 diagrams. 1947 Reinfeld-Bernstein text. Bibliography. xvi + 340pp. 5⅜ x 8. T463 Paperbound **$2.00**

THE PRINCIPLES OF CHESS, James Mason. This "great chess classic" (N. Y. Times) is a general study covering all aspects of the game: basic forces, resistance, obstruction, opposition, relative values, mating, typical end game situations, combinations, much more. The last section discusses openings, with 50 games illustrating modern master play of Rubinstein, Spielmann, Lasker, Capablanca, etc., selected and annotated by Fred Reinfeld. Will improve the game of any intermediate-skilled player, but is so forceful and lucid that an absolute beginner might use it to become an accomplished player. 1946 Reinfeld edition. 166 diagrams. 378pp. 5⅜ x 8. T646 Paperbound **$1.85**

LASKER'S MANUAL OF CHESS, Dr. Emanuel Lasker. Probably the greatest chess player of modern times, Dr. Emanuel Lasker held the world championship 28 years, independent of passing schools or fashions. This unmatched study of the game, chiefly for intermediate to skilled players, analyzes basic methods, combinations, position play, the aesthetics of chess, dozens of different openings, etc., with constant reference to great modern games. Contains a brilliant exposition of Steinitz's important theories. Introduction by Fred Reinfeld. Tables of Lasker's tournament record. 3 indices. 308 diagrams. 1 photograph. xxx + 349pp. 5⅜ x 8. T640 Paperbound **$2.25**

THE ART OF CHESS COMBINATION, E. Znosko-Borovsky. Proves that combinations, perhaps the most aesthetically satisfying, successful technique in chess, can be an integral part of your game, instead of a haphazard occurrence. Games of Capablanca, Rubinstein, Nimzovich, Bird, etc. grouped according to common features, perceptively analyzed to show that every combination begins in certain simple ideas. Will help you to plan many moves ahead. Technical terms almost completely avoided. "In the teaching of chess he may claim to have no superior," P. W. Sergeant. Introduction. Exercises. Solutions. Index. 223pp. 5⅜ x 8. T583 Paperbound **$1.60**

CATALOGUE OF DOVER BOOKS

MODERN IDEAS IN CHESS, Richard Reti. An enduring classic, because of its unrivalled explanation of the way master chess had developed in the past hundred years. Reti, who was an outstanding theoretician and player, explains each advance in chess by concentrating on the games of the single master most closely associated with it: Morphy, Anderssen, Steinitz, Lasker, Alekhine, other world champions. Play the games in this volume, study Reti's perceptive observations, and have a living picture of the road chess has travelled. Introduction. 34 diagrams. 192pp. 5⅜ x 8. T638 Paperbound **$1.25**

THE BOOK OF THE NEW YORK INTERNATIONAL CHESS TOURNAMENT, 1924, annotated by A. Alekhine and edited by H. Helms. Long a rare collector's item, this is the book of one of the most brilliant tournaments of all time, during which Capablanca, Lasker, Alekhine, Reti, and others immeasurably enriched chess theory in a thrilling contest. All 110 games played, with Alekhine's unusually penetrating notes. 15 photographs. xi + 271pp. 5⅜ x 8. T752 Paperbound **$1.85**

KERES' BEST GAMES OF CHESS, selected, annotated by F. Reinfeld. 90 best games, 1931-1948, by one of boldest, most exciting players of modern chess. Games against Alekhine, Bogolyubov, Capablanca, Euwe, Fine, Reshevsky, other masters, show his treatments of openings such as Giuoco Piano, Alekhine Defense, Queen's Gambit Declined; attacks, sacrifices, alternative methods. Preface by Keres gives personal glimpses, evaluations of rivals. 110 diagrams. 272pp. 5⅜ x 8. T593 Paperbound **$1.35**

HYPERMODERN CHESS as developed in the games of its greatest exponent, ARON NIMZOVICH, edited by Fred Reinfeld. An intensely original player and analyst, Nimzovich's extraordinary approaches startled and often angered the chess world. This volume, designed for the average player, shows in his victories over Alekhine, Lasker, Marshall, Rubinstein, Spielmann, and others, how his iconoclastic methods infused new life into the game. Use Nimzovich to invigorate your play and startle opponents. Introduction. Indices of players and openings. 180 diagrams. viii + 220pp. 5⅜ x 8. T448 Paperbound **$1.50**

THE DEVELOPMENT OF A CHESS GENIUS: 100 INSTRUCTIVE GAMES OF ALEKHINE, F. Reinfeld. 100 games of the chess giant's formative years, 1905-1914, from age 13 to maturity, each annotated and commented upon by Fred Reinfeld. Included are matches against Bogolyubov, Capablanca, Tarrasch, and many others. You see the growth of an inexperienced genius into one of the greatest players of all time. Many of these games have never appeared before in book form. "One of America's most significant contributions to the chess world," Chess Life. New introduction. Index of players, openings. 204 illustrations. xv +227pp. 5¾ x 8. T551 Paperbound **$1.35**

RESHEVSKY'S BEST GAMES OF CHESS, Samuel Reshevsky. One time 4-year-old chess genius, 5-time winner U. S. Chess Championship, selects, annotates 110 of his best games, illustrating theories, favorite methods of play against Capablanca, Alekhine, Bogolyubov, Kashdan, Vidmar, Botvinnik, others. Clear, non-technical style. Personal impressions of opponents, autobiographical material, tournament match record. Formerly "Reshevsky on Chess." 309 diagrams, 2 photos. 288pp. 5⅜ x 8. T606 Paperbound **$1.25**

ONE HUNDRED SELECTED GAMES, Mikhail Botvinnik. Author's own choice of his best games before becoming World Champion in 1948, beginning with first big tournament, the USSR Championship, 1927. Shows his great power of analysis as he annotates these games, giving strategy, technique against Alekhine, Capablanca, Euwe, Keres, Reshevsky, Smyslov, Vidmar, many others. Discusses his career, methods of play, system of training. 6 studies of endgame positions. 221 diagrams. 272pp. 5⅜ x 8. T620 Paperbound **$1.50**

RUBINSTEIN'S CHESS MASTERPIECES, selected, annotated by Hans Kmoch. Thoroughgoing mastery of opening, middle game; faultless technique in endgame, particularly rook and pawn endings; ability to switch from careful positional play to daring combinations; all distinguish the play of Rubinstein. 100 best games, against Janowski, Nimzowitch, Tarrasch, Vidmar, Capablanca, other greats, carefully annotated, will improve your game rapidly. Biographical introduction, B. F. Winkelman. 103 diagrams. 192pp. 5⅜ x 8. T617 Paperbound **$1.25**

TARRASCH'S BEST GAMES OF CHESS, selected & annotated by Fred Reinfeld. First definitive collection of games by Siegbert Tarrasch, winner of 7 international tournaments, and the leading theorist of classical chess. 183 games cover fifty years of play against Mason, Mieses, Paulsen, Teichmann, Pillsbury, Janwoski, others. Reinfeld includes Tarrasch's own analyses of many of these games. A careful study and replaying of the games will give you a sound understanding of classical methods, and many hours of enjoyment. Introduction. Indexes. 183 diagrams. xxiv + 386pp. 5⅜ x 8. T644 Paperbound **$2.00**

MARSHALL'S BEST GAMES OF CHESS, F. J. Marshall. Grandmaster, U. S. Champion for 27 years, tells story of career; presents magnificent collection of 140 of best games, annotated by himself. Games against Alekhine, Capablanca, Emanuel Lasker, Janowski, Rubinstein, Pillsbury, etc. Special section analyzes openings such as King's Gambit, Ruy Lopez, Alekhine's Defense, Giuoco Piano, others. A study of Marshall's brilliant offensives, slashing attacks, extraordinary sacrifices, will rapidly improve your game. Formerly "My Fifty Years of Chess." Introduction. 19 diagrams. 13 photos. 250pp. 5⅜ x 8. T604 Paperbound **$1.45**

Classics of Science

THE DIDEROT PICTORIAL ENCYCLOPEDIA OF TRADES AND INDUSTRY, MANUFACTURING AND THE TECHNICAL ARTS IN PLATES SELECTED FROM "L'ENCYCLOPÉDIE OU DICTIONNAIRE RAISONNE DES SCIENCES, DES ARTS, ET DES METIERS" OF DENIS DIDEROT, edited with text by C. Gillispie. The first modern selection of plates from the high point of 18th century French engraving, Diderot's famous Encyclopedia. Over 2000 illustrations on 485 full page plates, most of them original size, illustrating the trades and industries of one of the most fascinating periods of modern history, 18th century France. These magnificent engravings provide an invaluable glimpse into the past for the student of early technology, a lively and accurate social document to students of cultures, an outstanding find to the lover of fine engravings. The plates teem with life, with men, women, and children performing all of the thousands of operations necessary to the trades before and during the early stages of the industrial revolution. Plates are in sequence, and show general operations, closeups of difficult operations, and details of complex machinery. Such important and interesting trades and industries are illustrated as sowing, harvesting, beekeeping, cheesemaking, operating windmills, milling flour, charcoal burning, tobacco processing, indigo, fishing, arts of war, salt extraction, mining, smelting iron, casting iron, steel, extracting mercury, zinc, sulphur, copper, etc., slating, tinning, silverplating, gilding, making gunpowder, cannons, bells, shoeing horses, tanning, papermaking, printing, dying, and more than 40 other categories. 920pp. 9 x 12. Heavy library cloth. T421 Two volume set **$18.50**

THE PRINCIPLES OF SCIENCE, A TREATISE ON LOGIC AND THE SCIENTIFIC METHOD, W. Stanley Jevons. Treating such topics as Inductive and Deductive Logic, the Theory of Number, Probability, and the Limits of Scientific Method, this milestone in the development of symbolic logic remains a stimulating contribution to the investigation of inferential validity in the natural and social sciences. It significantly advances Boole's logic, and describes a machine which is a foundation of modern electronic calculators. In his introduction, Ernest Nagel of Columbia University says, "(Jevons) . . . continues to be of interest as an attempt to articulate the logic of scientific inquiry." Index. liii + 786pp. 5⅜ x 8.
S446 Paperbound **$2.98**

*DIALOGUES CONCERNING TWO NEW SCIENCES, Galileo Galilei. A classic of experimental science which has had a profound and enduring influence on the entire history of mechanics and engineering. Galileo based this, his finest work, on 30 years of experimentation. It offers a fascinating and vivid exposition of dynamics, elasticity, sound, ballistics, strength of materials, and the scientific method. Translated by H. Crew and A. de Salvio. 126 diagrams. Index. xxi + 288pp. 5⅜ x 8. S99 Paperbound **$1.75**

DE MAGNETE, William Gilbert. This classic work on magnetism founded a new science. Gilbert was the first to use the word "electricity," to recognize mass as distinct from weight, to discover the effect of heat on magnetic bodies; invented an electroscope, differentiated between static electricity and magnetism, conceived of the earth as a magnet. Written by the first great experimental scientist, this lively work is valuable not only as an historical landmark, but as the delightfully easy-to-follow record of a perpetually searching, ingenious mind. Translated by P. F. Mottelay. 25 page biographical memoir. 90 fix. lix + 368pp. 5⅜ x 8. S470 Paperbound **$2.00**

*OPTICKS, Sir Isaac Newton. An enormous storehouse of insights and discoveries on light, reflection, color, refraction, theories of wave and corpuscular propagation of light, optical apparatus, and mathematical devices which have recently been reevaluated in terms of modern physics and placed in the top-most ranks of Newton's work! Foreword by Albert Einstein. Preface by I. B. Cohen of Harvard U. 7 pages of portraits, facsimile pages, letters, etc. cxvi + 412pp. 5⅜ x 8. S205 Paperbound **$2.25**

A SURVEY OF PHYSICAL THEORY, M. Planck. Lucid essays on modern physics for the general reader by the Nobel Laureate and creator of the quantum revolution. Planck explains how the new concepts came into being; explores the clash between theories of mechanics, electrodynamics, and thermodynamics; and traces the evolution of the concept of light through Newton, Huygens, Maxwell, and his own quantum theory, providing unparalleled insights into his development of this momentous modern concept. Bibliography. Index. vii + 121pp. 5⅜ x 8.
S650 Paperbound **$1.15**

A SOURCE BOOK IN MATHEMATICS, D. E. Smith. English translations of the original papers that announced the great discoveries in mathematics from the Renaissance to the end of the 19th century: succinct selections from 125 different treatises and articles, most of them unavailable elsewhere in English—Newton, Leibniz, Pascal, Riemann, Bernoulli, etc. 24 articles trace developments in the field of number, 18 cover algebra, 36 are on geometry, and 13 on calculus. Biographical-historical introductions to each article. Two volume set. Index in each. Total of 115 illustrations. Total of xxviii + 742pp. 5⅜ x 8. S552 Vol I Paperbound **$2.00**
S553 Vol II Paperbound **$2.00**
The set, boxed **$4.00**

CATALOGUE OF DOVER BOOKS

*THE THIRTEEN BOOKS OF EUCLID'S ELEMENTS, edited by T. L. Heath. This is the complete EUCLID — the definitive edition of one of the greatest classics of the western world. Complete English translation of the Heiberg text with spurious Book XIV. Detailed 150-page introduction discusses aspects of Greek and medieval mathematics: Euclid, texts, commentators, etc. Paralleling the text is an elaborate critical exposition analyzing each definition, proposition, postulate, etc., and covering textual matters, mathematical analyses, refutations, extensions, etc. Unabridged reproduction of the Cambridge 2nd edition. 3 volumes. Total of 995 figures, 1426pp. 5⅜ x 8.   S88, 89, 90 — 3 vol. set, Paperbound **$6.75**

*THE GEOMETRY OF RENE DESCARTES. The great work which founded analytic geometry. The renowned Smith-Latham translation faced with the original French text containing all of Descartes' own diagrams! Contains: Problems the Construction of Which Requires Only Straight Lines and Circles; On the Nature of Curved Lines; On the Construction of Solid or Supersolid Problems. Notes. Diagrams. 258pp.   S68 Paperbound **$1.60**

*A PHILOSOPHICAL ESSAY ON PROBABILITIES, P. Laplace. Without recourse to any mathematics above grammar school, Laplace develops a philosophically, mathematically and historically classical exposition of the nature of probability: its functions and limitations, operations in practical affairs, calculations in games of chance, insurance, government, astronomy, and countless other fields. New introduction by E. T. Bell. viii + 196pp. S166 Paperbound **$1.35**

DE RE METALLICA, Georgius Agricola. Written over 400 years ago, for 200 years the most authoritative first-hand account of the production of metals, translated in 1912 by former President Herbert Hoover and his wife, and today still one of the most beautiful and fascinating volumes ever produced in the history of science! 12 books, exhaustively annotated, give a wonderfully lucid and vivid picture of the history of mining, selection of sites, types of deposits, excavating pits, sinking shafts, ventilating, pumps, crushing machinery, assaying, smelting, refining metals, making salt, alum, nitre, glass, and many other topics. This definitive edition contains all 289 of the 16th century woodcuts which made the original an artistic masterpiece. It makes a superb gift for geologists, engineers, libraries, artists, historians, and everyone interested in science and early illustrative art. Biographical, historical introductions. Bibliography, survey of ancient authors. Indices. 289 illustrations. 672pp. 6¾ x 10¾. Deluxe library edition.   S6 Clothbound **$10.00**

GEOGRAPHICAL ESSAYS, W. M. Davis. Modern geography and geomorphology rest on the fundamental work of this scientist. His new concepts of earth-processes revolutionized science and his broad interpretation of the scope of geography created a deeper understanding of the interrelation of the landscape and the forces that mold it. This first inexpensive unabridged edition covers theory of geography, methods of advanced geographic teaching, descriptions of geographic areas, analyses of land-shaping processes, and much besides. Not only a factual and historical classic, it is still widely read for its reflections of modern scientific thought. Introduction. 130 figures. Index. vi + 777pp. 5⅜ x 8.
S383 Paperbound **$3.50**

CHARLES BABBAGE AND HIS CALCULATING ENGINES, edited by P. Morrison and E. Morrison. Friend of Darwin, Humboldt, and Laplace, Babbage was a leading pioneer in large-scale mathematical machines and a prophetic herald of modern operational research—true father of Harvard's relay computer Mark I. His Difference Engine and Analytical Engine were the first successful machines in the field. This volume contains a valuable introduction on his life and work; major excerpts from his fascinating autobiography, revealing his eccentric and unusual personality; and extensive selections from "Babbage's Calculating Engines," a compilation of hard-to-find journal articles, both by Babbage and by such eminent contributors as the Countess of Lovelace, L. F. Menabrea, and Dionysius Lardner. 11 illustrations. Appendix of miscellaneous papers. Index. Bibliography. xxxviii + 400pp. 5⅜ x 8.   T12 Paperbound **$2.00**

*THE WORKS OF ARCHIMEDES WITH THE METHOD OF ARCHIMEDES, edited by T. L. Heath. All the known works of the greatest mathematician of antiquity including the recently discovered METHOD OF ARCHIMEDES. This last is the only work we have which shows exactly how early mathematicians discovered their proofs before setting them down in their final perfection. A 186 page study by the eminent scholar Heath discusses Archimedes and the history of Greek mathematics. Bibliography. 563pp. 5⅜ x 8.   S9 Paperbound **$2.45**

Biological Sciences

AN INTRODUCTION TO GENETICS, A. H. Sturtevant and G. W. Beadle. A very thorough exposition of genetic analysis and the chromosome mechanics of higher organisms by two of the world's most renowned biologists, A. H. Sturtevant, one of the founders of modern genetics, and George Beadle, Nobel laureate in 1958. Does not concentrate on the biochemical approach, but rather more on observed data from experimental evidence and results . . . from Drosophila and other life forms. Some chapter titles: Sex chromosomes; Sex-Linkage; Autosomal Inheritance;; Chromosome Maps; Intra-Chromosomal Rearrangements; Inversions—and Incomplete Chromosomes; Translocations; Lethals; Mutations; Heterogeneous Populations; Genes and Phenotypes; The Determination and Differentiation of Sex; etc. Slightly corrected reprint of 1939 edition. New preface by Drs. Sturtevant and Beadle. 1 color plate. 126 figures. Bibliographies. Index. 391pp. 5⅜ x 8½.   S306 Paperbound **$2.00**

THE GENETICAL THEORY OF NATURAL SELECTION, R. A. Fisher. 2nd revised edition of a vital reviewing of Darwin's Selection Theory in terms of particulate inheritance, by one of the great authorities on experimental and theoretical genetics. Theory is stated in mathematical form. Special features of particulate inheritance are examined: evolution of dominance, maintenance of specific variability, mimicry and sexual selection, etc. 5 chapters on man and his special circumstances as a social animal. 16 photographs. Bibliography. Index. x + 310pp. 5⅜ x 8.   S466 Paperbound **$2.00**

THE ORIENTATION OF ANIMALS: KINESES, TAXES AND COMPASS REACTIONS, Gottfried S. Fraenkel and Donald L. Gunn. A basic work in the field of animal orientations. Complete, detailed survey of everything known in the subject up to 1940s, enlarged and revised to cover major developments to 1960. Analyses of simpler types of orientation are presented in Part I: kinesis, klinotaxis, tropotaxis, telotaxis, etc. Part II covers more complex reactions originating from temperature changes, gravity, chemical stimulation, etc. The two-light experiment and unilateral blinding are dealt with, as is the problem of determinism or volition in lower animals. The book has become the universally-accepted guide to all who deal with the subject—zoologists, biologists, psychologists, and the like. Second, enlarged edition, revised to 1960. Bibliography of over 500 items. 135 illustrations. Indices. xiii + 376pp. 5⅜ x 8½.   T786 Paperbound **$2.25**

THE BEHAVIOUR AND SOCIAL LIFE OF HONEYBEES, C. R. Ribbands. Definitive survey of all aspects of honeybee life and behavior; completely scientific in approach, but written in interesting, everyday language that both professionals and laymen will appreciate. Basic coverage of physiology, anatomy, sensory equipment; thorough account of honeybee behavior in the field (foraging activities, nectar and pollen gathering, how individuals find their way home and back to food areas, mating habits, etc.); details of communication in various field and hive situations. An extensive treatment of activities within the hive community—food sharing, wax production, comb building, swarming, the queen, her life and relationship with the workers, etc. A must for the beekeeper, natural historian, biologist, entomologist, social scientist, et al. "An indispensable reference," J. Hambleton, BeES. "Recommended in the strongest of terms," AMERICAN SCIENTIST. 9 plates. 66 figures. Indices. 693-item bibliography. 252pp. 5⅜ x 8½.   T1137 Paperbound **$2.00**

BIRD DISPLAY: AN INTRODUCTION TO THE STUDY OF BIRD PSYCHOLOGY, E. A. Armstrong. The standard work on bird display, based on extensive observation by the author and reports of other observers. This important contribution to comparative psychology covers the behavior and ceremonial rituals of hundreds of birds from gannet and heron to birds of paradise and king penguins. Chapters discuss such topics as the ceremonial of the gannet, ceremonial gaping, disablement reactions, the expression of emotions, the evolution and function of social ceremonies, social hierarchy in bird life, dances of birds and men, songs, etc. Free of technical terminology, this work will be equally interesting to psychologists and zoologists as well as bird lovers of all backgrounds. 32 photographic plates. New introduction by the author. List of scientific names of birds. Bibliography. 3-part index. 431pp. 5⅜ x 8½.   T1128 Paperbound **$2.00**

THE SPECIFICITY OF SEROLOGICAL REACTIONS, Karl Landsteiner. With a Chapter on Molecular Structure and Intermolecular Forces by Linus Pauling. Dr. Landsteiner, winner of the Nobel Prize in 1930 for the discovery of the human blood groups, devoted his life to fundamental research and played a leading role in the development of immunology. This authoritative study is an account of the experiments he and his colleagues carried out on antigens and serological reactions with simple compounds. Comprehensive coverage of the basic concepts of immunolgy includes such topics as: The Serological Specificity of Proteins, Antigens, Antibodies, Artificially Conjugated Antigens, Non-Protein Cell Substances such as polysaccharides, etc., Antigen-Antibody Reactions (Toxin Neutralization, Precipitin Reactions, Agglutination, etc.). Discussions of toxins, bacterial proteins, viruses, hormones, enzymes, etc. in the context of immunological phenomena. New introduction by Dr. Merrill Chase of the Rockefeller Institute. Extensive bibliography and bibliography of author's writings. Index. xviii + 330pp. 5⅜ x 8½.   S299 Paperbound **$2.00**

CULTURE METHODS FOR INVERTEBRATE ANIMALS, P. S. Galtsoff, F. E. Lutz, P. S. Welch, J. G. Needham, eds. A compendium of practical experience of hundreds of scientists and technicians, covering invertebrates from protozoa to chordata, in 313 articles on 17 phyla. Explains in great detail food, protection, environment, reproduction conditions, rearing methods, embryology, breeding seasons, schedule of development, much more. Includes at least some species of each considerable group. Half the articles are on class insecta. Introduction. 97 illustrations. Bibliography. Index. xxix + 590pp. 5⅜ x 8. S526 Paperbound **$3.00**

THE BIOLOGY OF THE LABORATORY MOUSE, edited by G. D. Snell. 1st prepared in 1941 by the staff of the Roscoe B. Jackson Memorial Laboratory, this is still the standard treatise on the mouse, assembling an enormous amount of material for which otherwise you spend hours of research. Embryology, reproduction, histology, spontaneous tumor formation, genetics of tumor transplantation, endocrine secretion & tumor formation, milk, influence & tumor formation, inbred, hybrid animals, parasites, infectious diseases, care & recording. Classified bibliography of 1122 items. 172 figures, including 128 photos. ix + 497pp. 6⅛ x 9¼. S248 Clothbound **$6.00**

MATHEMATICAL BIOPHYSICS: PHYSICO-MATHEMATICAL FOUNDATIONS OF BIOLOGY, N. Rashevsky. One of most important books in modern biology, now revised, expanded with new chapters, to include most significant recent contributions. Vol. 1: Diffusion phenomena, particularly diffusion drag forces, their effects. Old theory of cell division based on diffusion drag forces, other theoretical approaches, more exhaustively treated than ever. Theories of excitation, conduction in nerves, with formal theories plus physico-chemical theory. Vol. 2: Mathematical theories of various phenomena in central nervous system. New chapters on theory of color vision, of random nets. Principle of optimal design, extended from earlier edition. Principle of relational mapping of organisms, numerous applications. Introduces into mathematical biology such branches of math as topology, theory of sets. Index. 236 illustrations. Total of 988pp. 5⅜ x 8.
S574 Vol. 1 (Books 1, 2) Paperbound **$2.50**
S575 Vol. 2 (Books 3, 4) Paperbound **$2.50**
2 vol. set **$5.00**

ELEMENTS OF MATHEMATICAL BIOLOGY, A. J. Lotka. A pioneer classic, the first major attempt to apply modern mathematical techniques on a large scale to phenomena of biology, biochemistry, psychology, ecology, similar life sciences. Partial Contents: Statistical meaning of irreversibility; Evolution as redistribution; Equations of kinetics of evolving systems; Chemical, inter-species equilibrium; parameters of state; Energy transformers of nature, etc. Can be read with profit even by those having no advanced math; unsurpassed as study-reference. Formerly titled ELEMENTS OF PHYSICAL BIOLOGY. 72 figures. xxx + 460pp. 5⅜ x 8. S346 Paperbound **$2.45**

THE BIOLOGY OF THE AMPHIBIA, G. K. Noble, Late Curator of Herpetology at the Am. Mus. of Nat. Hist. Probably the most used text on amphibia, unmatched in comprehensiveness, clarity, detail. 19 chapters plus 85-page supplement cover development; heredity; life history; speciation; adaptation; sex, integument, respiratory, circulatory, digestive, muscular, nervous systems; instinct, intelligence, habits, environment, economic value, relationships, classification, etc. "Nothing comparable to it," C. H. Pope, Curator of Amphibia, Chicago Mus. of Nat. Hist. 1047 bibliographic references. 174 illustrations. 600pp. 5⅜ x 8.
S206 Paperbound **$2.98**

STUDIES ON THE STRUCTURE AND DEVELOPMENT OF VERTEBRATES, E. S. Goodrich. A definitive study by the greatest modern comparative anatomist. Exceptional in its accounts of the ossicles of the ear, the separate divisions of the coelom and mammalian diaphragm, and the 5 chapters devoted to the head region. Also exhaustive morphological and phylogenetic expositions of skeleton, fins and limbs, skeletal visceral arches and labial cartilages, visceral clefts and gills, vacular, respiratory, excretory, and peripheral nervous systems, etc., from fish to the higher mammals. 754 illustrations. 69 page biographical study by C. C. Hardy. Bibliography of 1186 references. "What an undertaking . . . to write a textbook which will summarize adequately and succinctly all that has been done in the realm of Vertebrate Morphology these recent years," Journal of Anatomy. Index. Two volumes. Total 906pp. 5⅜ x 8. Two vol. set S449-50 Paperbound **$5.00**

A TREATISE ON PHYSIOLOGICAL OPTICS, H. von Helmholtz, Ed. by J. P. C. Southall. Unmatched for thoroughness, soundness, and comprehensiveness, this is still the most important work ever produced in the field of physiological optics. Revised and annotated, it contains everything known about the subject up to 1925. Beginning with a careful anatomical description of the eye, the main body of the text is divided into three general categories: The Dioptrics of the Eye (covering optical imagery, blur circles on the retina, the mechanism of accommodation, chromatic aberration, etc.); The Sensations of Vision (including stimulation of the organ of vision, simple and compound colors, the intensity and duration of light, variations of sensitivity, contrast, etc.); and The Perceptions of Vision (containing movements of the eyes, the monocular field of vision, direction, perception of depth, binocular double vision, etc.). Appendices cover later findings on optical imagery, refraction, ophthalmoscopy, and many other matters. Unabridged, corrected republication of the original English translation of the third German edition. 3 volumes bound as 2. Complete bibliography, 1911-1925. Indices. 312 illustrations. 6 full-page plates, 3 in color. Total of 1,749pp. 5⅜ x 8.
Two-volume set S15, 16 Clothbound **$15.00**

INTRODUCTION TO PHYSIOLOGICAL OPTICS, James P. C. Southall, former Professor of Physics in Columbia University. Readable, top-flight introduction, not only for beginning students of optics, but also for other readers—physicists, biochemists, illuminating engineers, optometrists, psychologists, etc. Comprehensive coverage of such matters as the Organ of Vision (structure of the eyeball, the retina, the dioptric system, monocular and binocular vision, adaptation, etc.); The Optical System of the Eye (reflex images in the cornea and crystalline lens, Emmetropia and Ametropia, accommodation, blur circles on retina); Eye-Glasses; Eye Defects; Movements of the Eyeball in its Socket; Rod and Cone Vision; Color Vision; and other similar topics. Index. 134 figures. x +426pp. 5⅜ x 8. S924 Paperbound **$2.25**

LIGHT, COLOUR AND VISION, Yves LeGrand. A thorough examination of the eye as a receptor of radiant energy and as a mechanism (the retina) consisting of light-sensitive cells which absorb light of various wave lengths—probably the most complete and authoritative treatment of this subject in print. Originally prepared as a series of lectures given at the Institute of Optics in Paris, subsequently enlarged for book publication. Partial contents: Radiant Energy—concept, nature, theories, etc., Sources of Radiation—artificial and natural, the Visual Receptor, Photometric Quantities, Units, Calculations, Retinal Illumination, Trivariance of Vision, Colorimetry, Luminance Difference Thresholds, Anatomy of the Retina, Theories of Vision, Photochemistry and Electro-physiology of the Retina, etc. Appendices, Exercises, with solutions. 500-item bibliography. Authorized translation by R. Hunt, J. Walsh, F. Hunt. Index. 173 illustrations. xiii + 512pp. 5⅜ x 8½. S979 Clothbound **$10.00**

FINGER PRINTS, PALMS AND SOLES: AN INTRODUCTION TO DERMATOGLYPHICS, Harold Cummins and Charles Midlo. An introduction in non-technical language designed to acquaint the reader with a long-neglected aspect of human biology. Although a chapter dealing with fingerprint identification and the systems of classification used by the FBI, etc. has been added especially for this edition, the main concern of the book is to show how the intricate pattern of ridges and wrinkles on our fingers have a broader significance, applicable in many areas of science and life. Some topics are: the identification of two types of twins; the resolution of doubtful cases of paternity; racial variation; inheritance; the relation of fingerprints to body measurements, blood groups, criminality, character, etc. Classification and recognition of fundamental patterns and pattern types discussed fully. 149 figures. 49 tables. 361-item bibliography. Index. xii + 319pp. 5⅝ x 8⅜. T778 Paperbound **$1.95**

Classics and histories

ANTONY VAN LEEUWENHOEK AND HIS "LITTLE ANIMALS," edited by Clifford Dobell. First book to treat extensively, accurately, life and works (relating to protozoology, bacteriology) of first microbiologist, bacteriologist, micrologist. Includes founding papers of protozoology, bacteriology; history of Leeuwenhoek's life; discussions of his microscopes, methods, language. His writing conveys sense of an enthusiastic, naive genius, as he looks at rainwater, pepper water, vinegar, frog's skin, rotifers, etc. Extremely readable, even for nonspecialists. "One of the most interesting and enlightening books I have ever read," Dr. C. C. Bass, former Dean, Tulane U. School of Medicine. Only authorized edition. 400-item bibliography. Index. 32 illust. 442pp. 5⅜ x 8. S594 Paperbound **$2.25**

THE GROWTH OF SCIENTIFIC PHYSIOLOGY, G. J. Goodfield. A compact, superbly written account of how certain scientific investigations brought about the emergence of the distinct science of physiology. Centers principally around the mechanist-vitalist controversy prior to the development of physiology as an independent science, using the arguments which raged around the problem of animal heat as its chief illustration. Covers thoroughly the efforts of clinicians and naturalists and workers in chemistry and physics to solve these problems—from which the new discipline arose. Includes the theories and contributions of: Aristotle, Galen, Harvey, Boyle, Bernard, Benjamin Franklin, Palmer, Gay-Lussac, Priestley, Spallanzani, and many others. 1960 publication. Biographical bibliography. 174pp. 5 x 7½. T1066 Clothbound **$3.00**

MICROGRAPHIA, Robert Hooke. Hooke, 17th century British universal scientific genius, was a major pioneer in celestial mechanics, optics, gravity, and many other fields, but his greatest contribution was this book, now reprinted entirely from the original 1665 edition, which gave microscopy its first great impetus. With all the freshness of discovery, he describes fully his microscope, and his observations of cork, the edge of a razor, insects' eyes, fabrics, and dozens of other different objects. 38 plates, full-size or larger, contain all the original illustrations. This book is also a fundamental classic in the fields of combustion and heat theory, light and color theory, botany and zoology, hygrometry, and many other fields. It contains such farsighted predictions as the famous anticipation of artificial silk. The final section is concerned with Hooke's telescopic observations of the moon and stars. 323pp. 5⅜ x 8. T8 Paperbound **$2.00**

Puzzles, Mathematical Recreations

SYMBOLIC LOGIC and THE GAME OF LOGIC, Lewis Carroll. "Symbolic Logic" is not concerned with modern symbolic logic, but is instead a collection of over 380 problems posed with charm and imagination, using the syllogism, and a fascinating diagrammatic method of drawing conclusions. In "The Game of Logic" Carroll's whimsical imagination devises a logical game played with 2 diagrams and counters (included) to manipulate hundreds of tricky syllogisms. The final section, "Hit or Miss" is a lagniappe of 101 additional puzzles in the delightful Carroll manner. Until this reprint edition, both of these books were rarities costing up to $15 each. Symbolic Logic: Index. xxxi + 199pp. The Game of Logic: 96pp. 2 vols. bound as one. 5⅜ x 8.   T492 Paperbound **$1.50**

PILLOW PROBLEMS and A TANGLED TALE, Lewis Carroll. One of the rarest of all Carroll's works, "Pillow Problems" contains 72 original math puzzles, all typically ingenious. Particularly fascinating are Carroll's answers which remain exactly as he thought them out, reflecting his actual mental process. The problems in "A Tangled Tale" are in story form, originally appearing as a monthly magazine serial. Carroll not only gives the solutions, but uses answers sent in by readers to discuss wrong approaches and misleading paths, and grades them for insight. Both of these books were rarities until this edition, "Pillow Problems" costing up to $25, and "A Tangled Tale" $15. Pillow Problems: Preface and Introduction by Lewis Carroll. xx + 109pp. A Tangled Tale: 6 illustrations. 152pp. Two vols. bound as one. 5⅜ x 8.   T493 Paperbound **$1.50**

AMUSEMENTS IN MATHEMATICS, Henry Ernest Dudeney. The foremost British originator of mathematical puzzles is always intriguing, witty, and paradoxical in this classic, one of the largest collections of mathematical amusements. More than 430 puzzles, problems, and paradoxes. Mazes and games, problems on number manipulation, unicursal and other route problems, puzzles on measuring, weighing, packing, age, kinship, chessboards, joiners', crossing river, plane figure dissection, and many others. Solutions. More than 450 illustrations. vii + 258pp. 5⅜ x 8.   T473 Paperbound **$1.25**

THE CANTERBURY PUZZLES, Henry Dudeney. Chaucer's pilgrims set one another problems in story form. Also Adventures of the Puzzle Club, the Strange Escape of the King's Jester, the Monks of Riddlewell, the Squire's Christmas Puzzle Party, and others. All puzzles are original, based on dissecting plane figures, arithmetic, algebra, elementary calculus and other branches of mathematics, and purely logical ingenuity. "The limit of ingenuity and intricacy," The Observer. Over 110 puzzles. Full Solutions. 150 illustrations. vii + 225pp. 5⅜ x 8.   T474 Paperbound **$1.25**

MATHEMATICAL EXCURSIONS, H. A. Merrill. Even if you hardly remember your high school math, you'll enjoy the 90 stimulating problems contained in this book and you will come to understand a great many mathematical principles with surprisingly little effort. Many useful shortcuts and diversions not generally known are included: division by inspection, Russian peasant multiplication, memory systems for pi, building odd and even magic squares, square roots by geometry, dyadic systems, and many more. Solutions to difficult problems. 50 illustrations. 145pp. 5⅜ x 8.   T350 Paperbound **$1.00**

MAGIC SQUARES AND CUBES, W. S. Andrews. Only book-length treatment in English, a thorough non-technical description and analysis. Here are nasik, overlapping, pandiagonal, serrated squares; magic circles, cubes, spheres, rhombuses. Try your hand at 4-dimensional magical figures! Much unusual folklore and tradition included. High school algebra is sufficient. 754 diagrams and illustrations. viii + 419pp. 5⅜ x 8.   T658 Paperbound **$1.85**

CALIBAN'S PROBLEM BOOK: MATHEMATICAL, INFERENTIAL AND CRYPTOGRAPHIC PUZZLES, H. Phillips (Caliban), S. T. Shovelton, G. S. Marshall. 105 ingenious problems by the greatest living creator of puzzles based on logic and inference. Rigorous, modern, piquant; reflecting their author's unusual personality, these intermediate and advanced puzzles all involve the ability to reason clearly through complex situations; some call for mathematical knowledge, ranging from algebra to number theory. Solutions. xi + 180pp. 5⅜ x 8.   T736 Paperbound **$1.25**

MATHEMATICAL PUZZLES FOR BEGINNERS AND ENTHUSIASTS, G. Mott-Smith. 188 mathematical puzzles based on algebra, dissection of plane figures, permutations, and probability, that will test and improve your powers of inference and interpretation. The Odic Force, The Spider's Cousin, Ellipse Drawing, theory and strategy of card and board games like tit-tat-toe, go moku, salvo, and many others. 100 pages of detailed mathematical explanations. Appendix of primes, square roots, etc. 135 illustrations. 2nd revised edition. 248pp. 5⅜ x 8.   T198 Paperbound **$1.00**

MATHEMAGIC, MAGIC PUZZLES, AND GAMES WITH NUMBERS, R. V. Heath. More than 60 new puzzles and stunts based on the properties of numbers. Easy techniques for multiplying large numbers mentally, revealing hidden numbers magically, finding the date of any day in any year, and dozens more. Over 30 pages devoted to magic squares, triangles, cubes, circles, etc. Edited by J. S. Meyer. 76 illustrations. 128pp. 5⅜ x 8.   T110 Paperbound **$1.00**

MATHEMATICAL RECREATIONS, M. Kraitchik. One of the most thorough compilations of unusual mathematical problems for beginners and advanced mathematicians. Historical problems from Greek, Medieval, Arabic, Hindu sources. 50 pages devoted to pastimes derived from figurate numbers, Mersenne numbers, Fermat numbers, primes and probability. 40 pages of magic, Euler, Latin, panmagic squares. 25 new positional and permutational games of permanent value: fairy chess, latruncles, reversi, jinx, ruma, lasca, tricolor, tetrachrome, etc. Complete rigorous solutions. Revised second edition. 181 illustrations. 333pp. 5⅜ x 8.
T163 Paperbound **$1.75**

MATHEMATICAL PUZZLES OF SAM LOYD, selected and edited by M. Gardner. Choice puzzles by the greatest American puzzle creator and innovator. Selected from his famous collection, "Cyclopedia of Puzzles," they retain the unique style and historical flavor of the originals. There are posers based on arithmetic, algebra, probability, game theory, route tracing, topology, counter, sliding block, operations research, geometrical dissection. Includes the famous "14-15" puzzle which was a national craze, and his "Horse of a Different Color" which sold millions of copies. 117 of his most ingenious puzzles in all, 120 line drawings and diagrams. Solutions. Selected references. xx + 167pp. 5⅜ x 8.   T498 Paperbound **$1.00**

MATHEMATICAL PUZZLES OF SAM LOYD, Vol. II, selected and edited by Martin Gardner. The outstanding 2nd selection from the great American innovator's "Cyclopedia of Puzzles": speed and distance problems, clock problems, plane and solid geometry, calculus problems, etc. Analytical table of contents that groups the puzzles according to the type of mathematics necessary to solve them. 166 puzzles, 150 original line drawings and diagrams. Selected references. xiv + 177pp. 5⅜ x 8.   T709 Paperbound **$1.00**

ARITHMETICAL EXCURSIONS: AN ENRICHMENT OF ELEMENTARY MATHEMATICS, H. Bowers and J. Bowers. A lively and lighthearted collection of facts and entertainments for anyone who enjoys manipulating numbers or solving arithmetical puzzles: methods of arithmetic never taught in school, little-known facts about the most simple numbers, and clear explanations of more sophisticated topics; mysteries and folklore of numbers, the "Hin-dog-abic" number system, etc. First publication. Index. 529 numbered problems and diversions, all with answers. Bibliography. 60 figures. xiv + 320pp. 5⅜ x 8.   T770 Paperbound **$1.65**

CRYPTANALYSIS, H. F. Gaines. Formerly entitled ELEMENTARY CRYPTANALYSIS, this introductory-intermediate level text is the best book in print on cryptograms and their solution. It covers all major techniques of the past, and contains much that is not generally known except to experts. Full details about concealment, substitution, and transposition ciphers; periodic mixed alphabets, multafid, Kasiski and Vigenere methods, Ohaver patterns, Playfair, and scores of other topics. 6 language letter and word frequency appendix. 167 problems, now furnished with solutions. Index. 173 figures. vi + 230pp. 5⅜ x 8.
T97 Paperbound **$2.00**

CRYPTOGRAPHY, L. D. Smith. An excellent introductory work on ciphers and their solution, the history of secret writing, and actual methods and problems in such techniques as transposition and substitution. Appendices describe the enciphering of Japanese, the Baconian biliteral cipher, and contain frequency tables and a bibliography for further study. Over 150 problems with solutions. 160pp. 5⅜ x 8.   T247 Paperbound **$1.00**

PUZZLE QUIZ AND STUNT FUN, J. Meyer. The solution to party doldrums. 238 challenging puzzles, stunts and tricks. Mathematical puzzles like The Clever Carpenter, Atom Bomb; mysteries and deductions like The Bridge of Sighs, The Nine Pearls, Dog Logic; observation puzzles like Cigarette Smokers, Telephone Dial; over 200 others including magic squares, tongue twisters, puns, anagrams, and many others. All problems solved fully. 250pp. 5⅜ x 8.
T337 Paperbound **$1.00**

101 PUZZLES IN THOUGHT AND LOGIC, C. R. Wylie, Jr. Brand new problems you need no special knowledge to solve! Take the kinks out of your mental "muscles" and enjoy solving murder problems, the detection of lying fishermen, the logical identification of color by a blindman, and dozens more. Introduction with simplified explanation of general scientific method and puzzle solving. 128pp. 5⅜ x 8.   T367 Paperbound **$1.00**

MY BEST PROBLEMS IN MATHEMATICS, Hubert Phillips ("Caliban"). Only elementary mathematics needed to solve these 100 witty, catchy problems by a master problem creator. Problems on the odds in cards and dice, problems in geometry, algebra, permutations, even problems that require no math at all—just a logical mind, clear thinking. Solutions completely worked out. If you enjoy mysteries, alerting your perceptive powers and exercising your detective's eye, you'll find these cryptic puzzles a challenging delight. Original 1961 publication. 100 puzzles, solutions. x + 107pp. 5⅝ x 8.   T91 Paperbound **$1.00**

MY BEST PUZZLES IN LOGIC AND REASONING, Hubert Phillips ("Caliban"). A new collection of 100 inferential and logical puzzles chosen from the best that have appeared in England, available for first time in U.S. By the most endlessly resourceful puzzle creator now living. All data presented are both necessary and sufficient to allow a single unambiguous answer. No special knowledge is required for problems ranging from relatively simple to completely original one-of-a-kinds. Guaranteed to please beginners and experts of all ages. Original publication. 100 puzzles, full solutions. x + 107pp. 5⅜ x 8.   T119 Paperbound **$1.00**

Fiction

FLATLAND, E. A. Abbott. A science-fiction classic of life in a 2-dimensional world that is also a first-rate introduction to such aspects of modern science as relativity and hyperspace. Political, moral, satirical, and humorous overtones have made FLATLAND fascinating reading for thousands. 7th edition. New introduction by Banesh Hoffmann. 16 illustrations. 128pp. 5⅜ x 8.
T1 Paperbound **$1.00**

THE WONDERFUL WIZARD OF OZ, L. F. Baum. Only edition in print with all the original W. W. Denslow illustrations in full color—as much a part of "The Wizard" as Tenniel's drawings are of "Alice in Wonderland." "The Wizard" is still America's best-loved fairy tale, in which, as the author expresses it, "The wonderment and joy are retained and the heartaches and nightmares left out." Now today's young readers can enjoy every word and wonderful picture of the original book. New introduction by Martin Gardner. A Baum bibliography. 23 full-page color plates. viii + 268pp. 5⅜ x 8.
T691 Paperbound **$1.50**

THE MARVELOUS LAND OF OZ, L. F. Baum. This is the equally enchanting sequel to the "Wizard," continuing the adventures of the Scarecrow and the Tin Woodman. The hero this time is a little boy named Tip, and all the delightful Oz magic is still present. This is the Oz book with the Animated Saw-Horse, the Woggle-Bug, and Jack Pumpkinhead. All the original John R. Neill illustrations, 10 in full color. 287 pp. 5⅜ x 8.
T692 Paperbound **$1.50**

28 SCIENCE FICTION STORIES OF H. G. WELLS. Two full unabridged novels, MEN LIKE GODS and STAR BEGOTTEN, plus 26 short stories by the master science-fiction writer of all time! Stories of space, time, invention, exploration, future adventure—an indispensable part of the library of everyone interested in science and adventure. PARTIAL CONTENTS: Men Like Gods, The Country of the Blind, In the Abyss, The Crystal Egg, The Man Who Could Work Miracles, A Story of the Days to Come, The Valley of Spiders, and 21 more! 928pp. 5⅜ x 8.
T265 Clothbound **$4.50**

THREE MARTIAN NOVELS, Edgar Rice Burroughs. Contains: Thuvia, Maid of Mars; The Chessmen of Mars; and The Master Mind of Mars. High adventure set in an imaginative and intricate conception of the Red Planet. Mars is peopled with an intelligent, heroic human race which lives in densely populated cities and with fierce barbarians who inhabit dead sea bottoms. Other exciting creatures abound amidst an inventive framework of Martian history and geography. Complete unabridged reprintings of the first edition. 16 illustrations by J. Allen St. John. vi + 499pp. 5⅜ x 8½.
T39 Paperbound **$1.85**

SEVEN SCIENCE FICTION NOVELS, H. G. Wells. Full unabridged texts of 7 science-fiction novels of the master. Ranging from biology, physics, chemistry, astronomy to sociology and other studies, Mr. Wells extrapolates whole worlds of strange and intriguing character. "One will have to go far to match this for entertainment, excitement, and sheer pleasure . . . ," NEW YORK TIMES. Contents: The Time Machine, The Island of Dr. Moreau, First Men in the Moon, The Invisible Man, The War of the Worlds, The Food of the Gods, In the Days of the Comet. 1015pp. 5⅜ x 8.
T264 Clothbound **$4.50**

THE LAND THAT TIME FORGOT and THE MOON MAID, Edgar Rice Burroughs. In the opinion of many, Burroughs' best work. The first concerns a strange island where evolution is individual rather than phylogenetic. Speechless anthropoids develop into intelligent human beings within a single generation. The second projects the reader far into the future and describes the first voyage to the Moon (in the year 2025), the conquest of the Earth by the Moon, and years of violence and adventure as the enslaved Earthmen try to regain possession of their planet. "An imaginative tour de force that keeps the reader keyed up and expectant," NEW YORK TIMES. Complete, unabridged text of the original two novels (three parts in each). 5 illustrations by J. Allen St. John. vi + 552pp. 5⅜ x 8½.
T1020 Clothbound **$3.75**
T358 Paperbound **$2.00**

3 ADVENTURE NOVELS by H. Rider Haggard. Complete texts of "She," "King Solomon's Mines," "Allan Quatermain." Qualities of discovery; desire for immortality; search for primitive, for what is unadorned by civilization, have kept these novels of African adventure exciting, alive to readers from R. L. Stevenson to George Orwell. 636pp. 5⅜ x 8.
T584 Paperbound **$2.00**

A PRINCESS OF MARS and A FIGHTING MAN OF MARS: TWO MARTIAN NOVELS BY EDGAR RICE BURROUGHS. "Princess of Mars" is the very first of the great Martian novels written by Burroughs, and it is probably the best of them all; it set the pattern for all of his later fantasy novels and contains a thrilling cast of strange peoples and creatures and the formula of Olympian heroism amidst ever-fluctuating fortunes which Burroughs carries off so successfully. "Fighting Man" returns to the same scenes and cities—many years later. A mad scientist, a degenerate dictator, and an indomitable defender of the right clash—with the fate of the Red Planet at stake! Complete, unabridged reprinting of original editions. Illustrations by F. E. Schoonover and Hugh Hutton. v + 356pp. 5⅜ x 8½.
T1140 Paperbound **$1.75**

CATALOGUE OF DOVER BOOKS

FROM THE EARTH TO THE MOON and ALL AROUND THE MOON, Jules Verne. Complete editions of two of Verne's most successful novels, in finest Edward Roth translations, now available after many years out of print. Verne's visions of submarines, airplanes, television, rockets, interplanetary travel; of scientific and not-so-scientific beliefs; of peculiarities of Americans; all delight and engross us today as much as when they first appeared. Large, easily readable type. 42 illus. from first French edition. 476pp. 5⅜ x 8.　　　　　T633 Paperbound **$1.75**

THREE PROPHETIC NOVELS BY H. G. WELLS, edited by E. F. Bleiler. Complete texts of "When the Sleeper Wakes" (1st book printing in 50 years), "A Story of the Days to Come," "The Time Machine" (1st complete printing in book form). Exciting adventures in the future are as enjoyable today as 50 years ago when first printed. Predict TV, movies, intercontinental airplanes, prefabricated houses, air-conditioned cities, etc. First important author to foresee problems of mind control, technological dictatorships. "Absolute best of imaginative fiction," N. Y. Times. Introduction. 335pp. 5⅜ x 8.　　　　　T605 Paperbound **$1.50**

GESTA ROMANORUM, trans. by Charles Swan, ed. by Wynnard Hooper. 181 tales of Greeks, Romans, Britons, Biblical characters, comprise one of greatest medieval story collections, source of plots for writers including Shakespeare, Chaucer, Gower, etc. Imaginative tales of wars, incest, thwarted love, magic, fantasy, allegory, humor, tell about kings, prostitutes, philosophers, fair damsels, knights, Noah, pirates, all walks, stations of life. Introduction. Notes. 500pp. 5⅜ x 8.　　　　　T535 Paperbound **$1.85**

Prices subject to change without notice.

Dover publishes books on art, music, philosophy, literature, languages, history, social sciences, psychology, handcrafts, orientalia, puzzles and entertainments, chess, pets and gardens, books explaining science, intermediate and higher mathematics, mathematical physics, engineering, biological sciences, earth sciences, classics of science, etc. Write to:

Dept. catrr.
Dover Publications, Inc.
180 Varick Street, N.Y. 14, N.Y.